Pain in the Belly

Pain in the Belly

The Haugean Witness in American Lutheranism

THOMAS E. JACOBSON

Foreword by GRACIA GRINDAL

WIPF & STOCK · Eugene, Oregon

PAIN IN THE BELLY
The Haugean Witness in American Lutheranism

Copyright © 2024 Thomas E. Jacobson. All rights reserved. Except for brief quotations in critical publications or reviews, no part of this book may be reproduced in any manner without prior written permission from the publisher. Write: Permissions, Wipf and Stock Publishers, 199 W. 8th Ave., Suite 3, Eugene, OR 97401.

Wipf & Stock
An Imprint of Wipf and Stock Publishers
199 W. 8th Ave., Suite 3
Eugene, OR 97401

www.wipfandstock.com

PAPERBACK ISBN: 978-1-6667-5978-5
HARDCOVER ISBN: 978-1-6667-5979-2
EBOOK ISBN: 978-1-6667-5980-8

For Theresa, Henrik, Helena, and Antonia, my beloved family

It was said many years ago by a leader in the Church: "We shall gobble the pietists [Hauge Synod] in a tremendous outward organization." "Yes," it was answered, "such an attempt can surely be made; but then the Church must be prepared to take the consequences. If the attempt is made to gobble the pietists for the purpose of getting rid of them, then it is to be feared they will cause tremendous pains in the belly of the Church."

—Theodore Graebner, "The Ghost of Pietism,"
Concordia Theological Monthly, April 1932, 16.

Table of Contents

FOREWORD | xiii
PREFACE | xvii
ACKNOWLEDGMENTS | xx
LIST OF ABBREVIATIONS | xxiii

INTRODUCTION | 1
    The Need for a Serious Study of Haugeanism within American Lutheranism | 3
        An Important Caveat | 3
        Articulating the Need for a Study of the American Haugean Tradition | 5
    The Shape of the Argument | 9

ESTABLISHING THE HAUGEAN IDENTITY | 16
    The Background of Hauge's Life and Work | 16
        The Introduction of Christianity in Norway | 17
        The Introduction of the Reformation in Norway | 18
        The Influence of Continental Pietism on Norwegian Church Life | 22
        Other Considerations | 25
        Summary | 27
    The Life and Work of Hans Nielsen Hauge | 27
        Hauge's Childhood and Youth | 27
        Hauge's "Conversion" | 30
        Hauge's Ministry | 33

TABLE OF CONTENTS

    From Hauge to Haugeanism | 38
        A Brief Look at Hauge's Theology | 38
            Biblical Understanding | 39
            Synergism | 41
            The *Triplex Munus* | 42
        Hauge's "Testament to His Friends" | 42
        The Impact of the Haugean Revival on Norwegian Society | 44
        The Evolution of the Haugean Tradition | 45
            The Grundtvigian and Johnsonian Revivals | 46
            Rosenian Influence | 49
    The Emergence of an American Haugeanism | 51
        Waves of Immigration | 51
            The "Sloopers" and the *Restauration* | 52
            The First Wave: 1836 to 1865 | 53
            The Second Wave: 1865 to 1915 | 54
        Elling Eielsen | 55
            Eielsen's Ordination and the "Evangelical Lutheran Church in America" | 58
        The Move toward Reorganization | 62
            Outside criticism | 63
            The first schism | 68
            The second schism | 69
            The reorganization | 70
    Conclusion | 74

LIFE WITHIN HAUGE'S SYNOD AND MERGER NEGOTIATIONS | 76
    The State of American Lutheranism as of 1876 | 76
        Outside Norwegian-American Lutheranism | 77
        Within Norwegian-American Lutheranism | 79
            The Norwegian Synod | 80
            The Conference and the Norwegian-Danish Augustana Synod | 83

TABLE OF CONTENTS

Issues within Hauge's Synod | 87
    Geography | 88
    Significant Personalities | 90
    Organizational Life | 92
        Polity | 93
        Worship | 94
        Lay Activity | 98
        Institutions of Mercy | 100
        Mission | 100
            Home mission | 100
            The China Mission | 101
            The Santal Mission | 103
            The Lutheran Orient Mission | 104
            The Zion Society for Israel | 105
        Education | 106
            Congregational education | 106
            Red Wing Seminary | 106
            Jewell Lutheran College and Camrose Lutheran College | 110
        Language | 111
        Publications | 113
            The periodical *Budbæreren* | 113
            The periodical the *Lutheran Intelligencer* | 114
            The periodical *Tidsskrift for Kirke og Samfund* | 118
        Ecumenical Activity | 118
            With other Lutherans | 119
            With non-Lutherans | 122
    Theological Identity | 126
        A Commitment to Lutheranism | 126
        Morality | 131
        The Nature of American Haugeanism | 133
Merger Negotiations Leading up to 1890 | 138

The Eau Claire Meeting | 138
The Scandinavia Meeting | 139
Merger Negotiations Leading up to 1917 | 142
Initiation of the Union Movement | 142
"Free" Conferences | 142
The Resolution of 1905 | 144
The Negotiations and Outcome | 147
Negotiations and *Opgjør* | 147
Reactions | 152
Implementation | 160
"Articles of Union" | 160
"An Interpretation" | 163
The consummation of the union | 166
Conclusion | 168

THE HAUGEAN PRESENCE WITHIN THE NLCA | 169
American Lutheranism after 1917 to 1960 | 170
Outside Norwegian-American Lutheranism | 170
Within Norwegian-American Lutheranism | 172
Haugeanism in the Early Years of the NLCA | 174
Early Signs of Discontent | 175
An Anecdote | 175
Wee's Illness and Resignation | 176
The Publication of *Haugeanism* | 179
The Hauge Lutheran Inner Mission Federation | 183
Wee's Later Publication | 185
The Fate of the Schools | 187
Jewell Lutheran College | 187
Red Wing Seminary | 192
Haugeanism in the Later Years of NLCA/ELC | 210
Seminary Life and Curriculum | 211
Mission and Evangelism Organizations | 217
The Lutheran Orient Mission Society | 218

TABLE OF CONTENTS

  The Zion Society for Israel | 219
  The World Mission Prayer League | 220
  The Lutheran Evangelistic Movement | 225
 Leadership within the NLCA | 234
 Later References and Apologetics for Haugeanism | 238
  In Periodicals | 239
  In Books | 245
Conclusion | 250

CONGREGATIONAL LIFE | 252
 The Impact of the Merger on Parish Life | 253
 Evaluation of the Fate of the Congregations | 257
 Categories of Congregations | 260
  The First Category | 261
   Emmanuel Lutheran Church of Kenyon, Minnesota | 261
   Blom Prairie Lutheran Church of Toronto, South Dakota | 264
   Jevnaker Lutheran Church of Borup, Minnesota | 266
   Zion Lutheran Church of Dexter, Minnesota | 267
   East Immanuel Lutheran Church of St. Paul, Minnesota | 269
   Kongsvinger Lutheran Church of Oslo, Minnesota | 271
  The Second Category | 273
   Singsaas Church of Hendricks, Minnesota | 273
   First Lutheran Church of Pontiac, Illinois | 275
   St. Paul's Lutheran Church of Minneapolis, Minnesota | 276
   Bardo Lutheran Church of Tofield, Alberta | 279

TABLE OF CONTENTS

        Franklin Lutheran Church of Viroqua, Wisconsin | 280

        South Zumbro Lutheran Church of Kasson, Minnesota | 281

    The Third Category | 282

        Emmanuel Lutheran Church of Beresford, South Dakota | 283

        Trinity Lutheran Church of Madison, Wisconsin | 284

        Scandia Lutheran Church of Centerville, South Dakota | 285

Conclusion | 285

HAUGEANISM TODAY | 287

    Overview of American Lutheranism after 1960 | 288

    Haugeanism in The American Lutheran Church | 292

        The Ministry of Seth Eastvold | 292

        Lutherans Alert | 296

        Affiliation of Lutheran Movements | 300

        The Lutheran Evangelistic Movement | 301

    Recent Developments | 306

        The Hauge Lutheran Inner Mission Federation | 306

        The Lutheran Evangelistic Movement | 311

        The World Mission Prayer League | 313

        China Service Ventures | 316

        Chosen People Ministries | 317

        Lutheran Lay Renewal of America | 318

    Conclusion | 320

CONCLUSION | 321

Appendix A | 327

Appendix B | 334

Appendix C | 344

Bibliography | 377

Foreword

IN THE 1950S, DURING my teenaged years, our Young People's society in the little Norwegian American Lutheran congregation my father served as pastor spent the full burden of its time arguing with the older folks, who were very much Haugeans, about dancing. Where in the Bible did it say "Thou shalt not dance" or that dancing was a sin? The older generation could not answer that to the satisfaction of most. They admitted that the Bible did not say dancing was a sin—Miriam and David after all danced—and agreed that it was not in and of itself a sin; it was rather what dancing led to. This was before "the pill." A girl who got pregnant out of wedlock at that time had a grim future before her. The boy who had gotten her pregnant, if he had any honor, would marry her. Often those marriages were unhappy.

The prohibition was something like a fence around the law. It gave most of us a very innocent and happy adolescence. Oscar C. Hanson, the father of a recent ELCA presiding bishop Mark Hanson, wrote a tract called *The Dangerous Dance*. One of my friends told my father in a heated exchange that she had never had a dirty thought about dancing until she read that tract. It was an astute comment. Later, despite the strict rules of her Haugean parents, the "dangerous dance" did get her into the trouble the Haugeans predicted. She had to marry the boy who got her pregnant. And it was an unhappy and violent marriage.

There are still today many of my age who resent Hans Nielsen Hauge for ruining their adolescence with "unnecessary" rules: no dancing, drinking, smoking, or playing cards. Many fled the Lutheran church, maybe even the Christian faith entirely. They are a diminishing number now, but I can hear it coming when an older person begins to criticize their upbringing in a Hauge influenced congregation. The speech is well rehearsed and angry, and their pride in what they have thrown off is clear.

There were also those who stayed in the Norwegian Lutheran Church of America but chose to be part of congregations that did not follow Hauge or his disciples. In seminary, many students made fun of Hauge and Haugeans, to the point of mocking him on his commemoration day by drinking and carousing to show their Lutheran freedom.

What they knew about Hauge was next to nothing, only his alleged legalism regarding certain amusements. They believed he was a conservative legalist who was not truly Lutheran. Theologians could win easy battles with him on their playing field. But not on his. He was an evangelist and an entrepreneur. His success was not in his theological work, but in his changing of the hearts of his countrymen. When I came to teach at the seminary and heard of the antics of the students in mocking Hauge, it made me angry. I began teaching about Hauge's concern for the spiritual lives of those around him, his building of industries that employed the poor and did good for Norway, his approval of women preaching and being spiritual leaders, his ability to read people and challenge them to new lives in service to God and their neighbors. It did little good with some, but serious students looking for their spiritual roots began to listen. But when I wanted to give them resources to study, there was little available other than old philio-pietist books from the 1930s. There were few if any resources that spoke to them. A few students here and there would read these books and find them helpful, but quaint.

Hence, Thomas Jacobson has done something in this book that is invaluable for scholars and people with a general interest in the history of Hans Nielsen Hauge and his impact on the people who emigrated from Norway. Hauge's revival swept Norway and changed it spiritually by awakening people from their spiritually dead lives, converting them and challenging them to obedient lives as they lived out their Christian vocations. His movement also broke the mercantilist system of the Dano-Norwegian monarchy with his entrepreneurial sense for the country as he walked from one end of it to the other. In many places, he would see possibilities for a paper mill, saltwork, or other industry. He had the moxie to choose the right people to build industries, giving many young people new ways to make money and improve their economic status. Even today, scholars are beginning to discover how vast the reach of his movement was in Norway and are coming to understand it in new ways.

The latest scholarship is pointing out Hauge's genius for organization and communication in his time, using letters, small groups, and gossip to bring his message to the mostly rural stock of early nineteenth century Norway. His small groups, the many lay people, men and women who became preachers of the gospel, traveled into the farthest reaches of the country. They gave many of these people and their descendants the courage to innovate and do things not imagined in their culture at the time.

Thus, when they heard of the opportunities in America, its freedom and its vast expanses of land available to them if they worked hard, they were well prepared to emigrate. They had acquired courage and a sense of God's part in their lives. With that, they made excellent citizens of the New Land and built churches, schools, colleges, seminaries, institutions of mercy, and a Norwegian American world located mostly in the upper Midwest.

Jacobson tells us of the origin of this movement and then does what has never been done before: he looks for evidence of Hauge's movement in America, not just the schools and missions, but the emphasis of the Haugeans as they worked to evangelize the world. His translating of the early documents, his following the ups and downs of Hauge's influence in the people, congregations, and institutions of America is sheer genius. It is almost as if he captured the evanescent colors of the rainbow and gathered them together in a thesis, now this book. Not only does he give us the story of the founding of these things which can be tracked and documented, he also finds those sparkling colors that are still alive today in people and congregations influenced by Hauge's movement.

This book is a massive work and deserves our respect and engagement. There are still places in Lutheran churches in North America where young people are challenged to live for Jesus, to turn their lives around and follow their Lord. There are Bible camps, youth gatherings, and special meetings where people are awakened and come to the knowledge of salvation through the preaching of the word and testimonies of others. It still happens, and Jacobson helps us trace those moments up to the present. The Haugean spirit still lives.

Like it did in that young friend of mine I mentioned in the beginning, now gone to her eternal reward. She suffered terribly in her marriage and subsequent life. Then God spoke to her, and she was converted. She told me later, in the language of her parents years before who had fervently prayed for her, that she now loved to go to the seaside and listen to the roaring waters and observe the grasses blowing in the wind and repeat Bible verses on the wonder of God's love. The faith planted in her long ago changed the direction of her life and led her to walk in the Master's steps. Pure Hauge.

Gracia Grindal
Professor Emerita of Rhetoric
Luther Seminary

Preface

AMERICAN LUTHERANISM HAS BEEN dissected and examined from numerous different angles. Yet the contributions and influence of the Haugean tradition—an integral part of the Norwegian-American Lutheran experience—has received scant attention from historians. This book, which is a slight revision of my doctoral dissertation from 2018 at Luther Seminary in St. Paul, Minnesota, is an attempt to fill that lacuna.

My first real experience with the name Hans Nielsen Hauge occurred during my "middler" (second) year in the Master of Divinity program at Luther Seminary in St. Paul, Minnesota. It was the spring semester of 2004, toward the end of March. Evening conversations between students in the fellowship area of our residence hall were not uncommon, but little did I know that the discussion that night would be for me a gateway to what would become my primary area of study.

It began when a group of my classmates asked me if I would be interested in joining them for an upcoming celebration to be held on the evening of March 29. This gathering, which I learned was to include the consumption of large amounts of alcohol, was ostensibly for the purpose of honoring the memory of Hans Nielsen Hauge, who is commemorated on that day. In reality, this attempt to "honor" Hague was intended to mock him and his legacy. I later discovered that this so-called "Hauge Forum" was a longstanding tradition at the seminary. The commemorative bust of Hauge, which was donated in the 1930s and is still displayed in the library of the seminary, would be "borrowed" each year for this event.

At the time, I knew little to nothing about Hauge's life and message. From the context of the conversation that evening, I deduced that Hauge was an influential Norwegian man, whose impact extended to the American Lutheran experience. I further deduced from the planned "celebration" to "honor" Hauge that at least some of his emphases were rooted in a pietistic variety of Christian expression, which presumably included condemnation of common amusements, such as drinking alcohol. Having as I do a tendency to root for the underdog, I sensed that the event planned for the evening of March 29 was inappropriate. Attempting to defuse the situation with humor, I responded to the invitation by saying, "I love Hauge; I own a complete collection of his works." Stifling laughter, one of my classmates said, "He doesn't have any works!"

This encounter piqued my interest in Hauge and the tradition that came after him. I soon discovered that my classmate's assertion regarding Hauge's lack of written works was incorrect. Hauge indeed wrote many books on spiritual and practical topics during his career, which in time were read by a large percentage of the Norwegian population. Most importantly, this encounter revealed to me that those who make a habit of mocking Hauge often do so ignorantly. This book is the culmination of that interest that began in 2004, and my hope is that, in addition to dispelling misinformation about Hauge and the tradition that followed him, it will create a greater and more nuanced understanding of both the man whose life and work revitalized his country, as well as the tradition bearing his name, which had no small influence on the broader American Lutheran tradition, an influence that continues today.

In the process of researching the history of Hauge's Norwegian Evangelical Lutheran Synod in America and the Haugean tradition in American Lutheranism more generally, I am sometimes asked whether I consider myself a Haugean. My response is always non-committal, and I somewhat jokingly refer to myself as "a Haugean who wears chasubles." Only those aware of the historic aversion of the Haugeans to clerical vestments will understand the joke. Nevertheless, there is a ring of truth to the joke; my experience of Lutheranism, along with many of my generation, is an amalgamation of many different emphases. Though my upbringing and experience in the Lutheran congregation of my childhood in Canby, Minnesota cannot be described as overly Pietistic or Haugean, and though I do not completely agree with every aspect of the Haugean tradition, I nonetheless find within it much that is commendable and worthy of study. In that spirit, I hope that this work will contribute to the knowledge base of American Lutheran history, but more importantly greater open-mindedness toward this important, influential, and

PREFACE

complex historical Christian movement among Lutherans. May we all display some openness to becoming Haugeans who wear chasubles!

Thomas E. Jacobson
March 29, 2023
Commemoration of Hans Nielsen Hauge, Renewer of the Church, 1824

Acknowledgements

THE PUBLICATION OF THIS book has been underwritten by the Lutheran Historical Conference through their Publication Grants program. I thank them for their generous support, by which the content of this book will find wider readership and without which the publication of the content would have been difficult.

Beyond this, compiling a list of acknowledgments for a work of this magnitude is a challenging task, as there is always the danger of omitting someone who has provided assistance in the course of my study. Therefore, I take Martin Luther's advice to Philipp Melanchthon to "sin boldly" as I attempt to enumerate the many individuals and organizations that have played a helpful if not invaluable role in my work.

First, I acknowledge my indebtedness to the scholars of previous generations who have plowed important ground in the area of Norwegian-American Lutheran history. Five deserve special mention: J. Magnus Rohne for his 1926 work entitled *Norwegian American Lutheranism up to 1872* and Eugene Fevold and E. Clifford Nelson for their joint work of 1960 entitled *The Lutheran Church among Norwegian-Americans*. My own work builds on the foundation that these scholars have laid and would be impossible without their efforts. More recent scholarship by Joseph Shaw and Todd Nichol has also informed my work in important ways. It is my hope that this study as well as my future scholarship will be a worthy addition to their important work and will contribute to a greater understanding of this field of history.

Second, I offer general thanks to the administration, faculty, and staff of Luther Seminary for their support and guidance. The individuals connected to Luther Seminary named below have been of great assistance and have made my work much easier. I thank Paul Lokken and Katherine Dahl, both formerly of the office of Graduate Theological Education. I

ACKNOWLEDGEMENTS

also extend thanks to Bruce Eldevik, Karen Alexander, and the rest of the library staff for their assistance in gathering necessary books and periodicals. Also deserving of special thanks are Paul Daniels and Kari Bostrom of the Luther Seminary archives. This work relies heavily on documents discovered in this archive and could not have been written without them. Kari, who lost her battle with cancer in late January of 2017, was of tremendous help, and her energy and encouragement are sorely missed by me and many others. Finally, my heartfelt appreciation goes to the following current and former faculty members of Luther Seminary who have played an important role in my doctoral coursework, research, and writing, leading to the dissertation on which this book is based: Lois Farag, Gracia Grindal, Mary Jane Haemig, Alan Padgett, Gary Simpson, Walter Sundberg, and most especially to my dissertation adviser Mark Granquist for his guidance and support during my degree completion.

Support for my research has come from individuals and organizations outside of Luther Seminary as well, and I wish to thank the following: Kerstin Ringdahl of the Pacific Lutheran University archives, Jeff Sauve of the St. Olaf College archives, the staff of the Center for Western Studies at Augustana University, and Charles Lindquist and the entire staff of the World Mission Prayer League. I also wish to thank Roy Harrisville Jr., James Knutson, David Preus, Joseph Shaw, and David Wee for their helpful insights on the history and enduring legacy of Hauge's Synod. Additionally, I thank the many former Hauge's Synod congregations that graciously provided me with access to their congregational histories and records. The one hundredth anniversary of the 1917 merger, which brought the life of Hauge's Synod to an end and produced the new church body of the Norwegian Lutheran Church of America, has come and gone as of June of 2017. In light of that significant observance, it is my hope that this work is a fitting tribute to the heritage and legacy of these congregations and the tradition they represent.

A word of thanks is also due to the congregations of Grace Lutheran Church and Our Savior's Lutheran Church in Menno, South Dakota, where my wife Theresa served as pastor from 2012 to 2021 and where we as a family resided during that time. They along with the entire community of Menno provided important friendship and a supportive environment in which to write the dissertation on which this book is based. I express a similar word of appreciation to the congregation of Good Shepherd Evangelical Lutheran Church of Lindy, Nebraska, where I served as pastor during much of this time, from 2015 to 2021. I also thank Grace

ACKNOWLEDGEMENTS

Lutheran Church of Thornville, Ohio, where I currently serve. In addition to the flexibility my congregations have extended to me in the process of writing and revising, serving as a pastor has reminded me of the main purpose of Christian historical scholarship, which is to be reminded of the "cloud of witnesses" (Heb 12:1) that surrounds us.

Finally and on a much more personal note, I must acknowledge my family and the important role they have played in my studies. I thank my wife Theresa for her support of me in myriad ways and her flexibility with my schedule as she has masterfully balanced attention to her own work with the care of our children. I also thank our three children Henrik Randolf, Helena Rakel, and Antonia Maren for their presence in my life and the joy they have brought me during my work. This work is dedicated to my family. Bearing in mind the imperfections of the Haugean Lutherans discussed in this book and the faults of any group of Christian people, however committed they might be, my prayer is that our children will demonstrate throughout their lives a similar seriousness of faith and commitment to the gospel that the men and women discussed here strove to demonstrate in former times.

List of Abbreviations

AALC	American Association of Lutheran Churches
AELC	Association of Evangelical Lutheran Churches
AFLC	Association of Free Lutheran Congregations
ALC	American Lutheran Church
ALMS	Affiliation of Lutheran Movements
ARC	Alliance of Renewal Churches
CALC	Canadian Association of Lutheran Congregations
CLBA	Church of the Lutheran Brethren of America
CSV	China Service Ventures
ELC	Evangelical Lutheran Church
ELCA	Evangelical Lutheran Church in America
ELCC	Evangelical Lutheran Church of Canada
ELCIC	Evangelical Lutheran Church in Canada
ELS	Evangelical Lutheran Synod
HLIMF	Hauge Lutheran Inner Mission Federation
JLC	Jewell Lutheran College
LBI	Lutheran Bible Institute
LCA	Lutheran Church in America
LCMC	Lutheran Congregations in Mission for Christ
LCMS	Lutheran Church – Missouri Synod
LCUSA	Lutheran Council in the USA
LEM	Lutheran Evangelistic Movement
LFRWS	League of Friends of Red Wing Seminary
LLRA	Lutheran Lay Renewal of America

LIST OF ABBREVIATIONS

LTC	Life Together Churches
NALC	North American Lutheran Church
NLC	National Lutheran Council
NLCA	Norwegian Lutheran Church of America
NLCSSW	National Lutheran Commission for Soldiers' and Sailors' Welfare
NRSV	New Revised Standard Version
PLC	Pacific Lutheran College
RWS	Red Wing Seminary
TALC	The American Lutheran Church
UDELC	United Danish Evangelical Lutheran Church
UELC	United Evangelical Lutheran Church
ULCA	United Lutheran Church in America
UNLC	United Norwegian Lutheran Church

1

Introduction

WRITING TO A TROUBLED situation in the early Christian communities in Galatia, the Apostle Paul quotes what was apparently a popular proverb to express his opposition to the Judaizing influence among those churches: "A little yeast leavens the whole batch of dough" (Gal 5:9).[1] He uses almost identical words when addressing the opposite crisis of libertinism in the Corinthian congregation (1 Cor 5:6). Jesus uses similar language when referring to "the yeast of the Pharisees and the yeast of Herod" (Mark 8:15).

In all three instances, the metaphor of yeast leavening a batch of dough is used in reference to negative influence among Christians, with the pure spiritual life of the community tainted by false teachings. As evidenced by the frequency of mocking and disparaging comments among North American Lutheran pastors concerning the Norwegian Lutheran lay preacher and entrepreneur Hans Nielsen Hauge and the subsequent Haugean tradition within American Lutheranism, it is fair to say that many consider Haugeanism a form of the negative yeast described by Paul, infecting church life with legalism, synergism, antiliturgical tendencies, and perhaps other perceived maladies.[2] Having, as I do, a ten-

---

1. Biblical quotations outside of quoted material from other authors are taken from the New Revised Standard Version (NRSV).

2. Though impossible to document, perhaps largely due to the lack of scholarly attention to the topic of Haugeanism, the frequency of such negative remarks is well attested in contemporary Lutheran circles, with Haugeanism viewed as a liability to "progress" in ecclesiastical developments and used as the punch line of jokes. A tradition persisted for a number of years at Luther Seminary in St. Paul, Minnesota where theological students would hold a "celebration" on the anniversary of the death of Hans

dency to root for the underdog, experiences with negative reactions to Haugeanism among my colleagues piqued my interest in this historical movement and led me to conclude that such negative reactions might actually be an indicator of the significance of this movement. Though I was not raised in an ecclesiastical environment heavily influenced by Haugeanism or Lutheran Pietism more generally, several questions began brewing in my mind: What role did Haugeanism play in the broader American Lutheran tradition? How did this spiritual movement find expression in the various Norwegian-American Lutheran church bodies of the nineteenth century? What were its distinctive emphases? Most significantly for the present, how were these emphases carried forward or rejected in the series of American Lutheran mergers of the twentieth century? Finally, who, if anyone, can be considered as carrying the banner of Haugeanism today, a little over a hundred years after the ecclesiastical merger of 1917 that united in a single body the vast majority of Norwegian-American Lutherans?

Considering the negative energy directed toward Haugeanism described above, is it possible to understand Haugeanism as a positive form of yeast that has in some ways contributed to vitality among American Lutherans over the years and even to the present? Indeed, the image of leaven in the Bible is not always negative, as in the following parable told by Jesus: "The kingdom of heaven is like leaven that a woman took and hid in three measures of flour, till it was all leavened" (Mt 13:33). Though not writing specifically about Haugean Pietism, but rather about historical Pietism more generally, biblical scholar Ernst Käsemann made the following comment about the German Protestantism of the twentieth century:

> We have every reason to not adopt a belittling attitude toward Pietism. Our church life still continues to draw its nourishment from its roots in Pietism. . . . [Its] weakening is undoubtedly leading to a very threatening crisis over the whole area of the Church's activity.[3]

Was the yeast of Haugeanism in American Lutheranism of the positive type, or was it rancid, leading to pain the belly of the consumer? The answer to that question depends on one's perspective and circumstances. Yet it can indeed be argued, in the spirit of Käsemann's comment, that

---

Nielsen Hauge (March 29) intended to mock him and his legacy.

3. Erb, *Pietists*, 1.

Haugean Pietism has nourished and provided important positive leaven in the American Lutheran tradition. Avoiding the extreme of uncritical exaltation, this book does not attempt to serve as a blind apology for the Norwegian Haugean tradition within American Lutheranism; many critiques of it, theological and otherwise, might well be valid. What this book does, however, is provide a more nuanced understanding of a numerically small though highly influential aspect of American Lutheranism that has often been neglected or dismissed. What is found in such a study might modify the view of Haugeanism as purely negative yeast and commend to contemporary Lutheranism an appreciation and perhaps implementation of some of its emphases as well as recognition of the ways that this tradition has already influenced broader church life.

THE NEED FOR A SERIOUS STUDY OF HAUGEANISM WITHIN AMERICAN LUTHERANISM

An Important Caveat

The image of yeast in a large batch of dough is an appropriate one for the Haugean tradition within American Lutheranism, but it is precisely this reality that makes historical study of Haugeanism in America challenging and perhaps partially accounts for the paucity of written works about the topic. Those influenced by the Haugean revival of Norway were not confined to a single church body in North America. Rather, Norwegian-American Haugeans exerted influence on all Norwegian-American Lutheran church bodies to varying degrees, at different times, and perhaps in different ways.[4] Even the "high-church" Norwegian Synod had at least some representatives of the Haugean tradition within its ranks.[5] Hence, an examination of Haugeanism in America can never be the history of a single church body. Of the various Norwegian-American Lutheran synods that existed in the nineteenth century, Fevold and Nelson note that the Norwegian Augustana Synod[6] and the Conference[7] viewed

---

4. Nelson and Fevold, *Lutheran Church*, 1:126.

5. Nelson and Fevold, *Lutheran Church*, 1:126.

6. Nelson and Fevold, *Lutheran Church*, 1:210. Fevold and Nelson note that the original name of this small synod that was formed in 1870 was "the Norwegian-Danish Augustana Synod in America," a title that was later changed to simply "the Norwegian Augustana Synod" in 1878.

7. Nelson and Fevold, *Lutheran Church*, 1:204. Fevold and Nelson note that the

themselves as American representatives of the Haugean tradition from Norway.[8] Even today, the Association of Free Lutheran Congregations (AFLC) considers its roots to be found in the Haugean revival of Norway.[9] It can also be argued that the Church of the Lutheran Brethren of America (CLBA), now headquartered in Fergus Falls, Minnesota, is an example of a contemporary Lutheran church body heavily influenced by Haugeanism.[10]

Bearing in mind the reality of the broad influence of Haugeanism on the Norwegian-American Lutheran tradition more generally, Fevold and Nelson do note, however, that it was primarily the Eielsen Synod and Hauge's Norwegian Evangelical Lutheran Synod in America[11] "that championed the principles historically associated with Hauge."[12] For this reason, in seeking to trace the continuation of the ethos of Haugeanism in American Lutheranism, this book will focus on the synodical body known as Hauge's Synod, all the while aware that Haugeanism did not fall neatly within the confines of any particular church body and that for most Haugeans particular synodical affiliation was of secondary importance to the concern for "experienced Christianity."[13] Hence, although the term "Haugeans" can at times refer to Norwegian-American Lutherans outside of Hauge's Synod, most often that designation will be used to refer to members or former members of Hauge's Synod. Indeed, as will

---

formal name of this body that was formed in 1870 was "the Conference for the Norwegian-Danish Evangelical Lutheran Church in America," which was usually shortened to simply "the Conference" in everyday communication.

8. Nelson and Fevold, *Lutheran Church*, 1:126.

9. Walker, *Standing Fast in Freedom*, 4. Headquartered in Plymouth, Minnesota, the AFLC understands itself as a representative of the Haugean tradition, but it also expresses appreciation for the Scandinavian pietistic and revival tradition more generally, including such individuals as Carl Olof Rosenius, Paavo Ruotsalainen, and Wilhelm Beck from Sweden, Finland, and Denmark respectively, despite the differences in emphasis among these revival leaders.

10. Nelson, *Lutheran Church*, 2:140. Nelson briefly discusses the origin of the CLBA in this volume.

11. As will be discussed later, this church body, henceforth known as "Hauge's Synod," resulted from an 1876 reorganization of the group known as Eielsen's Synod, which was constituted in 1846, the earliest Norwegian-American Lutheran church body to be formed.

12. Nelson and Fevold, *Lutheran Church*, 1:126.

13. Nelson and Fevold, *Lutheran Church*, 1:126. The phrase "experienced Christianity" serves here as a summary of the principles of Haugeanism, which will be discussed in a later chapter and which relate to the conviction that Christianity is something to be experienced and lived out, rather than simply a set of doctrines to which one assents.

be seen, documents from the historical eras under discussion sometimes use the label "Haugeans" to distinguish members of Hauge's Synod from the other Norwegian-American Lutheran church bodies.

Articulating the Need for a Study of the American Haugean Tradition

The negative attitude toward Haugeanism among many in contemporary American Lutheranism may account for the lack of scholarly attention to the topic. Whatever the case, though Hauge's Synod is frequently referenced in various works as a part of the larger narrative of Norwegian-American Lutheranism, little attention is given to its own concerns and internal deliberations leading up to the merger of 1917 that produced the Norwegian Lutheran Church of America (NLCA), with most attention given to the theological debates concerning the doctrine of election between representatives of the United Norwegian Lutheran Church (UNLC)[14] and the Norwegian Synod.[15] Of course, Fevold and Nelson's 1960 two-volume history of Norwegian-American Lutheranism does include significant discussion of Hauge's Synod leading up to the merger of 1917, but it says little about the continuation of the Haugean tradition after that. It is here that study of American Lutheran historiography becomes especially significant. Fevold and Nelson's work is invaluable for its detailed account of Norwegian-American Lutheran church life, especially the negotiations that made possible the merger of 1917. Yet their bias needs to be understood. The perspective of many American Lutherans of the middle twentieth century was one of optimism for the future, and they viewed the merger of various Lutheran church bodies as an expression of maturity in the American religious scene. Many thought that a large, merged synod was the destiny of American Lutheranism, which was moving away from ethnic enclaves and into a truly American identity that would carry considerable influence. Therefore, Fevold and Nelson's work was geared toward not only telling the story

---

14. The name of this church body is often shortened to simply the "United Church." To avoid confusion with the "United Lutheran Church in America" (ULCA), formed in 1918 as a merger of three eastern Lutheran synodical federations, this book will use the acronym "UNLC" to refer to this part of the Norwegian-American Lutheran tradition.

15. This group, founded in 1853, was officially known as the "Synod for the Norwegian Evangelical Lutheran Church in America," but was often referred to in shortened form as simply the "Norwegian Synod."

of Norwegian-American Lutheranism, but also toward justifying the participation of the Evangelical Lutheran Church (ELC)[16] in the 1960 merger that produced the American Lutheran Church (TALC). It was only natural, therefore, that they would tend to avoid discussion of internal conflicts within the new church organization after 1917, such as the struggle for maintaining the Haugean tradition discussed in this book. In his doctoral dissertation, on which the second volume of *The Lutheran Church among Norwegian-Americans* is based, Nelson argued in his conclusion that the significant accomplishment of the merger of 1917 was that

> it brought together, as no other major American denomination has done, and in quite the same way, the subjective tendencies of European pietism represented in Norwegian Haugeanism and the objective emphases of the Norwegian state church plus German Lutheran orthodoxy. Considering the intrinsic irreconcilability of some of the differing points of view in these two tendencies the achievement of 1917 was a notable success, *the working out of which after 1917 will be the task of future historians to observe and relate.*[17]

Writing over twenty years after Nelson's 1952 comment, historian Fred Meuser asserted in his brief mention of the 1917 merger that the "working out" of these two tendencies indeed was a success and that other than the small schism in the Norwegian Synod that produced the Evangelical Lutheran Synod (ELS), there were no difficulties between the two traditions that Nelson describes: "No other protest movement resulted, nor did the immediate postmerger years produce any great problems of adjustment. The Norwegians were convinced that they belonged together."[18]

Picking up where Nelson left off with his 1952 comment and in response to Meuser's 1975 assertion concerning the contented coexistence of members of the NLCA after the merger, one now needs to evaluate the truth of Meuser's comment, ask what happened to the Haugean tradition within the NLCA after 1917, and observe how it sought to perpetuate

---

16. The name of the church body formed from the Norwegian-American Lutheran merger of 1917 was originally the "Norwegian Lutheran Church of America," which was changed in 1946 after years of debate to simply the "Evangelical Lutheran Church" to reflect the transition from a Norwegian to an American identity.

17. Nelson, "Union Movement among Norwegian-American Lutherans," 619. The italics in this quote have been added for emphasis.

18. Nelson, *Lutherans in North America*, 373.

INTRODUCTION

itself. Despite Nelson's optimism about the coexistence of two different traditions in a single body and the movement toward merger more generally, the benefit of increased historical distance provides the opportunity to reevaluate earlier claims of historians. Indeed, the last half of the twentieth century and the initial years of the twenty-first century have been for American Lutherans in many ways a story of conflict and fragmentation. This sobering reality, certainly not envisioned by Nelson and his contemporaries, calls for a reexamination of some aspects of earlier written history, among which is the friction that existed between the Haugean expression of Lutheranism in America and its more formal and churchly counterparts, especially as Hauge's Synod entered the union of 1917 as a minority tradition and sought to express its identity within that body as leaven in a larger batch of dough.

Though there are some historical works devoted to expressions of Haugeanism in twentieth-century American Lutheranism, many of which are discussed in this book, there is no comprehensive work that ties them together into a cohesive whole. The closest thing to a history of American Haugeanism is the 1941 volume by the Hauge Inner Mission Federation entitled *The Hauge Movement in America*. In addition to being outdated, this book was intended more for internal edification among self-identified Haugeans than an attempt at an objective history. Aside from this volume, there is no single work devoted to an examination of the enduring legacy of Haugeanism after 1917. In addition, much has happened in American Lutheranism since 1941, which creates the need for an updated and more objective analysis.

The scant references to Hauge's Synod in more general works of American Lutheran history also reveal the need for a more in-depth analysis of the topic. Furthermore, these few references typically say little about the principles of historic Haugeanism and next to nothing about the enduring influence of this heritage, choosing instead to provide a superficial description of the participation of Hauge's Synod in the Norwegian-American Lutheran mergers of 1890 and 1917. Historian Abdel Ross Wentz does, however, make the following attempt at describing the character of Hauge's Synod in his 1955 work, revised in 1964:

> The oldest of these six bodies was Hauge's Synod, organized in 1846 by Elling Eielsen, a follower of Hans Nielsen Hauge, Norway's great evangelist-reformer. This group always insisted on definite marks of Christian experience, on positive and

courageous evangelism, and on vigorous development of lay leadership.[19]

Wentz goes on to note the involvement of Hauge's Synod in the social problems of the late nineteenth century, noting, however briefly, the involvement of Hauge's Synod in wider society:

> Early in the nineties the United Norwegian Church and the Hauge Norwegian Synod approved all Christian and legal efforts for prohibition and called on every church member to oppose "the godless and ruinous traffic" in liquor. Soon there were resolutions from those bodies on Sabbath reform and actions extending charity to immigrants.[20]

Although the 1975 work edited by E. Clifford Nelson entitled *The Lutherans in North America* mentions aspects of the life of Hauge's Synod, such as its involvement in the mission field in China and its establishment of Red Wing Seminary in 1879, it says a bit less than Wentz does in describing the character of Hauge's Synod and provides no specific examples of its organizational activity:

> Its roots were in the Haugean Awakening of Norway, and it promoted lay preaching, "living" Christianity, a "low-church" skepticism regarding formal worship and clerical vestments, and suspicion of clerical authority and ecclesiastical organization. . . . Increased organizational efficiency and churchliness meant no abatement of concern for Christian experience and lay activity.[21]

One also notes that Nelson's work frames the character of Hauge's Synod somewhat more negatively than does Wentz, using terms such as "skepticism" and "suspicion" rather than highlighting any positive contributions to American Lutheranism.

Finally, the most recent general history, *Lutherans in America: A New History* by Mark Granquist, says much less about Hauge's Synod than the two previous works, noting only the participation of Hauge's Synod in the merger process leading up to 1917:

> There had been one previous merger among the Norwegian American Lutherans, in 1890, which formed the United

---

19. Wentz, *Basic History of Lutheranism in America*, 249–50.
20. Wentz, *Basic History of Lutheranism in America*, 320–21.
21. Nelson, *Lutherans in North America*, 335.

Norwegian Lutheran Church, but sizable groups, namely the Norwegian Synod and the Hauge Synod, had remained outside this denomination. The theological issues of the nineteenth century, especially the election controversy and related topics, were still lively issues, and hard feelings and suspicions were still evident, particularly between the United Church and the Norwegian Synod.[22]

That this most recent general history of American Lutheranism says less about Hauge's Synod than the previous two works is understandable due to the smaller size of the book. Nevertheless, it is noteworthy that this quotation confirms the point made earlier, which is that greater attention is paid in discussions of Norwegian-American Lutheran history to the theological struggle primarily between the Norwegian Synod and the UNLC while saying nothing about the other significant concerns deliberated within Hauge's Synod leading up to the 1917 merger.

The purpose of highlighting these cursory references to Hauge's Synod in the three most recent general histories of American Lutheranism is not to disparage these important works. It is naturally beyond the scope of a history of such a complex topic to provide a highly detailed analysis of any particular church body, especially one as numerically small as Hauge's Synod. Indeed, references in these works to many other church bodies are similarly lacking in detail. Rather, it is simply to demonstrate that when viewed in light of the frequency of disparaging remarks about Haugeanism in contemporary American Lutheranism, these superficial references commend to readers the task of deeper research. What is found there might reveal an influence on American Lutheranism disproportionate to its size, one that might well endure to this day.

THE SHAPE OF THE ARGUMENT

Of the three Norwegian-American Lutheran church bodies that merged in 1917 to form the NLCA,[23] Hauge's Synod was the smallest, contributing about 8 percent of the total congregations, with the UNLC contributing 61 percent and the Norwegian Synod contributing 31 percent.[24] Though

---

22. Granquist, *Lutherans in America*, 222.

23. Nelson, *Lutheran Church*, 2:359. Occasionally, the name of this merged body is written as "in America," but the constitution of 1917 clearly uses the preposition "of."

24. *Shall Red Wing Seminary Be Closed?* 4.

sharing with the Norwegian Synod and the UNLC a common Norwegian and Lutheran identity, Hauge's Synod possessed some unique emphases bequeathed to it by its Haugean heritage that were not universally shared by the other bodies. For this reason, the Norwegian-American Lutheran merger of 1917 is a prime candidate for study among those interested in how smaller bodies with unique emphases fit into merged bodies and seek to continue their legacy.

This book serves two purposes. First, responding to the established point concerning the lack of information about Hauge's Synod as well as the Haugean tradition after 1917, the book seeks to contribute to the knowledge base of American Lutheran history by shedding light on this tradition, both before and after 1917. The endurance of this tradition within the NLCA after 1917 has been neglected by historians, a reality made nearly scandalous by the obvious awareness of this tradition, evidenced by the vitriol directed toward it. Only a few years after the merger of 1917, Gustav Marius Bruce, formerly of Hauge's Synod, wrote about the broad influence of Haugeanism on Norwegian-American Lutheranism that already existed in his time, and he expressed the hope that such influence would continue:

> Turning more specifically to the influence of Hauge on Christianity and church life among Norwegian immigrants, we must first mention the essential foundation of Hauge's work, personally experienced Christianity. In terms of Christian outlook, the Haugean influence has made a deep and, one hopes, ineradicable impression on Christian life on this side of the Atlantic. Personal conviction, a personal experience of grace and a decision to live for God are fundamental to the view of Christianity that the Norwegian people embraced through Hauge's work, and which we consciously continue to support and seek to promote.[25]

Bruce's words were written in 1926, and though he testifies to the influential nature of Haugeanism to that point, his expressed hope for the emphases of Haugeanism to continue their influence invites historical reflection on the fate of the tradition. As a minority in the 1917 merger, how did the Haugeans carry on their distinct emphases? Did the Haugean tradition survive, or was it defeated? Responding to the questions raised about the fate of this tradition, this book traces the history of Hauge's

---

25. Bruce, "Influence of Hauge," 92. A copy of this translated document is held in the Luther Seminary Archives.

INTRODUCTION

Synod from its origin in 1846 and attempts to identify the continuation of the Haugean spirit after the merger of 1917. More specifically, however, the book responds to the conclusion of Nelson's dissertation, where he highlights the coexistence of competing traditions as one of the significant accomplishments of the formation of the NLCA in 1917. The argument is made that Hauge's Synod, with its long history of friction with other aspects of Norwegian-American Lutheranism, entered the 1917 merger with significant reservations about the survival of Haugeanism within the NLCA. Far from a "happily ever after" scenario of merger, the minority Hauge's Synod element of the new church body often felt out of place, disenfranchised, and struggling to maintain its identity. In terms of the enduring institutional identity of Hauge's Synod, the tradition was certainly defeated, a loss at least partially self-inflicted as a result of the Haugeans' lackluster administrative talent. Yet the Haugean tradition was not entirely eradicated in that it continued to express itself through the various independent ministries and mission organizations to which the Haugeans contributed significantly. The book explores the attempt at coexistence between the Haugeans and their more churchly counterparts in the NLCA/ELC, the friction that often resulted, and the various ways Haugeanism continued to express itself within the "mainstream" church organizations, often in response to that friction. It will do so in the following ways:

Partially because the story of the Haugean revival of Norway is not widely known and numerous misunderstandings exist concerning Hauge's life and work, the book will begin, in the second chapter, by providing an overview of Hauge's activity in Norway. More importantly, this overview helps to establish what the Haugean tradition actually is before further discussion of how certain individuals and movements modified Haugeanism in Norway. A firm understanding of the Haugean tradition in Norway in all its complexity is essential for understanding the development of Haugeanism in North America. Considering the timeline of emigration from Norway to North America and the impact of the perspective of the later immigrants, this chapter will then discuss the emergence of an American Haugeanism and the move toward reorganization of the informal church body that was established in 1846 by Elling Eielsen. By addressing the internal conflicts of Eielsen's Synod leading up to the reorganization that produced Hauge's Synod in 1876, this part of the book will establish as much as possible the basic history and principles of Haugeanism, serving as a point of reference for the later parts of the book. Two other points in the second chapter are especially significant. First, one observes the friction that existed from the beginning between the Haugeans and their more formal, churchly counterparts with whom they would eventually merge. Second, one discovers that American Haugeanism itself was not a completely monolithic movement. Indeed, a bifurcation developed among the Haugeans due to recognition of the necessity of greater organization in the American environment, as well as influences in theology and piety from Scandinavia.

The third chapter will be devoted to evaluating the life of Hauge's Synod from 1876 to the 1917 merger. In addition to providing basic information about the church body, itself a valuable contribution given the paucity of information about Hauge's Synod, attention will be given to the unique identity of the organization among the broader field of Norwegian-American Lutheranism. The establishment of its educational institutions and missionary endeavors will also be noted, as will the ecumenical activity of Hauge's Synod, both with Lutheran and non-Lutheran entities. How and why the attitude of Hauge's Synod toward cooperation with other Christians differed from other Lutheran synods of the time will also be addressed as an important part of understanding its piety. Significantly, though Hauge's Synod possessed a synodical polity and an accompanying sense of the need for order in church life, it is evident that such organizational matters were of secondary concern to that of spiritual life, a reality with lasting repercussions for the continuation of the Haugean spirit in American Lutheranism. Finally, the book will focus here on the merger negotiations leading up to 1890 and 1917. How does one best understand the curious phenomenon of the withdrawal of Hauge's Synod from the merger of 1890 and the fact that Hauge's Synod initiated the merger negotiations that led to the merger of 1917? Especially important will be an evaluation of the concerns of Hauge's Synod in these merger negotiations and how its representatives sought to reconcile their Haugean heritage and practice with the idea of union with the two other synods. Note will also be made of opposition among the other synods, especially the Norwegian Synod, to the inclusion of Hauge's Synod in the 1917 merger and of different understandings of the "Interpretation" of Hauge's Synod concerning the union documents of 1917. All these issues will support the viewpoint that Hauge's Synod, although similar to the other synods in some ways, possessed a somewhat different spirit and entered this merger with some significant reservations among many in its ranks, fearful of the loss of its distinctive identity. That people from the other synods were also critical of Hauge's Synod meant that this merger, which was celebrated as uniting over 90 percent of Norwegian-American Lutherans, was rather uneasy, setting the stage for later conflict.

Despite reservations among many in Hauge's Synod about participation in the merger, Hauge's Synod ended its independent existence and became a part of the new NLCA in 1917. Therefore, the fourth chapter will address the former Hauge's Synod presence in this new body and its efforts to live out its principles. Taking note of a variety of issues, this chapter makes the argument that a sense of friction existed within the new NLCA between representatives of Hauge's Synod and the rest of the NLCA, which persisted decades into the life of the church body. By highlighting issues such as the perceived lack of adequate representation of Hauge's Synod among the leadership of the NLCA, the closing of Jewell Lutheran College in the 1920s, the closing of Red Wing Seminary in the 1930s, and the abandonment of the teaching of Haugean worship practices at Luther Seminary, this part of the book demonstrates that such occurrences contributed to a sense of disenfranchisement among some self-identified Haugeans, which appear to have led them to live out their unique heritage through other channels at various stages in the life of the NLCA. The existence of these independent channels will be discussed in a later chapter.

The fifth chapter discusses the experience of former Hauge's Synod congregations in the NLCA after 1917. A complete list of such congregations in existence as of 1916 is provided in Appendix C of this book. In keeping with the argument concerning friction and disenfranchisement made in the fourth chapter, an evaluation of this information reveals that a large percentage of former Hauge's Synod congregations departed from the NLCA at various points in its history to join other church bodies perceived as friendlier to their piety. This is demonstrated by an evaluation of various congregational documents and reminiscences. Also discussed in this chapter is the reason behind the fact that the defection of Hauge's Synod congregations took place slowly over time rather than as a single dissenting group, as was the case with the minority from the Norwegian Synod that formed in 1918 what is now known as the ELS. This chapter then proceeds to evaluate some specific examples of such former congregations of Hauge's Synod, dividing them into different categories. While some have remained within the mainstream church establishment, a significant number of existing former Hauge's Synod congregations have departed from the mainstream for church bodies friendlier to their piety.

At the same time, one observes on a congregational level a diversity of expression within the broader Haugean tradition, with some, while certainly considered theologically and socially conservative, exhibiting a focus on positive evangelism. Others, however, exhibit a darker and more legalistic piety. This distinction can perhaps be attributed to the earlier bifurcation among the Haugeans, discussed in the second chapter.

The sixth chapter discusses more recent developments in American Lutheranism and how the Haugean tradition can be understood to express itself today. Far from a single organization that can definitively be labeled as "Haugean," the tradition, with its historic concern in both Norway and North America to enrich the spiritual lives of people within the church establishment, lives on in the various organizations and ministries established by the Haugeans of previous generations. Especially after the transition to the English language was complete, the membership of these organizations was very often mixed, with former members of Hauge's Synod and their spiritual descendants serving with representatives of other synodical bodies. Though this is consistent with the lack of concern among the Haugeans for organizational life, it makes the enduring spirit of Haugeanism in such organizations difficult to demonstrate. It is, however, in keeping with the reality established early on that Haugeanism is a broad movement, not confined to a single church body. As Haugeanism began in American Lutheranism as a movement of "widely scattered faithful," so it remains today as leaven in a larger batch of dough, providing a continued witness to established church bodies of the importance of personal, experienced faith, a perspective that historians Fevold and Nelson claim "can never be entirely denied by those who take seriously the New Testament witness to Jesus Christ."[26]

Two important stylistic notes need to be made for readers. As already mentioned, the official title of the church body referred to in this book as "Hauge's Synod" was "Hauge's Norwegian Evangelical Lutheran Synod in America." At times, books, correspondence, and other documents in the eras under discussion refer to this church body as "the Hauge Synod" instead of "Hauge's Synod," and there is unfortunately a lack of uniformity in terminology. When such references are a part of quotations, the name used for the church body is preserved as it appears in the original document. However, the shortened form of "Hauge's Synod" is used by me in this book, as it more accurately reflects the official title. Second, it was

---

26. Nelson and Fevold, *Lutheran Church*, 1:150.

INTRODUCTION

common practice in Lutheran church organizations in the eras under discussion to refer to those involved in church affairs, both pastors and laypeople, by their last name, preceded by their first and middle initials. In general, the approach used in this book is to write the full name of an individual, when it can be determined, the first time the name of such an individual appears. Subsequently, the first and middle initial will be used in place of the full name. In determining the actual first and middle names of many of these individuals, I am indebted to a pastoral directory entitled *Who's Who among Pastors in all the Norwegian Lutheran Synods of America: 1843–1927*, the publication details of which are found in the bibliography.

2

Establishing the Haugean Identity

THOUGH NUMERICALLY ONLY A small part of the historic American Lutheran tradition, Haugeanism came to exert influence on this tradition disproportionate to its size. Yet American Haugeanism cannot be understood apart from its Norwegian origin, which was the result of centuries of ecclesiastical development in that kingdom. Therefore, this chapter examines the development of Christianity in Norway and how the life, work, and theology of Hans Nielsen Hauge himself were shaped by this background. It then turns its attention to the transplantation of the Haugean tradition to American soil, its struggle for self-understanding, and ultimately the development of the church body known as Hauge's Synod. Identifying the principles of Haugeanism as represented by this church body, this chapter sets the stage for the later interaction of Hauge's Synod with other parts of the Norwegian-American Lutheran tradition, as discussed in later chapters.

THE BACKGROUND OF HAUGE'S LIFE AND WORK

Hans Nielsen Hauge, a much derided historical figure in contemporary American Lutheranism is, according to Andreas Aarflot, viewed today more positively in Norway itself and looked upon as "an almost legendary figure in Norwegian church history."[1] This difference in attitude toward Hauge between Norway and North America is understandable given the broad impact of Hauge's work on Norwegian society, an impact

---

1. Aarflot, *Hans Nielsen Hauge*, 7.

not felt in North America. Aarflot acknowledges that Hauge's influence in Norway extended beyond ecclesiastical and spiritual life, having a broader impact on society, particularly its economic and political development. He calls for a sociological study to appreciate fully the impact of Hauge's work in different parts of Norway, which is beyond the scope of his work focused on the content of Hauge's preaching and its underlying theology.[2] As a testimony to Hauge's broad influence, efforts are currently underway in Norway to establish The Hauge Institute, which is being planned as an institution for the promotion of Hauge's vision for leadership, corporate communication, entrepreneurship, economic development, social responsibility, and business ethics.[3] With a figure such as Hauge often viewed as larger than life in at least some circles on both sides of the Atlantic, the temptation exists to ignore the history of his country and the tumultuous and troubled situation of late eighteenth- and early nineteenth-century Europe that is at least partly responsible for producing the "martyr's aura"[4] that surrounds him. As historical events and individuals are best understood in relation to the surrounding culture of their time, this chapter begins with a brief overview of Norway's history, as well as its relation to developments in the outside world at the time of Hauge's activity.

The Introduction of Christianity in Norway

Norway was first exposed to Christianity in the ninth century. The raiding activity of Vikings from the Scandinavian lands served unintentionally to introduce Christian faith and practice among the Norwegian people through the witness of Christian prisoners taken to Norway from England, Scotland, Ireland, France, and Spain.[5] Further Christian influence undoubtedly came from some Vikings themselves. After establishing permanent settlements in the lands they sought to plunder and, later, with whom they more peacefully traded, these Viking settlers adopted the Christian faith of their neighbors, apparently incorporating elements of Norse religion into their new faith. Any interaction that these Viking

---

2. Aarflot, *Hans Nielsen Hauge*, 7.

3. Hauge Institute, *Hauge Institute*, 3. Information on this endeavor can be accessed online at www.haugeinstitute.org.

4. Aarflot, *Hans Nielsen Hauge*, 7.

5. Irvin and Sunquist, *Earliest Christianity to 1453*, 373. The information in this paragraph is derived from pages 373 and 374 of this volume.

settlers had with their former homeland would have been a source of Christian influence there.

Though the ninth-century missionary monk Ansgar is popularly spoken of as "the apostle to the North" because of his activity in Denmark and Sweden, different individuals are credited with the more permanent establishment of Christianity in Norway. In the mid-tenth century, a newly elected Norwegian king from England named Haakon assumed his throne in Norway and spread the Christian faith in his territory. This was followed in the same century by another king named Olaf Tryggvason as well as the more famous Olaf Haraldsson[6] in the eleventh century. Hence, although Christian influence in Norway can be detected earlier, these monarchs were a critical part of establishing Christianity in the patchwork of kingdoms that comprised Norway in their era.

It is unclear the extent to which the people of Norway embraced the Christian faith at a personal level at the time of Olaf Haraldsson and before. Undoubtedly, many Norwegians continued their worship of Norse deities such as Freya, Odin, and Thor while being nominally Christian, a practice that likely continued for some time. At the same time, though the level of seriousness with which ordinary citizens took the new faith is difficult to determine, this imposition of Christian faith on Norway would clearly come to have an impact on broader society, one that trickled down in some form to influence common spirituality. One must bear in mind, however, that superstitious practices stemming from paganism apparently persisted for quite some time in Norway, even well beyond the era of the Reformation discussed below. Though this type of gradual conversion of a nation is certainly not unique to Norway, it is nonetheless an important part of the Christian heritage of Norway that shaped the practice of Christianity that Hauge encountered centuries later.

The Introduction of the Reformation in Norway

The Reformation of the sixteenth century in Norway was closely connected to developments in Denmark. There is no towering figure associated with the Reformation in Norway as there is in Sweden, where Olavus Petri has been given the title "The Swedish Luther." Though the title "The Norwegian Luther" has been bestowed on Jørgen Erickssøn, who became

---

6. This is the figure who came to be known as "Saint Olaf," for whom an American Lutheran college and various American Lutheran congregations are named.

the superintendent of Stavanger in 1571, because of his largely administrative reforms in that neglected diocese, it is clear that his influence was not nearly as wide and significant as that of Petri in Sweden.[7] Erickssøn's theological influence in Norway should not be completely dismissed, however, as is discussed below.

Evangelical[8] preaching appears to have been present in Norway to some extent in the 1520s; a friar named Antonius preached and taught theology associated with the Lutheran Reformation in the city of Bergen, on the western cost of Norway.[9] This is not surprising, as Bergen was the leading city of Norway at the time, a center of trade and commerce as a part of the Hanseatic League.[10] Nevertheless, there was no popular movement for evangelical reform in Norway at this time, with only scattered evangelical preaching occurring among some noble families throughout the rest of the decade.[11]

The Reformation would not take root in Norway until the country became a mere province of Denmark in 1536. Prior to this, Denmark and Norway were united by the Union Treaty of 1450, which stated that the two kingdoms would be eternally bound as equals under the same king.[12] After King Christian II of Denmark was exiled in 1523, partially as a result of his involvement with the Stockholm Bloodbath of 1520,[13] the new king Frederik I pledged to prohibit the Lutheran message from spreading in Denmark and Norway, which it nonetheless did. This reality possibly angered Archbishop Olav Engelbriktsson of Norway, who was a proponent of Norwegian independence as well as of the Catholic Church. Engelbriktsson was therefore involved in a plot for the exiled King Christian II to recapture Denmark and Norway. Though Christian II had at least some sympathies for the evangelical Lutheran message, he had apparently reconverted to Catholicism. This attempt at recapturing his former kingdom failed, however, and Christian II was himself

---

7. Grell, *Scandinavian Reformation*, 125.

8. The term "evangelical" refers here to the Protestant expression of the Christian faith in the time of the Reformation and not to its common usage in contemporary Christianity, which typically describes Protestant groups exhibiting moral and theological conservatism as well as an emphasis on adult conversion.

9. Montgomery, "Norway," 3:155–158.

10. Montgomery, "Norway," 3:155–158.

11. Grell, *Scandinavian Reformation*, 28.

12. Grell, *Scandinavian Reformation*, 28.

13. Dunkley, *Reformation in Denmark*, 19.

captured and jailed in 1531.¹⁴ After the death of Frederik I in 1533 and the subsequent Danish civil war that resulted in the victory of the new King Christian III, who was committed to the cause of the Reformation, Engelbriktsson lost influence and fled to the Netherlands. Perhaps in reaction to its role in the attempted coup, Norway's status was reduced from an equal to that of a province of Denmark, an arrangement that would endure until 1814.¹⁵ Therefore, after 1536, ecclesiastical developments in Norway would follow or at least be heavily influenced by those in Denmark. Accordingly, it can be said of the Norwegian Reformation that it came from above without popular movement for reform and was introduced gradually in 1537, not being complete until the introduction of a church order specific to the Norwegian situation in 1607.¹⁶

At the same time, the completeness of the Reformation at this point in Norway's history needs to be understood in light of the persistence of superstitious practices stemming from the earlier practice of Catholicism and perhaps even the paganism that preceded the introduction of Christianity. That Grell devotes an entire chapter in his book on the Scandinavian Reformation to the topic of the persistence of superstitious practices after the introduction of the Reformation is telling. Upon assuming his post as superintendent of Stavanger in the late sixteenth century, Jørgen Ericksson was faced with the challenge of eradicating superstitious practices that were associated with witchcraft, to which he refers in a book of sermons in 1592. Such practices, undoubtedly having developed over time in the late medieval era as a syncretism of pagan and Christian spirituality, were apparently opposed by the Reformers for leading people to place faith in things other than in God alone.¹⁷ The fact that Catholic priests simply continued serving in their parishes after the introduction of the Reformation in Norway likely accounts for this situation; with little opportunity for additional education, these clergy likely shared the beliefs of their parishioners. One example of the persistence of superstitious practices is the fact that King Christian IV renewed his prohibition of pilgrimages in Norway in 1622. It is also attested that visits to "sacred springs" were a part of Scandinavian folk religion in the decades following the Reformation. Though it is not clear the extent to which

14. Grell, *Scandinavian Reformation*, 28.
15. Grell, *Scandinavian Reformation*, 29.
16. Montgomery, "Norway," 3:155–158.
17. Grell, *Scandinavian Reformation*, 179. The information in this paragraph is derived from pages 179 to 187 of this volume.

such practices continued into the eighteenth and nineteenth centuries, it should be considered that such practices continued to be a part of folk religion throughout the generations. The state Lutheran church would come to play an important role in Norwegian society, but the persistence of these superstitious practices raises questions about the extent to which Norway's population internalized the message of the Reformation and even the Christian message more generally. In short, the religious situation of Norway after the introduction of the Reformation appears to have been an ideal environment in which a nominal church culture could develop, with people holding official membership in the church without a true faith commitment. An awareness of this reality is important for understanding the religious situation into which Hauge would enter in the late eighteenth and early nineteenth centuries.

A word must also be said concerning the type of Lutheran theology that took root in Norway with the introduction of the Reformation. As has already been noted, with no popular movement for reform in Norway, developments there closely followed those in Denmark. Lutheranism was and remains far from a theologically unified movement, and the Lutheran tradition that developed in the Scandinavian countries would be of a somewhat different flavor than that of the German territories. It has been observed that the earliest preachers of the Reformation in Denmark, active in the 1520s, preached a message that differed from the Wittenberg Reformers in some significant ways, having more in common with the Christian humanist tradition of Paulus Helie.[18] This tradition naturally placed more emphasis on the role of the human will in salvation.

Though the extent of this early humanist influence in the kingdom of Denmark and Norway should perhaps not be overstated, it is at least worth noting its presence amid further developments. Some scholars do, in fact, make a connection between the late medieval Christian humanism present in Denmark and Norway prior to the Reformation and the adoption of a Philippist variety of Lutheranism under the leadership of theologian Niels Hemmingsen.[19] As a part of the struggle between the Philippist and Gnesio-Lutheran parties in Germany, Hemmingsen was accused of crypto-Calvinism, especially concerning his view of the presence of Christ in the Lord's Supper.[20] Hemmingsen's influence in

---

18. Grell, *Scandinavian Reformation*, 26.
19. Grell, *Scandinavian Reformation*, 125.
20. Grell, *Scandinavian Reformation*, 120.

Denmark and Norway also showed itself in the treatment of the issue of the freedom of the human will. This Philippist emphasis on free will is evident in Hemmingsen's writings, and it appears to have been absorbed by Jørgen Erickssøn of Stavanger, with the focus of his preaching being on the necessity of "conversion."[21] Though the *Augsburg Confession* of 1530 was influential in Denmark and Norway, it would not be officially stated as normative for the kingdom until 1665.[22] Though the *Formula of Concord* of 1577 healed, at least on paper, the rift between Philippists and Gnesio-Lutherans in the German territories, King Frederik II, the son of Christian III, symbolically rejected this more detailed doctrinal statement by having copies of the *Formula of Concord* burned. This was mostly for political reasons, as a more precise doctrinal statement could potentially alienate Protestant allies of different confessions in other lands. It can be observed, therefore, that the desire for peace and unity in the kingdom of Denmark and Norway took precedence over potentially divisive theological disputes. This is perhaps the result of the Philippist focus on the responsibility of the king for both the spiritual welfare of his subjects as well as the regulation of society. Though this subordination of doctrine to other concerns in Denmark and Norway should not be overstated, it, along with the Philippist focus on free will, might at least partially account for the later flourishing of certain pietistic emphases in Norway discussed below as well as for Hauge's focus on Christian life, repentance, and conversion.

The Influence of Continental Pietism on Norwegian Church Life

The Pietist movement in the German territories, which is often, and perhaps artificially, considered to have begun with the publication of Philip Jakob Spener's *Pia Desideria*[23] in 1675,[24] did not remain confined to Germany. It took root in Denmark as well as in Norway by extension.

---

21. Quam, "Jørgen Erickssøn," 130.
22. Grell, *Scandinavian Reformation*, 117. The information in this paragraph is derived from pages 116 to 123 of this volume.
23. This is often translated as *Pious Desires* or *Devout Desires*.
24. That Spener's work was actually intended as an addition to a new edition of Johann Arndt's *True Christianity*, first published in 1606, indicates that Spener's concerns were not new. Ernest Stoeffler discusses the relationship between German Pietism and antecedent movements in his 1965 work *The Rise of Evangelical Pietism*.

This can be said to have begun during the reign of King Frederick IV of Denmark, whose court preacher R. J. Lütkens was involved in supporting pastors inclined toward the perspective of Pietism as well as the cause of foreign mission, recruiting Bartholomäus Ziegenbalg and Heinrich Plütschau from Halle in Germany to serve as missionaries to the Danish colony of Tranquebar in India.[25]

The influence of Pietism on Danish life manifested itself not only in the foreign mission field, but also at home. Endeavors mimicking those of Halle Pietism in Germany, such as orphanages and centers for the publication of Bibles and devotional literature, could be found in Denmark beginning with Frederick IV's reign. The Pietism that became established in the Dano-Norwegian kingdom was, unlike some manifestations of Pietism in the German lands, of the nonseparatist variety. This was because the leadership of the movement largely fell to pastors. When King Christian VI, who through marriage was influenced by German Pietism, assumed the throne in 1730, he succeeded in solidifying this "churchly," nonseparatist form of Pietism in his kingdom, issuing decrees in 1732 and 1741 that permitted conventicles[26] only under the supervision of an ordained minister. This "Conventicle Act" of 1741 would impact Hauge's life and work in a significant way decades after it was enacted.

This churchly Pietism in Denmark-Norway produced devotional and educational literature as well as hymns that would influence Hauge in his development and later work. This is significant, as it is often wrongly supposed that Hauge was the initiator of the pietistic tradition in Norway. In particular, Eric Pontoppidan, a Dane who later served as the bishop of Bergen, Norway, was influential through his work entitled *Sanhed til Gudfrygtighed*,[27] which was an "explanation"[28] of Luther's *Small Catechism*. This document, which contains in unabridged form 759 questions and answers intended for memorization,[29] was often used

---

25. Bergendoff, *Church of the Lutheran Reformation*, 159. Information in the following two paragraphs is also derived from page 159 in Bergendoff's work.

26. A conventicle is a gathering of Christians outside of regular worship, intended for edification in faith. This forerunner to modern "small group ministry" was proposed by Spener in *Pia Desideria*.

27. This is translated as *Truth unto Godliness* or *Truth unto Righteousness*.

28. In Norwegian, *Forklaring*.

29. Nichol, *Crossings*, 60. It is noted that it is not entirely clear if the entire document was used in confirmation instruction, as an abridged version by Peder Saxtorph from 1762 reduced the number of questions to 451.

in Norwegian and Norwegian-American Lutheran *barnelærdom*.[30] This work by Pontoppidan has been described as a work of "orthodox Pietism" that left a significant mark on Norwegian life, attaining semiconfessional status in the Church of Norway. Question 548 of this "explanation," which dealt with the issue of election or predestination, would go on to play a significant role in the American Lutheran theological controversy that divided the Norwegian Synod in 1887 and required resolution before the union of the vast majority of Norwegian-American Lutherans could be consummated in 1917. Other works, such as Pontoppidan's *Troens Spiel*,[31] collections of sermons by Luther, Johann Arndt's *Wahres Christentum*,[32] medieval works such as those by Johannes Tauler, works by Heinrich Müller, as well as hymns by Hans Adolph Brorson, Thomas Kingo, and others formed a canon of devotional literature that was a part of Hauge's ecclesiastical experience.[33] This churchly Pietism, while taking the Lutheran theological tradition seriously, expressed itself in ways that were often intensely personal and perhaps consistent with the greater emphasis on the human will in salvation stemming from the humanist and Philippist variety of Lutheranism in the Dano-Norwegian kingdom. The first and the last verse of Brorson's beloved Christmas hymn "*Mitt Hjerte Altid Vanker*"[34] serves as an example of this subjective focus:

> My heart is filled with wonder, to think how poor, forlorn, the manger was for Jesus the night that he was born. And yet it is my treasure, my hope, my faith, my light. I cannot ever leave you, O blessed Christmas night! . . . I would bring fresh palm branches to lay upon your bed. For you have come to save me, to suffer in my stead. My soul breaks forth rejoicing this happy Christmas tide. For you are born within me and make my darkness hide.[35]

---

30. This is best translated as "teaching of children" or "catechesis of children."
31. This is translated as *Mirror of Faith*.
32. This is translated as *True Christianity*. As mentioned earlier, Spener's *Pia Desideria* was intended as an introduction to a new printing of Arndt's work.
33. Aarflot, *Hans Nielsen Hauge*, 17.
34. This is translated as "My Heart Is Filled with Wonder."
35. Brorson, "My Heart is Filled with Wonder," 114.

Other Considerations

Though Norway was on the fringe of European life at the close of the eighteenth and beginning of the nineteenth centuries, it was not entirely isolated—largely due to its connection with Denmark—and outside ideas and events, such as the broad movement of the Enlightenment, missionary activity, and the Napoleonic Wars, would play a role in the development of Norwegian society. Aarflot remarks that Hauge's birth in the year 1771 placed him "in the century that bore both Pietism and the ideas of the Enlightenment in its womb."[36] Though the movements of Pietism and the Enlightenment are often understood to be antithetical, some scholars interpret aspects of Pietism as a part of the broader legacy of the Enlightenment. The Enlightenment ideal of individual freedom found expression in the desire of Pietists to practice faith in ways dictated by individual conscience, even when within the bounds of established state churches. Also, contrary to the caricature of Pietists as quietist and aloof from the concerns of society, they demonstrated a desire, often associated with the Enlightenment, to improve society through social ministries such as orphanages and other endeavors, as well as the strong missionary impulse that came from Pietistic institutions, discussed above.[37]

It should therefore come as no surprise that Norwegian society was undergoing a shift in this time. The greater focus on the individual from Pietism and the Enlightenment can be said to have contributed to a greater class consciousness and tension between state officials and wealthy citizens on the one hand and the farmers and laborers on the other. Also part of this shift in Norwegian society was a rising sense of national identity, distinct from Denmark. Though Hauge was himself influenced by this Pietistic and Enlightenment tradition, it has been said that his work actually fueled the process that led Norway to become a modern democratic society.

Yet the influence of the Enlightenment in Norway went beyond mere encouragement of personal initiative, progress in society, and movement toward independence. Enlightenment Rationalism impacted theology and preaching on the parish level. This tradition, which was exported from the University of Copenhagen,[38] tended to reject to varying degrees

---

36. Aarflot, *Hans Nielsen Hauge*, 15. Information in the following paragraph is also derived from page 15 of this volume.

37. Van Lieburg and Lindmark, *Pietism, Revivalism and Modernity*, 106.

38. It was not until the year 1811 that the University of Christiania (Oslo) was

traditional themes of Christian theology such as the Trinity, original sin, and the devil, replacing these with moralism and the discussion of practical topics.[39] Yet many rationalistic preachers sought to keep the peace by employing "the accommodation theory," where they would employ traditional theological terminology that would mask their true views, appeasing their more theologically conservative hearers and enabling them to preach according to their rationalistic convictions. It is not clear whether the average layperson of this era understood the rationalistic undertones of this preaching. Nevertheless, spiritual nourishment was available for the laity from the Pietistic devotional literature mentioned above. Hauge's supplementary religious gatherings would naturally come to find a willing audience in such an environment.

Another often overlooked foreign influence on Scandinavian life in this period that would influence Hauge's ministry and theology is the missionary presence of the Moravian tradition. Usually considered a part of the broader pietistic tradition because of their subjective religious tendencies, Moravians, also known as Herrnhuters, though tracing their origin to the tradition of Jan Hus after his execution at the Council of Constance in 1415, developed a distinct church culture under the leadership of Nikolaus Ludwig von Zinzendorf, himself a product of the Pietistic tradition of Halle, Germany.[40] This group demonstrated a strong world missionary impulse, through which they influenced Christians of other traditions, most notably John Wesley and his English Methodism. Because of their missionary activity, as well as their historical ties to the Lutheran tradition, Moravians and those influenced by them could be found in Norway, even among the clergy.

Finally, though Hauge's ministry began before the outbreak of the Napoleonic Wars, this conflict would impact his later work. This pan-European conflict, a product of the French Revolution, impacted even Norway; since the kingdom of Denmark-Norway allied with France, the resultant British blockade caused Norway to fall on hard times, with citizens resorting to consuming bread made of tree bark as well as creating a shortage of salt.[41] This crisis of war and shortages exacerbated

---

founded in Norway, meaning that Norwegian pastors were educated in Denmark prior to that.

39. Nelson and Fevold, *Lutheran Church*, 1:14. Information in this paragraph is derived from the same page in Nelson and Fevold's volume.

40. Engelbrecht, *Church from Age to Age*, 583.

41. Aarflot, *Hans Nielsen Hauge*, 39.

the growing sense of national identity and pride and also likely contributed to the greater religious seriousness that came with Hauge's spiritual movement.

Summary

From the brief historical survey above, one can see that the world into which Hauge entered in the late eighteenth century was colored by several influences. First, a "cultural Christianity" stemming from the royal imposition of the faith on Norway was pervasive, providing fertile ground for a religious awakening. Second, the form of Lutheranism that took root in Norway was of a less strictly confessional variety, possibly allowing for certain emphases of Pietism, notably the power of the human will, to find wide acceptance. Third, Norway, although a province of Denmark and located on the fringe of Europe, was by no means isolated, and outside influences, notably Enlightenment Rationalism among them, were contributing to ecclesiastical discontent and a shift in Norwegian society at the time that Hans Nielsen Hauge entered the scene.

THE LIFE AND WORK OF HANS NIELSEN HAUGE

Hauge's Childhood and Youth

In a now outdated biography, Wilhelm Pettersen lavishes praise on Hauge, labeling him "Norway's greatest man."[42] Though some might dispute this, it is worth looking more closely at the life of a man considered worthy by some of such a laudatory title. The life and experiences of Hauge, especially his operative theology and the persecution he faced, have played a large role in the ethos of the Haugean movement; understanding his experiences is important for understanding the movement that came after him.

Hans Nielsen Hauge was born in 1771 in the Tune parish, located seventy-five miles south of the capital city of Christiania.[43] He had four brothers and four sisters; the oldest sibling, a girl, died before Hauge was born.[44] In accordance with Norwegian naming customs, one of his

---

42. Pettersen, *Light in the Prison Window*, 5.
43. Named after King Christian IV, Christiania was renamed "Oslo" in 1924.
44. Aarflot, *Hans Nielsen Hauge*, 16.

surnames was based on his father's first name. As his father was Niels Mikkelsen, Hans was given the name "Nielsen," standing for "son of Niels." Also, as the farmstead on which he was born was named "Hauge," this was added as a second surname.[45] Norway did not have a standardized system of naming individuals until the "Naming Act" of 1923. Prior to that, people were typically named as the son or daughter of their father as well as from the farm or other location on which they were born or resided, and it was not unusual for people to have as many as four or more surnames throughout their life, depending on how often they moved.[46]

Despite the influence of Enlightenment Rationalism on theology in Norway described above, a more traditional Christianity fueled by the pietistic tradition remained a vital force among the laity. Hauge was baptized as an infant, as was customary, and his home life included morning and evening devotions based on the informal canon of devotional literature and hymns also described above. One commentator asserts that Hauge's eventual success and opposition is best understood in light of this dual background of Rationalism and lay spirituality.[47] Hauge reports that he became preoccupied with religious questions at the early age of eleven or twelve, pondering the afterlife and wondering about his salvation. At the age of thirteen, he along with his father and brother nearly drowned in the Glommen River while hauling hay, leading to greater introspection and awareness of his sin.

Though Hauge lacked formal university education like most people of his time, he was by no means unintelligent. He demonstrated skill as a farmer, carpenter, and blacksmith, as well as in academics, however infrequently he was able to attend school as a child.[48] His inquisitive nature perhaps contributed to his preoccupation with religious questions, which continued to raise doubts in his mind about his salvation.[49] He participated in the Rite of Confirmation at age sixteen, taking this "renewal of the baptismal covenant"[50] seriously, even admonishing his fellow students to do the same. Yet the sense of spiritual struggle that had developed within him led to theological conflict with his parish pastor

---

45. Arntzen, *Apostle of Norway*, 17.

46. Svendsbye, *I Paid All My Debts*, 16.

47. Hauge, *Autobiographical Writings*, 3. Other information in this paragraph is derived from pages 15 to 19 of this volume.

48. Arntzen, *Apostle of Norway*, 26–33.

49. Hauge, *Autobiographical Writings*, 4.

50. Arntzen, *Apostle of Norway*, 39.

ESTABLISHING THE HAUGEAN IDENTITY

in Tune; this pastor was heavily influenced by the Moravian[51] tradition, and Hauge found this Moravian form of Pietism to be inadequate, exhibiting "an emotional, sentimental piety" that was "lacking in ethical seriousness."[52] He retained this sense of spiritual seriousness in the following years, constantly examining his life in light of the words of the Bible, especially the Ten Commandments. From this, he became ever more aware of the division between "worldly things" and a pattern of life that was pleasing to God, yet he felt as though he was constantly drawn to such "worldly things," especially regarding the desire for material wealth.[53] He had further experiences where he narrowly escaped death, both on land and in water.[54] These situations awakened in him a greater consciousness of the physical as well as spiritual danger that surrounded him, expressed so well in Hans Brorson's hymn "*Jeg Gaar i Fare Hvor Jeg Gaar.*"[55]

As a young man, Hauge went to work in the city of Fredrikstad in southern Norway, not far from his childhood home, where he interacted with others of his generation and continued his practice of witnessing about spiritual matters, speaking of the reality of the sinful nature found in humanity as well as of the power of God's Word to change people, helping them to avoid sin.[56] While in the city, however, he succumbed to temptation from friends and became intoxicated after consuming liquor, an experience that created a spiritual crisis comparable in seriousness to the physical crisis of his brush with death in the Glommen River years earlier. After an experience of repentance, he returned home to the Hauge farm. The spiritual atmosphere of his childhood home was a refreshing break from his experiences in Fredrikstad. He found his work on the farm, which included clearing brush, pulling tree stumps, and breaking stones to be a fitting analogy to the work of the Holy Spirit in human life, "breaking stony hearts, uprooting stumps of sinful habits, cutting away the rank growth of evil desires, clearing the branching briars of wicked

---

51. Moravians of this era were often referred to as "Herrnhutters," after the name of the Moravian community established by Nikolaus Ludwig von Zinzendorf.

52. Molland, *Fra Hans Nielsen Hauge til Eivind Berggrav*, 11.

53. Hauge, *Autobiographical Writings*, 20 – 21.

54. Arntzen, *Apostle of Norway*, 40.

55. Hauge, *Autobiographical Writings*, 20. This hymn is translated by Ditlef Georgson Ristad as "I Walk in Danger All the Way."

56. Arntzen, *Apostle of Norway*, 51. Information in this and the following paragraph is derived from pages 51 to 83 of this volume.

thoughts, and cleansing the heart and soul from worldly rubbish, filth, and garbage."[57]

It was this view of the Christian life, namely, that faith brings with it a genuine change in a person's life, that at least partly caused Hauge to take offense at a revival that was taking place near his home. As mentioned earlier, the pastor of Hauge's congregation, Gerhard Seeberg, was influenced by the Moravian tradition. Several people became attracted to his preaching, but Hauge sensed something missing in the theological content of this revival. Though this preaching was not rationalistic and was a welcome break from such preaching that focused on agriculture, vaccination, social etiquette, and other practical topics, this Moravian preaching emphasized cleansing by the blood of Christ but did not focus on conviction of sin by the law and amendment of life, something that Hauge considered essential, which had been impressed on him by his study of Luther's *Small Catechism*. Furthering his suspicions about the quality of this revival was the fact that these "Seebergians" seemed to lift up the figure of Seeberg himself as a type of Christ-figure, focusing on his persecution from the church authorities in Christiania, creating a personality cult. For this, Hauge rebuked his former confirmation pastor in a letter that went unanswered.

Hauge's "Conversion"

While this Seebergian revival was taking place, Hauge himself would come to experience an awakening of sorts, one that differed significantly from that of the Seebergians, changed his life, and launched his itinerant preaching career. As a twenty-five-year-old on April 5, 1796, Hauge was "working outside under the open sky," presumably plowing, when he had an ecstatic experience as he sang the second verse of a familiar hymn from memory, "*Jesus, Din Søde Forening at Smage.*"[58] One English translation of the Dano-Norwegian translation of the original German verse reads as follows:

> Mightily strengthen my spirit within me, that I may learn what
> Thy Spirit can do; Oh, take Thou captive each passion and win

---

57. Arntzen, *Apostle of Norway*, 73.

58. Hauge, *Autobiographical Writings*, 41. This is often translated as "Jesus, I Long for Your Blessed Communion." Literally, the title speaks of "tasting union" with Jesus, leading some to place it in the "Lord's Supper" category in hymnals.

me, lead Thou and guide me my whole journey through! All that I am and possess I surrender, if Thou alone in my spirit mayest dwell, everything yield Thee, O Savior most tender, Thou, only Thou, canst my sadness dispel.[59]

The drama of this event rivals that of other famous conversion experiences in Christian history, such as Augustine in the Milanese garden, Luther's "tower experience," and Wesley's experience of a "heart strangely warmed" while visiting a Moravian gathering at Aldersgate Street in London. However, it seems as though Hauge's experience had more in common with the latter example than the first two.[60] Because of the temptation to dwell on the event in a sensationalistic way, it is important to understand this event properly and its meaning for Hauge's life and work. This event is sometimes referred to, even by Hauge himself, as a "conversion,"[61] but that description requires clarification.

Nearly twenty years after the fact, Hauge reflected on this experience and its meaning in his autobiographical writings. He described being "so exalted" that he was unable to express what took place.[62] Upon regaining his composure, he was filled with a sense of regret, feeling as though he had not, to that point, "served this loving transcendently good God." Beyond receiving a "changed mind" and "sorrow for sin," he described being filled with a love for God and for others, and this love carried with it a calling to help others "become partakers of the same grace." Indeed, a consequence of this "conversion" experience was an increased awareness of the division between the will of God and the reality of the world as "submerged in evil." This awareness effectively launched his ministry and provided its essential shape; his view of the sinful world in need carried with it a calling that he sensed from God: "You shall confess my name before the people; exhort them to repent and seek me while I may be found and call upon Me while I am near; and touch their hearts that they may turn from darkness to light."[63]

"Conversion" often implies a movement from a different faith tradition or none at all to allegiance to a new faith for the individual. This was clearly not the case in Hauge's situation. It was also not the case that

---

59. Hauge, *Autobiographical Writings*, 41.
60. Molland, *Fra Hans Nielsen Hauge til Eivind Berggrav*, 12.
61. Aarflot, *Hans Nielsen Hauge*, 21.
62. Hauge, *Autobiographical Writings*, 41. Information in this and the following paragraph is derived from pages 41 and 42 of this volume.
63. Hauge, *Autobiographical Writings*, 41.

this "conversion" moved him from a worldly to a godly way of life, even though he reports feeling convicted of sin and not truly loving God to that point.[64] With the exception of his experience with inebriation in Fredrikstad, Hauge was not a notorious sinner in the eyes of the world. Though his experience on April 5, 1796, was significant for him, it is clear that at no point did Hauge abandon the morality and piety he had inherited from his childhood; he occupied himself with religious questions from early on, and he participated uninterruptedly, before and after this event, in both the pietistic devotional life of his home as well as in the outward rituals and sacramental life of the Norwegian Church.[65] His "conversion" did not even involve a shift in perspective as large as the jump from his own pietistic background to the Moravian expression of the faith; his criticism of the Seebergian revival preceded his "conversion."

How, then, can the event of April 5, 1796, be best understood? First, it must be remembered that Hauge's own description of this event was nearly twenty years removed from its occurrence. It is possible that his description, given the benefit of historical distance, exaggerated its significance for his twenty-five-year-old self to some degree. With there being no way to determine this, one can only take Hauge at his word that he remembered the event "as clearly as if it had happened only a few days ago."[66] It is reported that this event changed Hauge's demeanor and filled him with joy.[67] But more specifically, he reports that this event supplied what he had found lacking in himself: a true spirit of repentance; a "changed mind," as he describes it; a desire to know God more deeply, especially through the teachings of Jesus; a desire to live an obedient and sanctified life; and a desire to work for the salvation of others by helping them to see their own need for repentance. Yet bewildering is that given the nature of his piety to that point, these concerns had occupied him for many years already; he was already in the habit of witnessing to others about the importance of taking faith seriously and of the necessity of repentance. His "conversion," therefore, is best understood as a decisive moment of clarity in his life, a "strengthening of spirit" as in the words of the hymn that was sung during his experience, a "convincing spiritual breakthrough,"[68] one that provided him with a sense of assurance that the

---

64. Molland, *Fra Hans Nielsen Hauge til Eivind Berggrav*, 11.
65. Aarflot, *Hans Nielsen Hauge*, 21.
66. Hauge, *Autobiographical Writings*, 42.
67. Arntzen, *Apostle of Norway*, 85.
68. Aarflot, *Hans Nielsen Hauge*, 21. Information in the next several paragraphs is

pattern of Christian life that he had learned, which involved a struggle to overcome sin, was indeed in line with God's will, all the while giving him a sense of purpose. Yet it does not appear to have changed his basic convictions about the pattern of Christian life, which he learned from his pietistic background and which involved the "objective anchoring in word and sacrament" as well as a "subjective appropriation" of that grace that expresses itself in a life of serious repentance in the midst of a sinful world.

Understanding the event of April 5, 1796, with the appropriate nuance is challenging, but the fact remains that this moment was significant for Hauge, and the continued significance of this moment of clarity in Hauge's life for the subsequent Haugean tradition cannot be overstated. His own experience informed the emphasis of the later Haugean movement; the existence of the Church of Norway and his view of the necessity of a subjective appropriation of faith led Hauge to focus his ministry on awakening nominal Christianity, on those within the Church of Norway whose commitment to the faith was limited to outward participation. His focus was not on non-Christians, but rather on an inadequate expression of Christianity. The fact that Norway was covered with Christian churches did not change the fact that the land was covered in darkness, in his view. It does not appear, however, that Hauge expected others to share in the same kind of ecstatic experience that changed his life in 1796, making attempts to link Haugeanism with the Pentecostal movement, at least originally, questionable. However, the expectation did exist that people would come to experience "conversion," in the sense of conviction of sin, repentance, and the leading of a sanctified life; this "experienced faith" meant that mere outward participation in the life of the church was inadequate. The view that the world, including the established churches, is a broad mission field would lead to Haugeanism taking on the role of leaven in a larger batch of dough rather than forming a sectarian group, leading to tension within the Church of Norway as well as within Norwegian-American Lutheran church bodies.

Hauge's Ministry

Hauge's impact on those around him after his moment of clarity was quickly felt; two of his sisters experienced a "change of heart" on the same

---

derived from pages 21 and 22 of this volume.

evening. Through individual conversations with those outside his family, his influence broadened. He also began to make use of the supplementary religious gatherings in his area to proclaim his message. Such gatherings, known as conventicles, were not a Haugean innovation, but were a part of the pietistic tradition in Lutheranism traceable to Spener's platform for reform articulated in his *Pia Desideria*.

Hauge's work was initially confined to his home region, but after a year he began to branch out to other communities, some of which had been touched by earlier forms of Pietistic revivals, including Moravianism, providing a point of contact with Hauge's own movement and adding to the number of his followers. As one example, the city of Drammen in eastern Norway was engulfed decades earlier in a radical pietistic revival under the leadership of a Dane named Søren Bølle.[69] During this time, Hauge also began his writing ministry, another means by which his influence spread. His first manuscript was entitled *The World's Follies* and contained harsh criticism of the clergy of the Church of Norway, chastising them for ineffectiveness at calling people in their charge to repentance and faithful living; the manuscript reveals Hauge's emphasis on holy living, demonstrating faith in daily life, as well as disapproval of rationalistic preaching focused on secular topics.[70] In general, Hauge's writings reflected his lack of formal education, demonstrating a lack of literary quality, all the while containing mature spiritual insights.[71] This, along with another aspect of his ministry discussed below, helps reveal that Hauge, though lacking formal education, was actually highly intelligent and creative.

As Hauge traveled, his vast knowledge of practical topics facilitated the building of relationships and provided occasions for spiritual conversation.[72] He held meetings by invitation or by his own initiative, and initially he sought to inform the local clergy of his plans for such meetings; at times the clergy were even in attendance. However, a little over a year after the beginning of his itinerant ministry, Hauge encountered his first serious opposition from the clergy, meaning that the encounter led to his arrest and release shortly thereafter, a pattern that would continue throughout the eight-year span of his ministry, until 1804. At issue was

69. Van Lieburg and Lindmark, *Pietism, Revivalism and Modernity*, 63.

70. Arntzen, *Apostle of Norway*, 86–88.

71. Molland, *Fra Hans Nielsen Hauge til Eivind Berggrav*, 13.

72. Aarflot, *Hans Nielsen Hauge*, 23. The following information is also derived from page 23 of this volume.

the Conventicle Act of 1741, described above, which forbade such gatherings without the presence of an ordained minister. Even prior to this first arrest, however, Hauge experienced opposition. During a conventicle meeting in his hometown of Tune at the beginning of his ministry, the pastors of the parish and the local bailiff interrupted the gathering and engaged in a dispute with Hauge. Both Hauge and the bailiff quoted the Conventicle Act, with Hauge arguing that the purpose of the law was actually to protect such nonseparatist "godly gatherings" and to restrain sectarian tendencies.[73] Hauge apparently did not intend his gatherings to lead to separation from the Church of Norway. He did, however, lift up this encounter as an example of the corruption of the established church, pointing out how such authorities, by hindering his activity, were focusing their energy in the wrong place, which perhaps contributed to the existing social cleavage between the civil and ecclesiastical officials on the one hand and the common folk on the other. Though this incident concluded with only a reprimand issued to Hauge, he would experience continued conflict with the clergy and civil officials between 1797 and 1804 over the same issue as well as over the violation of vagrancy laws, resulting in his arrest on ten different occasions.

The clergy and civil officials were not unanimous in their opposition to Hauge's activity, however. Some civil officials observed a positive shift in morality in Norwegian society that stemmed from the Haugean revival, and some among the clergy, notably Bishop Nordal Brun of Bergen, argued against the application of the Conventicle Law of 1741 in Hauge's situation, noting that since freedom of the press had been implemented in Norway in the meantime, the law prohibiting lay-led conventicles should be considered *de facto* repealed. Hauge also appealed to the existence of a law stipulating punishments for failure to attend church, arguing that since this law was not being enforced, the Conventicle Law should be regarded as similarly outdated. In his own reflection, Hauge justified his activity as a lay preacher by appealing to a work attributed to the German medieval mystic Johannes Tauler, which described a layperson instructing a member of the clergy in spiritual matters.[74]

Hauge's activity, which led him to traverse Norway, parts of it multiple times, took him as far north as the city of Tromsø as well as twice to Denmark. Yet his work was not confined to spiritual matters.

---

73. Molland, *Fra Hans Nielsen Hauge til Eivind Berggrav*, 16. Information in this and the following paragraph is derived from pages 16 and 17 of this volume.

74. Aarflot, *Hans Nielsen Hauge*, 24 – 25.

As mentioned, Hauge demonstrated talent in a variety of practical skills, which facilitated his ability to relate to people regarding spiritual matters. Though Hauge considered the world to be sinful and in need of repentance, this conviction did not lead to an otherworldly piety, and he always admonished his followers not to neglect their daily work, emphasizing the Lutheran doctrine of vocation by his words and example.[75] Wherever he stayed on his journeys, he assisted with farm chores as well as advising farmers on more efficient ways to conduct their work. He also knitted as he walked across Norway, maximizing his productivity.

Yet Hauge's involvement with things practical extended beyond these incidental matters. Attempting to secure all necessary business licenses where required, he established a number of commercial operations throughout Norway, and he assisted his friends in their own business development. In his view, this was a way of providing a Christian witness to those who were "worldly minded" by utilizing profit for good, thereby "letting their light shine" (Mt 5:16) and providing them with means to give rather than simply receive. In Bergen, Hauge directed business operations of his own, such as fishing and shipping operations and trading posts. Elsewhere, he assisted his followers in the establishment of various enterprises, such as lumber operations, mills of various types, and salt refineries. During this time, he also continued working toward the printing of his books, notably a hymnal consisting mostly of Brorson's hymns as well as a collection of his own sermons.[76] The pattern of arrest and release continued for Hauge, which provided him with time to focus on his literary activity; while in the Trondheim jail at Christmastime of 1799, he composed a hymn that has become emblematic of his attitude toward the persecution he faced, translated as follows: "With God in grace I'm dwelling, what harm can come to me from worldly pow'rs compelling my way thus closed to be? Though they in chains may bind me inside this prison cell, yet Christmas here can find me; within my heart 'tis well."[77]

For his writing ministry, Hauge had to that point utilized printers in Denmark as well as learning for himself the skill of bookbinding. The effectiveness of his writings in sowing the seeds of awakening inspired

---

75. Molland, *Fra Hans Nielsen Hauge til Eivind Berggrav*, 15. Information in this and the following paragraph is derived from pages 15 and 16 of this volume.

76. Aarflot, *Hans Nielsen Hauge*, 27. Information in this and the following two paragraphs is derived from pages 27 to 37 of this volume.

77. Aarflot, *Hans Nielsen Hauge*, 28.

him to establish a paper mill near Eiker in eastern Norway; the method of printing available at that time was primitive, involving printing on rags that were mixed with chemicals, providing motivation for an improved method. The building of the Eiker paper mill was completed in 1802. Leaving it in the hands of others, he spent more time in Bergen engaging in business and holding religious meetings. He traveled again to Denmark where he had contact with a Danish lay movement similar to his own and patterned after his revival in Norway. After leaving these "strong Jyllanders," he also spent a few days at a Moravian colony in Christiansfeld, where he developed a more positive image of the Moravian tradition than he had of the Seebergian expression of it in his earlier years.

Upon his return to Norway, Hauge experienced what would be his final arrest before his decade of captivity. While visiting the Eiker paper mill, Hauge was arrested on October 24, 1804. By then, Hauge's influence had been widely felt around Norway and even in Denmark to an extent, and although some civil and ecclesiastical officials were more sympathetic to Hauge, strong opposition from some led to his arrest; he was accused of fanaticism and sowing distrust of the pastors, and there was fear that this influence would spread even further into Denmark. There were four formal charges against him, the first involving alleged violations of the law against vagrancy, claiming that Hauge lacked the required merchant licenses to operate in various locations. The second accused him of misconduct in business ownership in Bergen. The third pertained to the rules governing the freedom of the press, which Hauge apparently pushed to the limit with his harsh criticism of the clergy. The final charge accused him of violating the Conventicle Act of 1741. He longed to be released and even expressed regret at the tone he used in some of his writings against the clergy, but the investigation into the charges against him was nonetheless lengthy, involving interviews with hundreds of people around Norway.

While Hauge languished in prison, conditions in Norway deteriorated as a result of the British blockade during the Napoleonic Wars; grain and salt were in short supply. Hauge was temporarily released from prison in order to construct a series of salt-works on the coast of Norway, extracting salt from the ocean in the time of shortage.[78] He was permitted some freedom after this time, but his case was not settled until December 23, 1814, when a court ruled that he was guilty only of the charges

---

78. Arntzen, *Apostle of Norway*, 264–68.

regarding the freedom of the press and the violation of the Conventicle Act. His punishment was a fine of a thousand *riksdaler*,[79] which was paid by friends soon thereafter.[80] During his period of imprisonment, Hauge's health suffered repeatedly. A nurse named Andrea Andersdatter Nyhus cared for him in 1811, and the two were married shortly after his release.[81] Their union produced one child, Andreas Hauge, who would also be influential in Norwegian ecclesiastical life.[82] Their family life was short-lived, however, as Andrea died from complications in childbirth. Hauge was later remarried in 1817, this time to Ingeborg Marie Olsdatter.[83] Unable to travel due to poor health, Hauge bought and settled on a farm named "Bredtvedt" near the capital city of Christiania where he continued his writings and correspondence with friends. He died on March 29, 1824, at the age of fifty-three.[84]

FROM HAUGE TO HAUGEANISM

With the death of Hauge, the movement he ignited was free to develop without his direct influence. As Haugeanism continued to impact Norway, other influences from home and abroad would color the expression of Haugeanism in the years that followed. Before examining these influences, it is important to evaluate Hauge's theological, ecclesiastical, and social legacy.

A Brief Look at Hauge's Theology

A complete examination of Hauge's theology based on his sermons and other writings is a task that was accomplished by Aarflot's book. To understand better Hauge's ministry and to clarify some misunderstandings about him, it is worth briefly discussing parts of his theological legacy here that appear significant for the later Haugean tradition. As already stated, however, though Hauge was by no means unintelligent, he did not possess a formal theological education, nor did he attempt to construct

---

79. This would be the equivalent of a few thousand dollars in modern US currency.
80. Aarflot, *Hans Nielsen Hauge*, 39.
81. Arntzen, *Apostle of Norway*, 286.
82. Aarflot, *Hans Nielsen Hauge*, 42.
83. Arntzen, *Apostle of Norway*, 289–90.
84. Molland, *Fra Hans Nielsen Hauge til Eivind Berggrav*, 18.

a systematic theology, all insights that must be taken into account when evaluating his theology. His theology is the product of influences from his pietistic background, notably from Johann Arndt and Erik Pontoppidan, as well as his independent reflections.[85] Discussion of Hauge's theology will take place under three broad categories that encompass the most significant points: biblical understanding, synergism, and the *triplex munus*.

Biblical Understanding

Those who mock Hauge in contemporary American Lutheranism sometimes refer to him as a "Fundamentalist." Though this term is used mostly imprecisely today as a blanket term describing conservative Christianity of any type, and though the use of the term is anachronistic in Hauge's situation, which was far removed from the American and British theological struggle against theological modernism in the twentieth century that produced the term "Fundamentalism," it is important to explore Hauge's understanding of biblical authority as a part of his larger theological legacy. Rigidity regarding biblical interpretation is the one of the five "Fundamentals" of 1910 that sets modern Fundamentalists apart from other theologically conservative Christians. The Fundamentalist understanding of biblical authority is itself a complex topic, and articulating its complexity is beyond the scope of this work. For the sake of simplicity, suffice it to say that modern biblical Fundamentalism is marked by a concern for "inerrancy" regarding the Bible's historical record.

Hauge certainly regarded the Bible as important. He read and studied it from childhood, and his writings record the following reflection: "Indeed, before I would give up the Bible, I would rather suffer to the utmost or lose my life."[86] His understanding early on was shaped by Pontoppidan's *Sanhed til Gudfrygtighed*, which articulates a doctrine of verbal inspiration, claiming that God's Spirit gave the biblical authors the ideas and the particular words with which to express the ideas. He also believed that the Bible and the message preached from it provided a "special revelation" to humanity in addition to the "general revelation" that is available to everyone in nature and in the individual conscience.[87] With

---

85. Aarflot, *Hans Nielsen Hauge*, 99.
86. Aarflot, *Hans Nielsen Hauge*, 67.
87. Aarflot, *Hans Nielsen Hauge*, 73.

this view of "special revelation," he affirmed Luther's teaching about the power of the Holy Spirit to call and enlighten people through the message of the gospel,[88] though he did affirm that God does, at times, provide revelations to people apart from the message of the Bible, as through prayer and through dreams, though such occurrences are abnormal.[89] It seems, however, that Hauge, in an effort to avoid the charge of heretical religious enthusiasm, expected that such "independent revelations" would take place within the context of a biblical faith, as was the situation with his own "conversion," or at least that the recipients of such "independent revelations" would come to express a biblical faith. He also spoke of the importance of hearing the Bible's message holistically, pointing out that Satan quoted the Bible selectively to serve his purposes.

As much as Hauge considered the Bible to be authoritative, he emphasized its authority as an active means to speak the Word of God to people, bringing about conversion and strengthening the daily life of believers. His view of biblical authority did not diminish his ability to look at the Bible critically and to lift up parts of the Bible, perhaps in the spirit of Luther, as more significant than others, all the while maintaining that each part of the Bible contains its own significance and remains a part of a cohesive whole. Hauge was aware of tension within the biblical canon, and he acknowledged that the reports of various events in the Bible, both in the Old and New Testaments, were not intended to be an exact historical record, actually demonstrating some affinity to Enlightenment theology on this point. Therefore, describing Hauge as a biblical Fundamentalist misses the mark.

The most significant thing that Hauge's biblical understanding reveals about his overall theology is his understanding of law and gospel. Hauge's ministry was carried out in a context with two competing themes. On the one hand, Enlightenment Rationalism fostered an environment of moralistic preaching, and on the other hand, the form of Moravianism with which he was familiar emphasized grace without law. Perhaps in reaction to this Moravianism, Hauge's preaching has been described as legalistic, though not in the same sense as Enlightenment moralism. Hauge's preaching was heavy on themes of law, repentance, and new life. He was also clear that the law of God was not confined to the Ten Commandments or the Old Testament more generally, but

---

88. Kolb and Wengert, *The Book of Concord*, 355.

89. Aarflot, *Hans Nielsen Hauge*, 75. Information about Hauge's theology on the next few pages is derived from pages 75 to 105 of this volume.

was also present in the New Testament, especially in the words of Jesus. In Lutheran fashion, Hauge emphasized the convicting function of the law while also lifting up the other side of the "two-edged sword" (Heb 4:12) of the gospel. Though he was clear that it is the gospel that contains the power to save sinners, Hauge, contrary to the Moravian expression around him, continued to emphasize the validity of the law of God for Christian life in discipleship and spiritual warfare. Applying the term "legalistic" to describe Hauge's theology makes some sense in light of the pervasiveness of such themes in his preaching, but one should not fail to consider his context and its influence on him or the important place the gospel occupied in his theology.

Synergism

Probably the most significant criticism directed at Hauge by modern Lutherans concerns his understanding of the human will and its ability to turn to God on its own power. Acknowledging that Hauge might depart from confessional Lutheranism on this point, one must emphasize again Hauge's lack of formal theological training, as well as bear in mind the type of Lutheranism that was present in the Dano-Norwegian kingdom at the time, discussed earlier in this chapter, which might account for Hauge's approach.

Hauge believed that human beings are distinct from the animal world, possessing an immortal soul, and that by virtue of this distinction, human beings are morally responsible. Though he believed in original sin as a breaking of God's plan for human life and a corrupting of God's image in humanity, he also believed that this sin does not negate, at least completely, the power of the human will. In his view, people still retain the ability to choose or reject the grace of God, and he cited biblical stories such as Mary "choosing the good portion" (Luke 10:42) as evidence. But his view of the ability of the human will to choose salvation should not be overstated. Original sin has corrupted the human will, and it is drawn toward evil, requiring the activity of the Spirit to intervene and enable a response. Yet it is the responsibility of human beings to respond affirmatively to the Spirit's call, as well as to engage in the continued struggle to maintain a relationship with God in the sinful world, which explains Hauge's emphasis on edifying gatherings, the continued function of the law in Christian life, and repentance. Even with this synergism, however,

Hauge was careful to avoid an overly positive appraisal of the human will, giving the example of two intoxicated men in a pub, which was in danger of collapse, requiring evacuation. One of the men accepted help out the door while the other refused and perished. Yet even the man who accepted help and survived had nothing for which to be proud.

The *Triplex Munus*

A brief look at Hauge's understanding of the person of Jesus Christ provides an important glimpse into his overall theology. Underscoring again Hauge's reliance upon and commitment to the inherited Christian tradition, he made use of the *triplex munus* when referring to Christ's person and work.[90] This understanding of Christ as possessing a threefold office of Prophet, Priest, and King has a long place in the Christian tradition, which helps defend Hauge against the charge of doctrinal innovation.

Although Hauge did not neglect the priestly role of Christ, as evidenced by his preaching on the atonement, his theology also gave equal or greater attention to Christ as a prophet, revealing God's will for life, as well as his role as King and Lord over life; the absence of any of these three parts of Christ's work led to an inadequate expression of Christianity.[91] Hauge's view of faith was that it must be "living," manifesting itself in a holy life and commitment to Jesus Christ as both Savior and Lord.[92] Hence, it is understandable that Hauge and his followers emphasized temperance and amendment of life regarding other vices.[93]

Hauge's "Testament to His Friends"

At the end of his life, Hauge apparently sensed that the awakening movement that he had ignited would have lasting significance for Norway. To provide direction to those who came after him, he felt compelled to address various issues in what became known as a "Testament to His Friends."[94] This brief statement demonstrates Hauge's chief concerns as well as his theological and ecclesiastical commitments.

90. Aarflot, *Hans Nielsen Hauge*, 136.
91. Aarflot, *Hans Nielsen Hauge*, 136.
92. Arden, *Four Northern Lights*, 66.
93. Hauge, *Autobiographical Writings*, 92–93.
94. Molland, *Fra Hans Nielsen Hauge til Eivind Berggrav*, 19.

When setting forth his will for his followers, Hauge began by invoking the Triune name of God, a simple act that demonstrated his allegiance to the established Christian tradition.[95] This same commitment is shown in his concern that people continue to uphold the authority of the Bible for Christian teaching and life. Specifically, he admonished his readers to continue to utilize the accepted catechism, presumably Pontoppidan's *Sanhed til Gudfrygtighed*, and other books that had been "tested and accepted as good," reading only with reservation those books that are "untested." By insisting that books be "tested," Hauge's concern was that the teachings therein conform to the chief doctrines of the Bible, notably an orthodox Trinitarian understanding of God, faith in Jesus as redeemer, and the importance of demonstrating faith in daily life by being "assiduous in good deeds." He also requested that his followers not publish or commend writings by themselves or others before such works are deemed trustworthy by the Christian fellowship and elders of the Haugean movement. All these instructions served to guard against any charge of religious enthusiasm and doctrinal innovation.

Addressing this concern even more directly, Hauge instructed his followers to remain in fellowship with the Church of Norway, pointing out that the Haugeans had never severed ties with the ecclesiastical establishment and had maintained their adherence to the teachings of the *Augsburg Confession*, thereby rendering accusations of sectarian behavior baseless.[96] He admonished them to continue to attend worship in the state churches, receive the Lord's Supper, and be married by the clergy. However, such instruction should not be interpreted as advocating uncritical allegiance to the Church of Norway. Hauge was careful to note that friction between his followers and the Church of Norway was at times justifiable, pointing out that the Haugean movement had earned its false reputation as a sect by standing against "vices with which many have dishonored the Christian Church." Hauge desired that those who came after him would stand as a positive witness of godliness to the Church of Norway from their position within it, serving as leaven in a larger batch of dough. In spite of the formal allegiance to the Church of Norway, the

---

95. Shaw, *Pulpit under the Sky*, 201. Information in these two paragraphs is derived from pages 201 to 204 of this volume.

96. As already noted, Hauge's theology, insofar as it can be constructed based on his writings and sermons, can be said to deviate at some points from the theology of the Lutheran confessions, especially regarding the freedom of the will. However, the point here is that Hauge and his followers understood themselves as standing within the boundaries of the established Lutheran tradition.

Haugean movement continued its practice of holding separate conventicles with Haugean lay preachers and the reading of devotional works in the absence of such preachers, all of which was in addition to attending church and receiving the Lord's Supper in the spring and fall.[97] Their participation in the sacramental life of the church was balanced, however, by maintaining this vigilant devotional life and "living faith," aware of the reality of spiritual danger and avoiding complacency.[98]

The Impact of the Haugean Revival on Norwegian Society

As noted at the beginning of the chapter, Aarflot alludes at the beginning of his work to the impact of the Haugean movement on society as a whole and not simply on church life.[99] It is easy and perhaps necessary for the purpose of discussion to divide Hauge's work between the spiritual and the practical, but such division is artificial. As a layperson who functioned as a preacher, he walked in both sacred and secular realms, uniting them by his own example and his encouragement of demonstrating faith in daily life, avoiding an otherworldly piety. Therefore, it is worth looking briefly at the impact of the Haugean movement on Norwegian society.

Hauge's movement has been credited with ushering in a new era in Norway's history where the common folk began to exert influence in both ecclesiastical and civil matters, changing the country for the better.[100] After the royal imposition of both Christianity and the Reformation, Hauge's movement marked a change by inspiring the laity, especially of the lower class, to make their voices heard in the church. Similarly, Hauge empowered the same laity in the development of business ventures and civic involvement. Amid the existing social cleavage between the official class and the lower class, consisting mostly of farmers and tenant laborers, Hauge's ministry primarily reached this lower class.[101] His encouragement of business ventures among the lower class helped change the Norwegian economy, and some of these people found their way into the cities, becoming prosperous. Over time, this translated into political involvement among the lower class, and three Haugean farmers

---

97. Molland, *Fra Hans Nielsen Hauge til Eivind Berggrav*, 20.

98. Shaw, *Pulpit under the Sky*, 180.

99. Aarflot, *Hans Nielsen Hauge*, 7.

100. Shaw, *Pulpit under the Sky*, 4.

101. Molland, *Fra Hans Nielsen Hauge til Eivind Berggrav*, 20. Information in this paragraph is derived from pages 20 and 21 of this volume.

were among the *Storting*[102] in 1814 when Norway achieved independence from Denmark and came under nominal Swedish rule at the conclusion of the Napoleonic Wars. In time, a "farming bloc" was formed in the *Storting*, which finally succeeded in 1842, contrary to the wishes of the king, in repealing the Conventicle Act of 1741, the law that had caused Hauge so much trouble during his ministry.

Hauge cannot be given complete credit for the transformation that occurred in Norwegian society. Outside factors such as the Enlightenment and the outcome of war can be credited with providing the immediate circumstances for Norwegian independence, but Hauge's role in empowering the lower classes through business development and "challenging old class privileges" was significant.[103] Hence, it can be argued that Hauge's work was instrumental in Norway's development as a modern democratic society.

The Evolution of the Haugean Tradition

After Hauge's death, the Haugean tradition continued to emphasize strongly God's law and obedience to it as well as the importance of continued struggle against sin and the importance of good works, rejecting the inwardly focused "blood piety" of the Moravians, which focused on contemplation of Jesus's wounds.[104] The Haugeans have been described as "puritans" in the sense that they rejected amusements such as dancing, card playing, and music making, being known to smash their violins. Yet the Haugean movement in Norway would continue to evolve, becoming less legalistic and more focused on evangelical proclamation. This shift has been credited to the Haugean lay preacher Anders Haave, who, in a moment of introspection and despair, felt that he could only trust in Christ's atonement for salvation and not in his own works. The legalistic focus continued to exert influence, no doubt, but this was tempered over time. Beyond this evolution, two other movements influenced Norwegian Haugeanism and, by extension, its American expression in significant ways.

---

102. This is the name of the Norwegian parliament.
103. Shaw, *Pulpit under the Sky*, 5.
104. Molland, *Fra Hans Nielsen Hauge til Eivind Berggrav*, 21. Information in this paragraph is also derived from page 21 of this volume.

The Grundtvigian and Johnsonian Revivals

The decades after Hauge's death witnessed other influences on Norwegian ecclesiastical life, one of which originated in Denmark under the leadership of Nikolai Grundtvig, a member of the clergy who was eventually given the title of bishop, but without the responsibilities of the office. Though critical of Rationalism, Grundtvig was a controversial figure with some theological views even considered questionable by others in agreement with his stance against Rationalism. Notably, though Grundtvig considered the Bible to be an expression of God's word, he emphasized instead the use of the sacraments and claimed that the Apostles' Creed predated the Bible and therefore held greater authority, which is sometimes referred to as Grundtvig's "churchly view." He also held to the possibility of an individual's conversion after death. This spiritual movement, in spite of the questionable theological emphases, appealed to some Haugeans in Norway, at least in part because of its rejection of Rationalism.[105] Yet Haugean support for Grundtvigianism diminished over time as it became apparent that the movement was of a different character than their own; the Haugeans felt that the "churchly view" did not take seriously their concerns for revival and conversion and were also dissatisfied with the Grundtvigian approval of what they considered to be sinful amusements.[106] Two theological professors of the newly created University of Christiania, Svend Hersleb and Stener Stenersen, had personal contact with and were influenced by Grundtvig in their rejection of Rationalism, but they came to reject his "churchly view." Nevertheless, their teaching rejected the practice of lay preaching so dear to the Haugeans, and pastors trained by them had a similar distaste for the practice. Therefore, the Haugean movement remained distanced from the officialdom of the Church of Norway.

Another important development in Norwegian ecclesiastical life in the first half of the nineteenth century was the founding of the Norwegian Missionary Society in 1842.[107] The religious energy of the Haugean movement likely contributed to this development. The mission meetings of the Society were partly responsible for another religious awakening in

---

105. Rohne, *Norwegian American Lutheranism up to 1872*, 16–17.

106. Nelson and Fevold, *Lutheran Church*, 1:29. Information in this paragraph is derived from pages 25 to 29 of this volume.

107. Molland, *Fra Hans Nielsen Hauge til Eivind Berggrav*, 32. Information in this and the following two paragraphs is derived from pages 32 to 34 of this volume.

Norway in the 1850s and 1860s. Sometimes referred to as the Johnsonian revival, this awakening movement had a different effect on Norway than Grundtvigianism.

Gisle Johnson was twenty-seven years old when he began serving as a theological professor in Christiania, and he remained a layperson during his service. His status as both a layperson and a theologian possibly contributed to his ability to relate to both the laity influenced by Haugeanism as well as the officialdom of the Church of Norway. He acknowledged the authority of the church officials, yet by virtue of his status as a theological professor, he developed a reputation as a preacher. As a part of the awakening that was taking place, Johnson, described as a quiet man, led devotional meetings and lectures on the Bible, first around the capital city and then around the entire country, and though his addresses were not fiery in their tone, he spoke to large crowds of the need for repentance. His message was well-received, and he at times cooperated with Haugean lay preachers, which helped heal the class division in Norwegian society.

Johnson's lasting impact, however, came through his students. Those educated by Johnson served as pastors around Norway, and they often sought to imitate not only Johnson's theology, but also his voice and mannerisms.[108] Through these disciples of Johnson and their communication with friends and relatives, the revival had a wide impact on the country, impressing upon both clergy and laity the importance of seriousness in spiritual matters and changing the character of entire cities with regard to their attitude toward cultural influences deemed as sinful.[109]

Theologically, Johnson's influence provided some justification for the practice of revival, which in turn provided some legitimacy for the Haugeans in their activity. In some cases, pastors worked with Haugean lay preachers, creating an appreciation for the Haugeans among the established church, yet Johnson's revival was able to reach those in the upper classes previously untouched by the Haugean revival.[110] Johnson was able to relate to the Haugeans through his careful articulation of theology. Desiring to "satisfy the strictest demands of Lutheran traditionalism" and confessional Lutheran theology, he nonetheless found ways to

---

108. Nelson and Fevold, *Lutheran Church*, 1:33.

109. Molland, *Fra Hans Nielsen Hauge til Eivind Berggrav*, 35.

110. Nelson and Fevold, *Lutheran Church*, 1:34. Information in this paragraph is derived from pages 34 to 35 of this volume.

affirm the subjective and experiential faith emphases of the Haugeans in what has been called "a combination of pietism and orthodoxy," which became the norm in Norwegian and Norwegian-American Lutheranism. One example of this blending of emphases is found in his theological writings:

> Despite the fact that the creation of faith thus is exclusively a work of God's grace, it is nevertheless impossible without a certain communication between divine grace and human freedom. No one can be forced into faith against his will. Converting grace cannot be any "irresistible grace" – it cannot work with any power that man cannot withstand. Within the concept of human freedom of the will there lies the possibility of an opposition to grace by which its action can be hindered. . . . The necessary prerequisite for the true occurrence of conversion, therefore, is a cancellation of the heart's natural opposition to converting grace. The heart must be made fit to be influenced by such grace through a preparation for conversion. Such working of grace must be subjectively made possible, and this preparation, just as much as conversion, can only be a work of God's saving grace.[111]

Hence, Johnson struck an important balance between the established confessional Lutheranism of his time and the Haugean revival activity. He insisted on using the term "Lutheran" to emphasize his confessional loyalty, but he also expressed a "somber pietism" in line with the Haugeans.[112] The cooperation of Haugeans and Johnsonian pastors produced the phenomenon of *bedehuser*,[113] where, as they were not officially congregations, laypeople could lead devotional meetings and preach; Johnson justified the practice of lay preaching according to what was known as "the emergency principle,"[114] attempting to sidestep the requirement of ordination for preaching derived from article fourteen of the *Augsburg Confession*.[115]

---

111. Granquist, *Scandinavian Pietists*, 73–74.
112. Molland, *Fra Hans Nielsen Hauge til Eivind Berggrav*, 37.
113. This is translated as "prayer houses."
114. Molland, *Fra Hans Nielsen Hauge til Eivind Berggrav*, 43.
115. Kolb and Wengert, *The Book of Concord*, 46.

Rosenian Influence

If the Johnsonian revival helped bring Haugeanism in Norway into closer fellowship with the established church and provided it with some theological legitimacy, it can be said that influence from the Rosenian revival in Sweden helped change the tone of Haugeanism. Carl Olof Rosenius, the son of a Swedish pastor, was born in 1816, when Hauge's life in neighboring Norway was drawing to a close. His father was influenced by the pietistic tradition within Lutheranism as well as by the revival movement that was taking place in Sweden at the time.[116] This revival in Sweden has been attributed to a reaction against the theological Rationalism of the established church as well as its detachment from the concerns of the common folk; Swedish pastors, functioning as state officials, were often preoccupied with record keeping, and the size of parishes often precluded regular visitation. The presence of Moravianism in Sweden in the previous century had helped popularize the practice of conventicles. It should also be considered, however, that the earlier revival movement under Hauge in Norway had some influence on developments in Sweden.

Sweden had experienced a number of separate revivals in different parts of the country in the late eighteenth and early nineteenth centuries. It was an English Methodist named George Scott who, serving as a missionary to Sweden, has been credited with providing some unity to these various movements. Scott did not emphasize confessional differences between different Christian traditions; like Hauge, he was more concerned with the quality of a person's spiritual life than with the institutional form of the church. While a student at Uppsala University, Rosenius fell under Scott's influence and experienced a spiritual awakening. With Scott's help, Rosenius was offered a position as an evangelist by an American missionary society, which allowed Rosenius the freedom to preach without ordination.

Yet Rosenius's contribution to the revival in Sweden came mostly from his writings. He and Scott began in 1842 the monthly publication of a magazine entitled *Pietisten*,[117] which also provided some unity for the Swedish revival movements and through which Rosenius's influence spread. The many hymns of Carolina Sandell-Berg, which have been described as "in complete accord with the Rosenian viewpoint," also

---

116. Arden, *Four Northern Lights*, 116. Information in this and the following two paragraphs is derived from pages 116 to 140.

117. This is translated as "The Pietist."

became popular and were an important part of the Rosenian revival. Rosenius emphasized traditional Christian themes such as creation, the fall into sin, the law of God, and the atonement of Christ. Though he did emphasize that faith brings about a new orientation in a person's life, Rosenius's piety can be described as "sweet," emphasizing "resting in quiet peace and sure confidence" through faith in what Jesus accomplished on behalf of humanity. This can be said to contrast with Hauge's harsher message of repentance and conversion.

The printing and popularity of Rosenius's writings in *Pietisten* led to his influence extending beyond Sweden. The Norwegian pastor Nils Laache, who became bishop of Trondheim in 1884, was active in the Johnsonian revival and translated many of Rosenius's writings for Norwegian readers.[118] Laache's appointment as a bishop in the Church of Norway itself carried symbolic significance, standing as a testimony to the deep and widespread influence of the Haugean and Johnsonian revivals on Norwegian ecclesiastical life, a changed situation from a few decades prior.[119] Specifically, however, Laache's influence was felt through his translation of Rosenius's works, which further colored the Norwegian ecclesiastical experience and influenced those known as Haugeans with Rosenius's emphases. In articulating the differences between the Rosenian and Haugean traditions, it has been said that the Rosenian message emphasized the joyful reception of salvation, whereas Hauge, based on his own experiences, emphasized a darker struggle for maintaining faith while in the world.[120] Furthermore, though Hauge emphasized repentance and continued obedience to God's law,[121] which was received by some as excessively legalistic and encouraging salvation through works, notably by A. Haave mentioned above, Rosenius articulated a more "evangelical" message of finding peace with God solely through the merits of Christ, as in this passage from *A Faithful Guide to Peace with God*:

> What is the end and purpose of repentance? God's purpose in your repentance is by no means that you are to make yourself fit and worthy of his pardoning grace, but rather that you be driven to Christ.... If you still seek salvation in your own betterment, the improvement of your character, your remorse, and your prayers, your knowledge of sin and guilt before the

---

118. Granquist, *Scandinavian Pietists*, 84.
119. Granquist, *Scandinavian Pietists*, 18.
120. Granquist, *Scandinavian Pietists*, 19.
121. Arden, *Four Northern Lights*, 71.

living God is sadly defective. But as soon as you find no peace; as soon as you cannot conform to the ways of the world, uncertain about the mercy of God, with no comfort in your heart, in your contrition, in your self-improvement, throwing yourself upon the mercy of God in Christ alone, just as you are, then is your repentance as it should be; for it attains its purpose, which was to drive you to Christ. In him you find peace and rest and safety.[122]

The coexistence and interaction between the Haugean and Rosenian pieties would come to play a significant role in Haugeanism as it became established in America, discussed below.

THE EMERGENCE OF AN AMERICAN HAUGEANISM

Waves of Immigration

An interesting coincidence is that Norwegian immigration to North America began in 1825, just over a year after Hauge breathed his last on the Bredtvedt farm south of Christiania. It is possible that Hauge's awakening influence on Norway played some role in stirring the Norwegian population to greater mobility, thereby serving as one factor among many in the decision of many Norwegians to seek a different life in North America.[123] Regardless, the fact that emigration from Norway began after Hauge's death helped ensure that Haugean influence would play a role in Norwegian-American Lutheranism from the very beginning. However, considering the developments and influences on Norwegian ecclesiastical life in the decades after Hauge's death that are noted above, Norwegian immigration to North America would carry with it different emphases at different stages of the immigration, which began in 1825 and continued well into the twentieth century. Therefore, to make sense of the development of Haugeanism in America, it is important to consider the different waves of the immigration during this time span as well as how they differed from one another.

---

122. Granquist, *Scandinavian Pietists*, 171.

123. Semmingsen, *Norway to America*, 35. Information in this and the following two paragraphs is derived from pages 10 to 35 of this volume.

The "Sloopers" and the *Restauration*

The first Norwegian move toward immigration to North America was taken on July 4, 1825, when 52 people left the coastal city of Stavanger on a sloop vessel named *Restauration*. Among these 52 immigrants were apparently a number of Norwegian Quakers who had been exposed to that sect during their imprisonment in England during the Napoleonic Wars; English Quakers visited and comforted these prisoners, which at times led to conversion. Quaker societies were therefore established in Christiania and Stavanger, and given that Quaker principles conflicted with the expectation of participation in the ritual life of the Church of Norway, their desire to emigrate is understandable.

Though this earliest example of Norwegian immigration to North America was numerically small, it reveals something significant about the Haugean experience in Norway shortly after Hauge's death and before the advent of Johnsonian and Rosenian influence. Based on an American newspaper report of the arrival of these "Sloopers" in New York, it appears that Haugeans were among the small group of Norwegian Quakers that arrived on the *Restauration*.[124] The apparent connection between the Quakers from Stavanger and the Haugeans is understandable because the Haugeans were well established in Stavanger and the surrounding area. More significantly, despite Hauge's admonition to his followers to remain connected to the Church of Norway in his "Testament to His Friends," it is reasonable to assume that the Haugeans of this period had an affinity to the Quakers, especially with their rejection of the ritual of the Church of Norway, resonating with the Quaker emphasis on internal, subjective appropriation of salvation. This connection between Quakers and Haugeans in Stavanger suggests that the relationship between the Church of Norway and the Haugeans was tenuous immediately after Hauge's death. It further suggests that the Haugean connection with Lutheranism in general was equally tenuous in this time, shown by their willingness to find kindred spirits among non-Lutheran sects such as the Quakers that rejected sacramental practice altogether. Further evidence of this loose connection to the Lutheran tradition among at least some early Haugean immigrants is demonstrated by the experience in the early Norwegian-American settlements of Fox River, Illinois; Sugar Creek,

---

124. Semmingsen, *Norway to America*, 13. Semmingsen notes that the newspaper report refers to members of a religious community termed "the holy ones," which is presumably a reference to a group of Haugeans.

Iowa; and Koshkonong in Wisconsin Territory, where Mormon missionaries from nearby Nauvoo, Illinois, succeeded in converting many Norwegians to the faith of the Latter-day Saints in the 1840s.[125] Of course, not all Norwegian immigrants in these settlements were rooted in the Haugean tradition. However, it is known that the Fox River settlement included many Haugeans, and it was from there that the Norwegian Mormons sent one among them, Endre Dahl, to Nauvoo to confer with Joseph Smith himself.[126] These examples of Haugean involvement with non-Lutheran groups such as Quakers and Mormons reveal the distance that existed between the Haugeans and established Lutheranism in the earliest years of the immigration, especially when transplanted from the state church environment of Norway to the voluntary religious environment of the United States.

The First Wave: 1836 to 1865

Though the famous "Slooper" ship voyage in 1825 is lifted up as the first example of Norwegian immigration to North America, immigration did not begin in earnest until 1836. Even then, however, estimates are that only a few hundred people emigrated from Norway annually, with the number increasing to over a thousand in 1843.[127] For the purpose of determining the motivations behind immigration, it must be observed that the number of immigrants gradually increased over the years, suggesting that "America fever" was spread in part by word of mouth and by letters to relatives and friends from those who had already made the journey. This also partially explains why some communities were relatively untouched by "America fever," as those without relatives in America naturally lacked such contacts. It can also be observed that immigration rose sharply during the depression years of 1849 and 1850, accounting for almost half of those who left Norway to that point. This suggests that lack of economic opportunities in Norway played a major role in the decision to immigrate. Those who immigrated to North America were not the poorest in Norwegian society, as some means were required to make the journey, but the concern of parents for opportunities for their

---

125. Mulder, *Homeward to Zion*, 7.

126. Mulder, *Homeward to Zion*, 8.

127. Semmingsen, *Norway to America*, 32. Information in this and the following two paragraphs is derived from pages 32 to 118 of this volume.

children in a country where farmland was scarce, especially when families were large, was a motivating factor in the decision, being encouraged by reports of a country with abundant land. Hence, this first wave of immigration included many families. Understandably, the Civil War in the United States between 1861 and 1865 led to a serious decrease in immigration, but the number would rise again after the war, with the Homestead Act of 1862 undoubtedly providing incentive.

Aside from the anomaly of a small number of Norwegian Quakers discussed above, it is clear that religion itself was not a major factor in the decision to immigrate. Semmingsen notes that active persecution of Haugeans ceased by the time serious immigration began in the 1830s and that the Conventicle Act was repealed in 1842, with a law concerning religious toleration being adopted in 1845. While this does not mean that Haugeans were fully integrated into Norwegian ecclesiastical life in this period, it does mean that they did not come to North America for the purpose of religious freedom. Many Norwegian immigrants, though formally connected to the church as citizens of the country, did not take their connection to the church seriously and felt free to join other religious groups in North America or none at all. At the same time, the social mobility and focus on individual conscience impressed upon Norway by the Haugean revival did play a role in "preparing the ground psychologically" for immigration. Hence, many Haugeans were among those who came to North America in this first wave of immigration, and they brought with them their loose connection and even suspicion of the established Church of Norway, which would be tempered among the Haugeans in the later years of this period with the advent of the Johnsonian revival.

The Second Wave: 1865 to 1915

The period between 1865 and 1915 has been described as a time of mass emigration from Norway, itself divided into three different waves, with only Ireland boasting a greater percentage of its population lost to emigration during this time. As the century progressed, the Norwegian population grew due to peace, improved diet from an abundance of herring and potatoes, and the smallpox vaccine. The improved conditions, however, brought burdens with them. When the population became too large, it precipitated a demographic crisis; the country was unable to support its people with opportunities for livelihood, and emigration served as a "safety valve," leading many to make the journey to North America, where immigrants were needed and opportunities were abundant. Although the earlier wave of immigration consisted mostly of families, in time, it was largely young and unmarried individuals who undertook the journey. This was possibly due to the need for work from the population increase, the greater ease of the immigrant journey resulting from friends and relatives who promised them shelter in the new country, as well as the youthful desire for adventure. Encouraging reports from those who had emigrated earlier, which were spread by newspapers and word of mouth, reports of abundant land available in the new country, as well as the possibility of avoiding military service were also contributing factors.[128]

As with the earlier wave of immigration, the desire for religious freedom was not a driving factor. Nevertheless, the immigrants carried their religious experiences in Norway with them, which would impact developments in North America. This second major wave of immigration coincided with the latter part of the Johnsonian revival, which witnessed at least a partial healing of the division between the Haugeans and the established church. Rosenian influence also began to be felt in this time from Laache's translations. These developments in Norway contributed to the evolution of the Haugean experience in North America, with the earlier immigrants exhibiting a "purer" Haugean message, greater antipathy to church organization, and a more tenuous connection to Lutheranism in general, whereas the later immigration brought with it Haugeans who had been shaped by the Johnsonian revival and Rosenian piety, exhibiting a greater desire for church organization and a more "evangelical" tone to their message.

Elling Eielsen

The Norwegian immigrant situation in the 1830s and 1840s has been described as chaotic, especially in the significant settlement of Fox River, Illinois. This report confirms the insight that the connection of many Norwegians to the Church of Norway and Lutheranism in general was tenuous in this time period, with immigrants, no longer constrained by the state church environment of Norway, choosing to belong to

---

128. Svendsbye, *I Paid All My Debts*, 19.

Quaker, Baptist, Presbyterian, Methodist, Mormon, Haugean Lutheran, and even "freethinker" societies, creating an environment of "inextricable disorder."[129] The Swedish Episcopalian Gustav Unonius also made his presence felt among these Norwegians, attempting to attract those who were dissatisfied with the chaos by providing an orderly church experience.

However, the task of providing some order to church life as well as preserving a connection to Lutheranism among these Norwegian settlements fell most significantly to a certain Elling Eielsen. Born near Bergen, Norway, in 1804, Eielsen experienced a spiritual awakening in 1829 during the Haugean revival. After a reckless youth and subsequent spiritual struggle, his contact with a Haugean family and his own study of Pontoppidan's *Sanhed til Gudfrygtighed* gave him a sense of peace that expressed itself in a somber piety that has been described as dark and legalistic; his piety was shaped by the Haugean movement before the advent of Rosenian influence. In the process of his conversion, he developed a deep dislike and distrust of the Norwegian clergy, sensing their lack of concern for the common people. He began a career as an itinerant lay preacher around Norway, and denouncements of the "long frocked" clergy and of "dead" orthodoxy were recurring themes in his message. He has been credited with invigorating Haugeanism in Norway, but his decision to immigrate to the United States meant that his aggressive style and tone would no longer serve as a barrier to healing the rift between the Haugeans and the Norwegian church establishment.

Eielsen came to the United States in 1839 and continued his itinerant lay preaching among his fellow Norwegians in Illinois and Wisconsin.[130] He brought with him his distrust and dislike of the church establishment in Norway, which extended to those who sought to perpetuate the state church order in the new land. He is described as having "little to no vision for congregational order or church management." Accordingly, the communities that gathered around Eielsen were only loosely organized and functioned without a church body to govern them; his followers of this time have been described as "widely scattered faithful." In Norway, Haugeanism was a movement that functioned within the established

---

129. Rohne, *Norwegian American Lutheranism*, 36. Information in this and the following paragraph is derived from pages 36 to 41 of this volume.

130. Norlie, *Norsk Lutherske Menigheter i Amerika: 1843–1916*, 2:681. A translation of the article quoted here is contained in appendix 1 in the dissertation on which this book is based. Information in this paragraph is also derived from page 681.

church, but the American situation had no such ecclesiastical framework wherein Haugeanism could function, and Eielsen himself began to recognize the need for greater organization in the early 1840s.[131]

Though Eielsen's legacy is generally considered one of disorder and minimal ecclesiastical oversight, this reputation might not be entirely justified. In view of the chaotic religious situation among these immigrants described above, Eielsen, despite his antipathy to state church order, provided these immigrants with a continued connection to Lutheranism. He vigorously defended Lutheran teachings against the various "sectarians."[132] He also provided them with a facility for worship in Fox River, which doubled as an immigrant hospitality center; this facility, though referred to as a *forsamlingshus*[133] rather than a church, nonetheless provided some sense of organization.[134] Eielsen's further commitment to organized Lutheranism in some form is demonstrated by his educational concern. Recognizing the need for books for religious instruction in Fox River, especially in the English language, which was being adopted by the youth of the community, Eielsen, possibly with some assistance, translated Luther's *Small Catechism* into English and secured printed copies in New York in 1841.[135] Shortly thereafter, in 1842, he made another arduous journey to New York and Philadelphia to secure printed copies in Norwegian of Pontoppidan's *Sanhed til Gudfrygtighed* in exactly the same type as the 1775 version. This version of Pontoppidan's *Forklaring*[136] of Luther's *Small Catechism* also included the first twenty-one articles of the *Augsburg Confession*.[137] Though his efforts to secure printed copies of these documents as well as his inclusion of the *Augsburg Confession* demonstrate Eielsen's commitment to Lutheranism in at least some form, his desire to reprint *Sanhed til Gudfrygtighed* in exactly the same format as the 1775 version demonstrates his continued friction with the establishment of the Church of Norway; the church establishment apparently utilized an altered form of Pontoppidan's work, which the Haugeans opposed.[138] The altered version reflected Grundtvigian emphases and was

131. Nelson and Fevold, *Lutheran Church*, 1:80.
132. Sovik, "Elling Eielsen," 16.
133. This is translated as "gathering house."
134. Nelson and Fevold, *Lutheran Church*, 1:76.
135. Norlie, *Elling Eielsen*, 16.
136. This is translated as "Explanation."
137. Sovik, "Elling Eielsen," 17.
138. Carlsen, "Elling Eielsen," 69.

viewed with suspicion.¹³⁹ This can be said to summarize the ecclesiastical situation of the Norwegian immigrants under Eielsen's leadership: a commitment to Lutheranism existed, but the aversion to church organization in the Norwegian settlements, a by-product of Eielsen's disdain for the Church of Norway, remained strong.

Eielsen's Ordination and the "Evangelical Lutheran Church in America"

Nevertheless, anticlericalism and aversion to the establishment of the Church of Norway was not uniform throughout the Norwegian-American settlements in the early 1840s. Though both the Fox River and Muskego settlements were familiar with Eielsen and were heavily influenced by Haugeanism, the Muskego settlement near Wind Lake, Wisconsin, had a bit more sympathy for ecclesiastical order than their counterparts in Fox River. The different origins of the immigrants in these separate communities might account for this difference.¹⁴⁰

Eielsen was therefore rejected as the leader of the Muskego community; they preferred at first the work of other lay preachers and then later decided to call and ordain a certain Claus Lauritz Clausen, a young man of Danish background, as the pastor of the congregation.¹⁴¹ Eielsen's decision to pursue ordination for himself is ironic given his harsh condemnation of the clerical class in Norway, and so it is important that the action be understood correctly. His own recognition of the difference between the Norwegian and American ecclesiastical environments and the need for some form of ordered ministry in the Norwegian-American settlements undoubtedly led him to seek official recognition to perform pastoral functions through ordained status. However, it should also be considered that his discovery of the intention of the Muskego community to ordain Clausen provided impetus, possibly desiring to remain competitive with Clausen for leadership in the settlements. The details surrounding Eielsen's ordination have been a source of controversy. At any rate, it is generally accepted that a German Lutheran pastor named Francis Alex Hoffman, who lived in the vicinity of Chicago, presided at

---

139. Nelson and Fevold, *Lutheran Church*, 1:78.

140. Rohne, *Norwegian American Lutheranism*, 48–49.

141. Nelson and Fevold, *Lutheran Church*, 1:80. Information in this paragraph is also derived from page 80 of this volume.

Eielsen's ordination service on October 3, 1843.[142] Documentation of Eielsen's ordination was placed on file at the circuit court of Dane County, Wisconsin, on May 11, 1845, signed by F. A. Hoffman as a representative of "the Union of Lutheran Ministers of Northern Illinois." However, the date of October 3, 1843, does not appear on this copy, which is possibly due to an oversight on the part of the recording clerk. Nevertheless, Eielsen's eventual opponent Johannes Wilhelm Christian Dietrichson, who insisted on examining Eielsen's ordination certificate, reported that the certificate that he viewed did indeed list the date of ordination as October 3, 1843. However, in 1862, Eielsen commented that the certificate contained a typographical error and should have read "October 31" instead of "October 3."[143]

Whatever the case, though Eielsen cited receiving a call from "many immigrants,"[144] the validity of his ordination was questioned by Clausen. Curiously, Eielsen had parted ways with Clausen in August of that year over the very issue of Clausen's intention to be ordained.[145] The validity of Eielsen's ordination was also questioned by another early leader among the Norwegian-Americans, the state church pastor J. W. C. Dietrichson, who made the Koshkonong settlement in Wisconsin his headquarters and claimed that Eielsen had not been properly examined, to which Eielsen responded that he had been "examined by the Holy Spirit" through the many trials that he had endured as he ministered to the immigrants.[146] If Eielsen's ordination took place on October 3, 1843, and is to be considered valid, he unquestionably holds the title of the first Norwegian Lutheran pastor ordained in North America, as his ordination preceded that of Clausen's by two weeks.[147] Yet Eielsen's status as an ordained pastor did little to change his attitude toward the clergy and the Norwegian church establishment. He continued to speak against the use of clerical vestments and the liturgy of the Church of Norway. He also continued to emphasize the traditional Haugean rejection of common amusements, such as "dancing and drinking, riotousness and revelry."[148] Further evidence that ordination did not change the character of the man

142. Norlie, *Norsk Lutherske Menigheter i Amerika*, 2:681.
143. Carlsen, "Elling Eielsen," 76–78.
144. Nelson and Fevold, *Lutheran Church*, 1:81.
145. Rohne, *Norwegian American Lutheranism*, 62.
146. Nelson and Fevold, *Lutheran Church*, 1:81.
147. Rohne, *Norwegian American Lutheranism*, 63.
148. Nelson and Fevold, *Lutheran Church*, 1:81.

comes from the meeting between Eielsen and Dietrichson in 1845. When Dietrichson questioned the validity of his ordination, Eielsen grabbed Dietrichson's beard in a dramatic display and defiantly exclaimed, "Listen to me, you pope, I intend to plague you as long as I live."[149]

In spite of his opposition to the clerical authority that Dietrichson represented, Eielsen's followers began to recognize the need for a somewhat more concrete organization by which to order church life; the "widely scattered faithful" desired to "come together more closely."[150] The increasing number of immigrants in the settlements accelerated the need for such an organization, especially since there were no ordained pastors from the homeland to serve them.[151] Yet Eielsen had little concern for church organization and administration, an attitude summarized by a quote attributed to him: "I have nowhere read that Christ kept a protocol when he traveled about and conducted meetings for the people."[152] His indifference to matters of administration might account for the fact that the exact timeline of the process leading to the establishment of his church organization is unclear. Nevertheless, various records indicate that a meeting was held on April 13 and 14 of 1846 in Jefferson Prairie, Wisconsin.[153] Two younger associates of Eielsen, Ole Andrewson and Paul Andersen, impressed upon Eielsen the need for a church body to govern the scattered congregations, especially in light of Dietrichson's competing organizational efforts. They were suspicious of Dietrichson's alleged affinity to Grundtvigian theology from Norway and desired an alternative.[154] Hence, at the Jefferson Prairie meeting in 1846, what is considered to be the first Norwegian-American Lutheran church body came into being, the name of which was first "The Evangelical Lutheran Church on Jefferson Prairie, etc., in North America" and then changed to the less cumbersome title the "Evangelical Lutheran Church in America"[155]

149. Nelson and Fevold, *Lutheran Church*, 1:103
150. Norlie, *Norsk Lutherske Menigheter i Amerika*, 2:681.
151. Sovik, "Elling Eielsen," 20.
152. Rohne, *Norwegian American Lutheranism*, 96.
153. Rohne, *Norwegian American Lutheranism*, 97.
154. Nelson and Fevold, *Lutheran Church*, 1:129.

155. This should not be confused with the church body of the same name that was formed in 1988 as the result of a merger of the Lutheran Church in America (LCA), the American Lutheran Church (TALC), and the Association of Evangelical Lutheran Churches (AELC). The wording of the title of this church body is inconsistent in various sources and sometimes even within the same source, sometimes being listed as "of America" rather than "in America."

at some point shortly thereafter. More commonly, this church body was known as "Eielsen's Friends" or "Eielsen's Synod."[156] Some outside of this organization referred to them as the "Ellingians."[157]

The founding document of Eielsen's Synod that was drafted and adopted at the Jefferson Prairie meeting came to be known as the "Old Constitution,"[158] though it was apparently modified significantly in 1850, as discussed below. This document, apparently Eielsen's work, was viewed by some American Haugeans in the following years as "strange" and "deficient," being overly focused on certain aspects of life in the congregation at the expense of a broader synodical vision and order,[159] having little concern for governance beyond the congregational level. In fact, it is not a constitution as much as it is a statement of faith that articulates certain convictions and principles. An examination of the contents of this "Old Constitution" confirms this criticism. The document consisted of twenty articles, the first of which established the confessional basis of Eielsen's Synod. It declared adherence to "God's Word in the Holy Scriptures," the Apostles' Creed, and the *Augsburg Confession*.[160] This article was itself criticized as Grundtvigian, as its wording could be interpreted as placing the Apostles' Creed on the same level of authority as the Bible, though that was likely not the intention; it was more likely a lack of nuance on the part of Eielsen. In keeping with the Haugean emphasis on experienced faith, the second article declared that only those who had experienced conversion or were on their way toward conversion could be members, a perspective that was criticized as "Donatist." Other articles dealt with issues of discipline within the congregation, the prohibition of the use of clerical vestments, the necessity of lay preaching, the place of English and Norwegian languages within the congregation, and the sinfulness of the practice of slavery. The "Old Constitution" concluded with an "Agreement" that described the proper procedure for a pastoral call in a congregation, with emphasis placed on the spiritual qualifications of the pastor. As noted, the "Old Constitution" would be criticized

156. Rohne, *Norwegian American Lutheranism*, 97. According to Rohne on page 106, the "Old Constitution" underwent some revisions between 1846 and 1850, taking final form in that year.

157. Preus, *Vivacious Daughter*, 119.

158. Nelson and Fevold, *Lutheran Church*, 1:129. The text of the "Old Constitution" is provided in Appendix A.

159. Norlie, *Norsk Lutherske Menigheter i Amerika*, 2:681.

160. Nelson and Fevold, *Lutheran Church*, 1:129. Information in this paragraph is derived from pages 129 to 131 of this volume.

both by those outside as well as within Eielsen's Synod, but it did bring Norwegian-American Lutherans together, however loosely, into some form of synodical organization for the first time.

The Move toward Reorganization

Given that record keeping on the nineteenth-century American frontier was a haphazard affair, especially considering Eielsen's lack of concern for administration, it cannot be precisely known how many congregations belonged to the scattered fellowship of Eielsen's Synod from 1846 to 1876, at which point the synod was reorganized and renamed. Records indicate that delegates from eight congregations in Illinois and eight congregations in Wisconsin were present at the 1846 meeting in Jefferson Prairie. However, there were some congregations that were not represented from Chicago, Milwaukee, and Racine.[161] A listing of all known Norwegian-American Lutheran congregations from this time period notes that Eielsen had organized and served between thirty-five to forty congregations during his ministry, but this does not take into account the reality that Eielsen cared little for institutional formality as he organized congregations nor the apparent unintentional omission from this listing of some congregations that were present at the Jefferson Prairie meeting.[162] There were also likely a number of informal congregations and "preaching points" within the circle of Eielsen's Synod, making it reasonable to assume that there were somewhere between fifty to a hundred "congregations" in Eielsen's group, even if not all of them were officially incorporated. Despite the limitations of the congregational listing, it does identify certain locations as significant pockets of Eielsen's activity. Five congregations are listed in Illinois, thirteen in Wisconsin, three in Iowa, five in Minnesota, six in South Dakota, and one each in New York and Texas.

Between the years 1846 and 1876, Eielsen and his "Evangelical Lutheran Church in America" were criticized by other Norwegian-American Lutherans, and the friction that Eielsen experienced with Clausen and Dietrichson was just the beginning. Eielsen's Synod also experienced internal controversies and schisms leading up to the reorganization of

---

161. Norlie, *Elling Eielsen*, 14. Information in this paragraph is derived from pages 14 and 15 of this volume.

162. The listing of congregations referred to is known as "The Congregational Calendar" (*Menighetskalenderen*).

1876. This outside criticism is important to consider, as it is the earliest example of American Haugeanism clashing with other forms of piety, a phenomenon that would continue even after the merger of 1917. The internal conflicts within Eielsen's Synod reveal the struggle of American Haugeans to strike a balance between experienced faith and ecclesiastical organization, an issue that also remained relevant as Haugeanism sought to function as leaven in the larger batch of dough of Norwegian-American Lutheranism.

Outside Criticism

Those Norwegian-American Lutherans who did not flock to Eielsen's banner remained firm in their criticism of Eielsen and the group that formed around him, even after Dietrichson had returned to Norway in 1850. Dietrichson, having attempted unsuccessfully to form a lasting church body in the United States, was replaced by Herman Amberg Preus in 1851. Preus played a leading role in the dissolution of Dietrichson's organization and in the establishment of the "Norwegian Evangelical Lutheran Church in America" in 1853, which was later renamed "The Synod for the Norwegian Evangelical Lutheran Church in America." More often, this group was known as simply the "Norwegian Synod" or the "Old Synod."[163] The use of the term "synod" rather than "church" to describe the organization reflected Preus's theological conviction that his particular church body did not in itself embody the fullness of the Christian church, which was a criticism he leveled against Eielsen and his followers.

In 1866, Preus returned to Norway for several months, the purpose of his visit being to describe the ecclesiastical situation among Norwegian immigrants in the United States, thereby encouraging pastors in Norway to take up service across the Atlantic. He therefore delivered a series of seven lectures in Christiania in 1867. In them, he sought to portray the Norwegian Synod as the closest "daughter" to the Church of Norway. Naturally, a part of these lectures was an attempt to discredit other competing groups among the Norwegian immigrants, one of which was Eielsen's Synod.[164]

163. Preus, *Vivacious Daughter*, 5. Information in this and the following paragraph is derived from page xii of the introduction to page 3 of this volume.

164. Preus also discusses and criticizes the "Augustana Synod." At the time, this group was comprised of Norwegians, Swedes, and some Danes, all of whom had

The Norwegian Synod criticism of Eielsen's Synod certainly was theological in nature, as discussed below. However, it seems that some of the animus between them was of a more personal nature, with the Norwegian Synod feeling victimized by Eielsen and his followers. In her diary entry for November 5, 1855, Preus's wife, Linka,[165] described her layperson's perspective of the "Ellingians" and the relationship of the Norwegian Synod to them, wherein she articulated feeling a sense of self-righteousness emanating from the Ellingians. She mentioned an unsuccessful effort made on the part of her husband and some other leaders of the Norwegian Synod to build bridges with the Ellingians that year, noting that they had, to that point, engaged in slanderous talk about the Norwegian Synod:

> So . . . the high church council – Hermann and Adolph Preus and three laymen – held their meeting . . . on the 20th of June, and the following day. At the exact same time the honorable Ellingians had their annual meeting at Langeteig, so the council decided to go down there to demand an explanation from the members of that group about many false accusations they have made about false teachings, etc . . . they returned . . . with great expectations of improvements in the Ellingians' hateful and slanderous behavior, and that they would now deal with other branches of the church in loving fellowship, as the others treat them. . . . The pastors and congregations are in a way Lutheran, but our community has the purer, truer teaching. We are "God's little flock," so no union with the "great mass" is desired – the good Ellingians use such great words to describe their community that I have difficulty finding any spirit of humility there to guide them.[166]

Linka Preus's report was undoubtedly influenced by her husband's perspective on Eielsen's Synod to some extent, and it should be remembered that those among the Ellingians quite likely felt the same way about the Norwegian Synod's attitude toward them. Nevertheless, her account of

---

separated themselves from the Synod of Northern Illinois in 1860 and established a purely Scandinavian Lutheran church body. Three years after Preus's lectures, the Dano-Norwegian contingent amicably separated from the Swedes, forming two separate Dano-Norwegian groups.

165. The full name of Herman Amberg Preus's wife was Caroline Dorothea Margrethe Keyser Preus. She was commonly known by the nickname "Linka."

166. L. Preus, *Linka's Diary*, 306–307.

the interaction of these two groups reveals the level of friction that existed at this time.

If the Norwegian Synod was on the receiving end of slander by Eielsen and his followers, Preus at the very least was not a passive recipient of such attacks. In his lectures in Norway, his comments about Eielsen and the practices of his followers were more than pointed. Preus's criticism of the Ellingians began with highlighting Eielsen's refusal to work under the authority of state church pastors. For that reason, Preus claimed that Eielsen was not really a Norwegian lay preacher, but rather "a false teacher and founder of an erring sect."[167] As evidence of this, Preus claimed that Eielsen had wrongly assumed pastoral authority for himself, having not been properly examined for the pastoral office as well as producing no evidence of a call from any particular congregation. He also called into question Eielsen's ordination, noting discrepancies between Eielsen's account of the event and that of some eyewitnesses. Most significantly, Preus portrayed Eielsen as an enemy of the Norwegian Synod and guilty of persecuting orthodox teachers, drawing members away from orthodox congregations, and insisting on perpetuating a separate church organization rather than deferring to the proper church authorities once they arrived in the United States.

Preus mentioned the various schisms that Eielsen's Synod experienced over the years, which are discussed below, as further evidence of the troubled nature of that church body. He spent most of his lecture, however, critiquing the errors that he saw in the "Old Constitution." His first criticism dealt with the imprecise wording of the first article of this document, which concerns the confessional subscription of Eielsen's Synod. He granted that it was likely not Eielsen's intention to articulate a Grundtvigian perspective on the authority of the Apostles' Creed in relation to the Bible. Preus was not so charitable regarding the second article, however. He accused Eielsen's Synod of the Donatist heresy and of equating the visible organization of their synod with the invisible church by requiring a "pure" or "converted" membership. This attitude explained, in Preus's view, the legalistic tone of preaching within Eielsen's Synod, being directed only toward existing members of the organization. Preus's conflict with Eielsen on this point is foreshadowing of the later struggle of Haugeans to find an ecclesiastical home among other

---

167. Preus, *Vivacious Daughter*, 121. Information in the next few paragraphs is derived from pages 120 to 136 of this volume.

Norwegian-American Lutherans after 1917 as they struggled to reconcile their focus on truly converted Christian life within a larger church organization.

Issues in subsequent articles of the "Old Constitution" were also the subject of Preus's critique. The sixth article, as one example, which prohibits the use of clerical vestments as well as the use of the laying on of hands with absolution, was wrong because of its conflict with the principle of article seven of the *Augsburg Confession*, which allows freedom in "human traditions, rites, and ceremonies." Furthermore, he criticized Eielsen and those in his group for failure to use absolution or of only using absolution in a conditional form as well as prohibiting private confession and absolution. Preus's criticism extended to matters of practice within Eielsen's Synod, and he spoke against their custom of "public" prayer and of their view of the ability to offer "public" or "free" prayer as proof of being truly converted. Such a practice invited disorder, often confused prayer and preaching, drew too much attention to the individual offering the prayer, and encouraged women to speak in the public assembly, which Preus viewed as a violation of proper order.[168]

Beyond this, his criticism of Eielsen's Synod centered around three theological points, the latter two of which would have more enduring significance for the Haugean tradition. The first concerned the wording of the third article of the Apostles' Creed. Two different versions were in use among the Norwegian immigrants, but apparently Eielsen's Synod objected to the use of the word "universal," as it could suggest the presence of "unconverted" members within the church. Hence, Preus noted that the Ellingians sometimes considered baptisms conducted with the word "universal" in the Creed as invalid. The second criticism had to do with the practice of lay preaching, something that Eielsen's Synod considered the right of every Christian by virtue of his or her "spiritual priesthood." Preus argued that this right only extended to private admonition, teaching, and prayer; in accordance with article fourteen of the *Augsburg Confession*, only the pastor has the right to publicly exercise the office of the ministry. Emergency situations might necessitate a layperson to function as a temporary pastor, but this is not because of the rights of a "spiritual priesthood." Presumably, Preus's criticism of Eielsen here lay in the latter's unwillingness to defer to the proper church authorities once they appeared in the Norwegian-American settlements. Finally, there

---

168. Preus cites 1 Cor 14 and 1 Tim 2 in criticizing the practice of women speaking publicly in the Christian assembly.

was a point of contention between the Norwegian Synod on the one hand and Eielsen's Synod and the Scandinavian Augustana Synod on the other concerning the doctrine of the Sabbath, an argument based on the third of the Ten Commandments. The Norwegian Synod, Preus claimed, considered that no particular day of the week was established by God for the purpose of Christian worship, and that the practice of worshipping on Sunday is a choice that congregations make out of Christian freedom. On the contrary, Eielsen's Synod and the Scandinavian Augustana Synod considered Sunday to be a divinely established Sabbath, an attitude possibly absorbed from Reformed influence in American society. Preus described representatives of the Norwegian Synod discussing this matter with the Ellingians, appealing to article twenty-eight of the *Augsburg Confession* to support their position, to which the Ellingians responded either that they did not recognize the last seven articles as authentic or did not know they existed.[169] This would have been yet another point that caused Preus and the Norwegian Synod to question the Lutheran identity of Eielsen's Synod.

Many of the above points of contention between the Norwegian Synod and Elling Eielsen would continue to play a role in the relationship between Haugeanism and other parts of the Norwegian-American Lutheran tradition, even after the merger of 1917. In light of these issues as well as the animus that Preus displayed against Eielsen, labeling him a "cunning seducer," accusing his followers as displaying "thoughtless credulity" toward him, and expressing relief that the two groups mostly keep their distance from one another, it is difficult to imagine the Haugeanism displayed by Eielsen's Synod ever coexisting peacefully with the perspective of Preus and his colleagues in the Norwegian Synod. That a union between these perspectives was ever consummated was the result of changing attitudes within Eielsen's Synod that led to reorganization of the church body as well as careful, nuanced negotiation and compromise, carrying with it the near certainty of continued friction in the new church body after 1917.

---

169. The version of Pontoppidan's *Sanhed til Gudfrygtighed* that Eielsen reproduced in New York contained only the first 21 articles of the Augsburg Confession.

The First Schism

It was only two years after the founding of Eielsen's "Evangelical Lutheran Church in America" that the loosely organized group experienced its first schism, one that would significantly impact the course of Norwegian-American Lutheranism through the eventual founding of the Scandinavian Augustana Synod in 1860 and the emergence of two Norwegian-American Lutheran groups out of this Scandinavian Augustana Synod in 1870. This first schism resulted from dissatisfaction on the part of Eielsen's two younger colleagues, the very people responsible for prodding Eielsen toward the founding of Eielsen's Synod in the first place: Paul Andersen and Ole Andrewson.

Andersen had been educated at "Beloit Seminary" in Wisconsin, which was actually a nontheological academy with Presbyterian ties.[170] His time at Beloit occurred around the same time that he began his association with Eielsen. This non-Lutheran experience opened his eyes to religious life outside of Scandinavian circles and also coincided with his growing dissatisfaction with Eielsen's leadership. Andersen and Andrewson described church life under Eielsen's authority as filled with "laxity and disorder," and the two began a friendship with representatives of the Franckean Synod, a small eastern group known for its "American Lutheran" tendencies.[171] Nevertheless, the Franckean Synod was friendly to the convictions of these two men at the time, upholding the importance of "living Christianity" and standing against slavery. Though it is not clear whether Andersen and Andrewson were aware of the tenuous connection to Lutheranism on the part of the Franckean Synod, at the very least they did not consider their association with them to prohibit their use of Lutheran confessional documents.

Andrewson, who was the secretary of Eielsen's Synod, called for a meeting on September 29, 1848, for the purpose of deposing Eielsen as president as well as bringing Eielsen's Synod into the fellowship of the

---

170. Nelson and Fevold, *Lutheran Church*, 1:132. Information in this paragraph is derived from pages 132 and 133 of this volume.

171. The Franckean Synod was often criticized for its imprecise confessional basis. For example, it did not contain an explicit reference to the Augsburg Confession in its constitution, and it held a symbolic view of the sacraments, among other points that deviated from the growing appreciation of confessional Lutheranism in that time. The phrase "American Lutheranism" came to be associated with Samuel Simon Schmucker's 1855 attempt to revise the Augsburg Confession to make it more acceptable to the American religious environment, and the position of the Franckean Synod anticipates Schmucker's "Definite Platform" of that year.

Franckean Synod.[172] Meeting at Middle Point, Illinois, Andersen, who had recently been ordained by the Franckean Synod, was elected president of Eielsen's Synod, at which point followed a list of complaints about Eielsen, read by Andrewson. The charges against him were vague, accusing Eielsen of "immorality" without strong evidence. Nevertheless, Eielsen removed himself from the meeting unfazed, apparently considering the attack on his character a sign of his faithfulness. Though Andersen, Andrewson, and their associates found a home within the Franckean Synod for a time, resonating with their focus on revivalism and "living Christianity" as opposed to "dead orthodoxy" as represented by Dietrichson, in time they rejected the lax confessional stance of the Franckeans. Under the influence of William Passavant of the General Synod, Andersen, Andrewson, and others cooperated with other Scandinavians like Lars P. Esbjörn first in joining with the Synod of Northern Illinois in 1851 and then in forming the Scandinavian Augustana Synod in 1860, with the Norwegians parting amicably from the Swedes in 1870 to form two separate groups: the Norwegian-Danish Augustana Synod and the Conference for the Norwegian-Danish Evangelical Lutheran Church in America. In all of this, Eielsen continued his own activity, and his sphere of influence was not seriously diminished by the departure of Andersen and Andrewson.[173] Hence, what was known as Eielsen's Synod continued its life.

The second schism

Controversy within Eielsen's Synod did not cease with the absence of Andersen and Andrewson, however. The year 1850 saw the arrival of a twenty-one-year-old schoolteacher from Norway named Peter Andreas Rasmussen, who was influenced by the Haugean tradition.[174] Initially meeting with Hans Amberg Stub in Muskego and intending to connect with Clausen, Rasmussen encountered Eielsen, who convinced him that Stub and Clausen were actually Grundtvigians who had no interest in evangelism because of their belief in the possibility of conversion after

---

172. Rohne, *Norwegian American Lutheranism*, 100. Information in this paragraph is derived from pages 100 and 101 of this volume.

173. Nelson and Fevold, *Lutheran Church*, 1:137–38.

174. Rohne, *Norwegian American Lutheranism*, 105.

death.[175] Rasmussen then associated himself with Eielsen's Synod, teaching school in Lisbon, Illinois, the following year and functioning as a lay preacher through the reading of postils. The Lisbon congregation called him as their pastor in 1853, yet he desired to have more thorough training for the office, which he obtained at the Missouri Synod seminary in Fort Wayne, Indiana.[176]

It is likely that Rasmussen's experience with the Missouri Synod impressed upon him the importance of greater structure in church life.[177] A part of this greater "churchliness" was responding to the need for an educational institution. Rasmussen founded Lisbon Seminary in Lisbon, Illinois in 1855; though short-lived, it was the first theological seminary among Norwegian-American Lutherans. In addition, he became the editor of *Kirkelig Tidende*, the periodical of Eielsen's Synod. During his work in these ventures, he became involved in discussions concerning the revision of the "Old Constitution," being critical of the perceived Donatism in the second article. Through continued discussion of this issue as well as continued contacts with Carl Ferdinand Wilhelm Walther of the Missouri Synod, Rasmussen's relationship with Eielsen deteriorated; the conflict over the issue of the revision of the "Old Constitution" as well as personality conflicts with Eielsen led Rasmussen and half of the 1856 assembly at Primrose, Wisconsin, to depart from Eielsen's Synod. Many of those who severed ties with Eielsen became members of the Norwegian Synod, and Rasmussen himself joined the Norwegian Synod in 1862, a move that contributed to his status as a pan–Norwegian Lutheran in America.[178] At least in part because of Rasmussen's presence in the Norwegian Synod, Haugeanism came to exert some influence on all Norwegian-American Lutheran church bodies.

The Reorganization

Eielsen continued his activity despite the losses incurred from the previous two schisms. He traveled as far as Texas on a mission and even

---

175. Nelson and Fevold, *Lutheran Church*, 1:138–39.

176. Rohne, *Norwegian American Lutheranism*, 105.

177. Nelson and Fevold, *Lutheran Church*, 1:138–39. Information in this and the following paragraph is derived from pages 138 to 143.

178. Rasmussen would later go on to join the Anti-Missourian Brotherhood, which separated from the Norwegian Synod in 1887, which in turn led him to membership in the UNLC, formed in 1890.

attempted the founding of a school in Deerfield, Wisconsin for training pastors, which failed after a short time. In article eleven, the "Old Constitution" spoke of the importance of establishing such schools, but the fact that this school, as well as Lisbon Seminary, floundered can perhaps be attributed to Eielsen's earlier fear of educated clergy and emphasis on "lay and unlearned men" serving as preachers.[179] A consequence of this lack of a central educational institution was that, in the time after the departure of the Rasmussen contingent, there were only a total of five people, Eielsen included, who held the status of ordained pastor in Eielsen's Synod,[180] creating a vacuum of educated leadership. In addition to the practical function of providing a means for raising up educated leaders for a church body, such educational institutions also provide church bodies, through such education, with a means to perpetuate an identity, creating a sense of group cohesion. The failure of Eielsen's Synod to respond to this need was one reason for its decline and the desire among many within it for a modest reorganization of the group that resulted in a stronger synodical identity rather than nearly exclusive reliance upon Eielsen's personality and leadership.[181]

Beyond this recognition of the need for greater churchly order, in part through the establishment of an enduring educational institution, the growing desire for reorganization throughout the 1860s and into the 1870s centered around two theological issues. The first was dissatisfaction with the second article of the "Old Constitution," which, because of its emphasis on a visible "converted" membership, had been criticized earlier as "Donatist" and was partly responsible for the departure of Rasmussen in 1856. One of the key leaders who arose in opposition to Eielsen regarding this question was Østen Hanson, one of the few ordained pastors in Eielsen's Synod, who would later serve as a significant leader in the reorganized Hauge's Synod after 1876. In fairness to Eielsen, a significant struggle for American Haugeanism lay in the fact that it could no longer function as leaven in the larger batch of dough of the Church of Norway, and the focus of Haugeanism on the importance of "conversion" understandably led to an ecclesiological crisis outside the state church

---

179. Norlie, *Norsk Lutherske Menigheter i Amerika*, 2:682.

180. Nelson and Fevold, *Lutheran Church*, 1:143. Information in this and the following three paragraphs is derived from pages 143 to 146 of this volume.

181. That those outside of Eielsen's Synod dubbed those who belonged to it as "Ellingians" reveals that Eielsen's Synod relied heavily on Eielsen's personal leadership in the absence of a concrete synodical order.

context. Hanson and others understandably sought to remedy the Donatist notion that it is somehow possible to create a church body that is entirely pure and "converted" this side of eternity; such a notion conflicts with article seven of the *Augsburg Confession*. Yet as Hanson and his followers corrected this issue with the reorganization of 1876, their continued focus on the importance of awakened, living, and converted faith would set the stage for continued friction as Hauge's Synod sought to relate to other Norwegian-American Lutheran church bodies.

The second issue related to the growing influence of Rosenian piety, presumably the result of such influence being carried to the United States from Norway by later immigration. With Rosenian piety carrying a "sweeter" message that emphasized "objective justification" and the primacy of God's grace in the process of conversion rather than a strong focus on human initiative in repentance and conversion, Eielsen feared that the proper emphasis on "living faith" was being compromised. Though Hanson did not wish to diminish the Haugean emphasis on experienced faith and subjective appropriation of salvation, he and others did wish to ground the Christian experience in the message of God's grace for the whole world and the work of the Holy Spirit in bringing people to repentance and conversion; presumably, Hanson and others considered Eielsen's theology to emphasize overly the work of the human will in salvation. Those who favored greater churchly order and a theological perspective that was more acceptable to the Norwegian Synod's emphasis on "grace alone" and "justification of the world" became known as adherents of the "New Tendency." Those who clung to Eielsen's insistence on retaining the "Old Constitution" in unaltered form were known as the "Old Tendency."

In time, after more than two decades of intermittent conflict, Eielsen's authority began to diminish in the synod that informally bore his name. Bernt Julius Muus, at the time a member of the Norwegian Synod and observer at the 1870 convention of Eielsen's Synod, remarked that the New Tendency was gaining strength and that members of Eielsen's Synod no longer simply deferred to Eielsen's leadership. Over the next few years, discussion centered on the creation of a separate constitution for the synodical organization and a model constitution for congregations; prior to this, the "Old Constitution" functioned as the sole governing document for the entire synod.[182] This explains the criticism of the "Old

---

182. Norlie, *Norsk Lutherske Menigheter i Amerika*, 2:688.

Constitution" as "deficient" and "one-sided." In spite of the desire among the New Tendency for revising the "Old Constitution," creating congregational constitutional orders separate from the synodical constitution, and thereby creating greater churchly order, such efforts were repeatedly resisted by Eielsen.[183] Though the New Tendency came to favor drafting an entirely new constitution, in the end, hoping to appease Eielsen and his minority and maintain the unity of the synod, the decision was made in 1875 to accept the "Old Constitution" in revised form. This revision changed the name of the organization from the "Evangelical Lutheran Church in America" to "Hauge's Norwegian Evangelical Lutheran Synod in America."[184] In early 1876, Eielsen and some followers, resisting the revisions to the "Old Constitution," gathered in Jackson, Minnesota to form their own group, which elected Eielsen as president. In June of the same year, the "Evangelical Lutheran Church in America" was officially reorganized under the revised constitution and new name.[185] Though Eielsen's small dissident group continued to exist for some time and was often referred to as the "Eielsen Synod," Hauge's Norwegian Evangelical Lutheran Church in America was the legal successor to the church body originally formed in 1846. The rationale behind the change of name for the church body cannot be precisely known. One assumes, however, that the addition of the name "Hauge" served a twofold purpose. First, it helped ensure that the spiritual life of the synod would continue to be grounded in the tradition of Hans Nielsen Hauge, thereby emphasizing the importance of Christianity as something to be experienced, with emphasis on repentance, "conversion"—in the sense of a committed faith—a sanctified life, lay preaching, and simplicity in worship.[186] Second, it sent the message that the church body, most often referred to as "Hauge's Synod" in subsequent years, should no longer be identified as a personality cult surrounding Elling Eielsen.

The reorganization of the "Evangelical Lutheran Church in America" as Hauge's Synod brought with it new opportunities for relations with other parts of the Norwegian-American Lutheran tradition, which would be tested in the following years. The absence of Eielsen's cantankerous

---

183. Norlie, *Norsk Lutherske Menigheter i Amerika*, 2:689.

184. Nelson and Fevold, *Lutheran Church*, 1:147. Information in this paragraph is derived from pages 147 to 150 of this volume.

185. The text of the revised constitution of Hauge's Synod is provided in Appendix B.

186. Nelson and Fevold, *Lutheran Church*, 1:126.

personality and autocracy made such conversations between various synods easier. The recognition of the importance of greater churchly order as well as the clearing up of certain theological issues also removed barriers between Hauge's Synod and the Norwegian Synod. Yet differences remained in the areas of the attitude toward lay preaching, the use of liturgy and clerical vestments, and the doctrine of the Sabbath. Most importantly, Hauge's Synod retained the historic emphasis of Haugeanism on "conversion" or "living Christianity." Even when correcting the Donatist tendency in the "Old Constitution" and nuancing the emphasis on "conversion" theologically in the tradition of Johnson and Rosenius, this focus on subjective appropriation of faith would continue to create friction in their relationships with other church bodies and influence how those shaped by Haugeanism lived out their faith within the NLCA after 1917. The insight of Nelson's volume concerning the life of Hauge's Synod rings true: "Increased organizational efficiency and churchliness meant no abatement of concern for Christian experience and lay activity."[187]

Eielsen himself died on January 10, 1883, and the small dissident group that looked to him for leadership retained the older name in the form of the "Evangelical Lutheran Church, Eielsen Synod," having five pastors, twelve congregations, and 1,350 members as of 1964.[188] The last congregation of this group, Immanuel Lutheran Church of French Lake, Minnesota, was still active as of the year 2007.[189] Though Eielsen criticized Hauge's Synod for "high-churchism and false doctrine," in time some members of Hauge's Synod renewed relations with him,[190] perhaps a testimony to his significance in the lives of many Norwegian-American Lutherans in spite of his difficult personality.

CONCLUSION

Haugeanism emerged in early-nineteenth-century Norway out of a state church environment heavily influenced by Lutheran Pietism, Rationalism, and an economic crisis precipitated by war. The nominal Christian environment provided fertile ground for a religious awakening that called for a Christian faith commitment within the established church, and

---

187. Nelson, *Lutherans of North America*, 335.
188. Wentz, *Basic History of Lutheranism in America*, 120.
189. Christofferson, "History of Immanuel Lutheran Church," lines 46–49.
190. Nelson and Fevold, *Lutheran Church*, 1:150.

Hauge, though emphasizing the importance of outward participation in the life of the Church of Norway, also emphasized edifying devotional gatherings while also expecting that Christians would display a true faith commitment that expressed itself in repentance and daily living, a phenomenon often called "conversion." After Hauge's death, his followers were among the many Norwegians that sought a new life in North America, and the absence of the state church environment in the new country created organizational difficulties for these Haugeans. Though Haugean influence was present to some extent among all Norwegian-American Lutherans, Elling Eielsen became its most vocal representative in the early settlements. Though Eielsen provided important leadership early on, his lack of concern for organization as well as his difficult personality led to many withdrawing from his loosely organized church body over the years. In part from the influence of modifications to Haugeanism in Norway carried by later immigrants, Eielsen's influence began to wane. Desiring to adjust to the voluntary religious environment of North America by creating a stronger organization, as well as continuing to emphasize the importance of a truly converted or awakened faith among church members, Eielsen's Synod reorganized itself as Hauge's Synod in 1876. From there, it was positioned to relate to other Norwegian-American Lutheran synods in the coming years.

3

Life within Hauge's Synod and Merger Negotiations

THIS CHAPTER WILL DISCUSS the internal life of Hauge's Synod before turning attention to its involvement in the merger negotiations of the late nineteenth and early twentieth century. Attention given to Hauge's Synod as a church body is a valuable contribution in itself given the limited amount of information about it currently available, but this analysis also serves the purpose of highlighting how the uniqueness of Hauge's Synod created some friction between it and the other church bodies in the merger negotiations, friction that would endure even beyond the merger of 1917.

THE STATE OF AMERICAN LUTHERANISM AS OF 1876

The "Evangelical Lutheran Church in America" that was founded in 1846, more commonly known as "Eielsen's Synod," took on new life with the reorganization of 1876. Though the life of Hauge's Synod is the focus of this book, it is important to remember that it occupied only a small part of the broader North American Lutheran tradition. For perspective, Hauge's Synod was a small group even within the subcategory of Norwegian-American Lutheranism. Awareness of the size of Hauge's Synod in relation to the surrounding Lutheran milieu is a part of understanding its struggle for self-identity as well as the disproportionate influence that Haugeanism exerted on the American Lutheran tradition as a whole. Furthermore, as has already been seen, Norwegian-American Lutherans did not exist in isolation from other American Lutherans, with contacts existing between them and the more Americanized Lutheranism of the east as well as with German-American Lutheranism, especially as represented by the Missouri Synod. Therefore, this chapter begins with a brief description of the state of affairs among Lutherans around 1876, when the reorganization of the "Evangelical Lutheran Church in America" produced Hauge's Synod.

Outside Norwegian-American Lutheranism

The period in question has been referred to as a time of "mass immigration,"[1] which witnessed tremendous numerical growth and geographic expansion of the United States. Immigration to North America from various European lands served to increase the Lutheran population, but it must be remembered, as has been discussed in the Norwegian situation, that immigrants from traditionally Lutheran territories in Europe did not automatically flock to or develop Lutheran congregations in North America. For many immigrants, their connection to Lutheranism was tenuous, and missionary activity among immigrant communities was responsible for keeping many but not even most of these immigrants within the Lutheran fold in the new country.

The conflicted political environment of the United States of this time, especially regarding the issue of slavery, naturally impacted American Lutheranism. Lutheranism in the east, with roots in the tradition of Henry Melchior Muhlenberg, felt this division acutely. The General Synod, itself a federation of smaller, independent synods, which was established in 1820 with limited authority over the affairs of its member synods, was divided in 1861 with the secession of eleven Southern states from the Union. Originally, the new Southern federation of Lutheran synods was commonly known as the "General Synod South," but the addition of the Holston and Tennessee Synods in 1886 after clarification of the federation's attitude toward the *Augsburg Confession* changed the name to the "United Synod, South." Discussion over the acceptability of slavery raged among Lutherans as it did in the country as a whole in the decades leading up to the Civil War of the early 1860s, with some Northern synods adopting abolitionist stances. Lutheran synods that found

---

1. Granquist, *Lutherans in America*, 171. This discussion of the broader Lutheran environment in North America is derived from pages 171 to 197 of this volume.

themselves within the newly formed Confederate States of America came to different conclusions, attempting to provide biblical and theological justifications for slavery. After the Civil War ended in 1865, the slavery issue within American Lutheranism largely abated. This phenomenon can be observed in the case of Hauge's Synod. The "Old Constitution" of 1846 that governed Eielsen's Synod explicitly condemned the practice of slavery in article fourteen. The constitution of the reorganized body of 1876 retained the condemnation of slavery,[2] but when the constitution was revised in 1910, the issue is not even mentioned.

American Lutheranism also experienced division of a more theological nature in this period. The issue at stake was the relationship between the American Lutheran adherence to the historic Lutheran confessional documents on the one hand and the broader American religious environment on the other. In 1855, a document originating from the hand of Samuel Simon Schmucker of Gettysburg Seminary, entitled the "Definite Synodical Platform," circulated; this was an "American Edition" of the *Augsburg Confession*. It mitigated some elements of the document deemed "too Catholic," attempting to make Lutheranism more acceptable to the rest of American Protestantism, all the while preserving Lutheran confessional identity in some form. Though this "Definite Synodical Platform" was widely rejected, the issue of confessional subscription among American Lutheran synods continued to be controversial. The Franckean Synod, which had no explicit reference to the *Augsburg Confession* in its constitution, applied for membership in the General Synod and was accepted in 1864, setting off a conflict that would lead to schism. This action prompted the formation of a new seminary in Philadelphia the same year as well as the formation of an alternative federation of synods known as the General Council in 1867. Henceforth, the eastern "Muhlenberg" Lutheran tradition was divided into three federations.

The formation of the General Council represented a move within American Lutheranism toward greater confessional clarity. Yet this move was still considered insufficient by some, especially German synods centered in the Midwest. These groups desired greater clarity on some issues, and the Galesburg Rule of 1875, though placing limits on altar and pulpit fellowship with non-Lutherans, was criticized by these German synods for appearing to allow some exceptions to the rule that Lutheran

---

2. Nelson and Fevold, *Lutheran Church*, 1:148.

pulpits are for Lutheran ministers only and Lutheran altars are for Lutheran communicants only. Chief among these confessional Midwestern German synods was the Missouri Synod, tracing its roots to Saxon German immigrants who established their organization in 1847. Perhaps in response to the trend of forming cooperative federations of synods in the east, a group of like-minded, less-Americanized synods centered in the Midwest, including the Missouri Synod and the Norwegian Synod, formed the Synodical Conference in 1872. Within this confessional group erupted a dispute about how to articulate the doctrine of election or predestination from a Lutheran point of view, with two distinct "forms" of election being held, resulting in the withdrawal of some from the Synodical Conference.

Hauge's Synod developed and began its reorganized existence amid this turbulent environment among American Lutherans. It is not always clear the extent to which Hauge's Synod was influenced by the surrounding Lutheran environment, but as with the question of slavery, one can see a possible parallel between Hauge's Synod and the rest of American Lutheranism regarding the desire for greater confessional and theological clarity, which was accomplished with the reorganization of 1876.

Within Norwegian-American Lutheranism

Though not isolated from other parts of the American Lutheran tradition, Hauge's Synod naturally had more contact with its Norwegian-American counterparts, and it occupied a small yet significant place in this fragmented ecclesiastical environment. Leaders of Hauge's Synod would come to have contact with representatives of these other synods, especially as discussions of merger progressed. Hauge's Synod also demonstrated willingness to cooperate with other Norwegian-American Lutherans as needed, as evidenced by their calling of John Nathan Kildahl, at the time a pastor of the Norwegian Synod, to serve as a temporary professor at Red Wing Seminary in 1885.[3] Kildahl's piety was apparently considered by the officialdom of Hauge's Synod to be congruent with theirs. Notably, Kildahl was shaped by the Rosenian piety that had influenced American Haugeanism, discussed in the previous chapter.[4] Even on a more local level, pastors and laity within Hauge's Synod developed relationships

3. Shaw, *John Nathan Kildahl*, 82.
4. Shaw, *John Nathan Kildahl*, 64.

with clergy and members of the other synods, which were fueled by a common language and ethnicity. For example, Ø. Hanson, the opponent of Eielsen and first president of Hauge's Synod after the reorganization of 1876, developed a strong friendship with B. J. Muus, a neighboring pastor of the Norwegian Synod and eventual leader in the Anti-Missourian Brotherhood.[5] It has been suggested that, at least in some cases on a local level, the ecclesiastical experience of Norwegian-American Lutherans from these various synods was actually similar. An examination of the sermons of one pastor of the Norwegian Synod reveals that he was also in the habit of preaching about the necessity of "conversion."[6] In all subsequent discussion of the relationship between Hauge's Synod and the rest of Norwegian-American Lutheranism, this reality of the pan-Norwegian influence of Haugeanism needs to be borne in mind, as it was one factor in the increasing rapprochement over time. This is not to deny, however, that differences existed between these groups, theological and otherwise, especially among the leadership of the synods. These synods, including Hauge's Synod, were not all of one mind either as they conducted their affairs. Setting the stage for later analysis, it is important to provide a brief overview of the state of Norwegian-American Lutheranism around the time of the emergence of Hauge's Synod, with attention to some of the points of controversy between the various groups.

The Norwegian Synod

The formation of the Norwegian Synod in 1853 has already been discussed in the previous chapter, as has its interaction and conflict with Eielsen's Synod. Said to represent "tradition and orthodoxism,"[7] the Norwegian Synod became a numerically strong church body in its first few decades, focusing on the importance of doctrine and an educated clergy. Sensing a theological ally in the Missouri Synod, a Norwegian professorship was established at Concordia Seminary in St. Louis, where Norwegian Synod pastors could be educated. The Norwegian Synod was undoubtedly influenced by the Missouri Synod in their approach to

---

5. Shaw, *Bernt Julius Muus*, 92.

6. Nichol, *Crossings*, 151.

7. Nelson and Fevold, *Lutheran Church*, 1:151. The information in this and the following two paragraphs is derived from pages 151 to 180 of this volume.

questions of slavery and lay preaching, two issues that created friction with Norwegian-Americans influenced by Haugeanism.

Regarding the issue of slavery, the Missouri Synod had some sympathy with the South in the 1860s because slavery was legal in Missouri, and C. F. W. Walther provided biblical arguments for the existence of slavery as an institution; though Walther did not believe that slavery was a sin in itself, he did believe that it existed as punishment on society for sin. Hence, the Norwegian Synod sought to balance their relationship with the Missouri Synod and the rest of Norwegian-American Lutheranism, which generally opposed slavery, by agreeing with the Missouri Synod that the practice of slavery is not in itself a sin yet conceding that it is a moral evil and a consequence of sin; it was therefore appropriate to work for abolition in the interest of Christian love. This nuanced approach was not enough to satisfy many other Norwegian-American Lutherans, especially those within Eielsen's Synod, who felt that slavery violated the command of Jesus for Christians to treat others the way they would like to be treated (Mt 7:12).[8] Though this controversy abated after the Civil War, long before Hauge's Synod emerged in 1876, the fact that the original constitution of 1876 retained the condemnation of slavery indicates that distrust lingered between members of Hauge's Synod and the Norwegian Synod as a result of this issue for quite some time.

Another point of controversy was the issue of lay preaching, especially how to define it and when it is appropriate. Furthermore, does public prayer led by laypeople fall under the category of lay preaching? From the perspective of the Missouri Synod, the issue was easily resolved by article fourteen of the *Augsburg Confession*, which prohibits "public teaching" without a "regular call." However, Norwegian-American Lutherans came from a much different background, where prayer meetings with lay preaching were a significant part of their heritage from the Haugean revival. P. A. Rasmussen, who had broken ranks with Eielsen earlier, hesitated joining the Norwegian Synod because of their opposition to the practice of lay preaching and public prayer. Norwegian Synod leaders were divided about the question and in 1862 enlisted the help of Walther of the Missouri Synod to resolve it. In short, Walther essentially articulated the position of Gisle Johnson from Norway, which was the "emergency principle," a way of maintaining the importance of the office of ministry yet conceding that emergency situations can call for a

---

8. See article fourteen of the "Old Constitution" in Appendix A.

layperson to function in such a capacity. This satisfied Rasmussen, and he joined the Norwegian Synod in that year. Though this temporarily ended the discussion, the question of what constituted an "emergency" would continue to present itself, and different attitudes toward the practice of lay activity in the church would continue to be a source of friction between Hauge's Synod and the Norwegian Synod, especially in the merger process leading up to 1917.

The Norwegian Synod, having changed its name in 1868 from "The Norwegian Evangelical Lutheran Church in America" to "The Synod for the Norwegian Evangelical Lutheran Church" as a reflection of its ecclesiological convictions,[9] formalized its relationship with the Missouri Synod in 1872, when both groups joined the newly formed Synodical Conference. It remained a part of this cooperative federation of synods until 1883, when it departed during the controversy on election or predestination. This "election controversy" of the 1880s that had begun among the German-American synods the decade before had seeped into the Norwegian-American field partially because of the Norwegian Synod's relationship with the Missouri Synod. However, the debate among Norwegian-American Lutherans about how to articulate the doctrine of election or predestination was also a part of disputes that had been occurring between the Norwegian Synod and other Norwegian-American synods over the previous two decades, all of which had to do with the tension between the objectivity of truth and the personal appropriation of that truth.[10] Whereas the Norwegian Synod, influenced by the Missouri Synod, spoke of God's objective "justification of the world" through the work of Christ, representatives of other synods feared that this emphasis diminished the importance of personal reception of justification through faith. Similarly, the controversy about the nature of absolution reflected the tension between objectivity and subjectivity, with the Norwegian Synod maintaining that absolution is a "powerful impartation" of grace. Others felt that this focus did not adequately address the necessity of faith for such grace to become effective. The conflict between these two emphases tore the Norwegian Synod itself apart in the 1880s as the dispute about election or predestination intensified. A full discussion of these theological issues would require significant space, but simply put,

---

9. Nelson and Fevold, *Lutheran Church*, 1:181. The information in this paragraph is derived from pages 181 to 190 of Nelson and Fevold's volume.

10. Nelson and Fevold, *Lutheran Church*, 1:242. The information in this paragraph is derived from pages 242 to 270 of Nelson and Fevold's volume.

the Missourian emphasis on objective justification as a way of maintaining God as the author of salvation led many within the Norwegian Synod to hold the view that God "elects people unto faith." A number of people felt that this was essentially an articulation of Calvinism, however, and opted for Pontoppidan's articulation of election, which claimed that God "elects people in view of foreseen faith." This division between adherents of the "first form" and "second form" of election divided the Norwegian Synod in 1887, with roughly a third of pastors and congregations departing to form a temporary organization known as the Anti-Missourian Brotherhood.

In these theological disputes, Hauge's Synod was rarely at the forefront, though they often participated in the discussions. In at least one instance, they actually made an important contribution to such discussions in the process of merger negotiations, discussed below. When they did participate, they understandably tended to side with those emphasizing the subjective appropriation of faith. That they were often not major players in the theological discussions is perhaps a combination of two factors: the smaller size of the group in comparison to the others and the greater focus among them on the quality of spiritual life rather than formulating exact theological definitions. At the same time, Hauge's Synod as a whole was not indifferent to theology. One observer noted similarities between Hauge's Synod and the Norwegian Synod, claiming that "the Hauges did not lay cavalier hands on orthodox theology."[11] Yet he also notes that "they emphasized personal experience of faith. However, they did not regard faith as a movement of the will, but rather as a gift. But they did emphasize the experience of faith and mission."[12]

The Conference and the Norwegian-Danish Augustana Synod

Adding to the number of Norwegian-American church bodies already discussed are two groups that have been described as forming "the middle way"[13] between the Norwegian Synod and Hauge's Synod, being repulsed by what they saw to be the extremes of Eielsen as well as of

---

11. Harrisville, Interview by Thomas E. Jacobson. Roy Harrisville Jr. was emeritus professor of New Testament at Luther Seminary in St. Paul, MN. His father Roy Harrisville Sr. and grandfather Lars Harrisville were both pastors in Hauge's Synod.

12. Harrisville, Interview by Thomas E. Jacobson.

13. Nelson and Fevold, *Lutheran Church*, 1:191. The information in this and the following two paragraphs is derived from pages 191 to 238 of this volume.

the Norwegian Synod.[14] The two groups known as the Conference for the Norwegian-Danish Evangelical Lutheran Church in America and the Norwegian-Danish Augustana Synod emerged out of the Scandinavian Augustana Synod, which was established in 1860. Norwegian, Swedish, and even some Danish Lutherans joined the Synod of Northern Illinois in 1851, which was a member of the General Synod. The Synod of Northern Illinois consisted of a large German-American membership, creating a lack of ethnic solidarity for the Scandinavian contingent. Furthermore, as already discussed, the General Synod's confessional standards were less than clear, reflected by the statement of the Synod of Northern Illinois that the *Augsburg Confession* was "mainly correct." Even after a Swede, Lars P. Esbjörn, was sent as the Scandinavian professor to the synod's seminary in Springfield, Illinois in 1858 and pledged to teach in accordance with the unaltered *Augsburg Confession*, theological and practical differences[15] between the Scandinavian section of the synod and the others became apparent. In 1860, following the advice of William A. Passavant a decade earlier, the Scandinavian section of the Synod of Northern Illinois formed their own separate synod with an explicit statement of their confessional commitment in the name of the organization: the Scandinavian Augustana Synod.[16] In this organization, Swedes and Norwegians coexisted, with some Danes, much fewer in number than their other Scandinavian counterparts, included among the Norwegian congregations. Like other Norwegian-Americans, the Norwegians of the Scandinavian Augustana Synod were influenced by the Haugean revival of Norway.

The unity of this Scandinavian Augustana Synod was short-lived, however. Intended as an organization for all Scandinavians, divisions along nationalistic lines began to appear, especially on the congregational

---

14. The focus of the Norwegian Synod on doctrine was often referred to pejoratively by this "middle way" as "Wisconsinism" because of the large concentration of Norwegian Synod congregations in Wisconsin.

15. Nelson and Fevold, *Lutheran Church*, 1:195. Language was obviously one practical difference, and Esbjörn reportedly disliked having to attend worship held in the English language. However, the theological struggle concerning American Lutheran identity as a result of the "Definite Platform" controversy was being felt, especially regarding the Lutheran view of the Lord's Supper. Additionally, Esbjörn was dissatisfied with the "lack of spirituality," as the "English" preaching assumed that everyone in attendance was a true believer, downplaying the need for repentance.

16. "Augustana" is simply the Latin form of the German name "Augsburg." The name of the new organization reflected their confessional commitment to the *Augsburg Confession*.

level, as Norwegians and Swedes tended to gravitate toward those of their own heritage. Language also presented a challenge, especially in seminary education. Though the Norwegian and Swedish languages are for the most part mutually intelligible, there are noticeable differences that would create some difficulties in the process of study. The arrival of August Weenaas from Norway in 1868 as the Norwegian theological professor at the synod's seminary, at the time located in Paxton, Illinois, exacerbated the division between the Norwegians and Swedes. With Weenaas's arrival, the move toward the formation of a separate Norwegian educational institution gained traction. In 1869, Augsburg Seminary was founded in Marshall, Wisconsin. The following year, the split within the Scandinavian Augustana Synod was amicably realized, with the Swedish contingent continuing its existence as the Swedish Augustana Synod based in Rock Island, Illinois.

The process of division with the Swedish Augustanans revealed divisions within the Norwegian contingent itself, which resulted in the formation of not one but two separate groups of Norwegian-American Lutherans out of the Scandinavian Augustana Synod. On a practical level, this split among the Norwegians was the result of different interpretations of the motion to separate from the Swedes at Andover, Illinois in 1870. One group, led by Ole Jensen Hatlestad, understood that the separate Norwegian and Danish group, naturally named the Norwegian-Danish Augustana Synod,[17] was constituted at that meeting. Others, notably including Weenaas, interpreted the motion to mean that the organization would be constituted at a later meeting. Yet the division between these two groups had more to do with different attitudes toward church polity and the surrounding American environment. The Norwegian-Danish Augustana Synod established a synodical polity and sought to move beyond the ethnic Norwegian enclave through the use of English where possible; their desire to be more American in outlook was also reflected in their decision to subscribe formally to the entire *Book of Concord* rather than the practice of the Dano-Norwegian Lutheran tradition, which was official recognition of only the *Augsburg Confession* and Luther's *Small Catechism*. This group combined a strong focus on Haugeanism—notably informal, nonliturgical worship—with its American outlook and remained small throughout the twenty years of its existence, boasting only around eighty congregations when it concluded its

---

17. The name was changed to simply the "Norwegian Augustana Synod" in 1878.

existence in 1890. In contrast to the Norwegian Augustanans, the other group of Norwegians devised a rather different organization that would significantly surpass the Augustanans in size as well as rival the Norwegian Synod. Led by Weenaas, Clausen, who had separated himself from Eielsen many years before, and others, they envisioned their organization as a "conference" of pastors, professors, and laity. Congregations, however, were to be considered free and independent entities, creating a congregational polity. Accordingly, this group adopted the name "The Conference for the Norwegian-Danish Evangelical Lutheran Church in America," most often known simply as "the Conference." Also influenced by the Haugean revival of Norway, the Conference differed from the Norwegian Augustanans in that they gave greater attention to their Norwegian heritage and use of the Dano-Norwegian liturgical form of 1685.

When the Anti-Missourian Brotherhood separated from the Norwegian Synod in 1887, there were, however briefly, six distinct church bodies of varying size among Norwegian-American Lutherans: the tiny "Evangelical Lutheran Church, Eielsen Synod," the Norwegian Synod, the Anti-Missourian Brotherhood, the Norwegian Augustana Synod, the Conference, and Hauge's Synod. This number of synods would change with the union of 1890, which united the Anti-Missourian Brotherhood with the Norwegian Augustana Synod and the Conference, producing the United Norwegian Lutheran Church. The UNLC itself would experience two schisms in its first decade. The first involved a dispute over the educational philosophy of the church body.[18] With mergers, compromises in the interest of satisfying the various parties involved need to be made, which nevertheless turn out to be unsatisfactory to some. To accommodate the Anti-Missourian contingent, the UNLC declared St. Olaf College to be the college of the church body while retaining Augsburg Seminary for pastoral training. This arrangement drew the ire of some who came from the Conference, who felt that the unified preparatory and seminary educational program offered by Augsburg College and Seminary was essential for pastoral formation. The "Friends of Augsburg" formed as a special interest group within the UNLC in 1893 and then departed from the church body in 1897 to form the Lutheran Free Church. Unrelated to this "Augsburg Controversy," a small group departed from the UNLC in 1900 to form the *Brodersamfund*,[19] known

---

18. Nelson, *Lutheran Church*, 2:38. Information in this paragraph is derived from pages 38 to 81 of this volume.

19. This is literally translated as "The Society of Brethren." Likely to avoid confusion

in English today as the Church of the Lutheran Brethren of America (CLBA). Partially a product of a revival among Norwegian-American Lutherans in the 1890s, those that formed the CLBA were critical of the phenomenon of nominal church membership and desired that congregations be "pure," consisting of "truly converted" members. The formation of the CLBA is yet another testimony to the broad influence of Haugeanism within Norwegian-American Lutheranism.

ISSUES WITHIN HAUGE'S SYNOD

As discussed in the introduction to this book, the internal life of Hauge's Synod has not received a great deal of attention from historians. Therefore, this portrait of Hauge's Synod serves the broad purpose of creating greater awareness of this part of the American Lutheran tradition. However, having established the place of Hauge's Synod within the broader American Lutheran environment, a portrait of this synod's activity and its explicit attempt to live out its Haugean heritage on American soil is also necessary before discussing its relationship with other synods that culminated in the merger of 1917. Though it must be remembered that Hauge's Synod shared with other Norwegian-American Lutherans a common ethnic heritage as well as to varying degrees a connection with the Haugean tradition of Norway, what follows will also highlight unique aspects of Hauge's Synod that distinguished this group from other synods, creating difficulties in the process of merger. The words of Martin Gustav Hanson, president of Hauge's Synod in 1900, though not entirely devaluing the work of other synods, express awareness of the small yet unique identity of Hauge's Synod and therefore serve as a helpful introduction to the following discussion of the life of this church body after its reorganization in 1876 and prior to the merger of 1917:

> Although our synod is small and insignificant as compared to other similar organizations, still our synod has branched out and grown until now its influence is not so very limited. It is felt through our schools, works of charity and missions, both home and foreign. When all of these blessings are arrayed before our eyes we ought to be prompted with a desire to praise God. But our praise must not consist only in words. A pure religion, a

---

with non-Lutheran religious groups using the title "Brethren," it became known in English as the "Church of the Lutheran Brethren of America."

worship in spirit and truth and the right attitude towards God, is what He looks for. He desires our whole heart.[20]

Mindful of Hanson's words regarding the influence of Hauge's Synod, it is important to understand them in light of other observations. Before providing a portrait of Hauge's Synod, it is critical to note the observation of Gustav Marius Bruce in his 1916 reflection. Bruce comments regarding the at times lackluster sense of organizational identity and contribution to the life of the synod among the members of Hauge's Synod:

> If it can confidently be said that the congregations on the whole have embraced the organizationally-related interests and tasks with affection and interest, then it must be admitted that a sense of unity and a consciousness of the organization has not been nearly as strong as could be desired, and this deficiency has significantly hindered the success of both the congregations and the organization as a whole. For an organization to endure and grow in strength, its sense of unity and consciousness as an organization must be awakened, strengthened, and demonstrated, so that the whole organization can grow together into organic solidarity.[21]

Bruce's comment testifies that despite the way that the 1876 reorganization brought a greater sense of organization to American Lutheran Haugeanism, the synod itself was not viewed as a matter of primary importance by a large part of Hauge's Synod. Placing more emphasis on personal and congregational spiritual life led to an indifferent attitude among many Haugeans concerning organizational life, which would have ramifications for the continuation of the Haugean tradition in American Lutheranism.

Geography

A sense of the geographic presence of Hauge's Synod across North America is a helpful part of a portrait of this church body before further

---

20. Hauge's Synod, *Reports to the 55th Annual Convention*, 6.

21. Norlie, *Norsk Lutherske Menigheter i Amerika*, 2:691. The translation of this article is provided in an appendix in the dissertation on which this book is based, the details of which are found in the bibliography. See: Jacobson, Thomas. "Hauge's Norwegian Evangelical Lutheran Synod in America and the Continuation of the Haugean Spirit in Twentieth Century American Lutheranism."

discussion of its internal affairs. Furthermore, information about significant pockets of congregations is useful for later evaluation of the enduring legacy of Haugeanism. Just prior to the merger of 1917, there were 342 active congregations of Hauge's Synod, not including "preaching points."[22] All of these congregations were founded at different times, and nothing short of extensive local research beyond the scope of this work can reveal the founding dates of all these congregations. This makes tracing the rate of growth and geographic expansion of Hauge's Synod from 1876 to 1916 difficult. However, for comparison, Hauge's Synod had a total of fifty-nine congregations as of 1876.[23] By 1890, that number had grown to 185 congregations.[24] What can be observed is that Hauge's Synod experienced significant growth over these years, not only from the handful of congregations of Eielsen's Synod in the 1840s described in the previous chapter, but also after the reorganization of 1876.

Norwegian-American Lutheranism as a whole was heavily concentrated in the upper Midwest. The sections of Norlie's two-volume *Norsk Lutherske Menigheter i Amerika* devoted to states such as Illinois, Iowa, Minnesota, North Dakota, South, Dakota, and Wisconsin constitute many pages, whereas sections devoted to other parts of the country require only a few pages, sometimes only one, to list the congregations in a particular state. This Midwestern concentration was also true in the case of Hauge's Synod. In total, thirteen US states and three Canadian provinces were home to its congregations.[25] Minnesota had the highest concentration of Hauge's Synod congregations, a total of ninety-eight. Though there were a number of congregations in the southern half of the state, a significant concentration of congregations could be found in the northwestern counties of Minnesota. The state with the next highest number of congregations was North Dakota with eighty-two. These congregations were somewhat evenly distributed between the eastern and western counties of the state, but there were notable concentrations in the northwestern and southwestern corners. South Dakota contained the third largest concentration of congregations with fifty-three. With the exception of five scattered congregations in the west and one significant concentration in the northwestern most Harding County, these congregations were all found east of the Missouri River. Other states with

22. See the table in Appendix C of this book.
23. Satre, *Striving for Ministry*, 88.
24. Fevold, *Lutheran Free Church*, 48.
25. See the table in Appendix C of this book.

larger numbers of congregations were Iowa with twenty-five, Wisconsin with twenty-two, and Illinois with seventeen. In Iowa, there was a significant concentration in the north-central counties of Humboldt, Wright, Hamilton, Hardin, and Story. In Wisconsin, the south-central counties of Columbia and Dane, home to the state capital of Madison, contained a significant concentration of congregations. In Illinois, the congregations were all found in the northeastern part of the state, especially in Cook County, home to the city of Chicago. Also noteworthy is the presence of a large pocket of congregations, twenty-five in total, in Alberta, Canada. Finally, though small, the presence of Hauge's Synod extended far west, with one congregation each in British Columbia, California, and Washington.

The above information reveals two important things about Hauge's Synod. First, as Eielsen began his preaching activity in Illinois and Wisconsin, it is clear that Hauge's Synod was active in the task of home mission throughout its existence, expanding far beyond the point of its origin in these two states, becoming numerically stronger in states further west. It has actually been observed that this western growth came partially at the expense of the vitality of older congregations in Illinois and Wisconsin, with many members of these congregations uprooting and establishing new homes further west.[26] Second, the concentration of congregations in various places indicates that urban experiences as well as rural were a part of the life of Hauge's Synod.

Significant Personalities

Briefly identifying significant leaders within Hauge's Synod is another important part of its portrait as well as a prudent task prior to discussion of future events. These personalities were often involved in the governance of the synod as well as negotiations with other synods. Furthermore, church bodies often develop familial dynasties, where the children and even grandchildren of the patriarch continue to exert influence in the synod and in successor church bodies. As Hauge's Synod ended its existence and became a part of the NLCA in 1917, awareness of these significant personalities and dynasties is helpful for observing the enduring legacy of Haugeanism, as the activities of their children and grandchildren in the new ecclesiastical situation reveal much about how

---

26. Norlie, *Norsk Lutherske Menigheter i Amerika*, 2:689.

this tradition was transmitted to later generations. The designation of certain persons as "significant" is in some ways subjective, but frequent references to these individuals in various works and publications serve as an indicator of their importance in the affairs of Hauge's Synod, making them worthy of mention here.

When Eielsen departed from Hauge's Synod with the reorganization of 1876, the synod could no longer look to him as patriarch. There appears to be no single person within Hauge's Synod that assumed the mantle of this towering personality. This is understandable given that the move toward reorganization was partially in response to dissatisfaction with the broad authority that Eielsen exercised. The earliest leader of Hauge's Synod, however, has already been mentioned: Ø. Hanson exercised authority intermittently over the years both through the office that he held and in his role as one of the initial editors of the synod's periodical *Budbæreren*.[27] Hanson was the chief challenger to Eielsen in the struggle of the 1870s between the Old Tendency and the New Tendency. While he continued serving as a pastor in Goodhue County, Minnesota, he was elected as the first president of Hauge's Synod during the process of reorganization, a position that he held for one year. He was elected to that office again, holding it from 1887 to 1893. His four sons all became pastors in Hauge's Synod as well, one of whom, M. G. Hanson, also became president of Hauge's Synod and served in that capacity for a time in the twentieth century.[28]

Another name that appears in many reports and other documents of Hauge's Synod is that of Nels Johnson Løhre. He served as a parish pastor and authored a book for the young people of one of his congregations,[29] but his name is known mostly because of his service as secretary of Hauge's Synod. Løhre was also active in the union movement and possibly because of this was elected as the first secretary of the NLCA in 1917, making him the only member of Hauge's Synod to serve on the initial board of executive officers of the new church body.[30] Also active in the union movement leading up to 1917 was Carl Johann Eastvold, who was yet another prominent personality in Hauge's Synod. C. J. Eastvold also served as president of the church body in the early twentieth

---

27. Nelson and Fevold, *Lutheran Church*, 1:145. Information in this paragraph is derived from pages 145 to 148 of this volume.

28. Curtiss-Wedge, *History of Renville County*, 1258–59.

29. The book is entitled *To Young Men and Young Women*, published in 1902.

30. Nelson, *Lutheran Church*, 2:223.

century and was again elected, for ceremonial purposes, to the office just prior to the 1917 merger,[31] perhaps a testimony to the important role he played in the merger negotiations.

Also deserving of mention is the surname "Rønning," a name with enduring significance after the 1917 merger. Three siblings were born on the Buskerønning farm in central Norway in the mid-nineteenth century. The two boys, Nils Nilsen Rønning and Halvor Nilsen Rønning, and their sister Torbjørg Nilsdatter Rønning, known as "Thea," immigrated to the US in the 1880s.[32] Halvor and Thea became known for their work in the China Mission of Hauge's Synod, while Nils contributed to church life through his literary activity.

Two other names deserve special mention because of their work within Hauge's Synod, which carried over into the NLCA. The first is G. M. Bruce. While serving as the pastor of First Lutheran Church and Rook's Creek Lutheran Church in Pontiac, Illinois, Bruce began an English language periodical for Hauge's Synod entitled the *Lutheran Intelligencer*, which endured for only a few years. Bruce was also active in the union movement, presumably as the result of his role as professor of practical theology at Red Wing Seminary prior to the 1917 merger. He continued to be a "significant figure"[33] in the NLCA until the 1950s, serving as one of the two professors from Hauge's Synod at Luther Theological Seminary in St. Paul, Minnesota. The other professor, also involved in the union movement, was Mons Olson Wee, who taught Hebrew and Old Testament, also at Red Wing Seminary and Luther Theological Seminary. Through his professorship, his personality also figured prominently in the NLCA until his death in 1942.

Organizational Life

A portrait of Hauge's Synod becomes much clearer when observing specific areas of its organizational life. Members of Hauge's Synod never forgot their roots in Eielsen's preaching activity in Illinois and Wisconsin in the 1840s,[34] but the reorganization of 1876 provided them with the

---

31. Nelson, *Lutheran Church*, 2:221.
32. Grindal, *Thea Rønning*, 11.
33. David Preus, Interview by Thomas E. Jacobson.
34. Norlie, *Norsk Lutherske Menigheter i Amerika*, 2:681. Much of the information in this section about the organizational life of Hauge's Synod is derived from an article by G. M. Bruce, the translation of which is found in an appendix in the dissertation on

level of organization necessary to establish an enduring identity. Before examining the formal merger negotiations between Hauge's Synod and the two other merging bodies, a clearer picture of its organizational life is necessary.

Polity

The constitution of Hauge's Synod states in article fifteen that "the Synod consists of congregations and individuals who have been admitted into the Synod and have subscribed to this constitution." The organization of Hauge's Synod stood in contrast to that of the Conference. Whereas the Conference held that congregations were free and independent entities, Hauge's Synod viewed congregations as members, creating a synodical rather than a congregational polity. It must be noted, however, that even with its synodical polity, evidence cited later suggests that congregations of Hauge's Synod cherished their right to govern their own affairs within the boundaries of the constitution rather than be dictated to, which is important to remember for later developments. In contrast to the Norwegian Synod, Hauge's Synod also considered its pastors to be members of the organization. As such, the pastors could vote at the annual meeting even when they were not serving a congregation at the time,[35] provided that they were "serving the synod in some capacity." Even pastors who were retired for reasons of age or ill health could vote. One or two lay delegates from each congregation, as well as the professors of Red Wing Seminary and members of the board of trustees, could vote at the annual meeting, intended to be held in June of each year.

An examination of the same constitution reveals that Hauge's Synod maintained the offices of president, vice president, secretary, and treasurer. Additionally, considered under the category of "officers" was the "board of trustees." This board of trustees handled the financial matters of the synod as directed by the annual meeting. Also significant in the governance of the synod was the church council, consisting of nine members, including the president of the synod, three pastors, and five laypeople. The church council served a variety of roles in the synod, such as examining candidates for ordination, implementing decisions of the synod, mediating congregational disputes, and calling special meetings

---

which this work is based.

35. Nelson and Fevold, *Lutheran Church*, 1:148.

of the synod as necessary.³⁶ That laypeople had greater representation in the governance of Hauge's Synod was perhaps a testimony to their Haugean heritage; the synod desired to empower the laity in exercising spiritual leadership. Hauge's Synod was also divided into regional groups of congregations known as "districts" or "circuits." The number of these districts fluctuated over time, depending on the expansion of the synod into new territories or occasional reorganization, but Nelson notes that there were usually eleven total districts in the church body.³⁷ These districts elected their own presidents, and reports of the state of affairs within them are included in the annual reports of the synod.

Also falling under the category of polity is the thorny issue of how Hauge's Synod reconciled its desire for a "converted" membership with their statement that "the Synod consists of congregations and individuals who have been admitted into the Synod and have subscribed to this constitution." Desiring to avoid the accusation of Donatism that was leveled at Eielsen and his "Old Constitution," Hauge's Synod avoided language that suggested that their particular synod was the full embodiment of the Christian Church on earth and that every member of their group was necessarily "truly converted." At the same time, the constitution did specify that for membership in Hauge's Synod, individuals, in addition to subscribing to the Scriptures and the listed confessional documents, must "live Christian lives." It went on to state that being a "true member of the Church" requires one to be "converted and regenerated" while "remaining in the state of grace" and "bearing the fruits of faith." The use of the word "Church" appears to refer to the existence of the invisible rather than the visible Church, a concept that can be derived from *Augsburg Confession* article eight.³⁸ They were therefore free to maintain their Haugean focus on "conversion" without the accusation of doctrinal error.

Worship

Haugeanism in Norway continued to function within the Church of Norway, and in accordance with Hauge's wishes, those touched by his awakening movement continued to receive the sacraments from the established congregations while maintaining their separate edifying

---

36. Nelson and Fevold, *Lutheran Church*, 1:148.
37. Nelson, *Lutheran Church*, 2:93.
38. Kolb and Wengert, *The Book of Concord*, 43.

gatherings, often held in "prayer houses." American Haugeanism did not have the luxury of such a state church environment and was therefore required to combine its tradition of edifying gatherings with sacramental worship. This resulted in a pattern of worship within Hauge's Synod that was somewhat distinct from what was typical in the Norwegian Synod and much of the UNLC.

Nelson reports that the typical layout of a Hauge's Synod church sanctuary was similar to what one would encounter in a congregation of the Norwegian Synod and the UNLC. Beyond this, the Haugean experience of worship differed significantly from their more formal counterparts. Whereas the Norwegian Synod and much of the UNLC and its predecessor bodies used, in at least some form, the "Ritual" from the Dano-Norwegian *Altar Book*,[39] worship that was carried out within Hauge's Synod was much less formal. The description "less formal" should not be taken to mean sloppy or irreverent; rather, it simply followed a less rigidly structured pattern, allowing for more flexibility and spontaneity. This spontaneity led on some occasions to the preacher being interrupted and challenged during sermons.[40] The most noticeable departure from the formality of the Norwegian Synod and much of the UNLC, however, was the lack of clerical vestments and liturgical chanting, also known as the "intonation." This rejection of formality in worship was carried forward within Hauge's Synod from article six of the "Old Constitution." Whereas Norwegian Synod and UNLC pastors typically wore a black robe and stole with a white fluted collar, Hauge's Synod pastors simply wore ordinary suits or a Prince Albert frock coat during worship.[41] Also, whereas the "Ritual" used by the Norwegian Synod and the UNLC frequently employed the intonation of parts of the liturgy, such as the collect prayer, the Lord's Prayer, and the words of institution for the Lord's Supper, Hauge's Synod congregations rejected such

---

39. Nelson, *Lutheran Church*, 2:124. This "Ritual" was established in 1685 and was a revision of "The Ordinance" of 1542. The 1685 version itself underwent a simplification in 1802 in response to Rationalism. In 1887, a new "Ritual," which was based on a Bavarian (German) order for worship, was adopted in Norway, which became widely used in Norwegian-American Lutheran churches. Information in this section on worship is derived from pages 124 to 128 of Nelson's volume as well as the translation of G. M. Bruce's article in an appendix to the dissertation on which this work is based.

40. Harrisville, Interview by Thomas E. Jacobson.

41. Morris Wee Sr., Interview by Morris Wee Jr. Wee notes that although the rejection of traditional vestments was intended to minimize the distance between the pastor and the congregation, the use of the Prince Albert frock coat by the pastor was counterproductive in this regard, as it was only the pastor who would be attired in such a way.

liturgical chanting. Nelson uses the word "repugnant" to describe the attitude of Hauge's Synod toward such formal liturgy, as they believed that it "hindered the free movement of the Holy Spirit." However, as Bruce notes, Hauge's Synod did prescribe the use of the 1685 and later revised "Ritual" of 1887 for the administration of the sacraments of baptism and the Lord's Supper.

Even with the aversion to formal liturgy within Hauge's Synod, a certain pattern, though not formally fixed, could be detected in their worship practice. Hymns were often sung from Magnus Brostrup Landstad's Norwegian hymnal of 1869. It was also common for the pastor to invite a layperson to offer a "free prayer" rather than a fixed prayer from a book, yet another testimony to the importance they placed on empowering the laity to exercise spiritual leadership, which was at the heart of the Haugean movement. Despite their desire for a simplified worship experience, Bruce notes that influence from the structured *Ritual* of 1685 and then 1887 began gradually to seep into the worship practice of Hauge's Synod. However, these elements of the *Ritual* were adopted piecemeal by congregations and certainly not uniformly throughout the synod. This imposition of elements of the *Ritual* in some places, coupled with the lack of concern among Haugeans for proper execution of liturgy, resulted in an odd hybrid of formality and informality as well as inconsistent practice throughout the synod. For example, in some congregations the pastor began to use the salutation before the collect prayer. However, after he spoke "The Lord be with you," the congregation would not respond with the customary "And with your spirit." A pastor might also use customs associated with the altar, as during the celebration of the Lord's Supper, but then reject the practice of turning himself to face the altar during "sacrificial"[42] parts of the worship service, such as the reading of the collect prayer. Questions regarding when the congregation or baptismal sponsors were to stand rather than sit also presented themselves in many congregations. In short, because of their reliance upon spontaneity and "the free movement of the Holy Spirit" rather than a set liturgical form, the experience of worship in Hauge's Synod was varied, more so than their counterparts in the Norwegian Synod and the UNLC. However,

---

42. It was and remains customary in some places for a pastor to face the altar during prayer as a way of demonstrating that prayer is being directed to God. In contrast to this "sacrificial" part of the worship service, the pastor turns to face the people for proclamation. This liturgical division between "sacrifice" and proclamation was apparently not adhered to within Hauge's Synod.

Nelson refers to the traditional Epistle and Gospel readings from the Bible in such worship services of Hauge's Synod, indicating that a common lectionary provided, at least in many places, some uniformity in worship practice across the spectrum of Norwegian-American Lutheranism.

Of greater theological concern regarding worship was the question of absolution. Eielsen's Synod early on rejected the practice of laying on of hands at the pre-Communion absolution, instructing people in the "Old Constitution" to examine themselves privately. Then, absolution was to be declared in conditional form "to penitent souls." Over time, Hauge's Synod generally sought to divorce absolution as a ceremony from the Lord's Supper, advising people to seek absolution privately. There was a fear that such absolution, even when pronounced in conditional form, gave false assurance to people and encouraged them to become unworthy partakers of the sacrament. In some places, however, the conditional absolution was retained in public worship. Regarding the Lord's Supper, one thing that Hauge's Synod would have shared with the Norwegian Synod and the UNLC was that the sacrament was generally offered only at set times throughout the year rather than weekly. The tradition of low-church worship, absolution, and the Lord's Supper was carried forward among former Hauge's Synod congregations after 1917 as evidenced by the example of John O. Gisselquist, who believed that the preacher's task was to preach the gospel and leave to the Holy Spirit the task of applying forgiveness to individuals. J. O. Gisselquist's administration of the Lord's Supper also reflected the Haugean focus on introspection and subjective appropriation of faith. The Lord's Supper was offered infrequently, and even then the number of those present who received it was few.[43]

It must also be observed that the worship life of Hauge's Synod extended beyond Sundays. In addition to regular worship, special preparatory worship services were often held on Friday evenings before the administration of the Lord's Supper on Sundays. Additionally, "altar call" services were sometimes held in various places within Hauge's Synod at different times during the week, reflecting their heritage of awakening and emphasis on the importance of "conversion."[44]

---

43. Gisselquist, *Called to Preach*, 76.
44. Morris Wee Sr., Interview by Morris Wee Jr.

Lay Activity

Haugeanism began as a lay movement in Norway, and it is therefore not surprising that the distinction between the clergy and laity was at times blurred within Hauge's Synod. As has been seen, laypeople exercised considerable authority on both the congregational and synodical levels. Of course, the founding of Red Wing Seminary in 1879 provided the synod with the means to maintain a distinct clerical class within the synod, preparing pastors with a spiritual calling as well as adequate education for their duties. However, in their effort to encourage the practice of lay leadership and preaching, the activity of the clergy was often undermined. Many districts within Hauge's Synod exercised an "ordered" program of lay ministry as opposed to the less formal "free" lay ministry that arose within congregations. As Bruce reports, a distinct class of lay "emissaries" operated within the synod; they were sent by the districts to work in congregations. Though these lay emissaries were not considered to be pastors, Bruce refers to the existence of "ordained laypeople" in the early years of Eielsen's Synod. This later practice within Hauge's Synod of sending out lay emissaries was apparently a continuation of the earlier practice of granting some status of "ordination" to laypeople. Harrisville comments that these lay pastors who had some "alternative of ordination" were referred to derisively by those in the Norwegian Synod and Missouri Synod as "paper pastors."[45] This attitude extended even to those pastors within Hauge's Synod who had proper seminary education. Harrisville goes on to say that his maternal grandfather, who was a member of the Norwegian Synod, wrote to Harrisville's mother upon news that she had entered into a relationship with Harrisville's father, who was a member of Hauge's Synod. The letter expressed his concern and suspicion of Hauge's Synod, asking Harrisville's mother "if she really wanted to marry a poor Hauge's preacher." This was apparently not an isolated incident. When M. O. Wee, who would become a significant figure in Hauge's Synod, was a seminary student and became engaged, his future wife's parents, who came out of the tradition of the UNLC, expressed dismay. M. O. Wee's son reports: "My mother's parents belonged to the United Church and they were very unhappy when my mother decided she wanted to get married to a seminary student from the Hauge Synod,

---

45. Morris Wee Sr., Interview by Morris Wee Jr.

and my grandmother consoled herself over the shame of it by saying, well it would have been worse if he had been a Methodist."[46]

This program of "ordered" lay ministry within Hauge's Synod created problems, according to Bruce. When lay emissaries came to work in congregations served by ordained pastors, at times a rivalry and power struggle ensued between the pastor and the lay emissary. Furthermore, the program of "ordered" lay ministry served the purpose of discouraging "free" and more spontaneous lay activity within congregations, with some feeling as though only the lay emissaries had the right to lead lay meetings for edification. This tendency toward "ordered" lay ministry is a testimony to the increased organizational effectiveness that was brought about with the reorganization of 1876. However, it also seems contrary to the original spirit of Haugean spiritual freedom, which encouraged lay activity and preaching outside of the restrictions of the Church of Norway. Bruce reported that this concern was addressed by the South Dakota District of Hauge's Synod in their decision to send such lay emissaries only to mission congregations where their presence would not interfere with the existing leadership of a pastor, thereby allowing a more organic type of lay leadership to arise within the established congregations. In 1911, Bruce articulated his vision for lay activity within the synod, apparently arguing against the "ordered" program of lay ministry, which he viewed as a challenge to pastoral authority. He desired to maintain the distinction between clergy and laity, arguing that lay activity should be congregationally focused and geared toward assisting the pastor in his work:

> We have been pratting and agitating for laymen's work, until we have lost sight of the most important work that the lay-christian [sic] has, that of assisting in the spiritual upbuilding of his own congregation and being an Aaron and a Hur to his own pastor. That is the kind of laymen's work that counts most, and that should be most encouraged and cultivated. Such laymen's work also contributes greatly to the success of the pastor's work, making it count for more and show better results. Let the pastor and the Christian layman work hand in hand, encouraging, stimulating, and strengthening each other mutually, and there shall, there must be results, tho [sic] they cannot always be reduced to a tabulated form.[47]

---

46. Morris Wee Sr., Interview by Morris Wee Jr.
47. Bruce, "Editorial," 1911.

Bruce's opinion is noteworthy. However, the fact that tension between such lay emissaries and educated pastors was worthy of mention by Bruce as late as 1916 indicates that suspicion of clerical authority held itself strongly within Hauge's Synod to the end of its existence and no doubt continued into the NLCA after 1917.

Institutions of Mercy

As a small church body, Hauge's Synod was not in a position to develop and maintain a large number of institutions of mercy. However, the synod eventually established an orphanage named Bethesda near Beresford, South Dakota, in the year 1897. As Bruce reports, this orphanage was a source of pride for the synod, and they devoted considerable financial resources toward its maintenance. Early on, as reported by President M. G. Hanson in the year 1900, the Bethesda Orphanage cared for thirty to thirty-six children. Instruction was provided for these children in both English and Norwegian.[48] As of 1913, this orphanage cared for around sixty children and did so until they reached the age of eighteen.[49] A brief note in the *Lutheran Herald* from 1906 stated that the Bethesda Orphanage was experiencing difficulty with its lighting system, which was deemed unsafe and that a larger schoolhouse was needed to accommodate the large number of children.[50] In 1914, late in the life of the synod, an elder-care facility was also erected in Beresford. These two endeavors were the official institutions of mercy within Hauge's Synod, but Bruce notes that congregations were also accustomed to supporting charitable causes outside of the synod.

Mission

Home Mission

As already mentioned, home mission played a significant role in the growth of Hauge's Synod, as was the case with other American Lutheran church bodies. In 1913, it was reported that there were thirty home-mission pastors within Hauge's Synod as well as a superintendent of

---

48. Hauge's Synod, *Reports to the 55th Annual Convention*, 22.
49. "Facts About Hauge's Synod," 115.
50. *Lutheran Herald*, 1906, 189.

missions. This was out of a total of 160 pastors in the entire organization.⁵¹ According to Bruce's reflection in 1916, there was strong interest around the synod in financially supporting both home and foreign mission work, with the women's organizations of congregations supplying much, though not all, the funding. In the year 1900, President M. G. Hanson sought to impress upon the synod in his annual report the importance of home mission:

> If we truthfully pray that "God's name be made holy, His kingdom come, and His will be done," then we must also work to see that the prayer be effective. This applies especially to the Home Mission. The mission must necessarilly [sic] have its first place with us as a synod. It must be the direct result of our Christian life as a synod, both for our own edification and the advancement of God's kingdom. The need of creating a favorable opinion of our Home Mission and its work, cannot be laid to [sic] much stress upon. May God awaken in us an enthusiasm for this work! ... The love that we bear to God and our fellow men, will not permit us to rest while any remain unsaved.⁵²

The China Mission

Regarding foreign mission, the field of activity of Hauge's Synod was China. It is reported that as of 1913 there were four main stations and nearly forty substations of activity in the China Mission, with Fancheng as the headquarters. At the headquarters existed an impressive complex with much activity, which included a high school, a hospital and medical dispensary, an orphanage, and a school for boys and girls. The China Mission employed seventeen missionaries as well as nearly ninety native workers as of 1913.

Planning for this China Mission began in 1890, and prior to that the involvement of Hauge's Synod in foreign mission work was limited to contributions made to the Norwegian Missionary Society in the old country, which had been founded in 1842. The willingness of Hauge's Synod to contribute to this work flowed naturally from the fact that the Norwegian Missionary Society owed its existence to the religious energy

---

51. "Facts About Hauge's Synod," 115. Much of the following information about mission within Hauge's Synod is derived from the 1913 article from the *Lutheran Intelligencer* cited above.

52. Hauge's Synod, *Reports to the 55th Annual Convention*, 7–8.

of the Haugean awakening. Understandably, however, Hauge's Synod desired a mission field of its own to which it could contribute directly. The interest in China among Norwegian-American Lutherans can be partially attributed to speeches given by the likes of non-Lutheran missionaries such as Hudson Taylor, who had spent time in China.[53] The desire for establishing a mission field in China grew throughout the 1880s, but the president of Hauge's Synod at the time, Ø. Hanson, was reluctant to begin a new initiative, given the many other costly and time-consuming projects with which he was already occupied. When the older leadership of Hauge's Synod declined to establish such a mission in 1890, referring the matter to a committee, younger pastors such as Ole A. Østby worked toward the development of an independent China Mission Society. Though this organization consisted largely of Hauge's Synod representatives, it also included members of the UNLC, which had just been formed that year, in 1890.[54] This intersynodical endeavor, led by members of Hauge's Synod, is one telling sign that, for many within Hauge's Synod, particular synodical affiliation was secondary to their spiritual concerns, which included mission work.

This is a sentiment that was expressed by Halvor Rønning, who, along with his sister Thea, was among the first missionaries to China, supported for a time by both the China Mission Society as well as Hauge's Synod. In a confusing situation, Hauge's Synod itself began in 1891 its own China mission committee, independent of the China Mission Society. The committee that had been appointed the previous year declared itself ready to begin a synodical mission in China and commissioned Halvor and Thea Rønning for the work. A request was made by the Hauge's Synod committee that the China Mission Society, which the committee considered a temporary and therefore currently unnecessary organization, dissolve at that point. This request encountered resistance, as the China Mission Society had grown by that point to include several members of the UNLC. The two organizations then continued to operate parallel to each other, and the Rønning siblings were asked to resign formally from the China Mission Society and join the Hauge's Synod China Mission, which they did.[55] Hauge's Synod again expressed the desire in 1894 for the China Mission Society to merge with its China Mission. It was felt that such an arrangement would create greater clarity and

---

53. Grindal, *Thea Rønning*, 36.
54. Grindal, *Thea Rønning*, 54.
55. Syrdal, "American Lutheran Mission Work in China," 23–26.

efficiency in funding the mission, allowing the UNLC to then assume sole responsibility for the Madagascar Mission, with the understanding that financial contributions for either mission would be welcome from members of both church bodies. However, this proposal from Hauge's Synod was rejected in 1894, and the two mission organizations in China continued to function separately.[56] Syrdal notes, however, that the particular affiliation of the missionaries in China mattered little in the eyes of the missionaries themselves. Members of the Hauge's Synod China Mission, the China Mission Society, the Norwegian Mission Society from Norway, as well as independent Norwegian Lutheran missionaries "all worked together in a brotherly spirit."[57] It is not exactly clear what led to the strained relationship between Hauge's Synod and the China Mission Society. It is likely that many Haugeans involved in the China Mission Society cared more about shared missionary zeal and were less than concerned for the need to support a specific mission endeavor of Hauge's Synod, having greater concern for the mission work itself and ambivalence about the synodical affiliation of the missionaries involved. However, it should be considered that synodical politics played a role, with at least some members of the UNLC and Hauge's Synod desiring to avoid supporting each other; Hauge's Synod had at the last minute pulled out of merger negotiations that led to the formation of the UNLC in 1890.

The Santal Mission

The roots of the Dano-Norwegian Lutheran mission to the Santal people of India and Pakistan were in the work of two men, a Dane named Hans Peter Børresen and a Norwegian named Lars Skrefsrud. Skrefsrud in particular came to assume a nearly legendary status for the Haugean tradition. His mother was apparently involved in the Haugean movement in Norway in the city of Faaberg.[58] Skrefsrud's significance stemmed not only from his reputation as an effective missionary, but also from his experience of "conversion" as a youth. As a young man, Skrefsrud engaged in unwholesome activities while in Oslo, as well as a series of burglaries.

56. Grindal, *Thea Rønning*, 128–35.
57. Syrdal, "American Lutheran Mission Work in China," 27. In 1903, the UNLC took control of the China Mission Society.
58. Rønning, *Lars O. Skrefsrud*, 12. This information about Skrefsrud is derived from pages 7 to 31 of this volume.

While in prison, he experienced peace with God during a time of prayer, and he was eventually released in 1861, becoming an example of "living Christianity." Applying for service to the Norwegian Missionary Society the following year, his application was refused, which prompted him to attend the mission school in Berlin, Germany. There he encountered Børresen, and together the two embarked on a mission to Santalistan. Skrefsrud is remembered as a powerful speaker, a linguist who provided the Santal people with a written language and translations of Christian documents, and also as a social reformer who eliminated corruption among the leadership of Santalistan.

Interest in the Santal Mission among Norwegian-American Lutherans became a part of the "mission fever" of the early 1890s through the witness of H. Bottolsen, who had been impressed by hearing Skrefsrud in Norway ten years earlier, being inspired by his example. Just as the work of Skrefsrud and Børresen in Santalistan was an independent venture, the American Santal Mission Committee formed in 1891 was similarly independent, described as having "the very minimum of organization and no constitution or by-laws."[59] The initial board of the organization came exclusively from the UNLC and Hauge's Synod, with three of the nine members from the latter: Pastors I. Eistensen, O. P. Svingen, and N. G. Petersen. In time, membership in the organization came to include some representatives from the Lutheran Free Church, the CLBA, and the Danish-American Lutheran tradition. That the American Santal Mission Committee continued to emphasize its independence is shown by Helland's comment that the 1917 merger had no impact on the course of the mission other than to bring the Norwegian Synod into some contact with its work.[60] This is further evidence of the distance that existed between much of the Norwegian Synod and the Haugean tradition of the time.

The Lutheran Orient Mission

Brief mention should be made of the Hauge's Synod representation in what was officially known as the Inter-Synodical Evangelical Lutheran Orient Mission Society. The impetus for this endeavor came from the ecumenical Protestant World Missionary Conference in Edinburgh, Scotland in 1910. This conference, when assigning to various Christian

---

59. Helland, *American Santal Mission*, 13.
60. Helland, *American Santal Mission*, 30.

denominational traditions responsibility for evangelism to different regions of the world, gave responsibility for the Muslim Kurdish people to Lutherans.[61] The man credited with responding to this call of the 1910 conference was Ludvig Olsen Fossum, a pastor connected to the UNLC. However, significant personalities in Hauge's Synod soon became connected with the Lutheran Orient Mission, and as of 1921, N. J. Løhre was the president, M. O. Wee was the vice president, and C. J. Eastvold was a member of the board. Also on the board was Erick E. Espelien, notably the last pastor ordained by Hauge's Synod prior to the conclusion of its existence in 1917. The organization endured for some time after the merger, and M. O. Wee in particular came to play a prominent role, spending time in the Kurdistan region himself.

The Zion Society for Israel

Yet another intersynodical mission endeavor worthy of note in the life of Hauge's Synod is the Zion Society for Israel. This organization was unique in that it is best described as simultaneously focused on "home" and foreign mission, as it sponsored missionary activity both among Jews in the United States and in other lands. Originally organized in 1878 by representatives of the Conference, participants in the Zion Society for Israel came from various Norwegian-American Lutheran church bodies, especially those strongly influenced by Haugeanism: the UNLC and its predecessor bodies, the Lutheran Free Church, and of course Hauge's Synod. In fact, one of the expressed hopes for the organization was that it would contribute to unity among the various Norwegian-American Lutheran synods, "breaking down the barriers, which so artificially have separated what should be united."[62] Eight of the forty-nine board members of the organization in its first fifty years of existence, from 1878 to 1928, are listed as members of Hauge's Synod, and C. J. Eastvold began serving as its president in 1923. With the exception of P. A. Rasmussen, an early associate of Eielsen whose movement between different Norwegian-American Lutheran synods is described in the previous chapter, there are no representatives from the Norwegian Synod on the board of the organization,[63] which is possibly an indicator of the distance that

---

61. Wee, *Inter-Synodical Evangelical Lutheran Orient Mission Society*, 4.
62. Solberg, *Brief History of the Zion Society*, 27.
63. Solberg, *Brief History of the Zion Society*, 130–32.

existed between Haugeanism in that era and many within the Norwegian Synod. Participation in the Zion Society for Israel was only one part of the enthusiastic support for home and foreign mission demonstrated by Hauge's Synod in the late nineteenth century.[64]

Education

Congregational Education

According to Bruce, Hauge's Synod was active on the congregational level in providing religious instruction for young people. This instruction was in addition to the Sunday schools of congregations. Participation in the public school system meant that the only opportunity for such religious instruction was during the summer months and perhaps on Saturdays. For both rural and urban contexts, this created challenges, as those children in rural areas were often occupied with farm work from early on in their childhood, leaving little time for extra education. Those in urban areas apparently disliked the summer heat and sought to avoid sitting in classrooms during that time. The expectation of extra religious education also set children who were members of Hauge's Synod apart from their non-Lutheran peers, leading them to view such instruction as a burden. Another challenge in maintaining this system of youth education was the difficulty in finding and adequately paying trained teachers, who were often students at Red Wing Seminary and Jewell College, which are discussed below. Often, the teachers were not able to earn enough money from the congregations during the summer to continue their own studies the next year. Yet another challenge was obtaining the necessary books for religious instruction as well as confusion regarding which version of Pontoppidan's "Explanation" to use, of which there were apparently many.

Red Wing Seminary

As already observed, even Eielsen eventually recognized the need for a theological school to train pastors, which resulted in the short-lived Lisbon Seminary, founded in 1854.[65] The closing of another short-lived

---

64. Nelson and Fevold, *Lutheran Church*, 1:286–89.

65. Solberg, *Lutheran Higher Education*, 213. This discussion about Red Wing Seminary is derived from pages 213 and 214 of this volume.

preparatory school in Cambridge, Wisconsin in 1867 led to the expressed desire of some to open a school in Red Wing, Minnesota. However, Trinity Lutheran Church in Chicago proposed to incorporate space for a college and seminary on its premises. A tie of seventeen votes on each side led to casting lots to decide on a location for the educational institution of Eielsen's Synod. The lot fell to Chicago, but financial problems in the wake of the Chicago fire as well as a poor farming season led to the closure of this "Hauge's College and Eielsen's Seminary" in 1877. After the reorganization of 1876, however, a donation from a mortgage by a layperson in Red Wing secured the necessary property for a preparatory school and seminary in that community, which was established in 1879. This filled the need for a consistent educational program for Hauge's Synod. Nevertheless, as Bruce notes, the fear of a "learned pastorate" endured in many congregations of the synod. However, educational institutions often contribute to the establishment of an identity for church bodies, and Red Wing Seminary (RWS) filled that role for Hauge's Synod for thirty-eight years, until the merger of 1917. Even after this, RWS was retained as a preparatory academy of the NLCA. Though RWS obviously was influenced by its Norwegian heritage to some degree, it carried forward the historic Haugean concern for moving beyond the Norwegian ethnic enclave. N. N. Rønning commented that RWS possessed a greater American spirit than Augsburg Seminary in Minneapolis, which was more Norwegian it its focus, and that it was his experience at RWS that impressed upon him the importance of developing English writing skills.[66]

The educational program at Red Wing Seminary was not without controversy within Hauge's Synod, however. Late in the life of the synod, there appears to have been a dispute about the relationship between the college and theological departments of the institution. Some felt the need to assert that what is known as "Red Wing Seminary" was not simply the theological department, but that the theological department was simply one part of the whole institution, which included the college department. In reaction to this, some in the synod felt that this statement devalued theological education for ministry, exalting the college department at the expense of the theological department and accusing the faculty of Red Wing Seminary of contributing to this state of affairs. Bruce denied

---

66. Gisselquist, *Called to Preach*, 45.

that the faculty favored the college department over the theological and insisted that the mission of the whole institution was

> to build manhood and character on the impregnable rock of Holy Scripture and its life-bestowing and life-sustaining truths, and do all we can by the help and guidance of God and his Holy Spirit to assist in the training of thoroly [sic] spiritual, consecrated, and well-equipped young men for the greatest and noblest of all callings, the Holy Ministry.[67]

The existence of this dispute is indicative of the continued struggle within Hauge's Synod over educational qualifications for ministry, which was present even prior to the reorganization of 1876. In his statement, Bruce sought to balance the concerns of all involved, noting the importance of candidates being "spiritual" and "consecrated," but also "well-equipped." This was apparently a response to many within Hauge's Synod who viewed educational qualifications for ministry as unnecessary or of secondary importance. Indeed, in this 1916 reflection, Bruce notes that the "fear of a learned pastorate held itself very strongly" in many places.

In a brief memoir, Julius Boraas described his experience as a student at Red Wing Seminary in the late nineteenth century.[68] This information provides a glimpse into an important aspect of the life of Hauge's Synod from the perspective of someone involved in both the undergraduate and theological departments in the waning years of the century. In the earlier years of Red Wing Seminary, the school year lasted only seven months, from October to the end of April. Later, the school year was apparently extended to nine months. It was also common for students to be absent from school for lengthy periods during their studies for the purpose of assisting their families with farm work. Many theological students did not remain for the entire four-year course of study, leaving the school after a year or two to serve congregations in need of pastors, citing a strong "inner call."

The cost of tuition, room, and board at Red Wing Seminary is described as "unusually low," catering to "boys with little money." The annual tuition at that time was twenty-five dollars a year. The only furnishing in student rooms was a heating stove, and wood for heat needed to be provided by the student. Other room furnishings were often purchased

---

67. Bruce, "Editorial," 1913, 53.

68. Boraas, "Red Wing Seminary." The information in the following few paragraphs is derived from this memoir.

from departing students. For meals, a cooperative boarding club among the students hired two women to prepare meals, and the cost of this service for students was a little over a dollar a week. Students also did much of the work in maintaining the campus, lighting the stoves in the winter and cleaning. Student life was characterized generally as pious, with the presence of theological students among the undergraduates contributing to an atmosphere conducive to Christian spirituality. This "sobering" influence of the theological students influenced the undergraduates, and students from both departments participated in and led regular prayer meetings. On Sundays, students often attended the nearby St. Peter's Lutheran Church of Hauge's Synod. However, they also attended other congregations, even those outside of the Lutheran tradition, such as the Presbyterian congregation of Red Wing, perhaps as a reflection of their greater focus on spiritual life than on doctrine.

Regarding instruction, theological students were expected to learn Greek and Latin as prerequisites for the theological department. Lectures in the theological department were given in both Norwegian and English, with courses in biblical exegesis in Norwegian and church history in English. Hence, students would often graduate with at least some facility in the English language. Instructors were often full-time faculty members, but local pastors also served in that role at times, including the Swedish and "English" Lutheran pastors in Red Wing.

In his memoir, Boraas makes one final, telling comment about the ecclesiastical environment among Norwegian-American Lutherans of his time, which highlights the different attitude and tension that existed between Hauge's Synod and the Norwegian Synod. He discusses his father's "disgust" with a group of students from Luther College in Decorah, Iowa, which was the college of the Norwegian Synod. He had requested that they give speeches at a particular occasion, which they declined to do because they did not have prepared comments. Boraas's father remarked that students from Red Wing Seminary of Hauge's Synod would have spoken even without advance preparation. Their heritage in the Haugean revival and their tradition of nonliturgical worship led to a willingness to offer testimony when asked and created a noticeable difference in character between students from Hauge's Synod and their more formal counterparts. The sense of friction that existed between the Haugeans and other Norwegian-American Lutherans in this time can also be demonstrated by the experience of Red Wing Seminary students, who were evidently referred to derogatorily as "hogs" and treated "in a discourteous fashion" by some members of the surrounding community. The exact origin of this moniker is unclear, though it seems to be a mispronunciation of the word "Hauge." It is suggested that it was indeed intended to mock the Haugeans and their tradition.[69]

Jewell Lutheran College and Camrose Lutheran College

Of course, Red Wing Seminary also had a preparatory college department, but Hauge's Synod was also active in education on the strictly college level through two different institutions. Curiously, however, Richard W. Solberg's *Lutheran Higher Education in North America* makes no reference to Jewell Lutheran College (JLC) in Jewell, Iowa. Hence, information on the origin and activity of this institution was difficult to locate. In 1913, it was reported that JLC was "a co-educational institution, offering academic, normal, musical, and commercial courses to young men and women."[70] Founded in 1893, originally as an independent Lutheran college, JLC was apparently focused more on preparing students for secular vocations than on preparation for ministry, with religion being taught though not required.[71] In addition to religion, subjects taught included Latin, mathematics, grammar, history, psychology, various sciences, literature, bookkeeping, rhetoric, government, and vocal music. Enrollment gradually increased from the original thirty students in the first year. Though independent at first, Hauge's Synod had a strong connection with this college from the beginning. The town of Jewell is located in Hamilton County, Iowa, one of the historic strongholds of Hauge's Synod. Notably, C. J. Eastvold was among both the board of directors and the board of trustees of the college at the outset. Understandably, when the local college association could no longer absorb the costs, the college property was transferred to the Iowa District of Hauge's Synod in 1897. In 1903, a fire destroyed the main building of the college, and two students perished in the blaze. Recovering from this tragedy, the student enrollment peaked at seventy-two in 1917, at which point the college became a part of the NLCA. However, the college only lasted a few more

---

69. Gisselquist, *Called to Preach*, 53.

70. "Facts About Hauge's Synod," 115.

71. Nass, "Jewell Lutheran College." The following information about Jewell Lutheran College is derived from this brief history.

years, not surviving budget cuts in the NLCA in 1924. The following year, the college property was transferred to the Independent School District of Jewell Junction, Iowa. Despite its short life, JLC played an important role in the life of Hauge's Synod through the education of many young people, and significant figures such as N. J. Løhre and C. J. Eastvold are included on the list of presidents of the college.

The other educational institution connected to Hauge's Synod in some form was Camrose Lutheran College of Camrose, Alberta, a reflection of the significant presence of the synod in that part of Canada. The school, which began as a high school with the initiative of the UNLC, was supported by a joint foundation of UNLC and Hauge's Synod congregations. In 1939, the school obtained junior college status and eventually became an undergraduate institution.[72] Hauge's Synod recognized its relationship with Camrose Lutheran College, with Norlie listing "Camrose College preaching point" among the list of Hauge's Synod congregations as of 1916.

Language

The roots of Hauge's Synod in Eielsen's preaching activity meant that concern for the English language was a part of their heritage from the beginning. As already noted, Eielsen was not concerned with preserving the Norwegian language for its own sake, but rather sought to encourage the use of both Norwegian and English for evangelistic purposes in the new land. He provided an English translation of the *Small Catechism*, and his "Old Constitution" spoke in article thirteen of the importance of children learning both Norwegian and English. Harrisville reports that the members of Hauge's Synod, because of their concern for quality of spiritual life rather than particular form, have been described as "more easily assimilated" and "more ecumenical,"[73] which contained implications for language. Harrisville's grandfather "attacked other members of the clergy for insisting on the Norwegian language." However, as Norwegian immigration continued and increased, the need for Norwegian remained to reach out to new arrivals.

This created a confusing situation for Hauge's Synod as well as the whole of Norwegian-American Lutheranism. Eielsen's early advocacy for

---

72. Solberg, *Lutheran Higher Education*. 243.
73. Harrisville, Interview by Thomas E. Jacobson.

English was not shared by all, with many Norwegian-American Lutherans advocating for Norwegian, fearing the English language as a source of sectarian religious influences. For example, leaders in the Norwegian Synod referred in the 1860s to the Scandinavian Augustana Synod as a "Yankified ecclesiastical company,"[74] critical of its ties to the more Americanized Lutheranism of the General Synod; as already noted, the Norwegian Augustana Synod was explicit in its desire to use English, which distinguished it from the Conference. Even in the UNLC, there existed fear of abandoning Norwegian for English as of 1914, claiming that through the use of English "younger pastors who do not read, hear or understand Norwegian are in danger of becoming Reformed in sentiment and doctrine."[75]

Though article thirteen of the "Old Constitution," which stated the need for young people to learn both languages, was not carried forward in Hauge's Synod after the 1876 reorganization, Hauge's Synod shared with the Norwegian Augustana Synod greater openness to the American environment through the use of English. This is demonstrated by Bruce's description of the difficulties surrounding language in 1916. There were apparently some members of the synod who felt obligated to use English on the congregational level as well as during annual meetings of the synod, even when there was no real demand or need for it. Bruce also notes that the question of language was a divisive one in some congregations, driving a wedge between older and younger members, occasionally alienating the younger members who desired English and leading them to seek a church home elsewhere. Naturally, the demand for English was not uniform throughout Hauge's Synod, with congregations further east and in urban areas seeing the greatest need. In 1901, C. O. Eittreim, a pastor of Hauge's Synod in Creston, Illinois, presented a paper at the annual meeting concerning the "Demand for English Work in Our Synod." In it, he argued that such a need is real, citing the difficult balancing act between Norwegian and English that he was required to strike in his congregation, concluding that even congregations that were currently unable to see such a need would be faced with the issue before long.[76] Curiously, however, in spite of the openness toward the use of English, Hauge's Synod ranked lower than both the UNLC and the Norwegian Synod in the overall congregational use of English as of 1916, at

---

74. Nelson, *Lutheran Church*, 2:244.
75. "The Language Situation in the United Church," 186.
76. Nelson, *Lutheran Church*, 2:100.

17.2 percent. The UNLC boasted 21.6 percent of its organization using English, and the Norwegian Synod 25.7 percent.[77] This indicates that, despite their heritage of openness to English, Hauge's Synod remained strongly Norwegian in its outlook and practice. This apparent disconnect can perhaps be explained by considering the rural and urban divide in the synod. Many of the oldest congregations of Hauge's Synod, located in Illinois and Wisconsin, were urban, as was the case with Eittreim's congregation in Creston, Illinois. Naturally, these older, urban congregations carried considerable influence in the organization while also experiencing greater need for English due to greater mobility found in cities. The strong majority of total congregations, however, were located in more isolated rural areas, where English would not be as important.

Publications

THE PERIODICAL *BUDBÆREREN*

The official periodical of Hauge's Synod was *Budbæreren*, translated as "The Messenger." As already noted, Ø. Hanson was one of the initial editors of this Norwegian language organ, and it began circulation even before the reorganization of 1876. Regarding *Budbæreren*, Bruce only notes in 1916 that it had a fairly large circulation, though there were still many homes of members of Hauge's Synod congregations that did not receive it. With the exception of lists of financial contributors to the publication or lists of various missionary stations and workers, the text of the periodical is written entirely in Gothic script, making it difficult to decipher.

True to its title, *Budbæreren* served the purpose of communicating matters of significance to members of the synod as well as to those outside of the synod. There are often reports about the activity of the China Mission, for example, as well as more controversial articles of theological interest. The fact that *Budbæreren* played a significant role in the disputes among Norwegian-American Lutherans of the late nineteenth and early twentieth centuries is demonstrated by the frequent references to *Budbæreren* in other publications. In an issue of the *Lutheran Herald* of the Norwegian Synod from 1906, the editor refers to developments within Hauge's Synod, referring to a recent article in *Budbæreren* concerning the practice of absolution in Lutheran churches. The editor of the *Lutheran*

---

77. Nelson, *Lutheran Church*, 2:248.

Herald notes the *Budbæreren* editor's conviction that absolution should not be connected to the Lord's Supper or given publicly, referring to public absolution as a product of Rationalism and encouraging private absolution as the only practice justified by the Lutheran confessional writings.[78]

More innocuously, though of no less importance for a portrait of the synod's activity, the pages of *Budbæreren* are filled with updates about home mission activity and news from various congregations. For example, a brief article in 1908 provided an update about the activity of Niobrara Hauge's Norwegian Evangelical Lutheran Congregation in Knox County, Nebraska. As one of only three congregations of the synod in Nebraska at the time and therefore located outside any significant pocket of congregations of the synod, the members of the Niobrara congregation expressed gratitude for those individuals and "sister congregations" that offered financial contributions for the construction of their new church building, as worship services to that point had been held in an old schoolhouse. The author concludes, "Wherefore, may God's kingdom extend over these donors as over this congregation. And may this house, which is built, be to the glory of the Lord."[79]

The Periodical the *Lutheran Intelligencer*

Connected to the issue of language discussed above, the *Lutheran Intelligencer* was begun as an independent English language periodical within Hauge's Synod in 1911. However, it was notably not an official undertaking of the synod. Originally, G. M. Bruce began this publication as a newsletter for his congregations of First Lutheran Church and Rook's Creek Lutheran Church in Pontiac, Illinois. Even so, this semimonthly newsletter made use of advertisements from the local community in addition to the subscription cost of fifty cents per year in order to pay for the publication. In the first issue, Bruce highlighted the importance of using print as a means of communication in church life, noting that far more people are reached through such publications than through sermons.[80] Although intended at first primarily for the members of his congregations, Bruce's newsletter apparently had wider circulation; it reached the

---

78. *Lutheran Herald*, 1906, 525.
79. *Budbæreren*, 1908, 257. This translation is my own.
80. Bruce, "Editorial," 1911.

community of Dell Rapids, South Dakota, where Bruce had once resided. Highlighting outside reactions to the *Lutheran Intelligencer*, Bruce included in the second issue a note from the Dell Rapids, South Dakota *Times-Tribune*, which described the content of the newsletter:

> We are in receipt of the initial number of The Lutheran Intelligencer, published by Rev. Gustav M. Bruce in the interest of the Lutheran churches at Pontiac and Rook's Creek, Ill., of which he is pastor. It is a neat little eight page paper three pages devoted to advertising. The reading matter speaks in Rev. Bruce's vigorous style, and indicates the grade of work he has entered upon there. His many Dell Rapids friends will be glad to know of his apparent successful work.[81]

At first, Bruce appeared to be encouraged in this work. He reported in that first year that the English Board of Hauge's Synod congratulated him on doing, through the publication of an "English paper," what they had to that point been unable to accomplish.[82] The *Lutheran Intelligencer* soon expanded beyond its narrow focus on Bruce's congregations in Pontiac, Illinois. Upon Bruce's appointment as professor of practical theology at Red Wing Seminary in September of 1911, the paper became devoted to the interests of Hauge's Synod as a whole, and the initial results were modestly encouraging. Bruce reported at the beginning of the second year of publication:

> With this number we begin Volume Two of The Lutheran Intelligencer. When we began the publication of the Intelligencer last April as a parish paper devoted to the interests of our churches at Pontiac, Ill., we had no idea that it would be turned into a general church paper before the close of the first year of its existence. Such has been the case, however, and the experiment has been fairly successful so far. Last August we sent out the first number of a general nature, and since then our subscription list has been growing steadily, tho [sic] not very rapidly.[83]

The pages of the *Lutheran Intelligencer* are best described as a combination of devotional and theological articles geared toward laypeople, updates on congregations and pastors of Hauge's Synod, and advertisements highlighting important synodical ventures such as Red Wing

81. "What Others Say," 1911.
82. Bruce, "Editorial," August 16, 1911.
83. Bruce, "Editorial," January 1912.

Seminary, Jewell Lutheran College, and the Hauge's Synod Book Concern. Bruce's editorial comments also provide an important glimpse into the life of Hauge's Synod of the time. Notably, he addressed the difficult issue of language. Acknowledging the importance of continued use of Scandinavian languages as needed, he also frowned upon the attitude of some within Hauge's Synod that "Norwegian and religion are synonymous" and that "English is only a business language," according to an author in *Budbæreren*. Above all, Bruce encouraged members of Hauge's Synod to be concerned first and foremost with the salvation of souls and not about the particular language used, arguing that the *Lutheran Intelligencer* serves the same purpose as *Budbæreren*, only to different linguistic audiences.[84]

In spite of the initial modest success of Bruce's English paper, it ran into difficulties finding a wide readership, and the issue of language continued to present itself in its pages. Bruce included, wherever he could, letters from readers highlighting the importance of an English language periodical for Hauge's Synod.[85] It still sought to play an important role in the life of the synod, publishing English language reports of the annual meeting of Hauge's Synod at Red Wing in June of 1912. During the annual meeting that year, Hauge's Synod officially endorsed the *Lutheran Intelligencer* as a publication of the church body.[86] However, this apparently was not enough to increase the demand for an English paper within Hauge's Synod, and Bruce gave one final appeal to the constituency of Hauge's Synod for support of his work. In May of 1913, he wrote, "This is our final appeal to our readers and to the Synod at large. Now or never is the time to act. Speak a word for the Intelligencer to your parishioners and neighbors." In the very next issue, however, Bruce provided sobering words about the lack of receptivity to an English paper within Hauge's Synod, announcing that it would thenceforth serve as an intersynodical English language paper:

> This final chance has been given, and while we did receive some encouragements during the conference just closed, encouragements which we appreciate very much, knowing that they came from such as have our Synod's best interests at heart, yet we do not feel that it is worth while [sic] to waste any further time and effort on what seems an almost hopeless field for English

---

84. Bruce, "Editorial," February 1912.
85. Bruce, "Editorial," April 1912, 52.
86. Bruce, "Editorial," July 1912, 117.

religious journalism. We have therefore, after due consideration, decided to enter a field yet unoccupied and launch the Intelligencer as an inter-synodical paper, devoted not only to the interests of one small synod, but to the entire Lutheran Church of America.[87]

The *Lutheran Intelligencer* continued its existence as an English language paper devoted to the interests of the entire Lutheran community in America until May of 1914, at which point it ceased publication. Though it continued to highlight news from Hauge's Synod as well as the rest of Norwegian-American Lutheranism, it also included news from other synods and often provided a "directory" of the various Lutheran church bodies in America, listing the title of the synod and the president and secretary of each church body. This indicates, at least from Bruce's perspective, which was likely shared by many others, that the Lutheran identity of Hauge's Synod was strong. Further evidence of this is provided in the April issue of 1913, where Bruce reprinted an article by L. S. Keyser from *Lutheran Church Work*, which argued that the various Lutheran church bodies in North America, though not identical to one another in all matters of practice, were "fundamentally united" in doctrine, more so than other denominational families. Keyser then argued for greater Lutheran cooperation and union. At the same time, Bruce's commitment to Lutheranism did not appear to exclude entirely non-Lutherans from the kingdom of God, and he warned his readers in 1912 against overreliance on Lutheran fealty:

> Furthermore, one is apt to become so enrapt in the historical and human side of the Reformation, that the divine and spiritual element is more or less entirely lost sight of. It is well enough to be an enthusiastic Lutheran ourself [sic] and then seek to enthuse others with Lutheranism, but it must always be borne in mind that it is not faith in nor loyalty to Luther and Lutheranism that saves, but only faith in and loyalty to Christ Jesus alone.[88]

The *Lutheran Intelligencer* is an important source of information about Hauge's Synod during the years of its publication. However, the story of this English language organ itself serves as an important example of the controversy surrounding the question of language within Hauge's

---

87. Bruce, "Editorial," June 1913.
88. Bruce, "Editorial," October 1912.

Synod and highlights the resistance to the use of English in some places in the synod. The disappearance of this publication from the Norwegian-American scene after 1914 is also important to consider in discussion of the enduring influence of Hauge's Synod after the merger of 1917. When the three largest Norwegian-American church bodies merged in that year, the English language publications of the Norwegian Synod and the UNLC, the *Lutheran Herald* and the *United Lutheran* respectively, also merged. Hauge's Synod, however, had no English language organ as of that point, perhaps one factor in the feeling of disenfranchisement among former members of Hauge's Synod in the NLCA. This situation also demonstrates possible disunity within Hauge's Synod itself, with Bruce serving as a representative of a more outwardly focused, ecumenical piety. Bruce himself, in his 1916 observation, noted that there existed within Hauge's Synod significant resistance to engaging in institutionally related activities, with many members of the synod presumably preferring to focus on the quality of spiritual life on a local level. It should be considered that this bifurcation was partially the result of the mixture of influences in American Haugeanism discussed earlier: Johnsonian and Rosenian pieties.

The periodical *Tidsskrift for Kirke og Samfund*

The February 1912 issue of the *Lutheran Intelligencer* makes reference to the existence of a third periodical within Hauge's Synod. This *Tidsskrift for Kirke og Samfund*, translated as "Periodical for Church and Society," was edited by M. O. Wee, Bruce's colleague at Red Wing Seminary. However, this periodical is never referred to again in the *Lutheran Intelligencer*, and no copies of it can be located, suggesting that it was a short-lived endeavor.

Ecumenical Activity

A picture of the organizational life of Hauge's Synod would not be complete without considering its relationship with other church bodies. Of course, much of the discussion of the synod's ecumenical activity is included in the discussion of merger negotiations below. However, there are some noteworthy issues in this category not covered by the synod's involvement in merger negotiations, issues which provide an important glimpse into the life of Hauge's Synod.

With other Lutherans

As evidenced by references to Lutherans of other ethnic backgrounds in the periodicals of the synod, Hauge's Synod certainly possessed an awareness of the broader field of American Lutheranism. Their heritage in Eielsen's activity meant that contact with German and "English" Lutherans was a part of their group from the beginning. As has been seen, "English" and Swedish Lutherans were also involved in Red Wing Seminary. However, as has also been seen, in spite of this openness to interaction beyond the Norwegian-American Lutheran environment, Hauge's Synod remained strongly Norwegian in its outlook. Therefore, ecumenical relations with other Lutherans took place largely within the Norwegian-American milieu.

Through discussion of educational institutions and missionary activity, the relationship between Hauge's Synod and other Lutheran church bodies has already been described to some extent. As already noted, the ethos of Haugeanism did not fall neatly within the boundaries of any particular church body, with all Norwegian-American Lutherans influenced by it to some extent. For example, even some within the Norwegian Synod advocated for the Haugean practice of lay preaching, arguing that it was healthy for their church body and contributed to the salvation of souls.[89] This meant that many within Hauge's Synod felt a spiritual kinship with members of other synods, even when other members of those same synods expressed suspicion of Hauge's Synod. Already discussed was the call of J. N. Kildahl of the Norwegian Synod to teach at Red Wing Seminary as well as the invitation of "English" and Swedish Lutheran pastors in Red Wing to do the same on an adjunct basis. Also already discussed was the cooperation that existed between Hauge's Synod and the UNLC through the China Mission and Camrose Lutheran College. Though the relationship between the China Mission Society and Hauge's Synod was strained, members of Hauge's Synod, the UNLC, and later the Lutheran Free Church worked together and focused on the work at hand rather than denominational politics. At home, members of both church bodies cooperated in a similar way, with significant "inter-pollination"

---

89. Svanoe, *Work of Laypersons*, 5.

between them noted especially in the Hauge's Synod stronghold of north central Iowa; some members of the UNLC also referred to themselves as "Haugeaners."[90] In these examples, the ecumenical activity of Hauge's Synod was carried out on an *ad hoc* basis, arising from below rather than from authorities on high.

In the earlier years, however, Hauge's Synod did engage in ecumenical discussion of a more formal nature. The Norwegian Augustana Synod, described by Fevold and Nelson as "laboring to perpetuate its Haugean and American spirit," naturally saw in Hauge's Synod a kindred spirit.[91] With the focus of the Norwegian Augustanans on "conversion," lay preaching, nonliturgical worship, the use of English, and a suspicious attitude toward certain common amusements, Fevold and Nelson are correct in stating that it is difficult to find any significant differences between the two groups. Attempts were made in the 1870s by the Norwegian Augustana Synod to come into closer fellowship with Eielsen's Synod and then Hauge's Synod, but the turmoil within the synod over its constitution that resulted in the reorganization of 1876 understandably prevented serious discussions of merger with the Norwegian Augustanans. Two years later, interest in such a union waned as the result of the decision of Hauge's Synod to call August Weenaas as a professor at Red Wing Seminary, which was in the process of being organized. Weenaas, it will be remembered, was involved in the dispute that divided the Norwegian Augustanans from the Conference and was therefore viewed unfavorably by the Norwegian Augustana Synod. His presence at Red Wing Seminary therefore brought an end to the possibility of a union between them and Hauge's Synod. It is ironic that the openness of Hauge's Synod to working with those outside of their group who were considered congruent with their piety led to the collapse of a more formal ecumenical endeavor.

Later in the life of the synod, Hauge's Synod also engaged in discussions regarding practical cooperation with the Lutheran Free Church. As already noted, the Lutheran Free Church had separated from the UNLC in 1897 as a result of the controversy surrounding the status of Augsburg College and Seminary. Fevold notes that Hauge's Synod was viewed by the Lutheran Free Church as a kindred spirit despite the differences in polity. Sharing identification with Haugeanism, the two church bodies,

---

90. Harrisville, Interview by Thomas E. Jacobson.

91. Nelson and Fevold, *Lutheran Church*, 1:211. The discussion in this paragraph is derived from pages 211 to 216 of this volume.

beginning in 1902, cooperated in an annual weeklong educational event for pastors, held at Augsburg Seminary.[92] By 1906, the Lutheran Free Church had apparently taken over responsibility for the Madagascar Mission. Committees appointed by both these church bodies discussed cooperation in foreign missions in 1906, concluding that missionaries from either group could participate in the China Mission and the Madagascar Mission. Furthermore, contributions for both mission endeavors were to be solicited in the publications of both church bodies.[93] This is yet another indicator of the willingness of Hauge's Synod to cooperate with members of other church bodies considered congruent with their theological commitments.

A final issue to be considered regarding the relationship between Hauge's Synod and other Norwegian-American Lutherans is the cooperative work on an English language hymnal. Prior to the merger of 1917, four members of Hauge's Synod were included in a committee that led to the publication of *The Lutheran Hymnary* in 1912. According to this committee of twelve members, four each from the Norwegian Synod, the UNLC, and Hauge's Synod, the stated goal of this hymnal was to provide in the English language a treasury of "genuine Lutheran hymns."[94] What this meant is that the purpose of such a hymnal was to meet the needs and "expectations of our Norwegian-American Lutheran Church people" and was not American in its outlook. It therefore contained primarily English translations of Dano-Norwegian and German hymns with which Norwegian-American Lutherans would have been familiar. The liturgy contained therein was also a translation of the 1887 liturgy of the Church of Norway.[95] The Norwegian outlook of this hymnal is further confirmed by the other stated goal of the hymnal committee, which was to be "no small factor in the efforts made to unify the various Norwegian Lutheran Church bodies of our land." Leading up to the merger, the *Lutheran Herald* of the Norwegian Synod made a similar comment on the unifying influence of the *Lutheran Hymnary*: "The book [*Lutheran Hymnary*] also seems destined to play no small part in the work for church union, which now seems a question of time with the three main church organizations among the Norwegians."[96]

92. Fevold, *Lutheran Free Church*, 134.
93. *Lutheran Herald*, 1906, 1091.
94. *The Lutheran Hymnary*, 4.
95. Nelson, *Lutheran Church*, 2:124.
96. "Church Union and the Synod," 1914, 315.

Though Hauge's Synod was included in the process that led to the publication of this hymnal, having in fact influence on the committee disproportionate to its size, it appears that Hauge's Synod was included in the project somewhat as an afterthought. The origin of the hymnal project lay in the separate work of both the Norwegian Synod and the UNLC to produce an English language hymnal, and the Norwegian Synod extended an invitation to the UNLC to begin a joint effort in 1908.[97] The preface of the hymnal refers to this cooperation between the Norwegian Synod and the UNLC, but no mention is made of the invitation extended to Hauge's Synod. This apparent lack of initiative on the part of Hauge's Synod for participation in the project and the omission of a detailed reference to their contribution could be attributed to the lack of interest in liturgy among the synod, but it should also be considered that the other church bodies, representatives of the Norwegian Synod in particular, might have been less than concerned with acknowledging the contribution of Hauge's Synod. As noted, many parts of Hauge's Synod were familiar with Landstad's *Salmebog*[98] and the Norwegian hymns contained therein, making such an English language hymnal useful for them in the process of language transition, but the liturgical piece of *The Lutheran Hymnary* would have been largely irrelevant, and friction between these different traditions of worship would have been understandable.

With non-Lutherans

Hauge's Synod seems to have walked a difficult balance between valuing its Lutheran heritage on the one hand and acknowledging the existence of true and "living" Christianity among other Christian traditions. More will be said in the discussion of merger negotiations leading up to 1917 about how Hauge's Synod differed from other Norwegian-American synods in its approach to non-Lutherans. However, some things can be observed in the preceding years.

Already noted was the willingness of many students of Red Wing Seminary to worship at the local Presbyterian congregation. Although an isolated example, this testifies to a certain spirit of openness within Hauge's Synod concerning relations with Christians of other denominational families, and this openness is important to bear in mind when

---

97. Nelson, *Lutheran Church*, 2:170.
98. This is translated as "hymnbook."

considering the enduring legacy of Haugeanism after 1917. However, it would be inaccurate to portray Hauge's Synod as doctrinally indifferent. As Harrisville noted, "orthodox theology" was a central characteristic of Hauge's Synod.[99] One also notes in the pages of the *Lutheran Intelligencer* an emphasis on the importance of Lutheran identity. Though it is possible that this emphasis reflects Bruce's perspective, which might not have been shared by other members of the synod, it should be remembered that Bruce attempted to write and print articles that would be of interest to laypeople and therefore generate a strong base of readership, making it unlikely that he would print overly controversial articles; the fact that the *Lutheran Intelligencer* failed to gain a wide readership was due to the issue of language, as has been noted.

Already referred to is an article in this periodical about the "essential unity" of Lutheranism in America, which noted this unity as a difference between American Lutheranism and other American denominations. In that same issue, yet another article was reprinted from *Lutheran Church Work*, a publication of the General Synod. This article listed the percentage of membership gain among American religious groups between 1900 and 1910, noting that Lutherans far exceeded all other Protestant groups, boasting a 35 percent gain.[100] Though the article is not antagonistic toward other religious groups, it does express pride in the Lutheran heritage as a result of this statistic, all the while being mildly critical of religious groups "that depend most largely upon the revival system" instead of comprehensive religious education, noting that such revivalist groups showed the smallest rate of membership increase. Though not explicitly stated, this appears to be a criticism of "evangelical" and Methodist churches. The relationship between Hauge's Synod and other Christian traditions is also demonstrated by Bruce's inclusion of a vigorous defense of the doctrine of baptismal regeneration. With the title "Baptism Is Necessary," he goes on to quote a brief note from the publication *Lutheran Young People*:

> If there were no other reason, we would say that baptism is necessary because Christ commanded it. But it is also necessary because He has connected with it the blessings of salvation. Those who neglect or despise baptism disobey Christ and deprive

---

99. Harrisville, Interview by Thomas E. Jacobson.
100. Clark, "An Interesting Statement," April 1913, 58.

themselves of the blessings which He has connected with this holy sacrament.[101]

Bruce's tendency to reprint, in the pages of the *Lutheran Intelligencer*, notes and articles from various other Lutheran publications is itself an indicator of the strength of Lutheran identity within Hauge's Synod. At the same time, one also detects a cautious openness to ecumenical cooperation, at least regarding matters external to doctrine. Reprinting an article from the *Lutheran Church Visitor* in the February of 1913 issue, Bruce sought to impress upon readers the value of interdenominational movements. The brief article, written by an anonymous layperson, makes an argument for faithful Lutheran involvement in certain movements such as the Student Volunteer Movement, the Missionary Education Movement, and the Layman's Missionary Movement, noting that Lutherans have both much to receive from such movements and much to provide them. The author was careful, however, not to advocate for uncritical involvement in non-Lutheran organizations, pointing out that sectarian groups such as Mormons should not be considered "churches." He went on to describe his vision for faithful Lutheran involvement in such interdenominational movements:

> I am not a theologian, but a plain layman. I believe firmly in the doctrines of the Lutheran Church as I understand them, catechetical instruction being freely practiced by my father as well as by my pastor. I have no sympathy whatever with the movements which say, "Abandon all your doctrines all ye who enter here." I want nothing to do with any movement that "pronounces every creed as sectarian and schismatic." But instead of carefully avoiding all interdenominational movements lest a "creedless," "spineless," "colorless" Lutheranism be ours, I do believe that a Lutheran can co-operate with the three movements mentioned above without sacrificing a word of his creed. . . . The Lutheran Church can co-operate in the three movements named as long as they stand on their present platforms, and take with her to every meeting the three ancient symbols . . . and the Unaltered Augsburg Confession of Faith; also the other symbolical books.[102]

This defense of limited interdenominational cooperation and Bruce's inclusion of it in the pages of the *Lutheran Intelligencer* indicates that the

---

101. "Baptism Is Necessary," August 16, 1911.

102. "Our Debt to Interdenominational Movements," February 1913, 23.

listed criticisms were likely leveled at Hauge's Synod from other Lutherans. This attempt at a nuanced approach toward such interdenominational involvement is an indicator of the difficult balance that the synod sought to walk.

One final area in which Hauge's Synod would have had contact with Christians of other confessions was in the field of temperance work. Throughout the nineteenth century, many American Protestants sought to discourage the use of alcohol, which they viewed as a danger to the health of society. Though some temperance organizations were denominationally specific, many were interdenominational.[103] Bruce himself was a leader in an interdenominational temperance movement during his earlier ministry in Dell Rapids, South Dakota, and he wrote with pride about the continued victories of this movement in Dell Rapids, keeping the town "dry" through votes prohibiting saloons.[104] The temperance movement continued to play a role in the life of Hauge's Synod; a lengthy article was included in the *Lutheran Intelligencer* arguing against the practice of licensed saloons in communities.[105] A pastor of Hauge's Synod in Beresford, South Dakota, Julius Anderson Quello, was reportedly "subjected to vicious attacks by the lawless elements of the community, on account of the stand he had taken against the liquor traffic."[106] Though Wentz notes that Lutherans of the late nineteenth and early twentieth centuries were for the most part focused on the salvation of individuals rather than groups and considered that "social reform must begin with individuals," he does note that certain Lutheran groups such as the Swedish Augustana Synod, the UNLC, and Hauge's Synod were aberrations, with the UNLC and Hauge's Synod approving resolutions in the 1890s in support of temperance and prohibition as well as charitable work toward immigrants.[107] Hauge's Synod obviously did not reject the concept of individual salvation, as its revival heritage attests, but there existed openness among the synod to extend the concept of "salvation" to wider society through laws seeking to enforce morality, which is consistent with their heritage in the Haugean revival of Norway; Hauge's own concern for societal transformation is well-attested. By way of conclusion, one can say that Hauge's Synod, although certainly not

103. Granquist, *Lutherans in America*, 159.
104. Bruce, *Lutheran Intelligencer*, May 3, 1911.
105. Keyser, "Objections to the Licensed Saloon," May 1912, 71.
106. "Other Lutheran Synods," 1914, 62.
107. Wentz, *Basic History of Lutheranism in America*, 321.

"laying cavalier hands on theology" in Harrisville's words, possessed a somewhat different spirit than what might be found among many in the Norwegian Synod, demonstrating greater willingness to cooperate with non-Lutherans and to advocate for social action.

Theological Identity

Many of the issues already discussed provide a glimpse into the theological identity of Hauge's Synod. However, important for a more complete portrait of the synod are some other noteworthy issues.

A Commitment to Lutheranism

The Lutheran identity of Hauge's Synod has already been well established, but it is worth noting the explicit commitment to the Lutheran tradition contained in its constitution. The second article states:

> As we united have by the grace of our Lord Jesus Christ united and joined ourselves together into an organized Church Society of the Lutheran Church in America, so be it hereby firmly resolved and declared that this our Church Society shall ever remain as it now is in accordance with the true Lutheran faith and doctrine, built upon the Word of God, the Holy Scriptures, the canonical books of the Old and New Testament, as the only source and rule for faith, doctrine, and life. We accept as a true exhibition of the principal doctrines of the Word of God the three oldest symbols, the Apostolic, Nicene, and Athanasian, the Unaltered *Augsburg Confession*, and Luther's *Small Catechism*.[108]

Of course, constitutional statements and the attitudes of organizational leadership do not always translate to the local, congregational level. However, it should be noted that out of the synod's 342 congregations as of 1916, 243 of them contained the word *lutherske* or its English equivalent "Lutheran" in the title of the congregation.[109] The congregation in Platville, Illinois, made its Lutheran commitment even more explicit, calling itself "The Norwegian Evangelical Lutheran Congregation of the

---

108. The entire text of the constitution of Hauge's Synod is found in Appendix B of this book.

109. See the table in Appendix C of this book.

Unaltered Augsburg Confession." It was not uncommon for Norwegian-American Lutheran congregations to be known simply by the title *menighet*, meaning "congregation," as in the *Bethania menighet* of Volga, South Dakota, or the *Sion menighet* of Leonard, Minnesota. This phenomenon is true within Hauge's Synod as well as the Norwegian Synod and the UNLC, and though the absence of the word "Lutheran" in a congregation's title does not necessarily mean that such a congregation lacked Lutheran theological identity, it is simply noteworthy that the vast majority of Hauge's Synod congregations chose to make their Lutheran identity explicitly known.

As has already been established, however, Lutheranism is far from a theologically unified movement, and the theological disputes within Norwegian-American Lutheranism already discussed testify to this. It is therefore necessary to articulate further the particular flavor of Lutheranism represented by Hauge's Synod. Comments by President M. G. Hanson in his 1900 annual report to the synod demonstrate both its Lutheran commitment as well as the way that the Haugean heritage of revivalism and mission were expressed within that theological commitment:

> At Newman Grove, Nebr., Rev. Nervig's parish, and at Sioux City, Ia., Rev. Quello's parish, there has, during the winter, been a general revival. May God promote the work and preserve those that have been regenerated! . . . There are still new fields, where the Word of God have not [sic] been preached nor the Sacraments administered. If these be neglected, they will soon be occupied by workers from other synods or sects. Just here we have a great work that we must do, if we believe our method of work and the spirit of true Haugianism [sic] to be completely Lutheran and Biblical, thus answering to the requirements for the advancement of the Kingdom of God among men. . . . We should gather the people about the Word of God, and the Sacraments, organize congregations and lead souls to the Lord.[110]

As is seen from this quote, Hauge's Synod made use of and encouraged the practice of revivalism, but it did not, as discussed above regarding relationships with non-Lutherans, rely exclusively on the system of revival. Care is taken in Hanson's words to emphasize the importance of establishing congregations rooted in Lutheran sacramental theology, which would, in turn, provide members with education, thereby "preserving those that have been regenerated." In this sense, the type of revivalism

---

110. Hauge's Synod, *Reports to the 55th Annual Convention*, 23.

used within Hauge's Synod can be regarded as distinct from the more spontaneous American revivals of the Second Great Awakening; indeed, M. G. Hanson testifies to this with his reference to "other synods and sects."

Some articles in *Budbæreren* are also helpful in observing the theological identity of the synod. An article in 1908, translated as "Morsels from Bardo in Alberta," describes the celebration surrounding the laying of the cornerstone of the church building of the *Bardo menighet* in Alberta, Canada. In describing this event, the author expressed joy and gratitude for the new church building for the congregation. However, he took care to emphasize that the "spacious" building was not an end in itself, but rather a means to an end, a place where those "hungry for grace" could occupy the new spacious building in order to be sustained by "God's everlasting Word of sin and grace" as well as be empowered to "live in the fear of God." He also lifts up the new church building as a place where "newcomers will become connected with God in holy baptism."[111] The example of this congregational "morsel" demonstrates the way that Lutheranism was lived out on a congregational level in Hauge's Synod. Notably, there was a commitment to Lutheran sacramental theology, as the reference to baptism testifies. Traditional Lutheran themes such as sin and grace are also present. However, there was also an emphasis on Christian obedience to God, which is perhaps a testimony to the importance they placed on personal discipleship. The church building was also understood in a functional way, serving as a center for outreach to unbelievers. This is consistent with one observation that members of Hauge's Synod were known for their work of personal evangelism in their communities, being enthusiastic "pamphleteers," often going house to house to share their faith and distribute leaflets, which distinguished them from many in the Norwegian Synod, which operated more on a "Christendom model," establishing churches and assuming that people would come to worship with the ringing of the church bells.[112] This example of the Bardo Congregation in Alberta reveals the Lutheran commitment of Hauge's Synod on a local level, yet it also reveals their tendency to emphasize the subjective appropriation of the faith through calling people to repentance and "conversion."

---

111. "*Smuler fra Bardo i Alberta*," 1908, 822. This translation is my own.
112. Harrisville, Interview by Thomas E. Jacobson.

This tendency is also demonstrated by an article from 1910, which was apparently a reaction to the discussions that were taking place in preparation for the church union of 1917. Translated as "The Blessed State of Justification," the article criticizes the notion of objective "justification of the world," arguing, based on Paul's letter to the Romans, that it is appropriate to speak of the "reconciliation" of the world, but that the term "justification" should be understood in the subjective sense. The author writes about "inner peace" that comes with "a believing heart."[113] This is presumably a reference to the fifth chapter of Romans (Rom 5:1). The article clearly demonstrates the friction that existed between the objective emphasis of much of the Norwegian Synod and subjective emphasis of Hauge's Synod and much of the UNLC. The opinion expressed also explains the strong focus, as in the above example of the Bardo Congregation, on local outreach.

Sermons are also an important source for ascertaining the theological commitments of a church body. Extant sermons from pastors of Hauge's Synod in the era under discussion are not easily accessible, though it is well attested that Haugean preaching frequently involved subjective "heart religion" and calls for spiritual "conversion."[114] At the same time, there was clearly a concern among some for Hauge's Synod to be rooted in the Lutheran confessional tradition. In 1909, the synod published a booklet containing a sermon by C. J. Eastvold on the topic of baptism. In the introduction to the sermon, the president M. G. Hanson warned of the temptation to forsake the Lutheran tradition and encouraged greater understanding of it. This testifies to the fact that Hauge's Synod experienced some difficulty balancing its confessional heritage and its focus on inward spiritual life:

> The more urgent is this in our time, when indifference and disregard for the true doctrine as set forth in the Confession of our beloved Evangelical Lutheran Church, which has been expressed in the Augsburg Confession, seems to become more apparent and prevailing.[115]

The sermon itself provides a lengthy apology for the practice of infant baptism as well as a section that rejects the requirement of baptism by immersion, with numerous references to the Bible, the Lutheran

---

113. "Den Retfærdiggjores salige Tilstand," 1910, 798.
114. Nichol, *Crossings*, 144, 151.
115. Eastvold, *Sermon on Baptism*, 2.

confessional writings, and quotations from early church fathers. No specific contrary teaching is mentioned, but the fact that C. J. Eastvold emphasizes baptism as a means of grace is perhaps telling of the theological tendency within Hauge's Synod to devalue this part of the Lutheran tradition in an effort to uphold the principle of subjective appropriation of God's grace.

A description of the opening sermon at the 1913 annual convention confirms the dual focus on Lutheran confessional theology as well as individual, subjective faith within Hauge's Synod. The sermon, preached by M. O. Wee, at the time a professor at Red Wing Seminary, addressed the topic of Christian "spiritual warfare" (Eph 6:10–13). According to Bruce's description, Wee's sermon focused on directing such "warfare" in the right direction, discouraging strife and contention "among brethren." Rather, energy should be directed toward standing on the foundation of Lutheran theology, education of the young, preaching by both clergy and laity, and maintaining the "low-church" tradition of worship, thereby contending with the false and pernicious influences of "the Catholic Church, the atheistic and irreligious tendency of the American public school system, and the secret societies." Wee went on to list the tools of spiritual warfare to be "the Means of Grace and prayer."[116]

Yet another sermon, preached by I. G. Aschim at the annual convention of 1903, spoke of the importance of bearing proper spiritual fruit. Basing his comments on 1 Peter 1:3–11, Aschim challenged his listeners by pointing out that they had received grace from God, but that grace necessarily takes shape in life in the form of shunning godlessness. He commented that the sin of covetousness in particular has the potential to "destroy the life that God by regeneration created in your soul for your eternal welfare." He further spoke of reading the Bible holistically, emphasizing the importance of combining the grace-filled words of Paul with exhortations to holiness in other parts of the Bible. Likening Christian life to that of a growing plant, Aschim exhorted the congregation:

> The hearts of the Christians ought . . . to be such a soil where the seed . . . may sprout, grow, and bear fruit pleasing to God. . . . By the abundant grace bestowed on us through Christ Jesus, we ought to give evidence of our faith and make firm our election. . . . He has, therefore, bestowed on us all that is necessary for a new life of godliness. . . . The spirit of God here presents the God-life in man as the great contrast to the worldly life of the

---

116. "Proceedings of the Sixty-eighth Annual Conference," June 1913, 86.

ungodly, which is to be shunned by the faithful. . . . The believing Christian has . . . become a regenerated and sanctified soul, a new and budding plant in God's own garden.[117]

One can see, therefore, that the commitment to Lutheranism among Hauge's Synod was not of such a nature as to encourage a lax and comfortable faith, but rather one of spiritual watchfulness and discipleship. At the same time, there was apparently some concern that a genuine commitment to Lutheran theology was in danger of being lost in the process.

Morality

An outgrowth of this concern among Hauge's Synod for spiritual watchfulness was their attitude toward participation in common amusements. Whereas many Lutherans in the time of the Haugean awakening of Norway considered participation in certain amusements to lie in the realm of *adiaphora*, things neither commanded nor forbidden for Christians, Norwegian Haugeans had a reputation as "the puritans of Norway." Norwegian Haugeans, as a mark of their "conversion," were often known for renouncing pleasures they had once enjoyed, such as dancing, music making, and card playing.[118] In its American expression, Haugeanism certainly did continue the tradition of emphasizing both "Christian teaching and Christian life," with Red Wing Seminary lifted up as an institution that would influence students in expressing Christian morality as well as imparting knowledge to them.[119] According to Preus's recollection of "some of the oldsters," meaning former members of Hauge's Synod in the NLCA after 1917, there existed among some Haugeans a spirit of moralism and legalism regarding their antipathy to certain perceived sins such as dancing, card playing, smoking, drinking, and other vices, which also included a judgmental attitude toward those who indulged in such *adiaphora*. At the very least, this is how the Haugeans were sometimes perceived by others, especially those who came out of the Norwegian Synod tradition. At the same time, Preus commended

---

117. Hauge's Synod, *Reports to and Minutes of the 58th Annual Meeting*, 104.

118. Molland, *Fra Hans Nielsen Hauge til Eivind Berggrav*, 21. The word "puritan" here refers to a "purity" of behavior, though the term was originally applied to certain English Protestants who sought to "purify" the Church of England of vestiges of the Roman Church.

119. Rholl, *Red Wing Seminary*, 27.

the "deep seriousness" that the Haugeans attached to "daily living and the expressing of faith in daily living." Such seriousness was an expression of their "total commitment to the Lord," which necessarily included "little things."[120] This suggests that, although some members of Hauge's Synod undoubtedly expressed a dead moralism, many, perhaps most, considered their attitude toward participation in amusements to be simply a consequence of their Christian discipleship.

Evidence of a lack of legalism regarding specific amusements within Hauge's Synod is found in an article in the *Lutheran Intelligencer* from June of 1912. The article, authored by Bruce, does not enumerate prohibited amusements, but rather provides some guidelines for members of the synod to follow: "What kind of amusements may the Christian indulge in? This is a most difficult question. Here we should be concerned rather with principles than the enumeration of specific forms of amusements."[121] The article acknowledges the importance of recreation in the life of a Christian, noting that one who has faith does not cease being a physical creature. Christians need at times things that will "divert the attention from the ordinary routine, duties, and worries of life, and produce sensations of relaxation, rest, mirth, and enjoyment." At the same time, he cautioned readers that Christians cannot engage in amusements that are "wicked or tend toward wickedness" and that they must be things that are "in harmony with and not contrary to the spiritual life of faith," being "conducive to the building up of that life." He encouraged responsibility, reminding readers that they shall have to give account of their activity before God and reminding them of the need to support "the weaker brother or sister" when engaging in amusements. Whether the attitude toward amusements within the synod was expressed legalistically or in the healthier way described by Preus and Bruce, as a natural outgrowth of a life of faith, the notion that one's behavior must be congruent with one's professed faith, an inheritance from Hauge's own experience of "conversion," cannot be ignored in any complete portrait of Hauge's Synod.

---

120. David Preus, Interview by Thomas E. Jacobson.
121. "Our Amusements," June 1912, 84.

The Nature of American Haugeanism

Considering all the above-mentioned issues, a final piece of the portrait of Hauge's Synod is the question of whether Haugeanism in North America can be considered a "pure" Haugeanism or whether other influences colored it in such a way that it took on a different character. First, it must be remembered that Haugeanism in Norway was itself not completely monolithic. As is noted in the previous chapter, Hauge's vision articulated in his "Testament to His Friends" regarding the continued loyalty of the Haugeans to the Church of Norway appears not to have been universally followed. Furthermore, the legalism expressed by many earlier Haugeans seems to have mitigated to some extent, with the likes of Anders Haave advocating for a more "evangelical" rather than legalistic message. Of course, the Johnsonian and Rosenian movements influenced Norwegian Haugeanism in important ways, providing it with greater theological clarity, incorporating the Haugean spirit into the Church of Norway, and serving as an important reminder to the Haugeans of the ultimate purpose of repentance, which was not to seek salvation through personal betterment, but rather to "drive one to Christ," thereby finding peace with God.

When attempting to define American Haugeanism, it would be artificial to apply a single descriptive label such as "pure Haugean," "Johnsonian," or "Rosenian." Having already acknowledged the difficulty in defining Norwegian Haugeanism, it is not surprising that American Haugeanism would contain similar diversity. The differences between the state church environment of Norway and the voluntary religious environment of the United States also account for differences in the expression of Haugeanism. Nevertheless, some things can be observed about American Haugeanism that might well relate to the developments of the Johnsonian and Rosenian movements in the old country. When considering these issues, the nature of American Haugeanism becomes clearer, even if there is not a single, overarching label to describe it.

Already discussed in the previous chapter was the conflict between the Old Tendency and the New Tendency in the years before the reorganization of 1876. A major part of this New Tendency was the rejection of the perceived Donatism in the "Old Constitution." This could be the result of greater theological clarity brought about from Johnsonian influence. However, Ø. Hanson's role in the New Tendency has been largely attributed to the growing influence of Rosenian piety, originally from

Sweden. This piety, which modified Norwegian Haugeanism to some extent, continued to champion an awakened and converted faith and life, yet it was overall a more cheerful message of peace with God as a result of Christ's atonement. It is therefore understandable that those influenced by Rosenian piety would be less concerned with legalistic prohibitions of certain activities and more concerned with general principles of Christian living. In Hauge's Synod, one can detect, especially in the discussion about morality directly above, the existence of different attitudes toward amusements that might be indicative of the enduring presence of Rosenian piety. The enduring influence of this New Tendency in Hauge's Synod is possibly the result of Hanson's legacy, especially through the presidency of his son Martin. Indeed, M. G. Hanson's synodical communications seem consistent with the focus of the New Tendency, encouraging evangelism, "fraternal concord," and unity of purpose through "good deeds." Notably, the "good deeds" are not specified. In his 1901 annual report, he articulates this Rosenian focus with the following words:

> We can say with rejoicing that we have had a blessed year from our Lord, inasmuch as the effects of the Word of God and the administration of the Sacraments have throughout our Synod brought sinners to repentance and salvation. Many have awakened from their sinful slumbers and have found peace in Christ's atonement.[122]

The influence of Rosenian piety on Hauge's Synod can also be demonstrated by the involvement of the Rosenian J. N. Kildahl in the education of its seminary students. However, it must also be borne in mind that not all expressions of Haugeanism in America carried this "sweet," outwardly focused tenor. A darker, more legalistic, and combative Haugeanism persisted in places, which is apparent in later developments.

One must also consider the influence of the Johnsonian revival and theology on American Haugeanism. Already mentioned is the possible Johnsonian influence on the New Tendency through the rejection of perceived Donatism. In his attempt to balance the objective and subjective emphases in justification, thereby providing greater Lutheran theological clarity to Haugeanism, Johnson provided an important caveat regarding the difficulty in determining the spiritual state of an individual, which can be interpreted as criticism of the notion that membership in a synodical organization must be restricted to "only those truly converted."

---

122. Hauge's Synod, *Reports to the 56th Annual Convention*, 7.

Johnson essentially articulates the concept of "simultaneously saint and sinner" in Christian life, with sin an ever-present reality:

> But here, too, it must be pointed out that the regeneration of the sinner is as yet only the beginning of his quickening. The seed of a new, blessed life that thereby has been sown in his heart cannot in its self-development avoid being hindered and disturbed by sin in the flesh. The believer's peace is as yet no perfect peace, nor is his joy as yet unmixed.[123]

The strong focus on Lutheran identity as well as a "churchly" focus in Hauge's Synod through its synodical polity is also arguably a product of Johnsonian influence. However, one must note an important possible departure from the Johnsonian tradition within the synod. Though the theologian Georg Sverdrup is associated with the tradition of the Conference and later the Lutheran Free Church rather than Hauge's Synod, his convictions concerning the relationship between a pastor and a congregation as an organic unity, which he understood to be a rejection of Johnson's emphases, shed light on how the tradition of Johnson manifested itself in Hauge's Synod. As has already been noted, the Johnsonian revival of Norway was focused on the clergy, and Sverdrup understood that the emphasis of Johnson's movement was on such pastors serving as missionaries to congregations. This was opposed to Sverdrup's conviction that a pastor should relate to a congregation not as a superior, "lording it over the congregation of God," but rather as a "brother among brothers."[124] Accordingly, Sverdrup's perspective on lay activity differed from Johnson's. Whereas Johnson articulated the "emergency principle," Sverdrup disliked this perceived grudging toleration for lay ministry in a congregation. According to Helland, Sverdrup considered that lay activity should be viewed as a normal part of congregational life and that the pastor and congregation should together be considered a missionary body. Sverdrup's convictions on this matter led to the "Augsburg Controversy" within the UNLC and the formation of the Lutheran Free Church, as already discussed, a dispute to which Hauge's Synod remained aloof. However, Sverdrup's insights reveal something significant about Johnsonian influence within the synod. Hauge's Synod, with its insistence on lay activity, can be said to demonstrate an affinity to Sverdrup's perspective and a rejection of the Johnsonian emphasis. However, as has also been

123. Granquist, *Scandinavian Pietists*, 81.
124. Helland, *Georg Sverdrup*, 250.

noted, the synod struggled with the implementation of lay activity, and the different perspectives within the synod have already been noted. As difficult as it is to assign a single label to characterize Hauge's Synod in terms of its theological identity, this tension between the perspectives of Sverdrup and Johnson regarding lay activity and the relationship between pastor and congregation is important to note and one that would continue to present itself as Hauge's Synod prepared to end its independent existence in 1917.

Though it is not possible to provide a single label to describe Haugeanism as expressed within Hauge's Synod, awareness of the differences between the Norwegian and American environments as well as of the influence of the Rosenian and Johnsonian traditions is essential. At the same time, it is important to note the congruence between much of American Haugeanism and the concerns of Hauge himself, discussed in the previous chapter. Most significantly, his concern for "converted" Christian life was shared by Hauge's Synod. The implications for this were wide ranging, with Hauge's Synod sharing with Hauge himself concern for the nurturing of Christian life within ecclesiastical establishments and the empowerment of laity in offering Christian witness. Also shared, as an outgrowth of this concern for Christian life, was a discriminating attitude toward amusements, especially the use of alcohol. However, this also led to an outward focus within the synod on social matters such as charity to immigrants and temperance, perhaps rooted in Hauge's own social focus in Norway. Another thing yet unexplored is the relationship between Hauge's flexible understanding of biblical authority and the attitude of Hauge's Synod toward biblical "inerrancy." It has been established that Hauge, though viewing the Bible as important and indispensable for Christian life, did not consider it to be an exact historical record. Of course, the work of Hauge's Synod was carried out mostly prior to the Fundamentalist controversy in American Christianity, making the absence of the word "inerrant" in its description of the Scriptures understandable. However, one observation is that at least some within Hauge's Synod expressed similar flexibility in their approach toward the authority of the Bible to the point of expressing openness to theistic evolution and a less literal reading of the early chapters of Genesis, which would not have been shared by most people in the Norwegian Synod.[125] Indeed, J. O. Gisselquist, ordained as a pastor by Hauge's Synod just prior to the

---

125. Harrisville, Interview by Thomas E. Jacobson.

1917 merger, has been described as teaching his family that the days described in first chapter of Genesis in the Bible could refer to great periods of time rather than literal twenty-four hour days.[126] G. M. Bruce also later demonstrated openness to higher biblical criticism, publishing an article in the late 1920s addressing the issue of the "synoptic problem." In the article, Bruce acknowledged the dependence of the Gospel writers on prior oral and written traditions, yet this was not incompatible in his view with an understanding of biblical inspiration and authority.[127] This is perhaps a consequence of the greater focus placed on the quality of spiritual life in the synod rather than on fine points of doctrine. Nevertheless, this point is important to establish for considering the lasting legacy of Haugeanism in American Lutheranism.

Bearing all the above points in mind, perhaps the best way to understand the nature of American Haugeanism is to note the comments of a significant figure in the tradition of Hauge's Synod. Writing in 1929, at the fiftieth anniversary of Red Wing Seminary, M. O. Wee sought to enumerate the "fundamentals of Haugeanism." Excerpts from these "fundamentals" effectively summarize the points made above:

> The Haugeans were generally referred to by others as "the awakened." (de vakte.) For this reason the burden of their message was a call to repentance and conversion. They demanded a conscious transition in spiritual experience from death to life. They were also referred to by some as the "Praying Lutherans," because they emphasized ... meetings of prayer. ... Much stress was laid on seriousness and self-denial in Christian life ... the so-called adiaphora – amusements not sinful in themselves – were rejected. Their view of life in general was decidedly of a serious character ... much emphasis was laid on the Law of God. The Haugeans demanded pure doctrine in accordance with the Word of God and the Confessions of the Lutheran Church, but warned against a dead orthodoxy and the false consolation sought by an outward participation in church services. The right and privilege of every Christian to testify of his faith was insisted upon, but Christian life in strife against sin and fervent service for God and humanity was also strongly urged upon everyone. ... In church polity the Haugeans demanded the right of

---

126. Gisselquist, *Called to Preach*, 87.
127. Nichol, "American Lutheran Church," 197.

the congregation to regulate its own affairs, and a simplification of the Church Ritual.[128]

MERGER NEGOTIATIONS LEADING UP TO 1890

Thus far, discussion of Hauge's Synod has not proceeded in a strictly chronological fashion. The existence of the UNLC, formed in 1890 as a merger of the Anti-Missourian Brotherhood, the Conference, and the Norwegian Augustana Synod, has already been noted numerous times. However, it is important to discuss briefly this earlier merger, as Hauge's Synod was involved in the negotiations. Though it did not ultimately participate in the merger that produced the UNLC, its presence in the discussions is an important part of the history of the synod and reveals matters of significance about its perspectives and relationships with other church bodies, at least in the earlier years of its existence.

The Eau Claire Meeting

The departure of the Anti-Missourian contingent from the Norwegian Synod in 1887 provided the impetus for the Norwegian-American Lutheran merger of 1890. Desiring to decrease rather than increase the number of church bodies among the Norwegian-Americans, the Anti-Missourians viewed their organization as temporary and assumed leadership in the union movement.[129] P. A. Rasmussen, the early associate of Eielsen who had broken with him and joined the Norwegian Synod in 1862, now found himself among the Anti-Missourian Brotherhood. As the chair of the Anti-Missourian committee on union, he extended an invitation to the Conference, the Norwegian Augustana Synod, and Hauge's Synod to form a joint union committee. Each church body contributed seven members to this committee, a mixture of professors, pastors, and laypeople. Named to the committee from Hauge's Synod were Professor Hans Hanson Bergsland from Red Wing Seminary; Pastors Ø. Hanson, Anfin Olsen Utheim, M. G. Hanson, and Ingvald Eisteinsen; and laypeople H. M. Sande and O. E. Boyum.[130]

---

128. Rholl, *Red Wing Seminary*, 28–29.

129. Nelson, *Lutheran Church*, 2:4. Unless otherwise noted, this information about the merger of 1890 is derived from pages 4 to 22 of this volume.

130. Nelson and Fevold, *Lutheran Church*, 1:334–35.

At the first union meeting held at Eau Claire, Wisconsin, in August of 1888, Nelson noted that Hauge's Synod was the only participating body that failed to send full representation, with only Bergsland and Eisteinsen in attendance, which he considered "unmistakable evidence of the lack of a genuine interest in Hauge's Synod for the proposed merger." The union committee gathered at Eau Claire drafted a complete plan for the union as well as a proposed constitution for the new church body. In this early stage of the union movement, Nelson reported reservations on the part of Hauge's Synod to parts of the plan. For example, the second paragraph of the plan stated that old doctrinal differences between the merging bodies had been adequately resolved, at least to the point of not prohibiting union. This paragraph was reported as having been unanimously accepted by the committee, but Bergsland later reported in *Budbæreren* that his opposition to this statement was not recorded. Furthermore, Nelson reported that the fifth paragraph of the plan was also criticized by some in Hauge's Synod. This paragraph, though speaking positively of lay activity and noting the conviction that it is not an infringement on the pastoral office, nonetheless does not speak of such lay activity as an essential part of congregational life, which was presumably the reason behind the criticism. These two things were early indicators of hesitancy within Hauge's Synod toward the merger.

The Scandinavia Meeting

The next major step in the union movement took place at Scandinavia, Wisconsin, in November of 1888. In addition to members of the union committee, this meeting was open to one lay delegate from each congregation of the merging bodies as well as independent congregations. Again, Nelson reports that objections to the plan for merger were raised mostly by members of Hauge's Synod. Many committee members, Ø. Hanson and M. G. Hanson included, voted against the first paragraph, which dealt with the doctrinal basis of the proposed church body. The reason for their dissention is not immediately clear, as the proposed confessional basis contains nothing that would have been controversial, calling for subscription to the Holy Scriptures and the confessions of the Norwegian Lutheran Church, namely the creeds, the *Augsburg Confession*, and Luther's *Small Catechism*. The proposal went on to state that "there is evidence of no official act on the part of the synods in denial of the Scripture and the confessions." It is possible that some members of Hauge's Synod, while not disagreeing with the text, felt that the proposed wording did not adequately address the issue of unity of spirit and practice of the merging bodies. Though the Anti-Missourian Brotherhood had separated from the Norwegian Synod over the issue of election and perhaps partly their stance on the question of slavery, thereby demonstrating their rejection of the Norwegian Synod's focus on the objective nature of justification, it is understandable that Hauge's Synod, given the rocky history between them and the Norwegian Synod, would harbor some suspicion toward the Anti-Missourian contingent.

As Nelson further reports, the paragraph concerning lay activity discussed above was also a point of contention, with members of Hauge's Synod opposing it as well as the sixth paragraph that "asked for the exercise of mutual brotherliness." Again, the reasons behind the opposition to paragraph six are not clear, though one might deduce that such a clause was viewed as a threat to the synod in that it would diminish their ability to contend for their unique concerns as a part of the new church body. Beyond this, Nelson reports that ten members of Hauge's Synod proposed three amendments to the plan for union. The first two amendments reflected their concern for clarity regarding the language of justification; they desired through these amendments to make even clearer their focus on the subjective nature of justification. Though these two amendments were accepted by the union committee, the third proposed amendment, which would have added a paragraph to the constitution "encouraging lay activity as practiced by 'the friends of Hauge,'" was not accepted.

The spirit of unity between the three other bodies at the Scandinavia meeting was visible through the intersynodical celebration of the Lord's Supper at the conclusion, a practice which Nelson notes was unprecedented. However, Hauge's Synod as a whole was less than enthusiastic about the merger. Though there were some voices within the synod in support of the merger, Nelson notes that opposing voices were much louder, objecting that there was not sufficient "unity of spirit" and practice between Hauge's Synod and the other groups, with some suspicious of the quality of spiritual life and the presence of "living Christianity" among the others. It was not clear to many in the synod if their unique practices would be honored in such a union, namely their aversion to liturgy and clerical vestments. An article in *Budbæreren* from 1888 reveals this concern for lack of unity of spirit, citing different "upbringings" of the merging bodies. The author writes about the desirability of union, but not if such union means a loss of identity. He further indicates that some were concerned about abandoning Red Wing Seminary and whether Augsburg Seminary, the proposed seminary of the new church body, would adequately prepare men for ministry.[131] Yet another article from the same organ addressed the concern as to whether the majority in a merged church body would force the use of the liturgy of the Church of Norway upon the Haugeans.[132] An article from the following year pointed out that although the union committee declared the negotiating bodies to be in concord concerning their doctrine and teaching, this did not establish unity of practice between the various synods.[133] The broad concerns of the majority were summarized by P. Ljostveit as centering on the following issues: whether being "out and out spiritual men" would be listed as a qualification for theological teachers in the merged body, whether "the work of awakening" or revivalism would continue to be a part of church life in the new organization, and whether lay activity and testimony would play a role in the new UNLC.[134] In spite of an appeal to enter the union by J. N. Kildahl, who had left the Norwegian Synod for the Anti-Missourian Brotherhood and who had a long relationship of trust with the synod, Hauge's Synod stepped away from the merger at their annual convention in June of 1889, with President Ø. Hanson offering the opinion that the synod was not ready to enter such a merger. However, the union movement occurred in such a quick time frame that some congregational records from the other merging bodies mistakenly report that Hauge's Synod entered the merger of 1890 that produced the UNLC.[135]

This summary of the union movement that led to the formation of the UNLC, based largely on Nelson's work, does not touch in detail upon every point of discussion, but the most important thing to note here is the strong resistance toward the merger within Hauge's Synod. Both the fact that Haugeanism did not fall neatly into the boundaries of one particular church body and the openness demonstrated by many within Hauge's Synod toward cooperation with those considered friendly to their concerns have been noted numerous times. However, this process of merger serves as a reminder that such openness should not be overstated. Deep

---

131. "*Foreningssagen*," 1888, 123–24.
132. "*Foreningssagen*," 1888, 134.
133. "*Mit syn paa Foreningssagen*," 1889, 379.
134. Ljostveit, *Innermission Church History*, 308.
135. "History of Kindred Lutheran Church."

reservations existed in many places within the synod about the quality of spiritual life in the other church bodies as well as concerns about the survival of Haugeanism in a large, merged church body.

MERGER NEGOTIATIONS LEADING UP TO 1917

Though the union of 1890 decreased the number of Norwegian-American Lutheran church bodies, the overall field was still fragmented. From six distinct groups just prior to 1890, there were four after the merger: the newly formed UNLC, the still sizable Norwegian Synod, the tiny Eielsen Synod, and of course Hauge's Synod. With the formation of the Lutheran Free Church in 1897 and the CLBA in 1900, both of which emerged out of the UNLC, the number of church bodies was brought back to six. However, another merger was on the horizon, in which Hauge's Synod would come to participate.

Initiation of the Union Movement

Shortly after the withdrawal of Hauge's Synod from the union that produced the UNLC, hope was expressed by President Gjermund Hoyme of the Conference, who would also become the first president of the UNLC, that Hauge's Synod would soon reverse course and join the new church body.[136] Of course, this did not happen, and Hauge's Synod continued its independent existence until 1917. However, though the UNLC committed itself from the beginning at its opening convention in June of 1890 to furthering the cause of union with both the Norwegian Synod and Hauge's Synod,[137] it was curiously Hauge's Synod that made the formal move toward union with the Norwegian Synod and the UNLC, a move that will be discussed in this section.

"Free" Conferences

Throughout the decade of the 1890s, discussions of further union occurred in sporadically held "free conferences" that involved participants from the Norwegian Synod, the UNLC, and Hauge's Synod.[138] These

---

136. Nelson, *Lutheran Church*, 2:21.
137. Nelson, *Lutheran Church*, 2:25–26.
138. Nelson, *Lutheran Church*, 2:132. Discussion of these preliminary meetings is

conversations, which came to be known as "free" because of the nonbinding nature of their resolutions and the fact that participation in them did not imply formal fellowship between church bodies, began with the invitation of the Norwegian Synod to the UNLC to begin discussions of union. The meeting finally took place in January of 1892 at Willmar, Minnesota, and though Hauge's Synod was invited, it did not participate. The conviction of the Norwegian Synod was that such "free" gatherings should not begin with prayer, as it viewed joint prayer as an expression of unity of faith. The discussion centered on the question of how to articulate the doctrine of biblical inspiration, with the UNLC appealing to Gisle Johnson's conviction that Lutherans have no particular theory of inspiration. Also discussed was the issue of confessional subscription, with Stub and Koren of the Norwegian Synod advocating for subscription to the entire *Book of Concord*, presumably a result of influence from the Missouri Synod.

Differences between these two groups at the Willmar meeting meant that "free" conferences were not resumed until 1897, when B. J. Muus, a former Anti-Missourian of the UNLC, obtained signatures from a number of pastors from all three church bodies to continue discussions. Meeting in Lanesboro, Minnesota that year, Hauge's Synod was represented by Ole Sjursen Meland. According to Nelson, the topic of discussion was the issue of human responsibility in conversion unto faith. Once again, the thorny question of how to uphold God as the author of salvation while not diminishing human responsibility presented itself. Siding with Muus in his desire to emphasize subjective appropriation of faith, Meland reportedly offered the insight that the Holy Spirit gifts human beings with the ability to turn toward God and that human beings thereafter permit God to do the work of conversion. To say otherwise, in his view, was to turn human beings into "a stick or a stone" rather than "a being with a will." No concord was reached at this meeting, and a subsequent "free" conference at Austin, Minnesota, in 1899 was poorly attended. The Norwegian Synod invited the seminary professors of the other two bodies to meet and discuss doctrine in 1901, but Hauge's Synod did not participate. Overall, Nelson reports that the first few years of the twentieth century were not fruitful for the cause of further union.

derived from pages 129 to 142 of Nelson's work.

The Resolution of 1905

Yet something significant and unexpected occurred in 1905. The minutes of the annual convention reveal that Hauge's Synod established a committee to confer with other Norwegian-American Lutheran church bodies about a possible union. At this convention, Hauge's Synod issued "fraternal greetings" via telegram to both the Lutheran Free Church as well as the UNLC, both of which were meeting simultaneously, in June of 1905. These fraternal greetings were reciprocated. President M. G. Hanson also moved for a committee of three to be appointed to work with similar committees from other Norwegian-American Lutheran groups for the purpose of publishing a joint Sunday school paper. These things, however small, demonstrate a spirit of openness and cooperation.

During the eighth session of the convention, on Saturday, June 17, the minutes indicate that "Prof. M. G. Hanson, Rev. G. O. Paulsrud, and Rev. T. J. Oppedahl were elected to draft resolutions regarding the union of the Norwegian church organizations in America."[139] The next day, this committee took action:

> On motion of the union committee, it was decided that a committee of five be elected to confer with the committees of other Norwegian church organizations that are willing to confer with it regarding union; that this committee be instructed to report the result of such conference in the "Budbereren," [sic] and that the secretary be instructed to notify those bodies now in session regarding the Synod's action.[140]

Indeed, Nelson reports that the UNLC and the Norwegian Synod received telegrams from the Red Wing convention of 1905 and responded by appointing union committees of their own. Telegrams were also sent to the smaller groups: the CLBA, the Eielsen Synod, and the Lutheran Free Church. Only the Lutheran Free Church responded, saying that since it was not a synod, but rather a fellowship of independent congregations, it was not in a position to discuss union but was interested instead in "spiritual cooperation"; they did appoint a committee to discuss cooperation with Hauge's Synod, which resulted in a number of practical agreements, including the mutual recognition of ordinations and exchange of pastors.[141] At any rate, Hauge's Synod breathed new life into the union

---

139. Hauge's Synod, *Reports and Proceedings of the 60th Annual Convention*, 33.
140. Hauge's Synod, *Reports and Proceedings of the 60th Annual Convention*, 35.
141. Fevold, *Lutheran Free Church*, 135.

movement through their action in 1905, which would culminate in the 1917 merger.[142]

It is not exactly clear what led to the dramatic reversal within Hauge's Synod: from withdrawal from the earlier merger to initiator of the latter. Different opinions have been suggested. One is that a revival of Norwegian nationalistic feeling in the United States as a result of the 1905 independence of Norway from Sweden contributed to the renewed desire for union among Norwegian-American Lutherans in the early twentieth century.[143] It is certainly possible that such ethnic solidarity played a role in the increasing rapprochement, especially considering the strong display of ethnic solidarity present at the union festivities in 1917. However, there is no evidence available that Hauge's Synod was particularly influenced by Norwegian nationalistic fervor. Another explanation of a more spiritual nature has been offered. In an address given many years after the fact, N. N. Rønning commented that "[the Haugeans] believed that a union would further the cause of Christ and that full freedom to preach and practice as before would be theirs." He went on to say that "the Haugeans did not enter into the union of 1917 blindly. They were neither forced nor fooled."[144] One can infer from this that the Haugeans assumed that their presence in a large, merged body would be that of leaven in a larger batch of dough, where Haugean spirituality would serve as a positive influence.

In fact, throughout the 1890s, according to Nelson, "certain internal dissentions" within Hauge's Synod prevented them from taking up the cause of union even earlier. Again, it is not clear what dissensions to which he is referring, but the presence of internal conflict can be inferred from comments in the sermons and synodical communications referenced above, with calls for "fraternal concord" and for directing "warfare" in a spiritual direction rather than toward other "brethren." Evidence suggests that part of the problem might have related to a struggle over the leadership of Red Wing Seminary. Writing some years later, Ljostveit refers to a conflict between O. S. Meland and H. H. Bergsland, both of whom served as presidents of Red Wing Seminary, with Bergsland succeeding Meland in 1889. Then, he claims that Bergsland was ousted as president in 1897. Ljostveit provides no further information about the nature of

---

142. Nelson, *Lutheran Church*, 2:142–44. Unless otherwise noted, information in the following paragraphs is derived from pages 142 to 146 of this volume.

143. Granquist, *Lutherans in America*, 222.

144. Rønning, "An Abiding Spiritual Influence."

this conflict, though he claims that it "nearly tore the Hauge Synod to pieces."[145] Noteworthy is the fact that the official history of Red Wing Seminary shows the office of president to be vacant for thirteen years after Bergsland's "ousting," being finally occupied by Edward W. Schmidt in 1910,[146] perhaps an indicator of the seriousness of the conflict. Also noteworthy is the fact that the official history of the institution is silent on the conflict, perhaps an indicator of the desire to conceal it to avoid embarrassment. Another source, however, does provide some information about the conflict between Meland and Bergsland, which sheds important light on the tension between theology and spiritual life that existed within Hauge's Synod. According to Ole H. Oace's 1932 book, the conflict between the two men centered on the issue of the power of the human will, with Meland accusing Bergsland of promoting synergism.[147]

Ljostveit cites the departure of Bergsland as president as one of the reasons that the move toward church union gained traction within Hauge's Synod. Ljostveit's bias, writing many years removed from the events, was against the union of 1917, as he considered larger church bodies to be "churches for the religious masses" rather than groups of authentic, converted believers. This bias needs to be understood, but his interpretation of the events might well have merit. He lifts up Bergsland as a "champion of Hauge principles." Accordingly, he claims that "spiritual life was on the wane" in Hauge's Synod "after that time," which, in his view, led to greater focus on institutional mergers than on the quality of spiritual life. Another reason he offers for the change in attitude within Hauge's Synod is the change of heart in the highly influential figure M. G. Hanson, who had opposed the earlier merger of 1890. Finally, Ljostveit comments that there was still "a great deal of spiritual life" in the UNLC, especially in former congregations of the Norwegian Augustana Synod. Hauge's Synod congregations that had relationships with the Norwegian Augustanans might have considered that the whole of the UNLC would be a kindred spirit. Connected to this issue is the existence of a pan–Norwegian-American Lutheran revival in the mid- to late 1890s. Driven by traveling pastors and evangelists, including the well-known Norwegian Haugean missionary Lars Skrefsrud, this awakening impacted all church bodies in the Norwegian-American Lutheran field to varying degrees,

---

145. Ljostveit, *Innermission Church History*, 311. Information in the following paragraph is also derived from this page in Ljostveit's work.

146. Rholl, *Red Wing Seminary*, 40.

147. Oace, *Hauges synode*, 38.

including Hauge's Synod, but even the Norwegian Synod to a lesser extent.[148] It is possible that the spirit of this revival created a greater sense of intersynodical cooperation through shared spiritual experiences. Indeed, one observer notes that "the Revival in the Nineties was a truly spontaneous movement of spiritual awakening, without a specific individual or institution as the outstanding instigator or leader."[149] One more factor that served as a catalyst for the union movement was the existence of secular Norwegian societies that included members of the different church bodies as well as some non-Lutheran Norwegian-Americans.[150] These groups were often devoted to special interests such as music, literature, temperance, or simply a desire to perpetuate Norwegian culture in North America. Membership in these various "lags" or societies helped create trust between members of different synods through appreciation of their common ethnicity. Whatever the case, because of its initiative, Hauge's Synod would be occupied with merger negotiations from 1905 until 1917.

The Negotiations and Outcome

A complete report of the merger negotiations between the three largest Norwegian-American Lutheran church bodies of the early twentieth century is something that has been accomplished by Nelson's work. Therefore, it is not necessary to enumerate every detail of the discussions here. However, it is important to note the contributions of Hauge's Synod in these discussions that led to the resolution of the merger process and the end of its independent existence.

Negotiations and *Opgjør*

Beginning in 1906, after the resolution of 1905, Hauge's Synod began discussions with the Norwegian Synod and the UNLC. Nelson reports that the early meetings were characterized by "friendliness and genuine good will."[151] Curiously, the Norwegian Synod did not object to the practice

---

148. Fevold, *Lutheran Free Church*, 88.
149. Lee, *New Springtime*, 53.
150. Nelson, *Lutheran Church*, 2:152.
151. Nelson, *Lutheran Church*, 2:144. Unless otherwise noted, information in the following paragraphs is derived from pages 144 to 182 of this volume.

of common prayer with the other conferring bodies, which marked a change from the discussions of the late nineteenth century. This is possibly the result of the revival of the 1890s as well as a generational shift, with new individuals involved in the discussions. Accordingly, as Nelson reports, the early meetings were productive, and the representatives, including C. J. Eastvold of Hauge's Synod, were able to come to agreement on the doctrine of absolution through a set of five theses. Reviewing the earlier disputes, they agreed on language that satisfied the desire to emphasize both the objective and subjective elements of absolution, noting that it declares grace to the sinner, yet is "appropriated by the sinner through faith." The old Norwegian Synod language of absolution as a "powerful impartation" of grace, which had been offensive to the Haugeans, was discarded. As a further concession to the concern for subjectivity, the last thesis spoke of the importance of sincerity on the part of those making their confession. The concern of Hauge's Synod on this issue was apparently the belief that overemphasizing the objective nature of absolution led to a lax and comfortable faith that diminished the importance of spiritual struggle and watchfulness. Though these theses on absolution resolved some of the difficulty, at least on paper, which Nelson understandably desired to emphasize in his work, it is important to note that certain issues of concern within Hauge's Synod related to absolution were not specifically addressed, such as whether absolution should be given publicly and whether it should be stated in conditional form. Therefore, the agreement on paper did not necessarily resolve the issue in actual practice.[152]

Indeed, evidence indicates that not all within Hauge's Synod viewed the merger negotiations positively. H. N. Rønning, serving as a missionary in China at the time, questioned the usefulness of such conferences. Reporting on Rønning's 1906 article in *Budbæreren*, the *Lutheran Herald* described his reservations. He claimed that outward unity achieved by written agreements is of limited value, and nothing short of shared spiritual experiences will accomplish true unity:

> He doubts seriously the possibility of ever accomplishing church union through conferences, claiming that experience has shown the futility of such conferences. He thinks a general spiritual revival will accomplishing [sic] church union, and advocates union prayer meetings and meetings for mutual edification as

---

152. Nelson, *Lutheran Church*, 2:344–45. The theses on absolution are included in an appendix on these pages in Nelson's volume.

> sure means of bringing about church union. It would seem, however, that external unity where unity of belief were lacking would hardly be desirable. . . . This method may take longer than the other method, but it will bring true harmony in the end among all who will bow before the word of God.[153]

This reflection by the significant personality of H. N. Rønning testifies to the presence among many Haugeans of a rather different perspective on church fellowship than was found among their more churchly counterparts. His comments can be considered foreshadowing of the struggles that the Haugeans would come to experience within the NLCA, described in the following chapter.

Nevertheless, the merger negotiations continued. Later that year, the union committees tackled the issue of lay activity and ministry that was so important to Hauge's Synod. In a series of eight theses, they acknowledged the importance of the actual office of ministry as something distinct from the laity, articulating the "emergency principle" of Johnson, saying that laypeople should not function as pastors unless emergencies required it. Yet they also spoke of the importance of laypeople serving as "priests in their own station" in life, conceding that this can include laypeople working for "edification" in "assemblies of the congregation," not simply in the home. For the sake of order, however, they stated that such lay preaching should be regulated by the congregation and pastor, presumably as a way of preventing charlatan pastors and preachers from exercising influence. However, Nelson also noted that a concession was given to the Haugeans that this prohibition did not include itinerant pastors and lay preachers of "good report," which therefore allowed for the work of traveling evangelists to continue. Again, though Nelson does not mention it, this appears to be the result of influence from the revival of the 1890s, where traveling missionaries and evangelists played a significant role in Norwegian-American congregational life. Nelson credits the moderating influence of the UNLC with helping to bridge the gap between the concerns of the Norwegian Synod on the one hand and Hauge's Synod on the other. Again, this agreement appeared to resolve the difficult issue of lay activity, but as has already been seen, the practice of "regulated" lay activity within Hauge's Synod created problems, and

153. *Lutheran Herald*, 1906, 474.

the question of who exactly could carry out pastoral functions would be carried forward into the NLCA after 1917.[154]

In 1907 and 1908, the union discussions continued by focusing again on resolving the tension between human and divine responsibility in people being called, converted, and justified. Hauge's Synod, rooted in what some consider to be the synergistic tradition of Hauge himself, naturally had an interest in preserving a focus on human responsibility, and Nelson's discussion of the theses produced by the union committees of the three church bodies reveals that this concern was addressed. Beginning with an emphasis on original sin and the inability of people to turn to God on their own power, the theses make clear that though God is the initiator of conversion, "the persons who are called cannot avoid perceiving in their hearts the operation of the call upon them through the Law and Gospel." This appears to be a concession to the Haugean concern for "experienced salvation." Furthermore, the theses acknowledge that God's call to human beings is connected to the preaching of the word of God, thereby maintaining the importance of mission in the life of the church. Finally, though making clear that God is the author of salvation through bestowing grace, people are not coerced into having faith and possess the ability to reject grace.[155] These theses appeared to address concerns of the Haugeans, but Nelson notes that some within Hauge's Synod still remained uninterested in merger. However, he notes that C. J. Eastvold, president of the synod at the time, was favorable toward the cause of union, and many parts of synod followed his leadership in expressing impatience that discussions were not progressing more quickly.

The major issue that remained to be resolved was the very issue that tore the Norwegian Synod apart in 1887, which was the doctrine of election. As a result, union discussions nearly ground to a halt in 1909. That year, Stub, of the Norwegian Synod, prepared a set of theses for discussion by a subcommittee of the church bodies. Unable to reach agreement, it was proposed by the UNLC in the full joint committee meeting that a new set of theses by Eastvold of Hauge's Synod be used as the basis of discussion instead of Stub's. Curiously, it was at this point that the Norwegian Synod backed away and demanded that agreement by the subcommittee was necessary before further discussions could be held. In

---

154. Nelson, *Lutheran Church*, 2:345-47. The theses on lay activity are included in an appendix on these pages in Nelson's volume.

155. Nelson, *Lutheran Church*, 2:347-55. The theses on call and conversion are included in an appendix on these pages in Nelson's volume.

LIFE WITHIN HAUGE'S SYNOD AND MERGER NEGOTIATIONS

1910, after Norwegian Synod district meetings revealed continued interest in union in their church body, another joint committee meeting was held. Something similar to the previous meeting occurred when a motion was made to use Eastvold's theses instead of Stub's. Nelson reports that Stub's response was that the Norwegian Synod would not continue discussions if this were the case. It is possible that this reaction by the Norwegian Synod was due to their concern for doctrinal clarity, but it should also be considered that, given the history of suspicion between the Norwegian Synod and the Haugeans, they were reluctant to use the theses of the Haugean Eastvold as the basis of discussion.

It is understandable that reconciliation between the Norwegian Synod and the UNLC would be difficult regarding the issue, but Hauge's Synod was in the unique position of having some distance from the earlier Anti-Missourian controversy. However, Hauge's Synod agreed with the position of the UNLC, which was the "second form" of election, stating that people are elected by God for salvation "in view of foreseen faith." After the Norwegian Synod withdrew from the discussions, the UNLC and Hauge's Synod adopted Eastvold's theses as the basis of their discussion. As Nelson reports, these theses differed from Stub's; whereas Stub's theses began with a discussion of God's predestination, Eastvold's theses began with stating God's desire that all people be saved. They went on to discuss the necessity of faith for election, and on this basis the two church bodies were able to declare doctrinal agreement.

Nelson credits the existence of the joint hymnal project, which has already been discussed, as well as the strong desire of the laity, who were naturally more insulated from the theological discussions, for the continuation of discussions for a unified Norwegian-American Lutheran church; the ethnic solidarity, created in part from the secular societies mentioned above, can also be partly credited for this. Yet he also credits the tenacity and desire of Stub, of the Norwegian Synod, for a merged church body in keeping the discussions alive. When the debate about the doctrine of election continued, it is noteworthy that Hauge's Synod elected to remain outside the discussions; already in agreement with the UNLC and not having been a part of the original controversy of the 1880s, Nelson reports that the synod felt it best to let the Norwegian Synod and the UNLC resolve the matter between them. This is a further indication that the priority of Hauge's Synod lay outside the realm of formulating exact theological definitions. Though not indifferent to theology, their concern in the theological debates was for creating space for "experienced faith" and "conversion."

Therefore, the debate concerning election continued between the Norwegian Synod and the UNLC in 1911 and 1912. Meeting in Madison, Wisconsin, February 14 to 22 of 1912, their joint committee studied both "forms" of the doctrine of election, the first stated in article eleven of the *Formula of Concord* and the second in question 548 of Pontoppidan's *Sanhed til Gudfrygtighed*. In the end, two representatives, one from each church body, were charged with providing a satisfactory statement that would resolve the dispute. In short, their resolution stated that both "forms" of the doctrine of election have a place in the historic Lutheran tradition and can be considered orthodox. Therefore, these different ways of expressing the doctrine are acceptable and should not prohibit church union, and this resolution made possible the eventual merger of 1917. Nelson himself notes that this *Opgjør*, or "Madison Agreement," was not "a flawless display of theological finality" and was partially the result of weariness on the part of the committee over theological debate and a desire to end it. Indeed, some within the Norwegian Synod refused to accept the *Opgjør*, claiming that it allowed for synergism, resulting in the departure of some pastors and congregations, leading to the formation in 1918 of what became known as the Evangelical Lutheran Synod (ELS). Though the Norwegian Synod experienced an open schism over this doctrinal issue, Hauge's Synod was occupied with different concerns and would come to carry those forward into the NLCA of 1917 rather than forming a separate church body.

Reactions

Though the Madison Agreement of 1912 paved the way for an eventual union of the three church bodies, a number of details still needed to be resolved before final approval was given for the union. Nelson reports that the UNLC reacted to the news of the Madison Agreement with jubilation, which is not surprising given that the UNLC had working toward further union as one of its stated goals in 1890. In 1915, the twenty-fifth anniversary of the establishment of the UNLC, the *United Lutheran* printed an article with an air of triumphalism concerning the accomplishments of the UNLC and its role in bringing about further union, highlighting the regrettable nature of past conflicts between Norwegian

LIFE WITHIN HAUGE'S SYNOD AND MERGER NEGOTIATIONS

Lutherans in America and emphasizing a merger as the destiny of the various church bodies involved:

> The tide of union among Norwegian Lutherans in this country is firm and strong. Nothing can stop it for it is of God. Some may prefer to be left on the banks among the wreckage, but the tide will sweep on resulting in the greater Norwegian Lutheran Church in America. The date is not far off. Many are earnestly praying and striving that it may be accomplished in the great reformation year, 1917.[156]

The reference to "some" who "prefer to be left on the banks among the wreckage" appears to be directed toward minority groups in both the Norwegian Synod and Hauge's Synod who were expressing misgivings about the merger.

The Norwegian Synod, however, had a much more mixed reaction to the upcoming merger made possible by the Madison Agreement. Already mentioned is the internal struggle of the Norwegian Synod regarding acceptance of the *Opgjør*, requiring their president, H. G. Stub, to clarify that the agreement did not mean that one needed to accept personally both "forms" of election, but rather simply recognize the possibility of subscription to one of the two forms.[157] Opposition to the Madison Agreement and the planned upcoming union continued within the Norwegian Synod, however, and it was noted in the *Lutheran Intelligencer* in 1913 that "a remonstrance is being circulated in the Norwegian Synod against taking final action in favor of synodical union at the upcoming meeting of the Synod."[158] The opinion of the minority that eventually elected to remain outside of the merger is important to note, but there was, especially among some laity of the Norwegian Synod, a strong desire for union. In the secular Norwegian-American newspaper *Decorah-Posten*, a lay author criticized theologians in the Norwegian Synod for creating conflict where none need exist, pointing out that Pontoppidan's "Explanation" and therefore the "second form" of election contained therein was a part of their heritage out of the Church of Norway and had therefore been recognized in the Norwegian Synod for many years. He further accused the theologians of ignoring the desires and needs of the laity, making their lives in the church more difficult:

---

156. "Historical Survey," July 2, 1915, 420.
157. Nelson, *Lutheran Church*, 2:184–87.
158. "General Notes," May 1913, 74.

> Quibbling over technical distinction [sic] too fine to be seen, has brought to [sic] much mischief and misery to our church people already. Mischief because it fixes the attention so strongly upon distant imaginary evils that might result from such or such form and expression, that present sins escape the attention that moral obligation demands. Misery because it begets hatred instead of brotherly love.[159]

Accusing the theologians of perpetuating a conflict "based upon mere technicalities," the author urged final action on the question of union.

Regarding the attitude within the Norwegian Synod specifically toward union with Hauge's Synod, however, there is much less documentation available. As noted in the introduction to this book, the conflict between the Norwegian Synod and the UNLC over the issue of election and the resolution of the *Opgjør* is well-documented, while issues related to Hauge's Synod have received less attention. However, there are some clues that suggest some friction between Hauge's Synod and both the Norwegian Synod and the UNLC in the process of merger. Nelson reports that M. O. Wee, secretary of the joint union committee and Hauge's Synod emissary to the Norwegian Synod, "encountered serious misgivings" at the Norwegian Synod convention in 1917 concerning the details of the Hauge's Synod "Interpretation" of the union documents, which is discussed below.[160] In an interview, M. O. Wee's son Morris Wee Sr. commented on the role that his father played in the merger process, which reveals this friction. M. O. Wee felt

> that he had an absolutely [sic] responsibility on that committee to represent the point of view of the Hauge Synod, which was not always a popular point of view, not fully accepted by members of the other two church bodies; so he felt, not only that he was the secretary to record minutes, but was also the champion, together with Professor Bruce, a champion of the Hauge point of view, and I think that the record will show that he was not fearful of anybody and always determined that the point of view of the Hauge Synod should be fully represented in the merger negotiations.[161]

On the side of Hauge's Synod, *Budbæreren* naturally included a number of articles between the years 1912 and 1916 addressing the topic

---

159. *Decorah-Posten*, May 26, 1916.
160. Nelson, *Lutheran Church*, 2:221.
161. Morris Wee Sr., Interview by Morris Wee Jr.

of the upcoming merger, with opinions in favor and opposed as well as simply reporting on the progress of the union committee. One article from 1912 criticized the focus placed on merger by arguing that outward unity would not produce a true unity of spirit and actual practice.[162] Other articles addressed theological issues of importance to the Haugeans, such as the issue of lay preaching[163] and the relationship between the Lord's Supper and absolution.[164] One article reported on a district meeting in Minot, North Dakota, in January of 1916, where the upcoming merger was recommended for its practical benefits; small and struggling congregations in a particular area from all three church bodies could unite as one congregation and be more effective in outreach.[165] References to the union movement in the *Lutheran Intelligencer*, however, are few. This is surprising given that the years of its publication coincide with the final years of preparation for the merger. However, brief reports and commentary on the union movement do appear in certain places. In June of 1912, it is simply stated in the report of the annual convention that the results of the union negotiations were approved and that a committee of five was to be elected to coordinate with similar committees from the other church bodies in preparation for the merger.[166] In June of 1913, there is a brief note that "no definite results had been attained during the past year, except the holding of several joint meetings"[167] as well as a note referring to a letter from Stub of the Norwegian Synod, asking that Hauge's Synod accept their interpretation of the Madison Agreement. The response from Hauge's Synod was that since the Madison Agreement was formulated by the Norwegian Synod and the UNLC, Hauge's Synod should not take any action on it before the two other bodies had settled the matter. In August of that same year, Bruce noted that an invitation was extended to and rejected by the tiny Eielsen Synod, meeting at Frost, Minnesota, to enter into the merger negotiations that were progressing at the time.[168] Brief notes about the progress of the union movement are made in the August and November issues of that year, but in February of 1914, Bruce made his desire for union explicitly known through his report on the action of

162. *"Foreningssagen,"* 1912, 326.
163. *"Forening og lägmandsvirksomhed,"* 1913, 485.
164. *"Foreningssagen,"* 1916, 20.
165. *"Kredsmöde, foreningssagen,"* 1916, 104.
166. *Lutheran Intelligencer*, June 1912, 95.
167. "The Union Question," June 1913, 89.
168. "Church News," August 1913, 139.

the union committee. Noting that the committee had decided to pursue the creation of an organic union rather than a synodical confederation, he expressed his hope for a quick resolution of the process:

> The prospects for an early consummation of the union project are very promising, and it is to be hoped that no obstacles will now appear to delay or prevent the work now so nearly accomplished. God speed the day when the Norwegian Lutheran Church of this country will be not only one in body, but also in spirit.[169]

Though this quote betrays Bruce's desire for Hauge's Synod to enter the union, his last comment is worth noting. His remark could be interpreted either as cautious optimism that the merged church body would allow for the free flowing of Haugean spirituality and that spiritual life rather than institutional life would be the primary concern within it or as concern as to whether this would actually be the case.

Though supportive of the merger, this concern of Bruce for maintaining Haugean spirituality and its traditions is revealed in his comments in April of 1914, where he refers to the work of the union committee that lay ahead. He refers to "liturgical matters," presumably whether the low-church Haugean tradition of worship would be honored after 1917, as well as to "the disposition of the three theological seminaries, the colleges, academies, and other institutions belonging to the negotiating bodies."[170] The continuation of the Haugean cultus understandably weighed heavily on the minds of members of Hauge's Synod as the merger approached. Of equal or even greater concern for the continuation of the Haugean tradition would have been the fate of Red Wing Seminary in the new church body, as it was at that school that the unique traditions of Hauge's Synod were imparted to future clergy. Though Bruce continued to be supportive of the merger in spite of some apparent reservations, it is important to note that Hauge's Synod did have, as Nelson calls it, a "minority problem" as late as 1917, which needed to be appeased.[171] Notably, one member of this "minority committee" was O. H. Oace, a layperson whose name is significant for the continuation of the Hauge's Synod tradition in the NLCA, discussed in the next chapter.

---

169. "Union of Norwegian Lutherans," February 1914, 19.
170. "The Union of Norwegian Lutherans," April 1914, 50.
171. Nelson, *Lutheran Church*, 2:221.

Apparently in response to this "minority problem," J. N. Sandven, a pastor from the large and therefore presumably influential Hauge's Synod congregation in Roland, Iowa, voiced his support in 1915 for the merger. He cited the practical benefits of such a union, such as the strengthening of home and foreign missions. Yet he also expressed concern for the impact that withdrawal from the merger process would have on the reputation of Hauge's Synod. The *Lutheran Herald* quoted Sandven's original article in *Budbæreren*:

> As to the position of Hauge's Synod, which in 1905 sent out the invitation to the other church bodies to confer about church union, and whose members have met with the joint committee, and as a church body has accepted the articles of agreement, I can not [sic] see but that we publicly and as a church body have declared that we desire to join the union, unless the practical questions remaining should be of such a character that we could not with good conscience join. If for other reasons we should withdraw, we would pass the death sentence upon ourselves. We would then bring down upon ourselves the well-deserved contempt of others as people who had merely pretended friendship, and this would bring our own church into a controversy which, at least, would end in a deplorable division; because a person who acts honestly in the sight of God and man can not [sic] act with levity.[172]

Sandven's comments in support of the merger therefore testify to the significance of the spirit of resistance toward the merger in Hauge's Synod.

It must be mentioned that although Nelson does not ignore the presence of this "minority problem" within Hauge's Synod, the strength of this minority appears to have been more significant than Nelson reports. In what was apparently an open letter to members of Hauge's Synod, G. O. Mona, a pastor in Newman Grove, Nebraska, appealed to his fellow Haugeans, attempting to inform them of problems he saw in the merger negotiations:

> Christ our peace: there is a large part of our people who cannot go along with this merger at all, who say strongly that there is no scriptural reason that it is directed by the Lord. Many have only recently become aware of what happened at the synod's meeting last summer.[173]

---

172. "Church Union," 1915, 11.
173. Open letter from G. O. Mona, 1916. The translation of this letter is my own.

Mona went on to criticize the manner in which the concerns of Hauge's Synod were being handled by the joint union committee. He appears to refer in his letter to the "Interpretation" mentioned below, which clarified the understanding of Hauge's Synod regarding a number of issues in the "Articles of Union." Mona's letter claimed that these concerns were not being taken seriously, and he expressed concern for the survival of the Haugean witness, calling for a meeting to discuss the matter. A newspaper report from Red Wing, Minnesota, from late in 1916 confirms the presence, strength, and resolve of the resistance movement within Hauge's Synod:

> MAY OPPOSE SYNOD UNION IN COURTS. Minority Members of Hauge Synod Plan Drastic Action, If Necessary. A meeting of the minority members of the Hauge synod was held at Minneapolis recently.... They are opposed to the taking over of the property of the Hauge synod by the union church body, and it is said, will make a fight to retain possession, through the courts if necessary.[174]

Writing to Oscar Seebach, a member of the Minnesota House of Representatives, G. M. Bruce, who was serving as the chair of the Hauge's Synod union committee, explained that the minority element of Hauge's Synod was attempting to exploit a legal loophole that would effectively render the merger impossible. As explained by Bruce, since both Hauge's Synod and the UNLC were incorporated under the laws of Minnesota, such laws did not provide for the amalgamation of general religious bodies. Proposed legislation sought to remedy the situation, and Bruce urged Seebach to support the bill. Bruce's comments reveal the mindset of those Haugeans who opposed the merger; they were fearful of the loss of congregational property:

> Since our meeting in June there has been some effort put forth by a few ministers and laymen in our Synod who are opposed to union to organize a minority faction to oppose the proposed union. It is a few of the leaders of this faction who are opposing the passage of this bill in the hopes of making the proposed union impossible. Some misrepresentations of the bill have also been made, among others, the statement that this bill if enacted into law will deprive the congregations who may not wish to join in the formation of the new body of their church and

---

174. Clipping from unknown Red Wing, MN newspaper, 1916, G. M. Bruce File, Luther Seminary Archives, St. Paul, MN.

> parsonage property.... Thanking you for the attention you have already given this matter and for any assistance you may give us in securing the passage of this bill.[175]

The attempt by the minority of Hauge's Synod to defeat the proposed bill and therefore the participation of Hauge's Synod in the merger was obviously unsuccessful, which was Bruce's hope. Yet Bruce, as the chair of the Hauge's Synod union committee, continued to receive communications from concerned members of Hauge's Synod. A letter exchange between Bruce and a certain layperson Carl Bjørnstad from Velva, North Dakota, sheds further light on the mindset of members of Hauge's Synod regarding the upcoming merger. Not only does this exchange reveal the existence of resistance on a local, congregational level, it also betrays Bruce's own lukewarm support for the merger and reveals his hope of what the participation of Hauge's Synod could accomplish in a new and larger church body. Bjørnstad first asked Bruce for a breakdown of the vote at the Hauge's Synod convention to approve the merger in 1916, namely how many lay and clergy delegates supported and opposed the motion. He then suggested that the union of Hauge's Synod with the other two bodies was tantamount to a union of God's children with the devil's children.[176] After answering his question about the vote, Bruce responded:

> They say that Jesus has never said that God's children and the devil's children should unite. It is completely true, but do you not go too far when you suggest that Hauge's Synod consists of God's children and the other organizations of the devil's children? Judge for yourself. I have had the opportunity over the last three years to speak to many people in both the United Church and the Norwegian Synod congregations in Wisconsin, Minnesota, Iowa, and even North Dakota, and I have not disregarded the truth either, but I must say that they have both been considerate and receptive audiences. That there is much that is awry in both of the other organizations is of course something that must be acknowledged, but is it not also the case among us?[177]

---

175. Personal letter from G. M. Bruce to Oscar Seebach on March 3, 1917, G. M. Bruce File, Luther Seminary Archives, St. Paul, MN.

176. Personal letter from Carl Bjørnstad to G. M. Bruce on March 8, 1917, G. M. Bruce File, Luther Seminary Archives, St. Paul, MN.

177. Personal letter from G. M. Bruce to Carl Bjørnstad on March 31, 1917, G. M. Bruce File, Luther Seminary Archives, St. Paul, MN. The translation of this section of

Bruce went on to write:

> It really pains me that we disagree about Hauge's Synod and that so many are so diligent at sowing the seed of suspicion, dissention, and strife among us, thereby preventing us from being as large and extensive as we otherwise could be and being salt and light in the new organization. As you know, I have not been enthusiastic about the merger, but when this decision is adopted by our organization, I think that it is nothing other than my duty to go and prevail upon Hauge's Synod to be as completely unified as possible going into the new organization. I believe that we have a future in which, like Hauge's people, we can only let our prejudices be endangered and stand together in charity and unity.[178]

With these comments, Bruce here acknowledges the difference of spirit that distinguishes Hauge's Synod from the other two organizations and seems to be aware of the potential difficulties that would await the Haugeans in the new church body. Just as the Norwegian Haugeans lived out their commitments within the Church of Norway, Bruce's vision here is of the former Hauge's Synod serving a similar function, being "salt and light" in the NLCA.

Implementation

"Articles of Union"

In late March and early April of 1914, the joint union committee began the work of drafting the "Articles of Union" for the NLCA.[179] Consisting of a preamble and nineteen articles dealing with theological, ecclesiastical, and practical matters for the new church body, this document attempted to address the concerns of the three merging bodies as well as honor their traditions. The preamble acknowledged that the road toward achieving concord was long and contentious, referring to "sin" and "unjust accusations," yet rejoicing that God had "brought them to the same faith and

---

the Norwegian language letter is my own.

178. Personal letter from G. M. Bruce to Carl Bjørnstad on March 31, 1917, G. M. Bruce File, Luther Seminary Archives, St. Paul, MN. The translation of this section of the Norwegian language letter is my own.

179. Nelson, *Lutheran Church*, 2:366–69. The "Articles of Union" for the NLCA are printed on these pages in Nelson's volume, though the Norwegian text has been translated and printed in other places, such as in the *Lutheran Intelligencer* of May 1914.

doctrine," leading them to "become one also in external matters." The key question in the next chapter is whether the former members of Hauge's Synod truly did consider themselves "one in external matters" with the other church bodies and by extension whether they truly held "the same faith and doctrine."

First acknowledging the Holy Scriptures as either the "inerrant" or "infallible" Word of God, depending on the translation of the union articles, as well as the "confessional writings of the Norwegian Lutheran Church," namely the *Augsburg Confession* and the *Small Catechism*, the second article then lifted up recognition of the 1912 Madison Agreement as a condition for union. Though the second article reflected the theological struggle primarily between the Norwegian Synod and the UNLC, the third article was more relevant to Hauge's Synod. It dealt with the question of unionism, or "churchly cooperation with the Reformed and others who do not share the faith and confessions of these bodies." Though the article stated that the NLCA would not practice such unionism, Stub, who would become the first president of the NLCA, was not successful in adding the first clause of the Galesburg Rule into the "Articles of Union,"[180] creating some ambiguity as to what actually constituted "churchly cooperation." Given the balancing act that Hauge's Synod sought to walk regarding valuing its Lutheran heritage as well as recognizing the presence of "living Christianity" in non-Lutheran church bodies, this article prohibiting "churchly cooperation" was controversial among Hauge's Synod.

The union articles then turned to questions of church practice, another significant point for Hauge's Synod. Citing the Lutheran confessional writings concerning freedom in church rites, "provided there is unity in doctrine," which would have provided some assurance to the Haugeans that their worship practices could continue, the article nonetheless recommended that congregations not alter or discontinue church rites that have been in use for some time, as they "provide peace and good order." It is not clear from the text if the Haugean cultus was intended to be included in the category of "church rites and ceremonies which are not contrary to the Word of God and which have been in use for some time." However, the same article recommends, for the sake of "general uniformity," that congregations use the modified ritual of the Church of

180. Nelson, "Union Movement among Norwegian-American Lutherans," 565. Already referred to, the Galesburg Rule stated that "Lutheran pulpits are for Lutheran ministers only" and that "Lutheran altars are for Lutheran communicants only."

Norway. Also, nothing was specifically stated in the article about the use of clerical vestments. Again, this article contains significant ambiguity regarding the tradition of Hauge's Synod and its enduring presence in the NLCA.

The final two points of this article address other issues of significance to Hauge's Synod, namely the practice of absolution and lay activity. Regarding absolution, the article acknowledged differences in practice in congregations and allowed for absolution to be administered through the laying on of hands or as a general declaration without such a physical gesture. Hauge's Synod in general frowned on the physical gesture as superstition, as they felt it suggested that forgiveness proceeded from the minister's hands.[181] The article also stated that the practice of private confession and absolution was to be retained. Curiously, however, no mention is made in the union articles of the conviction of many in Hauge's Synod that absolution should not be given publicly at all. Article fourteen of the Hauge's Synod constitution stated that confession and absolution shall be used, but not required, as a part of the liturgy of the Lord's Supper. Congregations were, however, permitted to continue the practice of public absolution if they chose. Nevertheless, the absence of any discussion in the union articles of this part of the Haugean tradition is noteworthy. Regarding the issue of lay activity, the union articles acknowledged the theses on the topic prepared some years earlier, claiming that the NLCA will "cherish" lay activity as presented in those theses. Furthermore, the article stated that "it shall not be considered unchurchly [sic] practice or religious fanaticism for people to come together for prayer and the earnest promotion of spiritual awakening and spiritual life," which was clearly a concession to the Haugean tradition of revival and edifying gatherings.

Finally, the union articles dealt with practical questions of operation for the NLCA. The sixth article established the plan for seminary education. The seminary was to be located on two campuses, the first of which was the United Church Seminary of the UNLC, located in the St. Anthony Park neighborhood of Saint Paul, Minnesota, and the second of which was the campus of Luther Seminary of the Norwegian Synod in the Hamline neighborhood of Saint Paul. Though the campus of Red Wing Seminary would not be a part of the official seminary, two professors from Hauge's Synod would join the four from the Norwegian Synod

---

181. Morris Wee Sr., Interview by Morris Wee Jr.

and the four from the UNLC on the faculty of the new Luther Theological Seminary. The small size of Hauge's Synod in comparison to the other two church bodies made understandable the lesser representation from Hauge's Synod on the faculty. Red Wing Seminary, however, was not to be completely abandoned, which would have been an encouragement to Hauge's Synod that its identity would play a role in the NLCA. Red Wing Seminary was to serve as a "pro-seminary" in the merged body, which meant that it was to serve as an abbreviated seminary preparatory course for those of "advanced age" who lacked a college degree.[182] In addition, "circumstances permitting," Red Wing Seminary was to serve as a "normal school," meaning a teacher-training school, and "the most prominent preparatory school of the Church for its colleges." Additionally, though Jewell Lutheran College was not listed as one of the "standard colleges" of the NLCA, that distinction being reserved for Luther College in Decorah, Iowa, and St. Olaf College in Northfield, Minnesota, it shared with Augustana College in Sioux Falls, South Dakota, the status of being "owned by the Church." Therefore, Jewell Lutheran College was to receive annual appropriations from the NLCA.

Remaining matters in the union articles dealt with the disposition of institutions of mercy, missions, and publications. In short, institutions of mercy and missions of Hauge's Synod were to be continued within the NLCA, and Hauge's Synod was to be given representation in the merged publishing house and in the publication and the editorship of the merged English- and Norwegian-language periodicals.

"An Interpretation"

The ambiguity of the "Articles of Union" evidently prompted a response in the form of "An Interpretation" of the articles from the perspective of Hauge's Synod. The "minority element" in the synod was strong in the two years immediately preceding the merger, to the point where it was unclear whether Hauge's Synod would ultimately participate.[183] As Nelson reports, this minority was even more significant than that which had developed in the Norwegian Synod. The fear was that the "theology and spirit" of the Norwegian Synod would dominate in the new church

---

182. Rholl, *Red Wing Seminary*, 47.

183. Nelson, "Union Movement among Norwegian-American Lutherans," 586. Unless otherwise noted, information in this and the following paragraph is derived from pages 583 to 593 in Nelson's dissertation.

body and that a merged body would "quench the spirit of true Haugeanism," allowing for "unconverted" ministers and "unworthy" partakers of the Lord's Supper. Hauge's Synod had referred the matter of merger to its congregations in order to gauge the overall attitude within the organization, and in the 1916 convention at Red Wing, Minnesota, it was revealed that although sixty-four congregations favored the union unconditionally and eleven favored the union with reservations, twenty-eight congregations were opposed to some degree, twenty-two of them unconditionally. When voting to approve the "Articles of Union" and the proposed constitution of the NLCA, the tally was 142 in favor and 103 opposed. The presence of this significant minority prompted further discussions at the convention for clarification of the union articles, with Lars Harrisville emphasizing that Hauge's Synod was not alone in its concern for spiritual life, while another pastor spoke for the concerns of the minority.

In response to this conflicted state of affairs, G. M. Bruce produced "An Interpretation" of the union articles, which originated from the hand of N. J. Løhre. This interpretation of the "Articles of Union" apparently had the desired impact, as the convention approved the text by a vote of 187 to 18, sending it to the other two church bodies for approval. The subsequent three "enabling acts" for the merger also passed at the Red Wing convention by significant majorities. The "Interpretation" had apparently served its purpose, which was to assure those wary of merger that their Haugean tradition would be honored and continued within the life of the NLCA.

The "Interpretation" began by addressing the question of what constituted unionism and "churchly cooperation." Qualifying the statement in the union articles, it made a distinction between "organized and continuous activity of a churchly character or also incidental and occasional reciprocal relations in the preaching of the Gospel and administration of the Sacraments" and occasional participation in special events such as weddings, funerals, and other celebrations that involve ministers of other confessional groups.[184] Furthermore, it stated that participation in various ecumenical Christian mission ventures such as the Student Volunteer Movement and similar organizations was not to be considered "churchly cooperation." The Lutheran identity of Hauge's Synod as well as its ecumenical spirit shone through in this part of the "Interpretation."

---

184. Nelson, *Lutheran Church*, 2:370. The "Interpretation" of Hauge's Synod is found on pages 370 and 371.

Desiring to address concerns about the status of the Haugean cultus after the merger, the "Interpretation" turned its attention to the ambiguous statement in the union articles concerning the use of the modified ritual of the Church of Norway. It stated that Hauge's Synod understood that the pattern of nonliturgical worship generally in use in its congregation has official recognition, would continue to be used, and would be "eligible to be employed in the official assemblies" of the NLCA. It also stated that Hauge's Synod considered that its practice of divorcing absolution from the liturgy of the Lord's Supper as well as offering absolution without the laying on of hands would continue to be honored. Also connected to the concern for the preservation of the Haugean cultus, the "Interpretation" stated the expectation that the seminary of the NLCA would continue to offer instruction in the low-church worship practices of Hauge's Synod. The stated reason for this was that congregations that desired to maintain this worship tradition would need pastors familiar with it.

In commending the "Interpretation" to the other two church bodies for approval, Hauge's Synod stated that the goal of the document was to remove possible misunderstandings and to state clearly its expectations. Bruce, serving as emissary to the UNLC, brought the "Interpretation" to its 1917 convention, which was approved unanimously. As already noted, however, Wee's reception at the 1917 Norwegian Synod convention was less than warm. The Norwegian Synod eventually agreed to acknowledge the "Interpretation," but only after Wee's explanation that such acknowledgment did not imply approval of the contents of the document; in giving its approval and acknowledging the convictions of the Haugeans, the Norwegian Synod maintained that it retained the right to witness within the NLCA against the practices contained in the "Interpretation."[185] This meant that, although the requirements for merger were satisfied, the union of 1917 would not be a complete union of spirit between the three church bodies, and friction would continue as the former members of Hauge's Synod sought to perpetuate their heritage.

---

185. Nelson, "Union Movement among Norwegian-American Lutherans," 607. Unless otherwise noted, the discussion in this and the following paragraphs is derived from pages 607 to 617.

The Consummation of the Union

The only mention that Nelson makes of the final annual convention of Hauge's Synod in 1917 is that it elected C. J. Eastvold as its president for ceremonial purposes so that Eastvold, a key figure in the merger negotiations, could represent Hauge's Synod at the union festivities. This sole reference, however, overlooks another important attitude within Hauge's Synod concerning the ending of its existence; other sources add color to the story. A lay preacher in Hauge's Synod, Søren Petterson, is remembered as a champion of the historic principles of Hauge's Synod, such as "low-church simplicity in worship, its stress on repentance and personal experience, evangelism, layman's activity and the personal testimony."[186] Based on his reading of church history, a subject in which he was reportedly well versed, he became convinced that the worship practices prevalent in much of the UNLC and the Norwegian Synod were "hangovers from the Roman Catholic period." By extension, he feared that seeking union with such organizations would lead to the loss of the Haugean spirit, replacing it with "ritualism, formalism and dead orthodoxy." At the final convention of Hauge's Synod on June 8, 1917, Petterson spoke from the floor against the upcoming merger. During his speech, he apparently suffered a stroke, being caught by two others before he fell to the floor. Petterson's apoplexy on the floor of the final convention of Hauge's Synod and subsequent death did nothing to prevent the merger of 1917 from being consummated, and though it must be remembered that not all or even most members of Hauge's Synod shared his level of aversion to the merger, his witness, given the ambiguity surrounding the continuation of the Haugean spirit as discussed above, is an important one to remember as Hauge's Synod continued its life as leaven in a larger batch of dough that was the NLCA. Even among those in Hauge's Synod who were supportive of the merger, it has been reported that their attitude at the meeting was one of desiring to bring "light and truth" to the other church bodies through the merger. Additionally, they trusted in "solemn promises" about the continuation of Haugean spirituality in the NLCA through the enduring presence of Red Wing Seminary.[187] These issues, added to the less than overwhelming vote to approve the "Articles of Union" at the previous convention and the fact that the "Interpretation"

---

186. Hauge Inner Mission Federation, *Hauge Movement in America*, 150. The discussion in this paragraph is derived from pages 150 to 152 of this volume.

187. Stageberg, "Red Wing Seminary."

was required to assure those leery about the survival of their tradition, set the stage for an uneasy coexistence between many Haugeans and others in the new NLCA.

The following day, June 9, was a Saturday, and the union festivities began, as each church body had formally ended its existence the day prior. The enthusiasm among much of the Norwegian-American community was demonstrated by the headline in *Decorah-Posten*, translated as "The Norwegian Lutheran Church of America: a half a million Lutherans in united formation. The union movement is finally victorious."[188] The festivities in St. Paul, Minnesota began with a procession of clergy from each of the bodies from the St. Paul Armory to the St. Paul Auditorium. As Hauge's Synod was the oldest of the three, its representatives were first in line, followed by the Norwegian Synod and then the UNLC. Despite the general enthusiasm for the union, awareness of the differences between the groups did not disappear amid the celebration. According to Nelson, an observer of the procession commented, jokingly or derisively, "Here come the Pharisees, the scribes, and the sinners." The comparison of Hauge's Synod to a group of legalistic Pharisees and the Norwegian Synod to a group of overly literal scribes indicates that the reputations of these traditions remained strong even with the merger and that the distinct traditions would continue within the NLCA.

Later that day, H. G. Stub of the former Norwegian Synod, J. N. Kildahl of the former UNLC, and N. J. Løhre of the former Hauge's Synod were nominated and elected unanimously as president, vice president, and secretary of the NLCA, respectively. Of the nine districts of the new NLCA, two were initially led by former members of Hauge's Synod. C. J. Eastvold was elected president of the Southern Minnesota District, and Gilbert Olson Paulsrud was elected president of the South Dakota District. In fact, given that former Hauge's Synod congregations and members comprised a relatively small percentage of the total NLCA, the representation of Hauge's Synod in NLCA leadership was proportionate to its size. On Sunday, the festival worship was conducted, and an obvious attempt was made to honor the formal as well as low-church traditions of the merging church bodies. Nelson reports that the Sunday morning worship service was conducted with liturgical chanting and vestments, yet the service of the Lord's Supper was carried out without vestments and the absolution given without the physical gesture of laying

---

188. *Decorah-Posten*, June 12, 1917. This translation is my own.

on of hands. Furthermore, the joint service of ordination at the celebration included candidates wearing vestments as well as those wearing ordinary suits, which was another attempt to acknowledge the different traditions that fed into the NLCA. These attempts to honor the minority of former Hauge's Synod members are noteworthy and commendable, but the underlying friction between the different traditions that fed into the NLCA cannot be forgotten as the NLCA began its existence and carried out its work.

CONCLUSION

Nelson was impressed that the union of 1917 succeeded in bringing together "the subjective tendencies of European pietism represented in Norwegian Haugeanism and the objective emphases of the Norwegian state church plus German Lutheran orthodoxy." He notes in the same breath that "considering the intrinsic irreconcilability of some of the differing points of view in these two tendencies the achievement of 1917 was a notable success, the working out of which after 1917 will be the task of future historians to observe and relate."[189] Picking up where Nelson left off with his 1952 comment, the next chapter turns its attention to the question of the enduring legacy of Haugeanism in the NLCA after 1917.

---

189. Nelson, "Union Movement among Norwegian-American Lutherans," 619.

4

The Haugean Presence within the NLCA

DISCUSSION OF HAUGE'S SYNOD and Haugeanism thus far has covered historical eras already well documented by historians, even if the tendency, as in the case of Nelson, was to emphasize the union of the three largest Norwegian-American Lutheran church bodies as positive, thereby minimizing the tension between different traditions. With this chapter, however, this book ventures into largely uncharted territory. Assuming the mantle of Nelson, this chapter begins to address the "working out" of the coexistence of the two tendencies that he identifies: the subjective tendency of the Haugeans and the objective emphasis of the Norwegian state church. Though Nelson describes the 1917 merger as a "notable success" that brought together these "intrinsically irreconcilable" tendencies, evidence of the interaction between these two tendencies in subsequent years can, at least in many cases, hardly be called successful. Indeed, significant friction and concern for the survival of Haugeanism existed early on between the Haugean element of the NLCA and its more formal counterparts, which endured late into the life of the NLCA/ELC, and this chapter highlights that friction. In the process, this chapter discusses how Haugeanism came to express itself within the NLCA; no longer burdened with the task of maintaining a synodical organization, the Haugeans turned their attention to the significant concerns of their tradition: evangelism, mission, and spiritual life.

AMERICAN LUTHERANISM AFTER 1917 TO 1960

Not losing sight of the place of the Haugean element of the NLCA in the broader field of American Lutheranism, it is important to consider briefly the surrounding ecclesiastical environment in the years after 1917, both outside and within Norwegian-American Lutheranism. Developments outside of the NLCA impacted the Haugeans in that body, and the ecumenical spirit of the Haugeans led them to have contact with those outside their own group over the years.

Outside Norwegian-American Lutheranism

As the year 1917 approached, American Lutherans were still divided into a number of separate synodical groups, mostly reflecting their respective ethnic backgrounds. Yet the year 1917 held symbolic pan-Lutheran significance as the four-hundredth anniversary of the beginning of the Reformation that had begun with the publication of the *Ninety-Five Theses* of 1517. This created a sense of solidarity among American Lutherans and provided occasion for joint celebrations.[1] In the case of the eastern "Muhlenberg" Lutheran tradition, planning for a joint celebration of the Reformation anniversary led to a rapid movement for union among the General Synod, the General Council, and the United Synod, South. In 1918, the United Lutheran Church in America (ULCA) was formed as a merger of these three federations. The Swedish Augustana Synod, which had historic ties to the General Council, elected to remain independent, however. Elsewhere, three largely Midwestern German synods—Ohio, Iowa, and Buffalo—would remain independent until a merger brought them together in 1930 to form the American Lutheran Church (ALC). That same year, a number of synods based largely in the Midwest, including the ALC, the Swedish Augustana Synod, and the NLCA, formed a cooperative federation called the American Lutheran Conference, which paved the way for the eventual merger of 1960 that produced TALC. The church bodies of the Synodical Conference, led by the Missouri Synod, continued to function in their cooperative federation rather than move toward organic union. Other smaller synods representing different ethnicities continued independent existences for the time. However, the Reformation anniversary celebration and movement toward merger was

---

1. Granquist, *Lutherans in America*, 225. Information in this section is partly derived from pages 224 to 226 of this volume.

considered among many to be a sign of the "coming of age" of American Lutheranism, representing a united expression of Lutheranism in North American and in some cases a move away from ethnic enclaves of the participating synods.

Yet it was not only the Reformation celebration that led to this "coming of age" into an American identity. The involvement of the United States in the First World War necessitated cooperation in the area of military chaplaincy and related religious services for military personnel, leading to the formation of the National Lutheran Commission for Soldiers' and Sailors' Welfare (NLCSSW), which included synods outside the Synodical Conference, which had itself established its own Army and Navy Board. The NLCSSW of 1917 led to the formation in the following year of the National Lutheran Council (NLC), which coordinated a number of supposedly "external" ministries for the participating ten synods. The war had other important and unforeseen impacts on American Lutheranism, however. Because of the war, immigration from European lands largely stopped, yet another factor in the "coming of age." Connected to this, the lack of new arrivals from the old countries diminished the incentive to perpetuate European languages. Though the older "Muhlenberg" Lutheran tradition had been shifting to the use of English for several years, much of Lutheranism centered in the Midwest, including Hauge's Synod, which was fueled by the second broad wave of immigration, was still using European languages. Also motivated by a desire to avoid the appearance of sympathy with the German enemy, most of these congregations began rapidly shifting to the use of English. Scandinavian languages were sometimes confused with German, and any congregation utilizing a European language could have been viewed with suspicion. The old languages often endured in some form for many years, but generally one notes that the shift to English as a primary congregational language began in the early 1920s; minutes of congregational annual meetings are often recorded in English for the first time in these years. A common language made relationships between various synods easier, and gradually American Lutherans stopped viewing themselves simply as transplanted Europeans.

Yet another development in these years that began outside of Norwegian-American Lutheranism but nonetheless came to involve its participation was the founding of the Lutheran Bible Institute (LBI) movement, the planning of which began in 1918. Though initiated by members of the Swedish Augustana Synod, with Samuel Miller from that tradition as its first dean, the LBI movement quickly came to involve many members of the NLCA, to the point where participation in this independent movement was evenly divided between Norwegians and Swedes.[2] Supported in large part by laypeople from an "orthodox, confessional, pietistic" Lutheran perspective,[3] its goal was to provide biblical education for young people, often catering to those preparing for missionary work. It has been noted that historians have tended to ignore this significant development in American Lutheranism likely because it was an independent endeavor not carried out under official auspices. Indeed, as has been noted in the case of Nelson, the tendency among historians of that era has been to emphasize harmony and merger in the process of "coming of age" and downplay continued friction. The LBI movement, however, was controversial among some because of its independence, with some in the Swedish Augustana Synod viewing it as unnecessary and influenced by traditions outside of Lutheranism, such as the Bible schools of Reformed Fundamentalism. Furthermore, the publication of the LBI movement, *Bible Banner*, frequently contained criticisms of theological modernism in the Swedish Augustana Synod while insisting on the Lutheran identity and importance of the LBI, lest Lutheran youth be drawn to such Reformed Fundamentalist institutions. What is significant to note is that at least some participation in the LBI movement among members of the NLCA came from those influenced by the Haugean tradition, perhaps an indication that many Haugeans after 1917 did not feel obligated to carry out their spiritual callings through official channels.[4] Perhaps they even felt the need to work through such independent organizations for the sake of faithfulness.

Within Norwegian-American Lutheranism

The merger of 1917 brought over 90 percent of Norwegian-American Lutherans into a single organization, and though it was celebrated by

---

2. Granquist, "The Sociological Factor," 160.

3. Kibler, "Lutheran Bible Institute," 31. Discussion in this paragraph is derived from pages 31 to 37 in Kibler's dissertation.

4. Lutheran Bible Institute, *L. B. I. Memoirs*, 27. A listing of present and former board members of the LBI as of 1934 reveals that Haugean Rev. B. K. Barstad of Radcliffe, IA served on the board. Additionally, laypeople Carl Opsahl and H. J. Rognmoe from the Haugean strongholds of Jewell, IA and Kenyon, MN, respectively, also served on the board.

many, reservations as well as strong opposition about the union existed within both the former Norwegian Synod and Hauge's Synod, yet for different reasons already discussed. From the outside, criticism of the *Opgjør* and the subsequent merger came from the Missouri Synod, which claimed that the formation of the NLCA had more to do with Norwegian nationalism than doctrine.[5] Given the role that participation in secular Norwegian societies or "lags" played in preparing the ground for merger, this criticism might not be entirely unfair. Furthermore, not all members of the Norwegian Synod were content to accept the *Opgjør*. Sensing that "nationalism had triumphed over truth," a small group of thirteen pastors and elements of various congregations formed a new church body called the Norwegian Synod of the American Evangelical Lutheran Church, often nicknamed the "little Norwegians," presumably to distinguish it from the much larger NLCA.[6] This group later became known as the ELS. Also, though small in comparison, the presence of the smaller synods that did not participate in the merger cannot be ignored. In addition to the small ELS, which joined the Synodical Conference in 1920, the Lutheran Free Church, the CLBA, and the tiny Eielsen Synod also continued to exist parallel to the NLCA. Therefore, even with the merger, there remained five distinct American Lutheran church bodies of Norwegian background.

Hauge's Synod, however, ended its existence in June of 1917. Led to believe that their distinctive traditions would be honored as a part of the larger church body and that their spiritual influence in this body would be significant, the Hauge's Synod convention gave approval in 1916, albeit not overwhelmingly, to join the new NLCA. Though there are undoubtedly many examples of the peaceful coexistence of the various streams that fed into the NLCA, the unfolding story of this new Norwegian-American church body is far from the "happily ever after" scenario implied by Nelson and Meuser, who asserted that aside from the minor schism that produced the ELS, "No other protest movement resulted, nor did the immediate postmerger years produce any great problems of adjustment. The Norwegians were convinced that they belonged together."[7] This work argues in part that Meuser's assertion is incorrect. Evidence indicates that many of the Haugeans within the NLCA harbored concerns about the survival of their tradition and experienced

---

5. Nelson, *Lutheran Church*, 2:238.
6. Nelson, *Lutherans of North America*, 373.
7. Nelson, *Lutherans of North America*, 373.

difficulties meshing with members of the other two more churchly groups. The Haugeans, less concerned with institutional life, then began to adjust to their new role as leaven in a larger batch of dough. But how was this leaven received upon consumption? Was it easily digested, or did it create pain in the belly of the new church body of the NLCA? The rest of this chapter responds to this question.

HAUGEANISM IN THE EARLY YEARS OF THE NLCA

As noted in the introduction, constructing the history of Haugeanism in North America is challenging. As has been established, historians of previous generations have tended to emphasize official movements that often led toward institutional merger; Haugeanism was less concerned with such official movements and more concerned with the quality of spiritual life. For this reason, documentation of how Haugeanism was lived out after 1917 is scarce. Therefore, one is required to consult a variety of sources such as correspondence, anecdotes, and certain publications of the era to tell this important part of the American Lutheran story. However, one can at times catch glimpses of Haugean spirituality in official records. From the Southern Minnesota District of the NLCA, whose president was the Haugean C. J. Eastvold, the 1924 district convention passed a number of resolutions that reflected this concern for morality and revivalism:

> Standing on the "Rock of Ages," God's inspired and eternal Word, we reaffirm our unreserved loyalty to our beloved Savior, Jesus Christ and his cause, and urge upon pastors and congregations to take a definite and consistent stand against every sinful and compromising attitude in doctrine, association, and life generally. . . . Believing in the priesthood of believers, we deplore the laxity in many of our homes in regard to the use of God's Word, and we recommend the establishment of the family altar in every home. . . . We deplore the worldliness prevalent in our communities.[8]

Regarding the Haugean concern for spiritual awakening in congregational life, the same district minutes record the following resolution from the committee on church affairs:

---

8. NLCA, *1924 Annual Report: District Conventions.*

We rejoice with the congregations which have experienced spiritual awakening. We feel the need of a greater outpouring of God's Holy Spirit upon pastors and congregations, and urge upon all true Christians that they prevail upon God that He may redeem His promise of the Spirit.[9]

Outside of official minutes, however, one can observe various references to Haugeanism within the NLCA in the early years of the NLCA. Though these references are often brief, one can infer from these pieces of information much about the environment of the NLCA and the concerns of the Haugeans of this era.

Early Signs of Discontent

An Anecdote

A brief anecdote from the life of M. O. Wee only a few years after the union of 1917 is a helpful place to begin when examining the "working out" of the relationship between the Haugeans and others in the NLCA. It will be remembered that Wee was one of the two professors from the former Hauge's Synod at Luther Theological Seminary. One of Wee's colleagues on the faculty was J. N. Kildahl, whose ministry and friendship with Hauge's Synod has already been mentioned. When Kildahl died on September 25, 1920, Wee was called upon to participate in one of the many memorial services held in a variety of locations.[10] At the memorial service at Bethlehem Lutheran Church in Minneapolis, Wee reportedly donned a clerical gown for the first time in his career.[11] Coming out of the Hauge's Synod tradition, which rejected the use of clerical vestments, Wee apparently chose to vest out of a desire and perhaps because of pressure to conform in that instance. The situation revealed by such an anecdote seems innocuous on the surface, but Wee's son reports that his father experienced a certain agony over the situation: "[M. O. Wee] wore a gown for the first time as an ordained clergyman, and he told me he felt very weird, very unclear about the rightness of it at that time."[12]

9. NLCA, *1924 Annual Report: District Conventions*.
10. Shaw, *John Nathan Kildahl*, 370.
11. Morris Wee Sr., Interview by Morris Wee Jr. M. O. Wee was ordained in 1898, meaning that he never wore clerical vestments for the first twenty-two years of his ministry.
12. Morris Wee Sr., Interview by Morris Wee Jr.

There is more at stake in this anecdote than the private discomfort experienced by M. O. Wee, however. This situation speaks volumes about the power of conformity and how the Haugean element of the NLCA expressed itself in the early years of the church body. Although the "Interpretation" of the union articles offered by Hauge's Synod asserted that the typical Haugean worship practices "have official recognition" and "are eligible to be employed in official assemblies," Wee's situation with Kildahl's funeral reveals that the informal minority tradition of Haugeanism began its struggle for recognition early on. Though unified on paper, interaction between representatives of these different traditions in the NLCA created practical difficulties and understandably resulted in the jettisoning of the Haugean tradition in many cases.

Wee's Illness and Resignation

Evidence of this early concern for the survival of the Haugean tradition in the NLCA comes also from the experience of M. O. Wee prior to the situation with Kildahl's funeral. In October of 1919, correspondence indicates that Wee experienced a health crisis of some nature, with a certain "disease" exacerbated by "nervousness."[13] Though specifics about the nature of his illness are not available, it was serious enough to prompt Wee to resign from his position as professor at the seminary of the NLCA and instead assume a pastoral call at a congregation in South Dakota.[14] According to his son, Wee's illness and desire to resign were connected to disappointment he experienced on the faculty of the seminary. Wee's son relates that M. O. Wee and G. M. Bruce were viewed with suspicion by the rest of the faculty, which was dominated by former members of the Norwegian Synod and the UNLC.

Wee's decision to resign prompted a response from many in the NLCA, especially former members of Hauge's Synod, and correspondence indicates that concern was expressed for the impact his resignation would have on the peaceful coexistence between the Haugeans and others and on the strength of the Haugean influence in the NLCA. An unknown writer, apparently not a Haugean himself, sought to persuade

---

13. Personal letter from unknown author to H. G. Stub on October 29, 1919, M. O. Wee File, St. Olaf College Archives, Northfield, MN.

14. Morris Wee Sr., Interview by Morris Wee Jr. Unless otherwise noted, information in the following section is derived from this interview.

H. G. Stub, president of the NLCA, of the importance of Wee's presence on the faculty, lest the Haugeans become dissatisfied:

> Dear President Stub: Several of the Hauge people have spoken to me about Prof. Wee's resignation from his position at the seminary. They are very much afraid that his leaving the seminary will create a good deal of dissatisfaction among the Hauge's people, and, in that way, hinder the real union from taking place among our people.... Would it not be the advisable thing to do now, that the Board of Education tell Prof. Wee to quit his work at the seminary for the rest of the year and take off the necessary time for his health, and let him do it on full pay.... There certainly are enough professors over at the seminary to carry on the work in spite of Prof. Wee's absence. I feel sure if this action is taken by yourself, the Hauge people will appreciate it very much.[15]

Another letter from apparently the same unknown author directly to Wee sought to dissuade him from leaving the seminary for his new South Dakota pastorate. The author avoided specifics, yet alluded to the importance of Wee's presence at the seminary for the well-being of the NLCA:

> Dear Prof. Wee: . . . I wanted to see you very much in regard to your accepting the call extended to you from South Dakota. I feel sure you are making a mistake when you look at it from the standpoint of the welfare of the Church, for which you have done so much. I know your action is being taken due to the condition of your health, but I do not feel that accepting work of that kind is going to solve the problem. The Church, I think, will be only too glad to do what it can to help you, and you ought to have the necessary time, with full pay, to do what is necessary for your health, whether it be one or two years. I have suggested this to Dr. Stub and the Board of Education, and I hope if they take such action it will be possible for you to continue your connection with the seminary. There are certain things which are at stake in our Church work today, and I feel it is only by remaining in the position you are in, that these matters can be solved.[16]

It is not clear what is referred to by the "certain things which are at stake in our Church work today," but one can infer based on context that

---

15. Personal letter from unknown author to H. G. Stub on October 29, 1919.

16. Personal letter from unknown author to M. O. Wee on October 29, 1919, M. O. Wee File, St. Olaf College Archives, Northfield, MN.

the author considered Wee's presence as a representative of the Haugean tradition indispensable for harmony between the Haugeans and others in the NLCA. Wee's son relates that the annual convention of the NLCA the following year formally asked Wee not to resign from the seminary, and in the meantime, Stub evidently responded to the suggestion that support should be given to Wee by authorizing an appeal letter for financial support during his illness. Notable former members of Hauge's Synod such as district presidents C. J. Eastvold and G. O. Paulsrud circulated a letter asking for small donations. This Norwegian appeal letter quoted Stub, expressing his support and hope that Wee would not be burdened by financial concerns, but rather that "with God's help can come back with improved health."[17] At least some responses were made to this appeal. One in particular enclosed five dollars and expressed appreciation for Wee's contributions. However, the unknown respondent emphasized that Wee possessed the right to make his own decisions regarding his future, which should be respected even if care for his health required his absence from teaching for "a couple years."[18]

In the end, Wee did remain at the seminary, though his son relates that he experienced continued difficulty meshing with the faculty members from the other predecessor church bodies. In particular, Wee was disappointed at how he perceived his Haugean colleague Bruce was treated by the other faculty members. After four or five years, Bruce reportedly complained to Wee that the others did not regard him as "a full-fledged theological professor" because of his Haugean background. Wee then advocated for Bruce, pointing out that he was a "true scholar" and warning them that Bruce would likely leave the seminary if he were not given a major subject to teach. Wee himself encountered similar difficulty upon the death of J. N. Kildahl. Since Kildahl's subject was dogmatic theology, someone on the faculty needed to assume that responsibility. Wee's major subject was Hebrew and Old Testament, but he had also taught dogmatic theology while at Red Wing Seminary. For that reason, Wee was called upon to teach Kildahl's courses for the remainder of the year. However, the faculty reportedly insisted that Wee use Kildahl's notes for the lectures. Wee's son said, "They didn't trust my father because of his Hauge background enough to let him use his own notes. And father, being more gracious probably than he should have been, agreed to it."

17. Eastvold et al., "*En Henvendelse til Prester og Menigheder*."
18. Personal letter from unknown author to Gilbert Knutson on February 13, 1920, M. O. Wee File, St. Olaf College Archives, Northfield, MN.

The Publication of *Haugeanism*

Causation in history is difficult to prove. However, it is worth considering the possibility that some of Wee's difficulties described above could be related to the publication of his brief book entitled *Haugeanism: A Brief Sketch of the Movement and Some of Its Chief Exponents* in January of 1919. It is also possible that the book was written as a reaction to some of the concerns that he sensed about the survival of the Haugean tradition based on his early experience at the seminary. There is no available evidence of reaction against this book by Wee's colleagues, but the timing of its printing is conspicuous considering the reported suspicion directed at Wee and Bruce by other faculty members at Luther Theological Seminary around that time. Though the content of the book is valuable in itself, its appearance shortly after the beginning of the NLCA and in light of the friction on the faculty indicates that Wee sensed the need to provide an apology for the Haugean tradition.

In seeking to provide a nuanced picture of the Haugean movement, Wee portrayed Haugeanism as a pan–Norwegian Lutheran phenomenon; this was possibly the result of a desire to emphasize the credibility of Haugeanism as well as its continued relevance for the entire NLCA. Indeed, after a lengthy introduction by O. M. Norlie, who notably did not come from the Hauge's Synod tradition, Wee began his book by providing brief biographies of significant figures in the Haugean movement in Norway and North America. Naturally, he included names associated with what became Hauge's Synod, but he also, as a part of his apology, included various figures from different synods as well as well-respected Norwegian personalities. For example, he highlighted the life and ministry of Nils Thorbjørnsen Ylvisaker of the Norwegian Synod as well as Gisle Johnson. Though differences have been noted between some of Hauge's and Johnson's emphases, Wee likely appealed to the name of Johnson because he was all but universally respected among Norwegian-American Lutherans. In yet another attempt to emphasize the broad influence of Haugeanism, Wee listed the contributions of Peter Lorentzen Haerem, among which was promoting the work of Jewish missions.[19] As noted in the previous chapter, the Zion Society for Israel included many members of Hauge's Synod throughout the years, yet it was initiated by the Conference.

---

19. Wee, *Haugeanism*, 45.

After establishing the pan-Norwegian influence of Haugeanism, Wee continued by outlining basic points of the movement. Given the at times defensive tone of the writing, one can reasonably assume that his comments were in response to common criticisms of Haugeanism. Naturally, he emphasized its heritage in the awakening movement and the importance that the Haugeans placed on an awakened faith through repentance and conversion. He acknowledged the accusation that some Haugeans devalued the sacramental tradition because of their subjective emphasis and admitted that some were guilty of this. Yet he defended Haugeanism as a whole, claiming that most Haugeans did not reject sacramental life but only warned "against the use of the means of grace as a sleeping potion."[20] He further acknowledged the reputation of Haugeanism as excessively legalistic, yet argued that such attitudes are not representative of the movement as a whole. Wee encouraged his readers to understand the legalistic attitudes of early Haugeans as a natural reaction to the libertinism of the Seebergian Moravians and not to judge a historical movement "by its eccentricities, but by its central truths." Indeed, Wee asserted that Hauge and his followers always held to faith in Christ as the source of salvation. Wee's discourse here reflects the relationship between Haugeanism and Rosenian influence regarding morality and amusements discussed in the previous chapter as well as the manner in which Haugeanism was perceived by those outside of the tradition.

Continuing with his apology for Haugeanism, Wee curiously defined it as something distinct from both Lutheran Orthodoxy and Pietism, emphasizing that it contained elements of both of these movements, yet was a combination of and an improvement on both of them. He claimed that Haugeanism shared with Orthodoxy a concern for being grounded in "pure doctrine, in accordance with the Word of God and the confessions of the Church." Notably, Wee did not offer direct criticism of Orthodoxy, presumably in an effort to appeal to critics of Haugeanism from that tradition. He did, however, distinguish Haugeanism from broader Pietism, arguing that while Pietism shared with Haugeanism a desire to see "a conscious change of heart" in believers, Pietism stressed "rest and tranquility," "always looking upward," whereas Haugeanism emphasized "Christian life in its activity and strife." Wee cited the industriousness of Hauge and his followers in all realms of life, from manual labor to political involvement, as evidence of this, which was presumably

---

20. Wee, *Haugeanism*, 53. Discussion in this and the following paragraph is derived from pages 53 to 59 of Wee's volume.

intended to emphasize the usefulness of Haugeanism within the NLCA. Whether Wee accurately understood historical Pietism is another question, but his attempt at drawing a distinction between it and Haugeanism is significant, indicating that criticism of Haugeanism in this era likely, just as today, took the form of criticism of "Pietists."

Wee then turned his attention to the question of lay preaching and other matters of church polity. Referring to the Conventicle Act of 1741 as a "monstrosity," he used the text of this law as yet another means by which he differentiated Haugeanism from Pietism, as the law originated from Pietists in Denmark and Norway prior to Hauge;[21] he argued that the Conventicle Act discouraged itinerancy and spiritual energy. Attempting to give credibility to the practice of lay preaching, Wee cited the examples of prominent Norwegian ecclesiastical officials such as Bishop J. C. Heuch and Pastor Jakob Sverdrup, who expressed their support of the practice. Most notably, he mentioned Sigurd V. Odland, a successor to Gisle Johnson at the *Norsk-Lutherske Indremissionsselskap*, as providing justification for lay preaching based on his understanding of the "gifts of grace" present in a congregation. In accordance with the historic Haugean tradition, Wee believed that "every believer has the right publicly to testify concerning his faith," which need not be regulated by church officials beyond the congregation. This perspective differed from that of Gisle Johnson with his "emergency principle," and so Wee's invocation of Odland as Johnson's successor was clearly an attempt to bolster his argument. Regarding the use of clerical vestments, Wee argued, quoting the Norwegian Haugean Fredrik Müller, that the rejection of such vestments stemmed from the desire for cultural relevance rather than a lack of sophistication. He pointed out that non-Christian movements in Norway, such as the socialist movement, "laughed at the clerical gown" and that "the means of grace have their power and sacredness in themselves for those who believe" without such addenda. Finally, Wee curiously mentioned the contribution of women in the Haugean movement, who at times preached and led awakenings. However, on the same page, he was quick to point out that the Haugeans were careful to exercise discipline in their activities as a way of guarding against fanaticism, "not accepting an unknown traveling preacher without good recommendation," which was likely an attempt to assuage the suspicions of Haugeanism in the NLCA.

21. Wee, *Haugeanism*, 62. Discussion in this paragraph is derived from pages 62 to 71 in Wee's volume.

Wee concluded his brief book with a triumphal note concerning the practice of lay preaching among Norwegian-American Lutherans: "This strife is now at an end, God be praised! Lay preaching has become a recognized and permanent function in our Church. May it in the future, as it has been in the past, be a source of great blessing to our people!"[22] The overall tone of Wee's apology, however, suggests that he was less than convinced that Haugeanism would find enduring expression in the NLCA. On the following page, he emphasized one final time the broad influence Haugeanism had already had on Norwegian Lutheranism and how it served as "Light and Salt to the Church and the people of Norway." He went on to state that "its benign influence has also been felt in the neighboring countries, on heathen mission fields, and especially among us Norwegian Lutherans in America." Yet on the final page, Wee responded to apparent skepticism about the continuing relevance of Haugeanism into the future: "Can the movement maintain itself under the present conditions among us, as American Lutherans?"[23] Apparently, some were of the opinion that the transition to the English language from Norwegian meant that Haugeanism was a thing of the past, as "[American] soil is foreign to its nature." Yet Wee argued that Haugeanism, with its emphasis on spiritual revival, testimony, and corresponding industriousness, was something that had universal relevance. Wee saw Haugeanism as serving an essential role in the well-being of the NLCA, as leaven in a larger batch of dough, and he called for a new awakening:

> And it should be a powerful incentive to Christians who have the well-being of our Church at heart, to pray God that He in His mercy will raise up prophets among us, who may go forth in the spirit and power of Hans Nielsen Hauge. Then let every one who believes in and cherishes what Haugeanism represents, diligently practise [sic] what he preaches and earnestly pray for the continuance of this precious element in our church life.[24]

---

22. Wee, *Haugeanism*, 70.
23. Wee, *Haugeanism*, 72.
24. Wee, *Haugeanism*, 72.

The Hauge Lutheran Inner Mission Federation

Perhaps one part of the desire for the "continuance" that Wee sought was the appearance of an organization among Norwegian-American Lutherans the following year. There is no evidence directly linking Wee to the founding of this organization, but its origin must be noted as a part of the continuation of the Haugean tradition in the period under discussion. The exact origin of the Hauge Lutheran Inner Mission Federation (HLIMF) is somewhat obscure; documents concerning its founding cannot be located. However, it is clear that the organization began in the year 1920, indicating that its appearance likely stemmed from the perceived need to preserve Haugeanism after the merger of 1917.

The HLIMF, though open to working with Lutherans of other synods and even acknowledging the presence of "living Christianity" in non-Lutheran groups such as Baptists, Methodists, Pentecostals, and the Salvation Army,[25] consisted mostly of former members of Hauge's Synod. Given the focus of Ljostveit's book, which is the history of lay preaching and prayer meetings within established churches, the title of "inner mission" was apparently meant to refer to a network of independent societies that sought to nurture such lay meetings for edification. Sensing that outward participation in the life of the established church body, though widely considered necessary, was insufficient, the HLIMF endeavored to continue the Haugean tradition of lay-led edifying gatherings within but independent of the NLCA. They therefore sought to serve as spiritual leaven in a larger batch of dough. In the minds of the members, however, an organization such as the HLIMF was not an innovation. They considered their work to be a continuation of a long tradition of "independent lay activity," dating back to 1825 in North America, under the leadership of O. O. Hettlevedt, and of course to the work of Hauge himself in Norway.[26] Apparently a key part of the ministry of the HLIMF was its monthly publication *Morning Glory*, which began in 1926, printed out of Grand Forks, North Dakota. Emblazoned on the front page of each issue was a statement of purpose for the HLIMF, which was to stand for the following Haugean emphases: "experienced salvation, Christian fellowship, simplicity in worship, stir up the gifts of grace, maintain the bond of union."[27]

---

25. Ljostveit, *Innermission Church History*, 313.
26. Ljostveit, *Innermission Church History*, 313.
27. *Morning Glory*, June 1934, 84.

Though no information about the HLIMF is available from the time of its founding in 1920, comments from later years shed light on the situation that led to its founding and the motives of those involved. In 1934, a pastor of the former Hauge's Synod Bjørn Kittelson Barstad, notably one of the delegates protesting the closing of RWS in 1932, provided a testimony in *Morning Glory* concerning how an inner mission society near Halstad, Minnesota was instrumental in sustaining him in faith after he was convicted of sin and "converted" in 1888. He referred to the same program of ordered lay ministry in Hauge's Synod to which Bruce referred in his 1916 reflection, noting that Hauge's Synod made such lay preaching a priority. Yet Barstad, though striking a conciliatory tone, noted the changed circumstances after 1917:

> We ought to thank God for the evangelistic work that the church-bodies still carry on their program. But the Christian laymen's work controlled by the circuits came to a tragic conclusion after the church union in 1917. That was, at any rate, the case in the circuit I have reference to.[28]

He went on to note that the founding of the HLIMF was directly related to the perceived need to preserve the Haugean tradition after 1917. Quoting from his own earlier writing, Barstad noted the friction that the Haugean element experienced with others in the NLCA:

> The treatment given the laymen's work by the Church-Body could not have any other result than to bring the Christian people, especially of the Hauge type, to join the Inner Mission Societies that just in those days made a marked progress. The desire for communion with one another and a more extensive and aggressive work for the salvation of souls led to the organization of the Hauge Lutheran Inner Mission Federation in 1920 that now embraces about 30 societies of laymen.[29]

However, though Barstad alluded to poor treatment of the Haugean element of the NLCA, he notably continued his conciliatory tone regarding the relationship between the HLIMF and the NLCA, perhaps reflecting Hauge's own experience with the Church of Norway:

> Something should be added about the relation between the free Inner Mission work and the organized church. My testimony in this matter after 38 years of personal experience, is that there

---

28. Barstad, "What the Inner Mission People," 87.
29. Barstad, "What the Inner Mission People," 87.

needs to be no friction between the two. If the pastor and the congregation stand for the salvation of souls, why should there be any antagonism toward another group of Christian Lutheran brethren who stand for the same thing? Away with such an idea! My testimony is that the Christian Laymen have been a great help to me in my work as a pastor. Most of them have been among the best supporters both in the local work and for the church at large.[30]

The HLIMF would continue to make its presence felt in the NLCA throughout the decades, and more will be said about it in later developments. Yet its appearance shortly after the union of 1917 is another indicator of the difficulty that the Haugean element encountered in seeking to maintain its tradition. That the HLIMF served as a type of safe haven for the Haugeans and even perhaps a defensive alliance as they lived out their faith within the NLCA is shown by the fact that the president of the organization for a time in the early 1930s, G. O. Mona, was one of the leading voices opposing the union of 1917 for fear that the Haugeans would lose their identity in a larger church body.

Wee's Later Publication

One final noteworthy piece from this period relevant for considering the mindset of Haugeans in the NLCA is another brief book by M. O. Wee entitled *Urgent Needs of Our Times*, published in 1923. Of course, it must be understood that Wee's perspectives reflected his own concerns and were likely not held by all the Haugeans in the NLCA. However, it has been established that the prospect of his leaving his position at the seminary created significant concern among the former Hauge's Synod element of the NLCA, and so Wee's voice apparently carried considerable weight among the Haugeans of that time, making him a significant representative of that constituency.

The content of this brief book articulates a vision of Christian life informed by the principle of spiritual warfare. Written on the heels of the First World War, this is not surprising, but it is also consistent with the historic Haugean emphasis on spiritual watchfulness, discouraging a lax and comfortable faith. Likely because of the aftermath of the war, Wee was convinced that the time of his writing was one of the critical periods

---

30. Barstad, "What the Inner Mission People," 87.

of human history, and he called for seriousness in faith and prayer and, notably, a discriminating attitude toward amusements:

> A serious age demands a serious generation. This holds true, of course, at all times; but especially it is true of *critical* periods. The human race has passed through several such periods, and that our own age is one of them is self-evident. Life is solemn; so are the hurts and wants of life. Merely trying to kill time is out of question. Play must serve only as a necessary recreation or change, in order that the work may be done quicker and better.[31]

Yet Wee's Haugeanism came across even more strongly when he discussed the need for greater spirituality in church life. Having made an argument for the continued relevance of Haugeanism in his earlier book on the topic, here he continued the argument with a criticism of the tendency to emphasize church organization at the expense of the quality of spiritual life, which is perhaps telling about the prevailing attitude in the NLCA after 1917 with its focus on institutional merger:

> But is there not also an unmistakable demand in our day for a greater spirituality? Our age is strong on organization. Is there not a danger of our becoming organized to death? We are, today, doing things on a grand scale; we do things by "drives." In imitation of affairs political and social, we also crystalize our religious activities in such a way as to become institutional. Church life being a business, devotions are apt to become perfunctory.[32]

Wee acknowledged the need for administration in church life, but he cautioned readers about the danger of overemphasizing institutional life, and he called for spiritual life to pervade all aspects of such administration lest the church lose its true focus. In vivid prose, he wrote of "the one thing needful," which was "the pervading influence of God's Spirit in all our activities." This is consistent with the principles of historic Haugeanism, being concerned for "living Christianity" rather than institutional life. He quoted an anonymous source, regarded as "one of our sainted Church fathers," whose words are reproduced in full here. By these words, Wee made no secret of his concern for the influence of Haugeanism as the NLCA continued to come of age. In accordance with Hauge's own situation in Norway, Wee understood mere outward

---

31. Wee, *Urgent Needs of Our Times*, 5. Italicized text is in the original.
32. Wee, *Urgent Needs of Our Times*, 16.

participation in the established church to be inadequate, and he used his own position of influence as a seminary professor to advocate for the building up of spiritual life within the NLCA:

> But our sincere wish is not only that our youth who are to be educated to occupy positions of leadership among our people should be orthodox, should become men and women who hold fast the right form of the sound doctrine; but our sincere wish is also that they might become true Christians, believing, live children of God in whom the spirit might rule, so that they in every truth might become a blessing among our people. For this the believers in our congregations must diligently pray.[33]

THE FATE OF THE SCHOOLS

With Wee's concern in the above quote for the incorporation of spiritual life into theological education in the NLCA, it is appropriate to turn attention to the educational institutions of the former Hauge's Synod and their fate after 1917. As mentioned in discussion of the union articles in the previous chapter, the Haugeans were aware of the significance of educational institutions for perpetuating their identity, and their expectation and hope was that Red Wing Seminary in particular would serve as important spiritual leaven in the NLCA. The closing of their two historic institutions was understandably controversial for the Haugeans of the era, leading to a sense of disenfranchisement and perhaps providing the impetus for the creation of ministries independent of official control of the NLCA.

Jewell Lutheran College

The fate of Jewell Lutheran College has already been mentioned in the previous chapter. Though owned by the NLCA after 1917, it did not, according to the union articles, share the status of "standard college" with Luther College and St. Olaf College. To be sure, other colleges and academies within the NLCA shared the same secondary status as JLC. However, it was to receive some funding from the NLCA, which was discontinued in 1924, resulting in the closure of the institution that year. Many years later, Haugean alumni of JLC blamed the closure on

---

33. Wee, *Urgent Needs of Our Times*, 17.

the leadership of the NLCA for failing to provide necessary funding. However, it should be noted that at least some interest from outside of the former Hauge's Synod was directed toward JLC after the merger. In July of 1917, Lars W. Boe, at the time secretary of the NLCA board of trustees, sought to create a college association for JLC modeled after the association for Augustana College in South Dakota.[34] This indicates that an attempt was made to help JLC become self-supporting through funding raised through a college association. Based on later reports, such an association was apparently established shortly thereafter, but this effort, in spite of the increasing enrollment in the early 1920s, was not enough "to put the school on a sound economic basis."[35] Iver Iversen, president of JLC at the time, provided a positive report about the work of JLC in 1923, noting a total enrollment of ninety-one students and highlighting that three of the graduates that year were considering entering ordained ministry. However, he referred to difficulties facing JLC that suggest tension between the Haugean tradition of the college and the surrounding environment, including the local NLCA district: "The main difficulties we have had to contend with are: (a) Worldliness on the part of the people. (b) Lack of understanding of the aim of the Christian school. (c) Lack of cooperation within the district."[36] The following year, Iversen's comments continued to reflect typical Haugean piety, which was notably absent from the comments of presidents of the other colleges of the NLCA, as well as a sense of disappointment at the lack of interest shown in JLC by "the church people." He referred to a spirit of revival among the student body, yet also lamented the financial reality resulting in the closure of JLC:

> Jewell Lutheran College had during the school year, 1923–1924 a very blessed season. The Lord Himself by sending us an extraordinary spiritual blessing, a revival which reached nearly the whole student body, demonstrated the value of the small Christian school for the advancement of His Kingdom. However the church people did not have the vision and the spirit of sacrifice to respond to this challenge. Because of financial difficulties it was decided last spring to lay down the school.[37]

34. Personal letter from Lars W. Boe to P. M. Glasoe on July 23, 1917, Presidential Correspondence, Center for Western Studies at Augustana University, Sioux Falls, SD.
35. NLCA, *1923 Annual Report*, 187.
36. NLCA, *1923 Annual Report*, 187.
37. NLCA, *1924 Annual Report*, 166.

One can infer from the reference to "lack of cooperation within the district" as well as the failure of "the church people" to support the school that the expectation existed among the Haugeans that support for JLC would come from the NLCA as a whole rather than simply the Hauge's Synod element. As much as there might be truth to Iversen's contention that the NLCA as a whole was not interested in preserving JLC, it must also be considered that the Haugeans themselves shouldered some blame, as some responsibility for raising funds rested with their college association. It is understandable that the Haugeans, who placed more emphasis on spiritual life than on building institutions, were less effective than their more churchly counterparts at building endowments. Indeed, in his 1916 observation, G. M. Bruce commented that even though members of Hauge's Synod "surrounded the schools with warm and vibrant interest," the interests of both JLC and RWS were not heavily promoted throughout the synod, with greater interest shown toward traveling missionaries and evangelists.[38]

Evidence indicates that the closure of JLC as a result of the revocation of funding created lingering resentment among former members of Hauge's Synod. In a brief document from likely the 1950s, Jesse Thompson, holding the title of historian of JLC, reflected with bitterness on the fate of the school. He noted that with the transfer of the school to the NLCA in 1917, there was a "tacit understanding" that financial support would be given to the college. Noting also that Red Wing Seminary was promised support on the same level as the other "standard colleges," Thompson suggested that the union negotiations prior to 1917 were carried out in a spirit of feigned appreciation for the Haugean tradition and the interests of its schools and that there was no real intention from the NLCA to continue its support for the schools of Hauge's Synod over time. He also criticized others from the Haugean tradition in the NLCA for failing to defend the interests of their heritage in an effort to maintain their own credibility within the NLCA:

> Naturally the permanent preservation of their schools was a prime consideration in the union arrangements. However this friendly attitude did not continue very long after the new church organization had obtained control and in 1924 this fine property was sold to the city of Jewell for a High School. All this leads one to wonder whether this was part of a cleverly planned plot to destroy the Hauges synod [sic] schools and their impact

38. Norlie, *Norsk Lutherske Menigheter i Amerika*, 2:690.

on the new church. If that be true the plan was diabolically clever and would have done credit to a Hitler, and it was executed with the finesse of a Caligula, Nero, Torquemada, or Stalin. All of this taking place with only token protests from the Hauge Synod former clergy members. Did they more or less willingly trade their birthright for the proverbial meal ticket?[39]

Thompson reflected on the various reasons that JLC failed to survive, suggesting that the lack of alumni support, combined with the somewhat isolated geographical location of Jewell, Iowa, played a role. Perhaps reflecting his Haugean concern for the empowerment of the laity, he also attributed the decline of the college to the increasing authority and presence of clergy on the board of directors. The implication was that distancing the laity from the governance of the institution led to decreased participation by laity in terms of enrollment. However, lack of support from the NLCA leadership figured prominently in his criticism; his words continue his stinging indictment of the NLCA leadership, accusing them of deception in their dealings with the former Hauge's Synod membership:

> There were also other factors involved such as financial assistance which in the case of JLC had been promised but later withdrawn. The despicable action of the Church educational authorities in withholding aid for JLC while spending millions in building up their other schools, such as buildings on the campuses of St. Olaf and Luther College, spelled a planned exit for JLC. It has been reliably reported that something like $14,000 would have enabled JLC to discharge its funded debt and keep going.[40]

Thompson then noted that other schools from other traditions comparable in size to JLC, Lutheran and otherwise, continued to receive financial support from their respective church bodies, leading the institutions to thrive. Comparing the experience of JLC to such institutions, he pointed out that these other church bodies "did not reneg [sic] as did the Norwegian Lutheran Church of America to their eternal shame and disgrace."[41] Whether Thompson's accusations concerning the motives of the NLCA leadership are justified is a debatable point. Though many factors receive consideration in budgetary decisions by church bodies and committees,

39. Thompson, "A Cursory History."
40. Thompson, "A Cursory History."
41. Thompson, "A Cursory History."

there is reason to believe that the Haugeans' sense of unfair treatment by the NLCA was legitimate; as noted in the previous chapter, JLC experienced its highest enrollment in 1917 and perhaps could have continued to thrive with further financial support and promotion by the NLCA. Whatever the case, Thompson's attitude and perspective is significant for understanding the disenfranchisement the Haugean tradition felt within the NLCA/ELC late in its existence.

One must ask whether Thompson's level of anger at the officialdom of the NLCA/ELC was shared by all the Haugeans in the church body. It is impossible to know for certain the attitudes of everyone involved, and as he himself suggests, many former pastors of Hauge's Synod did not express such vitriol at the closing of JLC and RWS, simply objecting and then choosing to continue their ministries peacefully. However, the official title of JLC historian held by Thompson, apparently as part of the JLC student association,[42] suggests that such an attitude was a sentiment shared by many. Indeed, an appeal letter from the JLC student association in support of the establishment of a Hans Nielsen Hauge memorial infirmary in Red Wing makes many of the same points as Thompson's brief history, yet understandably with a more respectful tone, avoiding direct criticism of the NLCA.[43] Furthermore, Thompson was not the only one to criticize the 1924 decision of the NLCA. Susie Stageberg, the widow of a RWS professor who was elected corresponding secretary of the JLC student association in the 1950s, also offered critical comments. In 1959, when the ELC was concluding its existence in order to participate in the merger that produced TALC the following year, a certain Olaf Holen prepared to write a history of the South Central District of the ELC, which included the state of Iowa. In a letter to Stageberg, he thanked her for the information she provided and referred to aspects of her communication that, by virtue of their critical nature, could not be included in the official history:

> Dear Mrs. Stageberg: I want to thank you most heartily for the information you gave me with reference to the defunct Jewell College. It gave me all the information I wanted, and I am going to include this in the history of South Central District. As you state in your communication, I cannot include the critical remarks, but undoubtedly there is much to what you wrote.

---

42. This was the alumni organization of JLC.

43. Notes from Jewell Lutheran College Association Meeting at Blue Earth, MN on July 12, 1953, JLC File, St. Olaf College Archives, Northfield, MN.

The two Hauge Synod Schools, at Red Wing and Jewell, did not survive the union, but with some financial and other help they could perhaps have been saved. But that is history now and we better let the dead rest in peace.[44]

In an unknown publication from around the same time, Stageberg reflected on the legacy of JLC with gratitude yet sadness at its demise:

> I never cease to marvel that the Jewell College students have continued to carry on for 39 years even though this promising school situated as it was in one of the richest Lutheran communities in the USA, was closed in 1924. That the closing was a sad mistake, many of us see now. But again it is a case of hindsight being better than foresight.[45]

Red Wing Seminary

Even more significant for the Haugean element in the NLCA was the fate of Red Wing Seminary. More so than JLC, RWS was central to their identity through pastoral formation informed by their traditions and piety. The union articles did guarantee RWS a place in the life of the NLCA. Though the theological department was ended, assurance was given that the Haugean spirit would continue to play a role in the broader NLCA through the pro-seminary, academy, and normal school departments.

Despite the assurance of the continued life of RWS, evidence indicates that former members of Hauge's Synod expressed concern early on about the survival of the school as well as skepticism about the promised support from the NLCA. In the autumn of 1918, a certain Edward Johnson, a member of the NLCA board of education and former Hauge's Synod member, corresponded with M. J. Wick, who was at the time the president of RWS. The letter prodded Wick to begin efforts at fundraising:

> Dear Rev. Wick, I have the future of Red Wing Seminary at heart. I desire to mention the following project at this time. Is it not possible to get the alumni of the Seminary to get behind the raising a fund for the school.... I believe there is an opportunity to raise funds from many old friends of the former Hauges [sic] Synod.... One thing is sure, we must push the school forward

---

44. Personal letter from Olaf Holen to Susie W. Stageberg on January 22, 1959, JLC File, St. Olaf College Archives, Northfield, MN.

45. Comments from Susie W. Stageberg in unknown publication [ca. 1950s], JLC File, St. Olaf College Archives, Northfield, MN.

from now on and the pushing must be done by us, from the former Hauges [sic] Synod.⁴⁶

Johnson went on to suggest that RWS could follow the lead of other schools in offering military training as a part of their curriculum, hoping that it could boost enrollment. Early the next year, Johnson communicated with Wick once more, stressing the need to enlist the support of the alumni and fight for the future of the school. More than implicit in his remarks is his perception that already as of 1919, RWS was being devalued by the NLCA:

> I want to say again that we must proceed on the supposition that Red Wing Seminary is worth something to the church, so much that she is worth working for and making sacrifices for. If we think that the new church body is going to put anything in the lap of the Seminary, without any effort on the part of those who are interested, we are much mistaken. . . . Let us go after the proposition of building up the school. . . . We can do it. It will be for our good. It will be helpful to the entire church. The Alumni should, if possible, help to advertise the school for the coming year. . . . P.S. We cannot afford to lay down our arms because some are not interested in the Seminary. The school has enough backing to give good success and render splendid service to the new church.⁴⁷

There is also evidence that the educational program of RWS was the object of some suspicion in the NLCA as a whole in the years after the merger. The union articles specified that RWS would serve as a "pro-seminary," where somewhat older men lacking a traditional college education could be prepared for study at the seminary and eventual ordination. In a brief article from the 1920s, Herman E. Jorgensen, at the time president of RWS, offered an apology for the pro-seminary program; his words were presumably meant as a response to criticism of the program. In light of his comments, it is reasonable to assume that the more churchly focus of much of the NLCA tended to look disapprovingly on an educational program that allowed for what they likely considered a shortcut to ordination through less rigorous academic standards. Perhaps echoing the comments of Eielsen when defending his ordination examination "by

---

46. Personal letter from Edward Johnson to M. J. Wick on September 27, 1918, RWS File, St. Olaf College Archives, Northfield, MN.

47. Personal letter from Edward Johnson to M. J. Wick on March 5, 1919, RWS File, St. Olaf College Archives, Northfield, MN.

the Holy Spirit" and the various trials he endured, Jorgensen emphasized the value of somewhat older men being prepared for ordained ministry due to their life experience:

> [Older men] have struggled with life's ugliest reality, sin; have found themselves beaten in the combat; and have thru [sic] the grace of God learned to know Jesus Christ as the only deliverer from sin's guilt and domination. It is this very experience which has made them such useful members of the church. They have become zealous for God's work. And with this zeal has come, in many instances, a secret longing to serve their Master as shepherds of the congregation.[48]

He went on to emphasize that the NLCA, through the establishment of the pro-seminary program, recognized that certain men who had not been educated in the traditional manner were eligible to hear "the still, small voice of God's call." Jorgensen's comments reflect the continued tension between "official" and "spiritual" qualifications for ministry, observable as early as the conflict between Eielsen on the one hand and Clausen and Dietrichson on the other. However, Jorgensen was careful to point out that the pro-seminary program was not lacking in its academic standards, all the while emphasizing the need for spiritual conviction among pastors:

> Let it be understood . . . from the outset: This is not an easy path to the ministry for the mediocre or the laggard. If by ill fortune such a person should in this way reach the pulpit, let it be remembered that he not only has done an injustice to the Church, but he has also served himself a bad turn. The ministry is increasingly becoming the place where consecration plus ability and training will be most demanded. . . . For the pro-seminary is to train men who are to go to the theological seminary to work side by side with men whose schooling in point of time is twice their own; and its special problem is to bridge as much of this chasm as possible. If this is to be done successfully the

---

48. *Lutheran Herald*, [clipping ca. 1920s], RWS File, St. Olaf College Archives, Northfield, MN. For perspective, it is important to understand what was meant by the designation "older." In his apology, Jorgensen considered the pro-seminary program to be intended for men between the ages of twenty-two to thirty who lacked a traditional college degree. Though this age range hardly seems "old" by the standards of the present, seminary students of the time were almost always young men directly out of college who began theological study at the age of twenty-two.

student must be a man of ability, purpose, and industry. But above all: he must be a sincere and humble follower of Christ.[49]

Twelve years after the union that produced the NLCA, RWS celebrated its fiftieth anniversary. In the collection of essays and sermons compiled for the celebration, held from September 15 to 17 of 1929, there exists a significant amount of anxiety about the future viability of the school, which is telling about the Haugeans' own perceived status in the NLCA. Indeed, the entire collection reads as an apology for RWS and the Haugean tradition more generally, suggesting that even before the financial crisis of the Great Depression, which began the month following the celebration, RWS was struggling for viability, and the possibility of its closure was real. Significant figures from the former Hauge's Synod offered their thoughts on the occasion, and their remarks and questions were often pointed. In fact, the comments highlighted in this section constitute only a small fraction of the overall tenor of Rholl's edited work. A repeated refrain in the sermons and speeches is the concern for the place of Haugeanism in the NLCA. There was suspicion of the NLCA leadership as to whether they truly intended to allow the Haugean tradition to have genuine influence in the organization. For the participants in the anniversary celebration, these concerns were intimately connected to the fate of RWS. Tellingly, one of the speeches scheduled for the last day of the celebration was entitled "Red Wing Seminary's Place in Our Church."[50] In the opening sermon for the celebration given by Iver L. Lasseson, anxiety over the future of the institution was made explicit, yet the concern for the survival of RWS was tied to the greater concern for the enduring legacy of Haugeanism in the NLCA and whether the former Hauge's Synod element was serious about contending for its principles: "Are we now through with Red Wing Seminary? Does its position as a representative of the Haugean movement belong to the past? The answer depends upon how much there is left of the spirit of Haugeanism in us, the children of the former Hauge's Synod."[51] Indeed, throughout his sermon, Lasseson emphasized the distinct character of the Haugeans, drawing a line between the institutional church and the genuine Christian faith contained therein. Notably not rejecting the need for an

---

49. *Lutheran Herald*, [clipping ca. 1920s], RWS File, St. Olaf College Archives, Northfield, MN.

50. Rholl, *Red Wing Seminary*, 7.

51. Rholl, *Red Wing Seminary*, 11.

institutional church organization, his comments reflected the historic Haugean focus on spiritual life within the established church. Accordingly, he articulated the continuing mission of RWS in the following way:

> We, as children of the former Hauge's Synod, must look upon it as our Christian task, that we, true to the Word of God and our Christian conviction, should also through the Red Wing Seminary, contribute our part to the upbuilding of the Kingdom of God within the Norwegian Lutheran Church of America, whose members we are.[52]

Several other comments by other preachers and speakers at this celebration reflected a feeling of disenfranchisement among the Haugeans specifically related to the funding of RWS. Thomas Hanson, one of the brothers of M. G. Hanson, referred to the large budget of the NLCA, yet intimated that the funding of RWS by the NLCA was inadequate and that the true value of the institution was not broadly shared in the organization.[53] Referring to the merger agreement in the union articles, M. J. Wick asked the question directly: "Was it the earnest desire of the new church body to maintain Red Wing Seminary?"[54] A. M. Mannes spoke about the role of the alumni in maintaining RWS, calling for capital improvements in order to attract students. Acknowledging that the NLCA did contribute funding for general expenses, he was critical of their lack of investment in improving the property. Furthermore, Mannes claimed that RWS was dropped from the list of schools to benefit from a planned endowment in the NLCA. What accounted for this state of affairs, according to Mannes, was disconnect between the Haugean element of the NLCA and their more institutionally minded counterparts, who did not truly appreciate the Haugean tradition:

> But her alumni cannot expect that the rank and file of our church can appreciate the traditions and sentiments associated with her past history. She may, therefore, unintentionally be neglected in critical moments and periods. Such a condition is real today.[55]

---

52. Rholl, *Red Wing Seminary*, 12.
53. Rholl, *Red Wing Seminary*, 13.
54. Rholl, *Red Wing Seminary*, 47.
55. Rholl, *Red Wing Seminary*, 70.

Summarizing the concerns of all in addressing the mission of RWS in the NLCA, M. O. Wee alluded to unfair treatment that RWS received in the church body in comparison to other schools:

> Shall this landmark . . . be maintained, or has it outlived its usefulness? Is there still room for Haugeanism, as a Christian view of life, in the Norwegian Lutheran Church of America, or should it be rooted out? . . . There are those, who do not restrain themselves in calling attention to the spirit of this or that school, and point with pride to the traditions of those institutions. Why should it be different when it comes to Red Wing Seminary, the school of the Haugeans? Perhaps some of our alumni reply, that we should boost Red Wing Seminary without stressing Haugeanism. But what to us is important, is not the place nor the buildings, but what the school represents first of all.[56]

Given the comments noted above as well as many others in Rholl's anniversary collection of sermons and essays, it is clear that as of the conclusion of the 1920s, the Haugeans in general harbored concerns bordering on bitterness concerning the state of RWS in the NLCA and the Haugeanism it represented. Apparently, enrollment numbers at the school were not strong in the years after 1917, which contributed to financial difficulty. According to former president M. J. Wick, several factors contributed to this state of affairs. Diplomatically acknowledging the challenge of honoring and supporting the many and various institutions that fed into the NLCA as well as the good intentions of those who engineered the merger, he noted that RWS faced an uphill battle for survival from the beginning. Because of the presence of the other colleges, finding an enduring contributing role for RWS in the NLCA proved difficult.[57] Prior to the union, RWS had academy, college, and theological departments, but with the merger the college department was merged with St. Olaf College, and the theological department was consolidated with Luther Theological Seminary. Only the academy remained. The addition of the normal school and the pro-seminary sought to create a useful place for RWS into the future, but Wick commented that such an arrangement created "grim problems in the after-union days" and that it was a "death blow" to the school. In addition to the established point that the pro-seminary program was viewed with suspicion by some, the exceptional

---

56. Rholl, *Red Wing Seminary*, 57.

57. Rholl, *Red Wing Seminary*, 44. Discussion in this paragraph is derived from pages 43 to 52 in Rholl's volume.

nature of the program ensured that the number of students enrolled in the program remained small, meaning that revenue from the program was limited. Outside factors such as conscription of young men for the First World War and an influenza epidemic also contributed to declining enrollment.

Furthermore, it was the intention of the union articles that the former Hauge's Synod and RWS would be integrated into the life of the whole NLCA, and the Haugeans expected that their influence would serve as important spiritual leaven. Yet enrollment numbers at RWS, presumably from 1928, indicate that the school continued overwhelmingly to serve students from the former Hauge's Synod. A total of seventy-six students were reported from the former Hauge's Synod, eighteen from the former UNLC, and only eleven from the former Norwegian Synod.[58] This lack of widespread appeal is evidence of continued tribalism in the NLCA, and the fact that RWS did not draw large numbers of students from the other merging traditions likely contributed to the question of the enduring value of the school for the NLCA.

Sensing the likelihood of a motion to close RWS, former members of Hauge's Synod mobilized in the early 1930s to stave off such an attempt, calling themselves the "League of Friends of Red Wing Seminary" (LFRWS).[59] Leading up to the 1932 general convention of the NLCA to be held in early June of that year, this group produced a short, fourteen-page booklet entitled *Shall Red Wing Seminary Be Closed? Why?* It was produced hastily in response to the decision of the NLCA board of education on March 11 of that year, which recommended to the upcoming general convention that RWS be discontinued and consolidated with Augustana College in South Dakota. Later, possibly because of closer proximity to Red Wing, St. Olaf College was substituted for Augustana College in the motion. The booklet was distributed at the convention so that voting delegates would have access to the perspective of the Haugeans. Indeed, the LFRWS made explicit their feeling that the concerns of the former Hauge's Synod minority in the NLCA had not been adequately heard throughout the previous fifteen years.

Disconnect that existed between the Haugeans and the rest of the NLCA in this era is revealed in a comment by the committee on church affairs of the NLCA in the 1932 annual report. On the fifteenth

---

58. Rholl, *Red Wing Seminary*, 48.

59. *Shall Red Wing Seminary Be Closed?*, 10. Information in this section is derived from this brief booklet.

anniversary of the merger, the committee reflected positively on the life of the NLCA:

> It is now 15 years since the eventful year of 1917, when the NLCA became a historic fact. Thanksgiving and praise coupled with fear and trembling marked the great union movement. But God has been with us and He has proved to us that it was His work. His marvelous blessings have increasingly rested upon our work these 15 years. We have grown together. The old party lines are gradually disappearing. The union movement was well-planned. The good Lord was permitted to guide our leaders, and now as a result, we can look upon a truly united church body.[60]

The inclusion of this remark is shocking when viewed in light of the drama surrounding the fate of RWS at the same convention. The comments from the LFRWS that were distributed to the delegates indicate that "the old party lines" were alive and well as of 1932. With a tenor best described as respectful irritation at the proposed motion to close RWS, the booklet sought to inform the delegates of the ways in which the Haugeans had felt slighted within the NLCA, especially regarding the treatment of their school. Acknowledging that circumstances might necessitate the closure of RWS, the booklet admonished delegates to make their decisions in light of the Golden Rule (Mt 7:12), indicating the Haugeans' sense of maltreatment.

The booklet began by appealing to the union articles from fifteen years prior, noting that the three merging bodies were "one in faith," yet "differed sufficiently in emphasis to have caused disagreement and sometimes even antagonism." It pointed out that the smallest of the three bodies, namely Hauge's Synod, comprising a total of 8 percent of the total NLCA membership, entered the union in good faith even while naturally fearful of the loss of its identity. The LFRWS suggested that the union articles were being treated as a "scrap of paper" in that RWS was being disregarded in its standing alongside St. Olaf College and Luther College. The document then went on to provide a litany of complaints about the manner in which RWS and the Haugeans had been treated in the previous fifteen years. The first point concerned the development of the pro-seminary program itself. Citing those present at the meeting prior to the merger, the booklet claimed that the attitude of some present toward

---

60. NLCA, *1932 Annual Report*, 61.

the pro-seminary course of study was nonchalant and the entire program was treated as "nothing but a makeshift." The document intimated that some in the NLCA resolved not to take the program seriously from the beginning. The LFRWS complained further that the choice of president for RWS by the alumni in 1920, A. M. Mannes, was disregarded by the NLCA convention that year. Similarly, when RWS sought in 1921 to establish a Bible school in the mold of LBI, viewing the initiative as "an opportunity for expansion and service," the person chosen as head of the school by the NLCA board of education was not met with approval by the Haugeans. This appointment prompted a failed petition to the board of education for a change in leadership, and the chosen leadership reportedly resulted in the floundering of the Bible school. All these examples indicate that the Haugeans felt a sense of broken trust by the NLCA.

This feeling continued as the LFRWS delved into financial issues, pointing out that RWS actually took up only a small percentage of the overall educational budget of the NLCA and was not the financial burden that some considered it to be. Already mentioned is that RWS was inexplicably excluded from the endowment drive of 1925, and the booklet pointed out that former Hauge's Synod congregations contributed significantly to this fund for the support of the other NLCA schools while receiving nothing for their own school. It also highlighted the declining financial support from the NLCA for RWS over the years, even prior to the onset of the Great Depression. Finally, responding to the reality of declining enrollment, the LFRWS acknowledged the Depression as one cause, but they also pointed to the disrespect RWS received over the years from the NLCA, which created an environment of uncertainty, resulting in "lack of confidence, lack of trust, lack of students." Emphasizing again that former Hauge's Synod members entered the merger in good faith, supporting the school closest to them from the other predecessor bodies and receiving assurance that RWS "would be taken care of by the Church," they accused President Stub of ignoring RWS in his annual reports even in the first few years after the merger.

Perhaps striking at the heart of the matter, the LFRWS acknowledged that the formation of their group had been perceived as a problem in the NLCA. The reason for this was that RWS was viewed as "a pietistic center," with the term "Pietism" understood by many in the NLCA in a pejorative sense. This is further evidence that "the old party lines" in the NLCA were still in place, and the Haugeans sought to emphasize that "Pietism" was not necessarily a negative thing, but rather integral to their understanding of how a Christian school should function. Regarding the labeling of RWS as "a pietistic center," they responded:

> Some of us would not dare to call the school by so great a name; to us the label is rather a pointed way of expressing the content of our vision of what our school ought to be. For we believe that piety, or pietism if you will, may well be wedded to scholarship. And this, in fact, constitutes the main reason for the existence of Red Wing Seminary.[61]

In support of the view that piety and scholarship can be successfully integrated, they pointed out that RWS academy students tended to perform just as well as other students at the colleges they attended. Finally, the document concluded by pointing out that RWS was not the only educational institution of the NLCA that had experienced challenges and wondering why, for that reason, RWS was being singled out for consolidation with another institution. Luther College had also fallen on hard times, and the LFRWS suggested that due to its close proximity to St. Olaf College, the two colleges could easily be consolidated. For the Haugeans, in view of that option, the consolidation of RWS with another institution was a sign of the low opinion placed on RWS and Haugeanism in the NLCA, and they viewed such action as a threat to their enduring identity: "To the overwhelming majority of the friends of Red Wing Seminary consolidation *means nothing more than loss of identity*."[62]

An indication that the defensive tone of the Haugeans was rooted in actual criticism is the fact that the matter of the survival of RWS caught the attention of Lutherans outside the Norwegian-American field. In April of 1932, theologian Theodore Graebner, formerly of the Norwegian Synod and who was educated at Concordia Seminary of the Missouri Synod, published a critique of the LFRWS in the Missouri Synod publication *Concordia Theological Monthly*. In the article, entitled "The Ghost of Pietism," Graebner considered the Haugean element in the NLCA to be a nuisance, that Haugeanism was losing influence in the NLCA, and that the movement, focused as he understood it on lay preaching and revivalism, had long outlived its usefulness. Graebner referred to the words of M. J. Wick from the previous year, where Wick highlighted the resolve of the Haugeans to continue to serve as leaven in the larger batch

---

61. *Shall Red Wing Seminary Be Closed?*, 11.
62. *Shall Red Wing Seminary Be Closed?*, 14. The italics are in the original.

of dough of the NLCA despite the intention of others in the NLCA to cut off Haugean influence:

> It was said many years ago by a leader in the Church: "We shall gobble the pietists [Hauge Synod] in a tremendous outward organization." "Yes," it was answered, "such an attempt can surely be made; but then the Church must be prepared to take the consequences. If the attempt is made to gobble the pietists for the purpose of getting rid of them, then it is to be feared they will cause tremendous pains in the belly of the Church."[63]

It is clear that in the process of discussing the fate of RWS, Wick and presumably other Haugeans operated according to the view that much of the wider organization of the NLCA sought to marginalize them from the beginning. Yet Wick remained undaunted in his efforts to preserve Haugeanism at RWS, an effort which Graebner mocked as a lost cause. Graebner also quoted the Haugean C. K. Solberg, who was active in the leadership of the Zion Society for Israel, as complaining about "the high-church tendency" of the rest of the NLCA. Though Graebner wrote with appreciation about Hans Nielsen Hauge and his work amidst opposition and persecution from corrupt church authorities in Norway and conceded that the early generations of Norwegian-Americans had, as a result of the power of the movement, sufficient reason to perpetuate Haugeanism on American soil, he claimed that circumstances had changed and that "to-day there is no justification, except that of sentiment, for continuing the Haugean movement. The Norwegian Lutheran Church has had these many years orthodox and conscientious preachers."[64] It is not clear the extent to which Graebner's opinion was shared among many in the NLCA. However, given Graebner's roots in the Norwegian Synod, it is reasonable to assume that many of the former Norwegian Synod shared his opinion. That Graebner was aware of the situation and devoted an article of considerable length to the topic indicates the seriousness of this conflict among those involved.

Inevitably, the matter of the fate of RWS came to the floor of the 1932 annual convention of the NLCA. Unfortunately, there is no record of the content of the remarks made. Apparently, Arthur Rholl, the president of RWS at the time, made a motion that those speaking to the

---

63. Graebner, "Ghost of Pietism," 16.
64. Graebner, "Ghost of Pietism," 244.

matter from the floor be limited to three-minute comments.[65] The motion failed. Presumably, Rholl's intent was to allow for as many voices as possible to state their views. Noting only that "several people took part in the discussion," before a motion could be made to end the independent existence of RWS, a motion was made by the alumni association of RWS "to continue RWS at its present location." This motion also failed by a vote of 268 in favor to 299 opposed, sealing the fate of the school. The following motion to merge RWS with St. Olaf College then passed by a vote of 358 to 130. After this vote, the minutes note that several delegates went on record protesting the action taken to close RWS, notably among them J. O. Gisselquist, a pastor whose ministry would come to be significant when considering the enduring legacy of Haugeanism.[66]

Those protesting the action indicate the unhappiness of many and perhaps most of the Haugeans, but attempts were made at the convention to honor the legacy of RWS and look positively toward the future. Regarding the merger of RWS with St. Olaf, the record states that L. W. Boe, at the time president of St. Olaf, "extended a hearty welcome to the alumni and friends of Red Wing Seminary and assured them that everything possible would be done to make them feel that they are a real part of St. Olaf College."[67] Later, a resolution was presented and adopted, which honored those involved with the administration of RWS:

> The Church hereby expresses its high appreciation and sincere gratitude to the president of Red Wing Seminary, Dr. Arthur Rholl, the staff of teachers, the business manager and all others who have labored in the school, for the efficient, loyal and faithful services they have rendered Red Wing Seminary in the past. We wish them God's richest blessings for the future and sincerely hope that new doors may soon open for them where they may continue to labor in the service of our Church.[68]

The latter part of this chapter tells the story of how at least some from the Haugean tradition did continue to "labor in the service of [the] Church,"

---

65. NLCA, *1932 Annual Report*, 61. Discussion in this paragraph is derived from the information on this page.

66. A complete list of the delegates from 1932 protesting the action to close RWS is as follows: Rev. A. J. Evenson, lay delegate Olaf R. Kelly, Rev. S. K. Knutson, lay delegate O. A. Skeie, Rev. J. O. Gisselquist, Rev. P. M. Trelstad, Rev. B. K. Barstad, Rev. O. J. Malkewick, Rev. J. J. Lee, Rev. B. M. Guldseth, Rev. J. M. Johnson, Rev. O. J. Nesheim, Rev. Nils Klungtvedt, and Rev. Harvin N. Christensen.

67. NLCA, *1932 Annual Report*, 61.

68. NLCA, *1932 Annual Report*, 84.

though their service was notably often outside of the official auspices of the NLCA.

Even after the closure of RWS and its merger with St. Olaf College, the alumni continued to advocate for the preservation of its legacy and the Haugeanism it represented. In one instance, one detects a note of bitterness about the fate of RWS several years after its closure. On an unknown date sometime after 1946, Susie Stageberg, whose husband had once taught at RWS, gave a radio address over the station KAAA of Red Wing. She provided an overview of the history of Hauge's Synod and RWS, emphasizing the uniqueness of Haugeanism in the Norwegian-American Lutheran environment and highlighting the difficulty of finding a theological professor who stood for the Haugean principles of "low-church spirituality, christian [sic] testimony, prayer meetings, and simplicity of worship."[69] By appealing to Hauge's ministry to the working class in Norway, Stageberg highlighted the differences between Hauge's Synod and the other two merging bodies; less concerned with formality and status than the others, the focus of Hauge's Synod and RWS was on bringing "Light and Truth" to the other church bodies in the merger. Yet she suggested that the good intentions of those involved kept them from recognizing that a merger would mean the loss of the Haugean identity and the "dismemberment" of RWS. She highlighted the example of Søren Petterson as one who predicted this in 1917, yet whose warning was not heeded.

Her address was not only focused on reliving the past, however. Lamenting the sad condition of the buildings on the site of the defunct RWS, Stageberg provided a vision for how the spirit of Haugeanism could continue to live on and still utilize the campus of RWS. She called for the establishment of a Christian vocational school that would serve the working-class laity within the NLCA and the broader community, which would integrate learning with training in piety, also carrying on part of the tradition of the Haugean revival of Norway, which was empowerment of the working class:

> My own late husband . . . never ceased to urge the establishment of a christian [sic] vocational school where young men and women of small means could come to learn trades and vocations fitting them for efficient service in the common walks of

---

69. Stageberg, "Red Wing Seminary." In this radio address for station KAAA of Red Wing, Stageberg refers to her "late husband," and as O. O. Stageberg died in 1946, this address must have been given at some point after that time.

life in an atmosphere of "Light and Truth" which would lend to Labor the ethical standards essential to good citizenship. Our beloved church has no such other vocational facilities.... The world still needs Light and Truth.... Our Lutheran Church at large needs a new demonstration of service to the working class that would not only provide a popular educational issue but would be a fitting tribute to the common layman who served the Norwegian peasants and people with his hands as well as his heart, Hans Nielsen Hauge.[70]

Stageberg's vision did not come to fruition, and the site of the former RWS was eventually occupied by a nursing home facility, which still exists today under the name "Seminary Home." The decision of the NLCA to put the grounds of RWS to use at some point rather than let them fall into disrepair was appreciated by some of the Haugeans in a 1938 article in *Morning Glory*, though it expressed such appreciation grudgingly:

> To see, as we have seen, the buildings neglected and used for untoward purposes has been such a crucifixion to those of us who still love the old school and its traditions, that it is a great relief to know that the Church has at last given up the idea of wrecking it and instead has determined to make use of it for some useful purpose even though it is not what some of us had hoped and expected according to the sacred contract of 1917.[71]

Nevertheless, Stageberg's vision is testimony to the continuing recognition among the Haugeans in the NLCA of the importance of a school for an enduring identity, one that would replace RWS in that role. Such a vision for a school that would embody Haugean principles was not new as of 1946, however. One finds in *Morning Glory* a 1934 observation about the campus grounds of RWS and a longing for the reopening of the school:

> I found the steps of the main building covered with filth.... Instead of educating young people in the way of salvation, the school ... is now used to educate the chickens to lay more eggs. It is a disgrace to the church that such things should be permitted.... God open again the doors of Red Wing Seminary and pour the blessing upon the school, that it may be like in the days of old!"[72]

70. Stageberg, "Red Wing Seminary."
71. "Farewell, Red Wing Seminary," June 15, 1938.
72. Johnson, "The School on the Hill That Was Closed," March 1936, 67.

Also in 1934, some involved in the HLIMF began discussion about the possibility of establishing a school that would stand for "pietistic principles." The article by J. O. Reitan in the July 1934 issue of *Morning Glory* lists Nils Klungtvedt, notably one of the pastors protesting the closing of RWS, as the driving force behind the initiative. Noting that such a plan was not intended to compete with Bible schools such as LBI, the hope was that such a pietistic Lutheran institution would serve as a "bond of union" for "true Christian people" in the tradition of Spener and Francke in Halle, Germany. Curiously, no mention is made of the particular topics to be studied at the proposed school, only noting that young people need training in piety, as "their spirits are continually contaminated by the influence pervading the public school and their surroundings." Though not explicitly stated, one can assume that Klungtvedt's vision was that such a school would fill for the Haugeans the void created by the closing of RWS. Reitan's words drip with longing for a place where Haugean principles could find an institutional home, and they underscore the sense of homelessness that they felt within the NLCA in the wake of the 1932 convention. He also alluded to the Haugean element of the NLCA feeling out of place in church politics. Perhaps most significantly, he viewed such an institution as promoting "living Christianity" among the people of the NLCA itself, as well as reaching nonmembers. This is a testimony to the Haugean concern for "experienced salvation" rather than mere nominal membership:

> The Morning Glory has become a bond of union between us, and we are thankful to God for it. . . . But we look for more. How wonderful it would be to have a place to get together, where we could feel at home. Feel that we are all brothers and sisters in the Lord. A place where all suspicion and fear of political intrigues and calumnies would be banished and where spiritual enjoyment might be had in fellowship with one another on the foundation of principles mutually cherished. A place where we could send our children and where spiritual impressions indelible for time and eternity might be made on their minds and hearts. . . . It is our hope that such a school may be started soon, and that out from it may flow a mighty spirit that will promote a Revival of Christianity among our own people especially, and also reaching out to others.[73]

---

73. Reitan, "A Pietistic Lutheran Institution," July 1934, 121–22.

Klungtvedt continued his campaign in the following years for the RWS alumni association to obtain the school property, to "get hold of the school and use it for some good purpose in our Church." Noting that a committee of seven was appointed to press the relevant boards in the NLCA for a resolution of the matter, the proposition to the board of trustees requested that the property be turned over to the RWS alumni association and that the property would be used "for a Luther Camp, a spiritual retreat, and, or a school that will carry out and perpetuate the Haugian [sic] spirit, and laymen's work, as soon and in such a way as may be found practical."[74] The article went on to state that the proposition was rejected by the board of trustees. Klungtvedt's response in the same article, perhaps demonstrating a note of bitterness at how the needs and concerns of the Haugean element of the NLCA had been ignored, was that the ultimate goal of the RWS alumni association was not the obtainment of the property, but rather, "We desire to further the principles of Red Wing Seminary and to perpetuate the spirit of Haugianism [sic] among us. And there should be place in our Church for one [such] institution."

This vision for establishing a school or facility of some kind rooted in the Haugean tradition was not realized. However, evidence indicates that many of the Haugeans did, in accordance with the decision to merge RWS with St. Olaf College, attend and contribute to the life of St. Olaf. In a 1939 letter to attorney Oscar Ronken, who was apparently a part of the RWS alumni association, L. W. Boe, president of St. Olaf, highlighted the significant contributions of former members of Hauge's Synod, assuring him that the merger of the two institutions was more than simply a "paper proposition." Rather, the Haugean influence left a genuine mark on St. Olaf:

> The children from Hauge's Synod homes, both parsonages and otherwise, have been here in larger numbers than the proportion of Hauge's people in the Norwegian Lutheran Church, and they have held leading positions. Many of them have made very fine records scholastically. I have tried to give them at all times perfect freedom for the manifestation of the Hauge's spirit. N. N. Rønning once said that he had the impression that they had exercised a greater religious influence at St. Olaf than any other group. I have taken this attitude not merely because I think it fair and right when churches and institutions are consolidated,

---

74. Klungtvedt, "Red Wing Seminary," February 1937, 77.

but my traditions on my father's side go back to Hauge's Synod. ... We count Red Wing as an integral part of St. Olaf. I often speak of the present-day St. Olaf as something different from the school that was established in 1874. It is a flowing together of all those streams that were influenced by Hauge's work in Norway.[75]

That same year, as the alumni of RWS debated how to dispose of the Hauge Memorial Fund that was established before the closing of the school, there appears to have been some question concerning how the money would be used. According to O. O. Stageberg, the Hauge Memorial Fund "was established as an endowment fund for Red Wing Seminary in honor of its pioneer founders."[76] Given the unanticipated closing of RWS and the ambiguity of the fund's statement of purpose, O. O. Stageberg sought to provide clarity. Citing his many conversations with former members of Hauge's Synod, he argued that "keeping faith with the consecrated hope and desire of the donors" required that the fund be used in such a way as "to perpetuate the principles of personal and experienced Christianity, emphasized by Hans Nielsen Hauge."[77] In the end, the alumni decided to turn over their existing funds to St. Olaf College, as well as request that the alumni endowment that was in the possession of the NLCA be similarly turned over to St. Olaf College to be used for the construction of the new college library. As a part of the motion to execute this plan, the RWS alumni requested that a "Hauge Room" be set aside in the new library, where books, pictures, and other memorabilia from RWS could be held and where the alumni association of RWS could meet into the future.[78] To this day, the "Hauge Room" exists in the Rølvaag Memorial Library on the campus of St. Olaf College.

There is one final exchange to note in the context of the fate of the RWS property. In 1952, J. A. Quello, formerly a Hauge's Synod pastor in Beresford, South Dakota, wrote a circular letter to fellow former Hauge's Synod pastors from his new location in Red Wing. Telling of the mindset of some former members of Hauge's Synod in the NLCA/ELC, Quello's letter called for a meeting in June of that year to revive the board of

---

75. Personal letter from Lars W. Boe to Oscar Ronken on August 16, 1939, RWS File, St. Olaf College Archives, Northfield, MN.

76. Red Wing Seminary Alumni Association, "Seminary Newsletter," June 1939.

77. Red Wing Seminary Alumni Association, "Seminary Newsletter," June 1939.

78. Motion of the RWS Alumni Association [ca. 1939], RWS File, St. Olaf College Archives, Northfield, MN.

trustees of Hauge's Synod in an attempt to gain control of the property of RWS.[79] Since Quello was the only living member of the board of trustees at the time of the 1917 merger, he claimed that "this mantle has fallen" on him to exercise leadership. Curiously, Quello's letter claimed that the merger of 1917 "did not in any sense dissolve the Hauges [sic] Synod as a legal entity" and that the reviving of the board of trustees of Hauge's Synod was justified in light of the fact that the closure of RWS had in his opinion violated the "Articles of Union."

In a subsequent circular letter from the following month, Quello further articulated his purpose in seeking this course of action:

> Under these circumstances, it would seem that we should meet to protect what we may have left, not in the interest of any personal or collective grievance, but as a dedicated service to Haugean principles and Haugean traditions or individual christian [sic] responsibility for the salvation of souls. The question before us then is, what methods can we use to provide such protection?[80]

In encouraging attendance at the meeting, Quello alluded to, in reference to his attempt to advertise the meeting, resistance he had experienced in carrying out this action:

> I would urge all congregations who have not changed their status since the Union to send delegates. These may be the same as the ones sent to the ELC convention. Due to the refusal of the editor of the Herald to advertise our meeting, we are using the facilities of the Morning Glory and Indre Mission's Vennen [sic] to announce our meeting to be held at the Hauge Memorial Home, 2741 Park Ave., Minneapolis, Minn. On Tuesday, June 4th at 10 A. M. for as much of one day as we find necessary.[81]

In response to Quello, G. M. Bruce, presumably one of the recipients of the circular letters, disputed the claims made therein in a sharply worded response:

> Dear Brother Quello: I have read your circular letter . . . with a great deal of surprise. You should know better than to assume

---

79. Circular letter from J. A. Quello on March 6, 1952, G. M. Bruce File, Luther Seminary Archives, St. Paul, MN.

80. Circular letter from J. A. Quello on April 22, 1952, G. M. Bruce File, Luther Seminary Archives, St. Paul, MN.

81. Circular letter from J. A. Quello on April 22, 1952.

that the "mantle" of the late Prof. Elstad as chairman of the Board of Trustees of the Hauge's Synod has fallen and [sic] you and that it is incumbent on you to get Hauge's Synod and its Board of Trustees "able to function." You should also know that the church corporations which were merged in 1917 are not subject to dissolution by district court or other judicial action, for they all joined in the merger as corporations under the special act of the Legislature providing for such merger. . . . Hauge's Synod does not exist except as a corporate part of the present Evangelical Lutheran Church, and any meeting of former members of Hauge's Synod for the purpose you mention would not revive Hauge's Synod as an independent and sovereign corporation.[82]

Bruce concluded his letter by admonishing Quello against creating further conflict within the ELC. This exchange is further evidence of the existence of friction between the Haugeans and others in the ELC late in the life of that church body:

> Furthermore, you know very well both the history and the circumstances connected with the closing of Red Wing Seminary. It was not a willful and arbitrary act on the part of the Norwegian Lutheran Church to violate any part of the Union Agreements, but a case of forced necessity on account of an impossible situation that had arisen. No good can come from the agitation which you have started, but it may do an infinite amount of harm among some who are easily emotionally disturbed.[83]

HAUGEANISM IN THE LATER YEARS OF NLCA/ELC

Though Boe's words about the contribution of the Haugeans to the life of St. Olaf after 1932 should be taken seriously, the closing of RWS can be said to have marked a turning point in the Haugean tradition within the NLCA. The Hauge's Synod institutions of mercy in Beresford, South Dakota, Bethesda Orphanage and Bethesda Nursing Home, continued to exist and do so to the present, with the legacy of the orphanage now expressed in the "child and adolescent" department of Lutheran Social Services in Beresford. However, with the closure of both JLC and RWS, the Haugean element was left institutionally homeless in terms of an

---

82. Personal letter from G. M. Bruce to J. A. Quello on March 12, 1952, G. M. Bruce File, Luther Seminary Archives, St. Paul, MN.

83. Personal letter from G. M. Bruce to J. A. Quello on March 12, 1952.

educational facility that could provide them with identity into the future. Interestingly, it is around the year 1932 that one observes the development of some independent ecclesiastical initiatives to which many of the Haugeans contributed, and it should be considered that the decline and eventual closing of RWS played a role in the desire of many Haugeans to carry on their tradition through such endeavors. The following section discusses these initiatives as well as other issues related to the continued struggle to maintain the Haugean spirit within the NLCA.

Seminary Life and Curriculum

Without their own educational institutions to perpetuate their ethos, one then wonders about the Haugean presence at the seminary of the NLCA after the earlier years. It has already been established that some friction existed between Professors Bruce and Wee and the rest of the faculty in the years immediately after the merger, and one would assume that such friction continued to some degree over the years. As already stated, one of the challenges of the union movement leading up to 1917 was the question of liturgical practice in the new church body, with Hauge's Synod and some within the UNLC seeking to carry forward their tradition of low-church simplicity in worship. In keeping with the "Interpretation" of the union articles produced by Hauge's Synod prior to the merger, Nelson reports that "Hauge's Synod expected the instruction at the seminary to include a presentation of the Haugean worship practices."[84] He notes that some special lectures in Haugean worship practices were indeed held at the seminary in the years after the merger. At the same time, he states, notably without further comment, that "very few congregations retained the practices of Hauge's Synod."[85] This could be due to a lack of demand for such low-church worship leadership among the congregations, a testimony to the triumph of formalism in the NLCA among former Hauge's Synod congregations. It could also be a testimony to the lack of emphasis placed on such practices in the seminary instruction itself, with graduates emphasizing adherence to the Dano-Norwegian "Ritual" and its English language counterpart in *The Lutheran Hymnary*. These two possibilities are interconnected, of course.

---

84. Nelson, *Lutheran Church*, 2:213.
85. Nelson, *Lutheran Church*, 2:128.

There is much that is unclear about these "special lectures" in Haugean worship practices to which Nelson refers. In examining the catalog of Luther Theological Seminary in the years after 1917, one finds no specific reference to such lectures. For the academic year of 1919–1920, Professor Dahle is listed as teaching "Liturgy and Chanting." The course description states the following: "Study of the Ritual, according to both Forms. Drilling in the Norwegian and English Collects of the Church Year and the other Liturgical Services. Training in the right Use og [sic] the voice."[86] What is meant by "both Forms" is unclear, though it likely refers to the two orders for the morning service in *The Lutheran Hymnary*, both of which are expressions of liturgical formality derived from the Dano-Norwegian *Ritual*. This liturgical curriculum remained unchanged until the academic year of 1930–1931, when Professor Brandt assumed the role of liturgical instructor, at which point the catalog simply stated, "*Liturgics*. History and Principles. The Common Service. The Ministerial Acts."[87] In 1936–1937, Herman Preus, grandson of the Herman Amberg Preus mentioned in the second chapter and newly appointed professor, apparently assumed sole responsibility for liturgical instruction, with the lengthy course description containing no reference to Haugean worship practices:

> *Liturgics*. A study of the Lutheran Liturgy, including its historical background and development, its content and use, its purpose and value. The Liturgy is traced from its beginnings in the Old Testament Church, up through the Early Church and the Medieval Church, through the Roman Mass and Luther's Formula Missae and Deutsche Messe, and up to the present day. Special consideration is also given to Church Music, with practical exercises in Chanting.[88]

However, from early on after 1917, the catalog also stipulated that students participate in "occasional addresses and lectures given by speakers invited by the Faculty or student societies. These are usually given Monday evenings and the attendance of all students is expected. They are an important factor in the training of the minister."[89] It is reasonable to assume that if special lectures in the Haugean cultus were given at

---

86. *Luther Theological Seminary Catalog: 1919–1920*, 18.
87. *Luther Theological Seminary Catalog: 1930–1931*, 27.
88. *Luther Theological Seminary Catalog: 1936–1937*, 24. Italicized text is in the original.
89. *Luther Theological Seminary Catalog: 1922–1923*, 27.

the seminary as Nelson claims, they would have been presented at these Monday evening gatherings. However, the academic year 1936–1937 is the first catalog of the seminary that provides a list of these planned "occasional addresses and lectures." In the list, the topics of lectures ranged from health and medical issues to issues of church music and chanting, with no reference made to Haugean worship practices.[90] What can be stated is that as far as can be determined from the seminary catalog, instruction in the low-church worship tradition among Norwegian-American Lutherans was not embedded in the main curriculum, likely a contributing factor in the declining influence of that tradition among congregations.

The faculty minutes from Luther Theological Seminary throughout the years are also silent on the issue, and so it is not clear when such lectures were held, who conducted them, and when the practice of holding such lectures ended at the seminary. David Wee, grandson of M. O. Wee, suggested that the practice likely ended with the retirement of G. M. Bruce from the faculty in the 1940s.[91] M. O. Wee had died in 1942, making Bruce at the time the sole faculty representative of the former Hauge's Synod. Nevertheless, comments from individuals present at the seminary from around that time shed some light on how the older traditions were carried forward in the instruction and in the broader NLCA. James Knutson, a student at the seminary in the early 1950s, does not mention specific lectures in Haugean worship practices at that time, but he does mention that the daily chapel services were simple in their form, with no vestments or elaborate liturgy. What he describes, however, is not Haugean style informality with free prayer, but rather a formal structure in simplified form; he notes that *The Lutheran Hymnary* was used, even though the worship services were not elaborate. The exception was when daily chapel worship was led by Herman Preus, who was sometimes mocked for leading "mass" during such services. Knutson also notes that when the student body petitioned T. F. Gullixson, president of the seminary, to have a monthly service of the Lord's Supper for the students, the faculty agreed, with the stipulation that the service be held across the street at St. Anthony Park Lutheran Church, as the understanding at the time was that the administration of the sacraments needed to be connected to a congregation. In that location, the pastors

---

90. *Luther Theological Seminary Catalog: 1936–1937*, 25.

91. David Wee, Interview by Thomas E. Jacobson. Northfield, MN, November 28, 2016.

did use vestments and more traditional liturgy.[92] From the perspective of David Preus, who was ordained in 1950, vestiges of the traditional Haugean practices were still evident as of that point, "but barely."[93] He notes that some older pastors still resisted the use of vestments, and only a handful of congregations at that point prohibited vestments. With the coming of a newer generation, "some of the oldsters" adhered to the historic practices of Hauge's Synod, "but it was not … continuing." By the time that he was ordained, Preus notes that at least from his point of view it was difficult to identify pastors as representatives of any of the three merging traditions. Depending on one's perspective, this could be interpreted as a sign that the union of 1917 finally succeeded in creating a new church culture. It could also, in light of the dwindling influence of historic Haugean practices already mentioned, be understood as a loss of Haugean influence in the NLCA.

The triumph of formalism in the NLCA can be observed in the early 1930s through correspondence between T. F. Gullixson as president of the seminary and Johann Arndt Aasgaard, at the time president of the NLCA. In a letter from 1933, Gullixson expressed his frustration to Aasgaard concerning liberties taken by seminary students during their time on summer assignment in congregations. Gullixson's concern was that nonordained seminary students were in many cases essentially functioning as ordained pastors and portraying themselves as such through the wearing of vestments and administration of pastoral acts in situations that could not be considered emergencies. He blamed not only the students but also the supervising pastors for blurring the line between ordained and lay ministry, and he called upon Aasgaard to "crack down" on those failing to maintain the distinction, fearing that it would lead to chaos in church life:

> In short then, there is developing with us an attitude which would rapidly erase the distinction between a man ordained and not ordained. I have urged upon the young men here that if those distinctions are broken down they themselves and the ministry of their day, will be the chief victims of that loss of distinctive regard.[94]

---

92. Knutson, Interview by Thomas E. Jacobson.

93. David Preus, Interview by Thomas E. Jacobson.

94. Personal letter from T. F. Gullixson to J. A. Aasgaard on October 13, 1933, T. F. Gullixson File, Luther Seminary Archives, St. Paul, MN.

Accordingly, the Luther Theological Seminary catalog began addressing the situation in its 1936–1937 issue. Under the title "The Theological Student in Relation to Liturgical Practice," the section admonished students to exercise care not to portray themselves as ordained pastors when on "parish year assignment" or when serving as a "vacation time assistant." The stated principle was that a student was to function as a "layman" and "wear no vestment." Furthermore, such students were to "assume no part in the administration of the Lord's Supper," only "administer baptism in cases of real emergency," use the shorter form of the morning service without chanting, and conduct funeral services omitting the final "commitment service," explaining to those present that an ordained minister would conduct the "commitment" at a later time. Concluding the section, the statement made clear that

> the theological student should always conduct himself within as well as outside the sanctuary so as to be in keeping with good taste, and so as quietly but definitely to convey to others the impression that he also holds the view that in and about the house of God there is a distinction between an ordained pastor and a layman.[95]

To be sure, the statement acknowledged the principle of congregational freedom in worship practice, but it also quoted the NLCA constitution, which strongly recommended use of the formal "Ritual" and accompanying principles "in order that there may as a whole be uniformity." Of course, there is no specific reference to Haugeanism in the controversy discussed between Gullixson and Aasgaard, but noteworthy is the absence of any reference to Haugeanism in the official response. Historically, Hauge's Synod did maintain a separate office of ministry from the laity, though that distinction was at times blurred within the synod as has been observed. Yet the official response published by the theological faculty strongly assumed that congregations would carry out worship within the framework of the formal "Ritual," and no mention is made of Haugean worship practices, which the Haugeans considered in their "Interpretation" of 1916 "to have official recognition." This state of affairs is telling of the status of Haugeanism in the NLCA as of the early 1930s.

As the years went on and the older personalities on the faculty of the seminary began to retire, the question arose about how to maintain on the faculty the balance of the historic emphases that fed into the NLCA.

---

95. *Luther Theological Seminary Catalog: 1936–1937*, 31.

According to Harrisville, when Herman Preus was added to the faculty in 1936, Preus clearly stood in the tradition of his grandfather, representing the heritage of the Norwegian Synod and accompanying liturgical formality. In 1939, to fill the void of the heritage of Haugeanism on the faculty and maintain the balance, Gullixson, though himself a member of the Norwegian Synod prior to 1917, tapped George Aus, who was at the time pastor of Trinity Lutheran Church of Brooklyn, New York. According to Norlie, this congregation, *Den norsk lutherske Trefoldigheds menighet* in Brooklyn, was founded in 1890 as a member of the UNLC.[96] Though Aus was not a descendant of anyone from the former Hauge's Synod, he clearly represented its historic emphases of experienced salvation and evangelism.[97]

The HLIMF, upon hearing the news of Aus's appointment, felt encouraged in its role within the NLCA. The editor of *Morning Glory* emphasized the importance of contending for Haugean principles within the established church and dismissed any suggestion that concern for spiritual life necessarily excludes attention to Christian scholarship. In keeping with the historic dual concern of Haugeanism for revivalism and spiritual life on the one hand and Lutheran confessional commitment on the other, the editor lauded Aus's selection as a professor at Luther Theological Seminary:

> Dr. Aus . . . has a scholarly education; but what means more from a Christian point of view, he has also a warm heart for the kingdom of God. We do not at all sympathize with that certain kind of anti-intellectualism often so prevalent in some pietistic circles. . . . The Church needs Christian scholarship just as it needs evangelism and the things for which we as a group of lay people stand. . . . No, friends, it is most emphatically not a matter of indifference to us in whose hands our future pastors are entrusted.[98]

Far from the peaceful coexistence of the two historic emphases of objectivity and subjectivity in faith that Gullixson perhaps envisioned, Harrisville reports in the interview that "a battle ensued" between Preus and Aus. In another place, Harrisville comments that the Preus and Aus conflict was "the most fascinating and raucous period in Luther's

---

96. Norlie, *Norsk Lutherske Menigheter i Amerika*, 1:853.
97. Harrisville, Interview by Thomas E. Jacobson.
98. "An Introduction…with Remarks," February 16, 1939, 52.

history," which required the intervention of Gullixson, telling them to "cease and desist."[99] Apparently, the debate between them spilled over to the student body, with two different camps supportive of each professor. In the interview, Harrisville notes that Preus accused Aus of synergism in that he emphasized human responsibility for faith too strongly. At one point, Preus explained to Harrisville that Aus denied that faith was a gift from God: "I argued with George for two and a half hours over that. He believed that faith was initiated by the believer then later comes the Holy Ghost."[100]

Another recollection of Aus comes from the experience of James Knutson as a student in the early 1950s. Aus served as the faculty advisor for a student group devoted to street evangelism that involved preaching by upperclassmen, singing, and passing out tracts. In this sense, Aus carried forward the banner of Haugeanism through the practice of local evangelism as opposed to the "Christendom model." However, Aus's conflict as a representative of the subjective tendency on the faculty was not confined to his earlier dispute with Preus. In later years, Carl Braaten and Robert Jenson did not consider Aus to be sufficiently sophisticated theologically, critical of him because his doctorate was in Christian education.[101]

Mission and Evangelism Organizations

Even after the 1917 merger, the historic Haugean emphasis on mission continued, and in the case of the mission work in China, for example, Syrdal makes no reference to the 1917 merger having any impact on the work of the missionaries. Naturally, the separate Hauge's Synod mission and the China Mission Society of the UNLC became a united effort after that time, but even prior to that, Scandinavian and Scandinavian-American missionaries cooperated on a practical level. Syrdal notes, "Though the homeland organizations maintained their separate identities distinct [sic], differences were minimized on the foreign field."[102] He went on to describe cooperative efforts of the various Norwegian, Swedish, and

99. Harrisville, "Luther Theological Seminary," 47.
100. Harrisville, Interview by Thomas E. Jacobson.
101. Knutson, Interview by Thomas E. Jacobson.
102. Syrdal, "American Lutheran Mission Work in China," 457. This discussion is based on pages 457 to 465 of Syrdal's work.

Finnish missions, including a joint Chinese translation of Pontoppidan's *Forklaring* of Luther's *Small Catechism* and a joint theological seminary, efforts which they hoped would culminate in the establishment of an independent Lutheran Church of China. Harrisville reports that the Haugeans in the NLCA, especially the laity, contributed heavily to the China mission work, noting as well that the missions in Madagascar, Sudan, and other places "were stocked with *Haugeanerne*."[103]

Though many Haugeans participated in these denominationally sponsored missions of the NLCA and emphasized the work in the foreign field, remaining somewhat aloof from the church politics at home, there is evidence in three cases in particular that the Haugean element of the NLCA expressed reluctance to work with such official missions, choosing instead to pursue an independent course.

The Lutheran Orient Mission Society

Begun in the year 1910 intentionally as an intersynodical mission organization that came to involve many Haugeans, the Lutheran Orient Mission Society continued its existence after the merger of 1917. Writing on behalf of the organization in 1921, N. J. Løhre expressed the vision for the Lutheran Orient Mission by emphasizing its voluntary and intersynodical nature. Curiously, he took care to point out the importance of the intersynodical basis of the organization. The benefit of such an arrangement according to him was that it thereby "avoids the possibility of becoming involved in or of creating synodical conflicts. Such conflicts would seriously interfere with the work of the society both at home and abroad. Complications of this nature are not impossible should the relation become official."[104] It should be considered that this approach was at least partially the result of the desire to avoid the complicated church politics observed in the China Mission. Such an approach is also consistent with the historic emphasis of many of the Haugeans, which was to place priority on the mission itself rather than on synodical sponsorship. However, the fact that Løhre, writing in 1921, only a few years after the 1917 merger, emphasized the independence of the organization indicates a possible lack of trust in the NLCA. After all, with the merger, the number of separate church bodies among Norwegian-American Lutherans

---

103. Harrisville, Interview by Thomas E. Jacobson.
104. Wee, *Inter-Synodical Evangelical Lutheran Orient Mission Society*, 2.

was reduced, and those that remained outside of the NLCA were quite small in number.

The Zion Society for Israel

From its founding in 1878, the Zion Society for Israel, a pan–Norwegian-American Lutheran outreach to Jewish people at home and abroad, was not tied to the work of any particular church body, and the official history of the Society, written by the Haugean C. K. Solberg in 1928, expresses pride in this fact.[105] While the initiative for the founding of the society came from the Conference, it involved many members of Hauge's Synod in its leadership, and the Haugean participation continued after 1917. The Society continued for many years to operate independently, yet in service, of the NLCA and other church bodies. In a letter from the general superintendent of the Society G. A. Peterson to the church council of the ELC in 1947, one can infer his view that the role of the Society as an independent mission endeavor was to lift before the NLCA the importance of Jewish missions. He viewed the independent Society as providing a service to the church body as leaven in the larger batch of dough, and he was encouraged that this work appeared to have borne fruit, with the NLCA eventually placing Jewish missions on its own agenda. He wrote:

> By the resolution passed at the Annual Convention of the Norwegian Lutheran Church of America in 1942, it was decided to place Jewish Missions on "our official missionary program." Was not this the result of a steadily growing conviction that this is where it belongs?[106]

However, Peterson was disturbed that the ELC in 1947 was preparing to abdicate its responsibility for Jewish missions, to which it had committed itself in 1942. Evidently, the ELC was planning on turning over its own Jewish mission program to the NLC. Peterson considered this a mistake, as such a course of action would take ministry further away from the people of the ELC and diminish responsibility for personal evangelism. Peterson urged the ELC church council to remember that "Jewish people

---

105. Solberg, *Zion Society for Israel*, 57. Some Swedish-American Lutherans were also involved in the Society over the years.

106. Letter from G. A. Peterson to Church Council of the ELC, February 1947, Zion Society for Israel File, Luther Seminary Archives, St. Paul, MN.

are in our midst," rather than simply being a distant mission field. He suggested that the work of Jewish missions should be handled by an elected board of the ELC, which would be supported and encouraged by the work of the Zion Society for Israel, thereby preserving responsibility for mission among the people of the ELC. Otherwise, he suggested that the ELC should simply endorse the work of the Zion Society for Israel.

Peterson acknowledged that the NLC had carried out important work in the past, but he considered it wrong for a church body such as the ELC to turn over so much of its responsibility to a large cooperative federation. When the ELC failed to take Peterson's suggestions into consideration the following year, instead proposing to take over the work of the Zion Society for Israel entirely, which would presumably result in the exclusive NLC administration of the work of Jewish missions, Peterson resigned in a sharply worded reply.[107] In this incident involving the Zion Society for Israel, there is no specific mention of Haugeanism. However, given the strong Haugean base of the Society, one can infer that Peterson's convictions were informed by the Haugean desire to serve as leaven in the larger batch of dough of the NLCA/ELC, a conviction the he perceived to be rejected by the action of the ELC leadership.

The World Mission Prayer League

The World Mission Prayer League (WMPL) formally came into existence in 1937, originally known as the South American Mission Prayer League before its expanded focus on the entire world in 1939, though the initial vision for the organization began with Ernest Weinhardt while serving as a missionary in Sudan in 1929. It should be noted, however, that the WMPL in present form considers its roots to be found in the American board of the Santal Mission, mentioned in the previous chapter as an effort of the Haugeans founded in 1891. According to WMPL records, the WMPL merged with the American board of the Santal Mission in 1972, making the Haugean roots of the organization unmistakable. To be sure, a portrait of Hans Nielsen Hauge hangs prominently in the headquarters of the WMPL in Minneapolis.

But the influence of Haugeanism on the WMPL is evident in ways other than simply its roots in the Santal Mission. There does not appear

---

107. Letter from G. A. Peterson to the board of the Zion Society for Israel, [unknown date in 1948], Zion Society for Israel File, Luther Seminary Archives, St. Paul MN.

to be a "smoking gun" that connects the rise of the WMPL to the conflict between the Haugeans and the rest of the NLCA in the 1930s described above, but the appearance of the organization at this time along with its emphases and connections to other movements of the time leads one to conclude that the WMPL is indeed a part of the continuation of the Haugean tradition. Though a "smoking gun" is difficult to find in this situation, it should be noted that the two prominent individuals involved in the development of the WMPL initially sought sponsorship for their desired missionary work to South America from the relevant boards of the NLCA, which was denied. John Carlsen, a Norwegian immigrant and graduate of the LBI who worked with Weinhardt in the early years, approached the NLCA, but was told that they "do not feel ready at this time to begin work in South America."[108] The reasons for the decision of the NLCA are not clear, but the situation reveals that the beginning of the WMPL was rooted in the spiritual energy of the Haugean movement, which persisted despite the lack of support from the officialdom of the NLCA.

Indeed, Mildred Tengbom interpreted the formation and work of the WMPL as a part of the long tradition of independent pietistic movements within various Lutheran church bodies in Europe and North America, beginning with Spener and Francke in Germany and prominently including Hans Nielsen Hauge. She emphasized that what she terms "new life movements" existed in service to the established church bodies yet were often in tension with them. The characteristics that she describes of these "new life movements" are congruent with the principles of Haugeanism already established:

> Criticized the state churches which they considered bogged down in institutionalism, dogmatism and polemics; 2. Called for reform; 3. Emphasized conversion and rebirth; 4. Stressed holy living; 5. Underscored the importance of individual; 6. Preferred a simply liturgy; 7. Emphasized the priesthood of believers, or, in other words, held that all Christians could preach, witness, pray and engage in work to which they believed God had called them; 8. Considered the church to be the born-again believers and felt more unity with those who made this confession than with members of their own denominations who did not.[109]

---

108. Tengbom, *Spirit of God Was Moving*, 26.

109. Tengbom, *Spirit of God Was Moving*, 17–18. The discussion in the following

She also noted the ecumenical spirit of these "new life movements" as well as their affinity for "revivalistic [sic] preaching and Bible study." Noting that many within established churches mocked these pietistic movements as legalistic and that some embraced them, she also described the various ways that the Pietists themselves reacted to rejection. Some reacted defensively and removed themselves from the established church bodies, she acknowledged, and some were focused on their work in such a way as to remain oblivious to criticism. Yet she noted that most participants in these "new life movements" continued to function within the established churches despite the tension that at times existed.

Tengbom made the connection between the "new life movements" of the old countries and similar types of independent ministries in North America in the early part of the twentieth century. She mentioned that most of these movements in North America were rooted in the Scandinavian revival tradition. Hence, they were often, though not exclusively, carried out by Norwegians of the Haugean persuasion. Missionary impulse from these pastors and laity was strong as was a commitment to social ministry, an example of which is the Bethphage Mission of Axtell, Nebraska, which cared for individuals with physical and mental disabilities. She also included the Lutheran Colportage Service, which published religious tracts, the LBI of Minneapolis, and the Lutheran Evangelistic Movement, considered below, as a part of the growing influence of independent ministries. She acknowledged that in addition to the Holy Spirit working "overtime," this movement toward independent ministries functioning within the broader established church produced at times "excesses, sometimes critical, judgmental attitudes and a tendency to set up rules and regulations." Yet on the whole, she argued that those who sought to express themselves through these channels did so in a spirit of love. This bifurcation, taking the forms of both a darker, at times combative, and legalistic expression of faith, as well as a positive message of repentance and faith leading to inner peace is consistent with the history of Haugeanism and the influence of Rosenian piety.

In the history of the early years of the WMPL, Tengbom did not emphasize Haugeanism in particular, which is understandable given that the attitude of many Haugeans, as has been established, was one of emphasizing spiritual life and cooperation rather than particular institutions and titles. In fact, a part of the early vision by Weinhardt for what

---

two paragraphs is derived from pages 17 to 21 of this volume.

became the WMPL was that "God will take out of the Lutheran church a large number of men and women as missionaries to bring his gospel to the great unoccupied areas of the world" and "that these be taken out directly by Him, independently of and without the intervention of ecclesiastical organizations." A part of the vision was an independent society that would "eventually involve all the Lutheran churches in America."[110] This phenomenon of independence yet commitment to Lutheranism is also congruent with historic Haugeanism. Regarding the work of these independent movements of which the WMPL became a part, Tengbom quoted the Haugean C. K. Solberg as articulating the kind of organization that the WMPL sought to be: "Synodical lines were forgotten. One . . . objective was uppermost: How can we best develop, encourage, and practice a scriptural evangelism. . . . Loyalty and cooperation with synod and local congregations were stressed. Separatistic [sic] tendencies away from church or agitations in opposition to the church were warned against."[111]

At the same time, while stressing cooperation with the established church bodies, evidence suggests that the very existence of such independent ministries was an indication of dissatisfaction with the quality of work being carried out by the officialdom of the various synods. A part of the initial vision for the WMPL articulated by Weinhardt while in Sudan was that such an independent mission endeavor would "be a mighty factor in uniting the believers of the various synods of the Lutheran church in one heart, mind and spirit . . . that these things be a source of quickening and blessing to other churches in the homeland as well."[112] One can infer from this criticism of the tendency to emphasize mere institutional unity as well as a desire for Lutherans to experience true unity of faith, manifested in spiritual energy for mission.

This tension between the WMPL and the official work of the synods is also discussed in further detail by Tengbom in the context of the organization's "Prayer House" in Minneapolis, established as its headquarters in 1940. The "Prayer House" served the function of preparing new missionaries for their experiences in other parts of the world. In this communal living environment, it was stated that the conversations often turned to criticism of the ecclesiastical establishments and whether the church bodies truly possessed a desire "to preach the gospel to every

110. Tengbom, *Spirit of God Was Moving*, 9–10.
111. Tengbom, *Spirit of God Was Moving*, 22.
112. Tengbom, *Spirit of God Was Moving*, 10.

person."[113] Furthermore, WMPL members questioned the priorities of the leadership of the various synods, the NLCA prominent among them, concerning the construction of elaborate church buildings and the unnecessary duplication of efforts in the areas of broadcasting and publication. For the WMPL, such money would have been better spent on world mission to those who had never heard the gospel. The criticism continued concerning the various foreign missions of the established church bodies. The WMPL, perhaps reflecting the Haugean focus on assimilation for the sake of proclamation, looked down upon these synodical missions for "building walled-in, secluded missionary compounds where missionaries, after working hours (credit was given them for being hard workers and sincere), would relax comfortably, enjoying a standard of living many, many times higher than that of those to whom they ministered." Hence, a complex relationship existed between the WMPL and the NLCA from the beginning, which carried over to TALC after the merger of 1960. David Preus, who served as president of TALC beginning in 1973, makes the following comment:

> I always treasured, thought it was an important part of my ministry in the office of president, to encourage these spontaneous groups that were not a part of the official church's life, so Lutheran Youth Encounter, and stuff like that. I tried to encourage it. Or the World Mission Prayer League. We made sure we stayed in good standing with them. Sometimes I have the feeling they maybe didn't quite feel the same way about us but liked to have our money nonetheless.[114]

One final indicator of the tension that existed between the Haugean tradition and the official ecclesiastical establishment can be observed regarding the fate of the Santal Mission and the decision of that organization to merge with the WMPL in 1972. In 1970, discussions were held between the leadership of the Santal Mission and the board of world missions of TALC concerning the possibility of incorporating the work of the Santal Mission into the official denominational mission program, thereby ending the independent existence of the Santal Mission. A complete collection of correspondence between the various entities involved is not available, but the fragments that exist suggest that some concern was raised about whether TALC would faithfully represent the heritage of

113. Tengbom, *Spirit of God Was Moving*, 57. Discussion in this paragraph is derived from page 57 of this volume.

114. David Preus, Interview by Thomas E. Jacobson.

the Santal Mission and its principles. A document from late in 1970 from the board of the Santal Mission outlined their expectations of the board of world missions of TALC. In addition to pointing out that TALC would assume the outstanding financial responsibilities of the Santal Mission, they were clear to point out that they expected the board of world missions to represent faithfully the missionary zeal of the Santal Mission: "We act in the confidence that DWM-ALC has the missionary cause close to its heart."[115] The Santal Mission continued to discuss the benefits and drawbacks of such a merger into the following year, continuing to insist that the name of the Santal Mission be used by TALC in its dealings with the Santal people of India and Pakistan.[116] It is not clear what led to the dissolution of the proposed arrangement between the Santal Mission and TALC, but the fact that the Santal Mission chose in the end to merge with the WMPL instead of TALC leads one to consider the possibility that the Haugean roots of the Santal Mission played a role in the desire to remain outside the control of the denominational authorities.

The Lutheran Evangelistic Movement

The Lutheran Evangelistic Movement (LEM), yet another important part of the overall picture of the enduring legacy of Haugeanism in American Lutheranism, emerged in the 1930s amidst the complex web of organizations and individuals influenced by that tradition. Though it came to include participants from various synods, including some outside of the Norwegian-American tradition, in the earlier years much of the energy behind the development of the LEM came from those nurtured by Hauge's Synod.

It has been suggested that the LEM represented a "reappearance of pietism" in American Lutheranism.[117] This suggests that the influence of Pietism, broadly understood, was at some point absent from the American Lutheran tradition, an assertion that is questionable. Elsewhere in her thesis, Louise Burton uses the word "revival" to describe the work of the LEM, which is more appropriate; as has been observed, historic Pietism, especially as expressed by Haugeanism, influenced the Norwegian-American environment in different and significant ways. It is true,

---

115. "Proposed Conditions from Santal Side."
116. "Proposal for Merger of the Santal Mission."
117. Burton, "Lutheran Evangelistic Movement," 1.

of course, as has been observed in many cases, that significant friction existed between the Haugeans and others throughout the years, both before and after 1917, and that the Haugeans often felt that their tradition was in danger of being lost, making the LEM one example of a "revival" of Haugean emphases. In addition to being an expression of the historic Haugean desire to evangelize on a local level, the origin of the LEM can at least partially be understood in light of that friction between Haugean emphases and the officialdom of the NLCA.

Any discussion of the LEM needs to take into consideration the background of the practice of preaching evangelism in the NLCA/ELC. In a 1963 observation, reflecting on the history of evangelism in the NLCA/ELC after that body ended its existence and became a part of TALC in 1960, Fevold pointed out that the practice of evangelism had a place in all three predecessor bodies of the NLCA. Yet he also noted that there existed different opinions concerning the manner in which evangelistic work should be carried out, with the Norwegian Synod emphasizing the role of the parish pastor as an evangelist on the one hand and Hauge's Synod and much of the UNLC encouraging an evangelistic program carried out by laity as well as pastors on the other.[118] The "paper pastors" or "emissaries" in Hauge's Synod discussed in the previous chapter were in reality lay preaching evangelists, and the formation of the HLIMF has already been attributed at least partially to the perceived devaluing of the practice of lay preaching and evangelism in the NLCA.

To be sure, the NLCA did sponsor its own program of preaching evangelism, administered under the auspices of the board of home mission. In fact, the early influence of the Hauge's Synod tradition in the NLCA is shown through this initiative, as is the continued tension between the different emphases of the predecessor bodies. Shortly after the merger, John Johnson Breidablikk, a pastor of Hauge's Synod who had been chosen as chief evangelist of Hauge's Synod in 1917, was named as the synodical evangelist of the NLCA at the time of the merger. Yet Fevold's remarks indicate that this attempt to honor the tradition of Hauge's Synod did not erase the tension. The board of home mission acknowledged the following year that Breidablikk's appointment was controversial among some. Further evidence of this tension between the Haugeans and others is the fact that the Iowa District of the NLCA, apparently

---

118. Fevold, *History of Evangelism in the Evangelical Lutheran Church*, 2. This discussion of evangelism in the NLCA in this and the following two paragraphs is derived from pages 2 to 14 in this volume.

rejecting the synodical evangelism program, appointed its own evangelist from the Norwegian Synod tradition. Perhaps a testimony to the taxing work of a traveling evangelist, Breidablikk resigned after a short time, being replaced by another Haugean, H. N. Rønning, in 1921.

This tension that existed between the more churchly emphasis of the Norwegian Synod and the more spontaneous and lay-oriented emphasis of Hauge's Synod continued in the early years of the NLCA, with J. N. Kildahl seeking to strike a balance and avoid the kind of rivalry between pastors and evangelists articulated by Bruce in his 1916 observation. When describing the life of the NLCA in the earlier years, Nelson points to this evangelism program of the NLCA as a "strong indication that the Haugean emphasis on 'living Christianity' and 'edifying meetings' was a continuing emphasis in the new church."[119] However, as already discussed, Nelson sought to paint the merger of 1917 in a positive light and therefore downplayed continuing friction in the NLCA. The differences in emphasis between clerical and lay evangelism were a continuing source of tension, according to Fevold, and some in the NLCA regarded the entire focus on evangelism in congregations "with some suspicion and with reservations" regarding the "emotionalism" that they associated with much of American Protestantism. One of the evangelists employed by the board of home mission was Enoch L. Scotvold, a Haugean lay preacher who began his work with the NLCA in 1923 due to an increase in congregational requests for such preachers. Previously, he had served in a similar capacity with the HLIMF,[120] and it should therefore be considered that his appointment by the NLCA was a strategic move intended to appeal to the Haugean element of the organization and discourage separatist activities. Indeed, there is reason to believe that the officialdom of the NLCA sought to give at least token acknowledgment to the Haugean element fairly late into the life of the organization. In 1931, the faculty of Luther Theological Seminary voted to welcome a group of speakers to the seminary, all of whom were Haugeans and some of considerable note, to present a series of speeches on topics reflecting Haugean piety. Furthermore, the program was proposed by the Haugean C. K. Solberg. At least three of these speakers were connected to evangelism ministries, either officially recognized by the NLCA or independent. However, the

---

119. Nelson, *Lutheran Church*, 2:260.
120. Gisselquist, *Called to Preach*, 103.

minutes suggest that Solberg's proposal was not accepted uncritically and that the faculty felt the need to monitor the event:

> After considerable discussion it was voted that the themes and speakers be approved with the reconsideration that the program be carried out during the week set apart as Consecration Week under the joint auspices of the Faculty and the Student Body, the President of the Seminary presiding.[121]

Fevold notes that in 1932 the Great Depression necessitated the downscaling of the NLCA evangelism program, reducing the staff of evangelists from four to two. Jonathan D. Anderson, historian of the LEM, suggests that this situation might have provided impetus for Scotvold, though still connected with the NLCA evangelism program, to begin work toward the development of an independent, intersynodical evangelism program.[122] The move toward the widespread use of English facilitated such ecumenical endeavors, and many Haugeans in the NLCA took advantage of the new situation to find kindred spirits from other traditions. Anderson notes that Scotvold gathered around him in the autumn of 1936 a group of like-minded evangelists representing four different church bodies: John Carlsen, also a Haugean from the NLCA; Jens Halvorson of the Lutheran Free Church; Joseph Stump of the ULCA; and Evald Conrad of the Swedish Augustana Synod. Together, they planned an evangelism conference to be held in January of 1937 at Conrad's congregation, Trinity Lutheran Church of Minneapolis. This event became an annual tradition known as the Midwinter Evangelistic Conference of what became known as the Lutheran Inter-Synodical Evangelistic Committee. In 1945, this organization changed its name to the LEM. In the summer, the LEM held similar evangelism gatherings known as Deeper Life Conferences on Medicine Lake near Minneapolis. Occasionally, the LEM held its gatherings in other locations. Reflecting the Haugean base of the organization, a 1938 summer gathering was held in Eagle Grove, Iowa, located in one of the historic strongholds of Hauge's Synod.

---

121. Luther Theological Seminary Faculty Minutes, October 14, 1931, Luther Seminary Archives, St. Paul, MN. The proposed speakers were Dr. Arthur Rholl of RWS; Pastors H. N. Rønning, Odd Gornitzka, and Alfred B. Anderson; and layperson E. L. Scotvold. The topics of their lectures were "Lay Activity in the Light of History," "Personal Soul Winning," "What Is Meant by Lay Activity," "The Priesthood of Believers," and "Scriptural Evangelism."

122. Anderson, *Our Fathers Saw His Mighty Works*, 29. Information in this paragraph is derived from pages 29 to 30 of this volume.

With the appearance of the LEM, the field of evangelism related to the life of the NLCA became even more complicated. As already noted, the HLIMF, which was a network of independent so-called "inner mission societies" that functioned within the NLCA, carried out its own work of preaching evangelism, which ran parallel to the official evangelism program of the NLCA, and Enoch Scotvold served in that organization before joining the NLCA program in 1923. Evidence of the tension between the official and unofficial programs is found in the 1920 evangelism policy of the NLCA, which suggests awareness of alternative activities perceived as a threat to its work:

> The men (either pastors or laymen) designated to be evangelists shall have the special gifts required for this work, in addition to such self-evident qualifications as evidence of Christian character, knowledge of the Bible, loyalty to the confessions, and loyalty to the synod, its principles and practice.[123]

In light of the presence of the HLIMF throughout the years as a Haugean alternative to the official program, one wonders about the reasons behind the emergence of the LEM. It should be considered that the existence of the two organizations is a reflection of the bifurcation discussed earlier between a darker and more legalistic form of Haugeanism and the "sweeter," more evangelically oriented Haugeanism colored by Rosenian influence. Burton suggests that though the work of the HLIMF was largely congruent with what became the LEM, the HLIMF was deeply rooted in its Norwegian background and had been slow to switch to English, therefore remaining isolated from the rest of American Lutheranism. This hesitance to embrace English language work among some Haugeans was established in the previous chapter. In fact, the English language publication *Morning Glory* was first printed in 1926, and in the six years prior to that, the sole publication of the HLIMF was the Norwegian language *Indremissionsvenner*. Furthermore, the HLIMF was a layperson's organization, which was often critical of the clergy and viewed with suspicion by them. As an organization, it was viewed by many as legalistic.[124]

All these factors contributed to the desire of some to create a new, intentionally intersynodical organization for evangelism, even though there was crossover in terms of personnel between the two as well as

---

123. Fevold, *History of Evangelism in the Evangelical Lutheran Church*, 5.

124. Burton, "Lutheran Evangelistic Movement," 30. *Indremissionsvenner* is translated as "Inner Mission Friends."

with the official NLCA program. Scotvold was involved in the HLIMF in the early years of its existence, was an official evangelist of the NLCA, and was a leading personality in the formation of the LEM. J. O. Gisselquist, during his pastoral work in Centerville, South Dakota, was influenced by Scotvold's work with the HLIMF and was extended a call to serve as an evangelist by that organization in 1937. At the same time, he was associated with the LEM from the beginning and was eventually offered a call as an evangelist with the LEM in 1945.[125] Through it all, he continued to function as a pastor of the NLCA, having apparently favored the merger of 1917 at the time. He was, however, one of the individuals who went on record as protesting the action of the NLCA convention of 1932 to close RWS. Though there is no "smoking gun" connecting Gisselquist's involvement in the HLIMF and the LEM to a sense of disenfranchisement among the Haugeans as a result of the RWS incident, it has been established that Gisselquist, reflecting his Haugean background, placed little emphasis on synodical structures during his ministry, which set him apart from most pastors of the NLCA.[126] It is therefore reasonable to assume that Gisselquist felt a sense of spiritual homelessness in the NLCA after the closure of RWS and that participation first in the HLIMF and later in the LEM filled a void left after RWS became defunct. Indeed, Fevold notes that despite the connection of many in the LEM to the NLCA and the impact of that organization in stimulating interest in evangelism within that church body, a certain tension existed between the two organizations, with the LEM serving as a type of haven for those who had "not been entirely satisfied with the type of evangelism found in the ELC."[127]

The Haugean roots of the LEM can be seen in its emphasis on preaching evangelism, which was directed toward not only those outside the church but also, and perhaps primarily, at those within the established churches. Though American Haugeans were active in foreign mission work to those from outside the Christian fold, they also continued the historic Haugean concern for truly converted membership within their own organization of the NLCA, reflecting the subjective focus of their tradition. Scotvold himself was an example of someone who had been a church member for a number of years yet did not consider himself to be

---

125. Gisselquist, *Called to Preach*, 103.
126. Gisselquist, *Called to Preach*, 60.
127. Fevold, *History of Evangelism in the Evangelical Lutheran Church*, 12.

a true Christian until he had experienced conversion.[128] Nominal church membership and mere participation in the sacraments was inadequate, and the work of LEM sought to remedy the situation in the NLCA and other synods. This emphasis was central to the content of the LEM tent revival meetings, where Joseph Stump of the ULCA advertised himself as "eleven years a Lutheran pastor and unconverted." Stump reportedly threatened his audience with damnation if they were unable to articulate a precise moment of conversion, an emphasis that Harrisville describes as "Haugeanism gone rancid."[129]

Yet the focus of the LEM was not always as dark and confrontational as the content of Stump's preaching. Fevold reports that C. K. Solberg, who also participated in the LEM, articulated the purpose of the LEM evangelism conferences in the following way:

> To assemble those "who are interested in Biblical and practical evangelism, for the purpose of discussing the various phases of evangelistic activity, its need and importance in bringing about, under the guidance of the Holy Spirit, a spiritual awakening and a more fruitful spiritual life and service."[130]

The concern for grounding these evangelism conferences in the Lutheran theological tradition, while maintaining the Haugean focus on awakening and conversion, is shown by the presence of M. O. Wee at the first such event in 1937. Wee articulated the traditional Lutheran theme of preaching the Word of God as law and gospel, arguing that people must first be awakened by the law before being comforted by the gospel. A discussion ensued that drew on the experiences of Haugean missionaries in China with the conclusion that both those outside the Christian world and those within it share the need to be convicted and awakened by the law of God.[131]

In spite of the care taken by some within the LEM to carry out its work within the framework of Lutheran theology, evidence suggests that its work was not received positively by the NLCA leadership and its evangelism committee. The 1936 report of this committee contained a resolution to the annual convention of the NLCA that sought to promote the official evangelism program of the church body. Acknowledging the

---

128. Anderson, *Our Fathers Saw His Mighty Works*, 31.
129. Harrisville, Interview by Thomas E. Jacobson.
130. Fevold, *History of Evangelism in the Evangelical Lutheran Church*, 11.
131. Anderson, *Our Fathers Saw His Mighty Works*, 36–37.

desire of many congregations to participate in evangelistic meetings, the resolution called upon the NLCA to support its own evangelists and called upon the district presidents to hold "properly planned and conducted Spiritual Life Conferences." The resolution did not directly name the LEM or the HLIMF, but reference is made to competing evangelistic efforts among the people of the NLCA that were not to be trusted, lamenting the fact that the work of evangelism in the church body was not "unified":

> Believing that the Gospel of Jesus Christ, rightly preached and taught, is the only means of saving souls, and, believing that there is an increasing need and desire in our congregations for the type of evangelism afforded by properly planned and conducted Spiritual Life Conferences; and, believing that the need for a unified program of evangelism with a true Evangelical Lutheran stamp is made more urgent by the fact that in some congregations of our Church there is an increasing tendency on the part of some members to take part in certain evangelistic movements originating outside of our Church and which are not truly Lutheran in spirit . . .[132]

The reference to plural movements indicates that the resolution likely referred to the earlier work of the HLIMF as well as the developing plan for the LEM that same year. There is no specific discussion in the resolution concerning the content of these movements that were viewed as theologically objectionable. Nevertheless, this resolution is further evidence of the existence of friction between the NLCA leadership and the Haugean element of the church body.

The work of the LEM continued through the following decades, through evangelism, spiritual life conferences, and youth work, continually emphasizing the historic Haugean emphasis on repentance, personal faith, and corresponding peace with God. The work of the LEM was, according to Anderson, especially powerful in the areas of northwestern Minnesota, south central Minnesota, and north central Iowa,[133] all of which, as has been established, were strongholds of Haugeanism. It is understandable that a movement devoted to spiritual awakening within the established church bodies would find good reception in those areas accustomed to such an emphasis. As time went on, the LEM continued to experience some friction with church leadership concerning the

132. NLCA, *1936 Annual Report*, 45.
133. Anderson, *Our Fathers Saw His Mighty Works*, 192–94.

perceived "liberalism" that led to a devaluing of repentance and living faith. One LEM evangelist who served in the 1970s describes the difficulty of his work in ministering to those raised in Lutheran congregations without coming to a true faith commitment. Notably, he attributes much of the difficulty to clergy who claimed to have been "liberated" from "Fundamentalism" while studying in seminary. Such pastors had little time for the evangelism work of the LEM.[134] He also expresses surprise at the number of LEM supporters he encountered during his ministry that had forsaken their Lutheran heritage altogether, joining Assemblies of God, Baptist, and Evangelical Free congregations out of dissatisfaction with the spiritual life in the "mainstream" Lutheran bodies. Also suspect in LEM circles was the strong focus on merger that they perceived in the ELC in the 1950s. *Evangelize*, the publication of the LEM, lamented the focus on institutional merger, which threatened to "stifle and smother spiritual life and expression," hindering "the free and spontaneous movements inspired by the Holy Spirit."[135]

The LEM reflected its Haugean heritage not only through its work of evangelical revival and insistence on personal conversion but also through its insistence on working within the established church bodies, especially the NLCA. Though the relationship between the LEM and the NLCA was characterized by suspicion on both sides, the LEM, true to the heritage of Norwegian Haugeanism, saw itself as providing an important supplement to the church establishment, working within the organization as spiritual leaven. Evangelist Steven Lombardo commented that "the ministry of evangelistic preaching was always to supplement the evangelistic ministry of the local congregation. It was not to replace it."[136] Yet at times the source of friction was realization on the part of the traveling evangelists that congregational evangelism was in fact nonexistent. In a 1964 sermon printed in *Evangelize*, originally preached at the Eastern LEM Midwinter Conference that year, Herbert Franz spoke critically of the phenomenon of pervasive cultural Christianity, arguing that people do not find salvation through morality or participation in church activities. Rather, they despair of themselves as they recognize their sinful state, repent, and trust in the Savior for redemption. He contrasts "dead faith," which does not involve true repentance, with "living faith," which involves living an obedient life, singing "a new song, the song of

134. Gray, *Rise Up and Build*, 14.
135. Anderson, *Our Fathers Saw His Mighty Works*, 208.
136. Gray, *Rise Up and Build*, 15.

the redeemed."[137] Hence, morality was understood not as an end in itself, but as an outgrowth of a living faith, an understanding that is consistent with Haugeanism, especially as colored by Rosenian emphases. However, possibly reflecting the lack of theological precision of the Haugean movement, Franz's sermon can be said to contain some synergism with its emphasis on the human role in confession of sin. Indeed, the title of the sermon is "Will You Come?" The content of this sermon, with its exhortation to repentance and faith, can be said to be typical of evangelistic sermons of the LEM, which helps explain in part the resistance to the movement from early on in parts of the NLCA.

Leadership within the NLCA

Another important part of evaluating the continuation of the Haugean tradition after 1917 is to observe the presence of former Hauge's Synod members in the leadership of the NLCA. Given that Hauge's Synod contributed around 8 percent of the membership of the NLCA at the time of the merger, it is understandable that its representation in the leadership of the new church body would not be equal to that of the Norwegian Synod and the UNLC. Initially, effort appears to have been made to ensure that representatives of the three merging bodies occupied positions of leadership in the NLCA. N. J. Løhre was elected as secretary of the whole NLCA from the beginning, a position he continued to hold until 1933. Naturally, G. M. Bruce and M. O. Wee exercised some authority in the church body through their role as seminary professors, though their work was at times fraught with difficulty. At the outset, two district presidents, C. J. Eastvold and G. O. Paulsrud, from southern Minnesota and South Dakota, respectively, were members of Hauge's Synod.[138] All of the rest were from the Norwegian Synod and the UNLC. Nevertheless, one observes over time a decrease in the representation from the former Hauge's Synod in official leadership positions. By 1926, none of the district presidents were former members of Hauge's Synod, though

---

137. Gray, *Rise Up and Build*, 105.

138. Malmin, *Who's Who among Pastors*, 121. This volume contains information on every Norwegian-American Lutheran pastor from the years stated, and the particular synodical affiliation of the district presidents is found in their respective listings. For example, the listing for C. J. Eastvold is found on page 121. Additionally, since the first and middle names of many clergy are often abbreviated, this resource has been used throughout the writing of this thesis to discover their full names.

one of the vice presidents, A. M. Mannes of Volga, South Dakota, was a former member of Hauge's Synod.[139] That same year, G. M. Bruce began serving as the second vice president of the NLCA, a position he held until the late 1940s.[140] After 1926, lists of district officers demonstrate no move toward greater inclusion of former members of Hauge's Synod, though Seth Clarence Eastvold, son of Haugean C. J. Eastvold, occupied the office of vice president of the South Dakota District. In 1948, the same S. C. Eastvold, who was at the time serving as president of Pacific Lutheran College in Tacoma, Washington, began serving as first vice president of the ELC, holding the position until the end of the organization in 1960. Nevertheless, among those with living memory of the life of the ELC, the Haugeans were not strongly represented among the significant leadership, with S. C. Eastvold being a notable exception.[141] David Preus also mentions Bruce as "kind of a significant figure" and notes the presence of S. C. Eastvold, but otherwise draws a blank when asked about Haugean leadership in the NLCA.[142] This state of affairs can perhaps be attributed both to a lack of interest among the Haugeans for occupying administrative roles and lack of interest among the people of the NLCA for electing them.

Evidence exists that the perceived lack of Haugean representation in the NLCA/ELC weighed on the minds of at least some members of the church body. When the presidency of J. A. Aasgaard neared its end in 1954, the question of who would be elected to occupy that office generated much discussion. Writing to G. M. Bruce for input, Johannes Hoifjeld, pastor of First Lutheran Church in Orland, California expressed his desire that the Haugeans finally have an opportunity to hold the presidency of the NLCA. Noting that he experienced joy as a newly ordained pastor when the union of 1917 was consummated, he expressed disappointment at the negative attitudes he encountered when suggesting a Haugean for the office. Hoifjeld himself did not come from the Hauge's Synod tradition, but he felt that fairness dictated that a Haugean should be the next president:

---

139. NLCA, *1926 Annual Report*, 66.

140. The office of second vice president was subordinate to that of the president and first vice president. The second vice president would represent the office of the president in places where the president or first vice president needed to be absent. Although not an insignificant office, it did not carry the same prestige as the higher offices.

141. Harrisville, Interview by Thomas E. Jacobson.

142. David Preus, Interview by Thomas E. Jacobson.

> We elected a Norwegian Synod man our president, namely Dr. H. G. Stub. If I am correct, it was then understood that chairmanship should be rotated. This was done when Stub was to be succeeded as Dr. J. A. Aasgaard was one of the "United". [sic] Then we heard that the "Hauge" was to have the next turn. This was also done as far as the General Secretary was concerned, namely Lohre [sic], Bergsaker, and now Hove. Dr. Ylvisaker was so determined about the latter that two years ago he nominated Hove from the floor although we had at least four or five candidates before. The convention seemed to understand the fairness of the demand.[143]

Hoifjeld continues in his letter by noting his perception that things had changed in the ELC regarding this understanding of rotation of office between the three merging bodies:

> However, it seems to have taken a turn now in favor of "United" and "Synod" men. Not a single "Hauge" man has been mentioned to us out here on the Coast. How come? When I have mentioned Dr. Morris Wee as a possible, probable, and potential presidential candidate so many peculiar, unfair, and illogical reasons are presented. Even more eyebrows are lifted and heads shuck [sic] when I mention Dr. Seth Eastvold. I am not of the former "Hauge's Synod" as you possibly know, but I believe in being fair and give all a chance.[144]

He concludes the letter by lavishing praise on Morris Wee, the son of M. O. Wee, as an ideal candidate, yet laments that "I cannot do a thing to get him nominated." He suggests that Morris Wee is the person God intended to serve in the office of president but that some in the NLCA, out of determination to keep a Haugean out of the office, are not willing to "let the Lord actually act free-handedly in the matter."

In response to Hoifjeld, Bruce curiously refutes the assumption that the office of president was to be rotated in such a manner. In attempting to move the question of the presidential election away from concerns of the past synodical affiliation of the candidates, Bruce suggests in his response that the concern raised by Hoifjeld was not isolated:

> We are very fortunate in our Church at the present time to have a number of very capable and acceptable men for that position

---

143. Personal letter from Johannes Hoifjeld to G. M. Bruce on May 14, 1954, G. M. Bruce File, Luther Seminary Archives, St. Paul, MN.

144. Personal letter from Johannes Hoifjeld to G. M. Bruce on May 14, 1954.

available, regardless of past synodical backgrounds. In my opinion, that ever bobbing up question of where is he from synodically? [sic] is quite unimportant at this time, for no matter who is elected, he will be a product of the post-union theological seminary. To me the personal qualifications, spiritual and administrative, are of prime importance, and I trust the Holy Spirit will be permitted to guide the election of the right man for this position.[145]

Bruce then provides his perspective on the history of nominations and elections in the NLCA. Though attempting to downplay the factionalism in the early years of the NLCA, his response indicates that there was indeed some bias against the Haugeans early on related to the office of president of the southern Minnesota district:

> You intimate that there was some understanding at the very outset that the principal offices should rotate among the men of the different bodies that merged in 1917, and that, accordingly, the next president should be chosen from among those whose backgrounds rooted in the former Hauge's Synod. There was no such understanding at the time of the merger. We, as a Joint Union Committee, took pains to provide for an equitable distribution of the offices among men belonging to the several bodies at the first election, and our recommendations were followed by the merging convention. There was only one attempt made to upset that program, and that attempt was made by the friends in the U. C. of President T. H. Dahl, who tried to get him in as president of the Southern Minnesota District instead of Pastor C. J. Eastvold, but that plot failed.[146]

It is possible that Bruce, having retired by that point, nevertheless felt the need, possibly the result of his extensive involvement in the church life of the NLCA/ELC, to downplay continued tribalism and hard feelings on the part of the Hauge's Synod tradition. However, the correspondence between him and Hoifjeld indicates that the union envisioned by H. G. Stub in 1923 was not fully realized as of 1954:

> As we look back upon developments in our Church body during these six years, we are constrained with gratitude to recognize that the Lord hath done great things for us, and that our

---

145. Personal letter from G. M. Bruce to Johannes Hoifjeld on May 19, 1954, G. M. Bruce File, Luther Seminary Archives, St. Paul, MN.

146. Personal letter from G. M. Bruce to Johannes Hoifjeld on May 19, 1954.

unified church has prospered marvelously and produced a great and blessed fruitage. . . . The three Church bodies no longer make war upon one another. . . . The great purpose for which we labor, the common means and methods which we use to attain this purpose, are a guarantee that we shall amalgamate more and more in our views and that the old synodical lines will ultimately disappear, with the result that the consciousness of being one great unified church body, will overcome all tendencies to hold fast to synodical peculiarities which may not in every instance be of a beneficial character.[147]

In the end, S. C. Eastvold was a nominee for the office of president of the ELC. According to Harrisville, he "ran" for the office against Fredrik A. Schiotz, whose roots were in the UNLC. When Schiotz was elected on the second ballot in absentia in June of 1954, he reported to the Minneapolis convention where he was greeted and congratulated by S. C. Eastvold and Lawrence M. Stavig, both of whom had been nominees.[148]

Later References and Apologetics for Haugeanism

In the later decades of the NLCA, references to Haugeanism in its official publication of the *Lutheran Herald* are few. As many of the Haugeans remained aloof from the official life of the NLCA and expressed their convictions through independent initiatives and mission organizations, this can perhaps be expected. Nevertheless, in addition to Haugean-related periodicals such as *Morning Glory*, Haugeanism makes an appearance in a few places in these later decades in the official periodical and in books. These appearances are important to note for what they reveal about Haugean life and self-understanding in the later decades of the NLCA. It is possible to understand these appearances as apologies for the Haugean tradition, even if they differ in character. Some apologies are intended to create greater understanding of the tradition, whereas some apologies are intended for internal edification among Haugeans.

It has already been observed that M. O. Wee attempted to provide apologies for Haugeanism within the NLCA in the early years of the organization. As time went on, there clearly was continued consciousness of the different traditions that originally formed the NLCA, and "the old synodical lines" did not "ultimately disappear" as Stub had hoped for in

147. NLCA, "Report of the General President."
148. Schiotz, *One Man's Story*, 130.

1923. As well, one also notes an attempt to downplay continued tribalism within the NLCA/ELC and even offer implicit critiques of Haugeanism, and this is also discussed.

In Periodicals

In 1932, president of the NLCA J. A. Aasgaard, whose roots were in the UNLC, was called upon to deliver an address at Luther Theological Seminary. The occasion was the presentation of a bust of Hans Nielsen Hauge by the family of Ole N. Hendrickson in his memory, which remains in the Luther Seminary library to this day. It is not clear if the Hendrickson family's roots were in Hauge's Synod, but the choice of the gift coupled with its timing is curious. With 1932 witnessing the closing of RWS, it should be considered that one motivation for the choice of gift was to perpetuate the memory of Haugeanism itself. Yet Aasgaard, possibly out of a desire to minimize discontent, made no reference to the controversy surrounding RWS and its impact on the Haugean element of the NLCA. Instead, he chose to provide a brief biographical sketch of Hauge that emphasized his positive contributions and pan-Norwegian influence: "Our Norwegian Lutheran synods all have had as their backgrounds the results of Hauge's labors for that strength of confession and uniformity in belief of God's Word which have been stressed among us."[149]

The address expresses appreciation for Hauge and emphasizes his nonseparatist attitude toward the Church of Norway as well as its rites and ceremonies. Again, no reference is made to former members of Hauge's Synod, but one can infer from some of Aasgaard's emphases that he perhaps sought to address a potentially divisive situation regarding the Haugean element of the NLCA. His statement that Hauge did not advocate for changing policy, customs, ceremonies, and rites of the church does not take into consideration the changed situation of Haugeanism as it expressed itself in North America. His address also emphasizes Hauge's lack of emotionalism and sensationalism, pointing out his commitment to the Lutheran confessions. Also of significance is Aasgaard's comment concerning the past use of Hauge's legacy to advocate for anticlericalism:

> To me, the great thing about Hauge's contribution was not the fact that he was a layman. Some have stressed this so that it has been construed that it was doubtful whether the message could

---

149. Aasgaard, "Hans Nielsen Hauge," 1257.

be presented with the same fervor, earnestness and sincerity by those who were theologically trained. Hauge never entertained this notion. Wherever he met clergy who preached the truth or taught the truth, he encouraged the people to support them and to hear them gladly. The great thing about Hauge was neither his humble origin, nor lack of theological training, but the message that he proclaimed and his own attitude toward that message, in a day when it meant suffering, self-denial and shame to keep the faith.[150]

Aasgaard's role as NLCA president required him to hold together different and at times competing visions in the church body. He was no doubt sincere in his appreciative words about Hauge, which would undoubtedly have been encouraging to the Haugeans. Yet implicit in some of his comments, especially in light of the RWS controversy that same year, is a critique of some of the perceived emphases associated with parts of the Haugean tradition: devaluing of distinctly Lutheran theology, anti-clericalism, and overemphasis on emotionalism in evangelistic preaching. Aasgaard's critique of emotionalism in his address about Hauge was likely a criticism of tendencies he encountered among some Haugeans. This can be demonstrated by the fact that the criticism of emotionalism in evangelism, presumably directed at the independent evangelism ministries influenced by Haugeanism operating parallel to the official program of the ELC, can be found in later years as well. Selmer A. Berge's *Evangelism in the Congregation*, a publication from the official evangelism program of the NLCA, contains a similar criticism: "Evangelism is not bare emotionalism. It is not a superficial arousing of the inner emotional life by means that are artificial and tricky, so that a subject becomes the plaything of a strong leader."[151]

In the early 1940s, there appears to have been some confusion over when the NLCA would celebrate its centennial. Of course, the NLCA did not officially begin until 1917, but members of the NLCA understood themselves as continuing the earlier history of Norwegian-American Lutheranism. Therefore, the year of the centennial celebration depended on when the predecessor bodies of the NLCA were understood to have been founded. Confusion about this matter can be observed in the *Lutheran Herald* as early as 1914, when the comment was made that "the Synod of the Norwegian Evangelical Lutheran Church in America, commonly

---

150. Aasgaard, "Hans Nielsen Hauge," 1258.
151. Berge, *Evangelism in the Congregation*, 7.

called the Norwegian Synod, is the oldest such organization among the Norwegians in the United States,"[152] having been formed in 1853. As established in the second chapter, however, what became known as Hauge's Synod was founded by Eielsen in 1846 as a loosely organized church body. With the reorganization of 1876, Hauge's Synod became the legal successor to the original organization. Eielsen's small splinter group was therefore actually a new schismatic group. Accordingly, some references in the *Lutheran Herald* assume that the true centennial of the NLCA was to be recognized in the year 1946. In 1942, Knut Olafson Lundeberg, the pioneer of the CLBA in 1900 who returned to the UNLC in 1911, having apparently softened his views on the qualifications for church membership, wrote in the *Lutheran Herald* about the tradition of Haugeanism. The article is presented in such a way as to assume that readers are largely unfamiliar with Haugeanism, perhaps only being acquainted with a negative caricature of the movement. The tone of the article is not defensive, yet it does emphasize that Haugeanism is congruent with the Lutheran confessional tradition, perhaps in reaction to accusations to the contrary. It also points out that Haugeanism in Norway was a reaction against both "dead orthodoxy" as well as Rationalism, possibly an attempt to expand the understanding of Haugeanism for readers accustomed only to a negative portrayal. Lundeberg was obviously confused about the exact year of the founding of Hauge's Synod, but he did tie the beginning of the NLCA to the work of Eielsen in the 1840s: "In preparing for the centennial celebration of our church in 1943, we turn our eyes to the past to trace its development from the early beginnings."[153]

When the year 1946 arrived, another prominent Haugean felt the need to remind the entire ELC of its Haugean roots. N. N. Rønning pointed out in the *Lutheran Herald* that Hauge's Synod held the honor of the oldest Norwegian American Lutheran church body:

> When we write the history of our own church body, we must go back to the year 1846, for the Eielsen Synod which was then organized revised its constitution and adopted the name, the Hauge Norwegian Evangelical Synod in America [sic] in 1875, and the Hauge Synod together with the Norwegian Synod and the United Norwegian Lutheran Church organized the Norwegian Lutheran Church in America in 1917.[154]

152. "The Union and the Synod," 315.
153. K. O. Lundeberg, "Haugeanism in Norway."
154. N. N. Rønning, "Our First Church Body."

Like Lundeberg's article, Rønning's tone is not defensive, yet he does go to great pains to emphasize that Eielsen's Synod, though lacking in organization, was committed to Lutheranism as expressed in the *Augsburg Confession*. In light of other evidence presented in this chapter regarding the status of Haugeanism, these brief articles by Lundeberg and Rønning are likely indicative of widespread devaluing of the Haugean tradition in the NLCA/ELC as a whole and can therefore be understood as small attempts at providing a positive apology for Haugeanism.

Yet the issue of when to understand properly the origin of the NLCA did not die away. Although seemingly a minor issue, there is some evidence that misunderstanding of the history of Hauge's Synod was present in the NLCA, which elicited a negative reaction among some sympathetic to the Haugean tradition. In 1953, a book entitled *Norsemen Found a Church: An Old Heritage in a New Land* was published. The book was intended to honor the heritage of the Norwegian Synod, a hundred years after its founding in 1853. To be sure, the book does not ignore Hauge's Synod and Haugeanism in general, nor does it explicitly claim that the Norwegian Synod is the oldest Norwegian-Lutheran church body. However, when discussing the missionary zeal of Hauge's Synod, the book erroneously claims that "the Hauge Synod came into being in 1876."[155] Though not critical of the book specifically for this reason, the J. Hoifjeld mentioned above took note of the book in his correspondence with Bruce. While appreciative that at least part of the book faithfully represented Haugeanism, he noted that the publication was evidence "that the old synodical lines have not been totally obliterated."[156]

A few years later, an article in the *Lutheran Herald* erroneously claimed that Hauge's Synod, identified as the "strongest group" of the "low wing" of Norwegian-American Lutheranism, was "established in 1875" rather than in 1846.[157] It is likely that *Lutheran Herald* editor Olaf Gabriel Malmin was simply misinformed about the details of the reorganization that began in 1875 and was concluded the following year. Nevertheless, the response of G. M. Bruce to this error is worth noting. As can be observed throughout this work, Bruce was a significant figure in the life of Hauge's Synod, especially as it prepared to merge in 1917. He clearly cared for his Haugean heritage all the while expressing openness

---

155. Preus et al., *Norsemen Found a Church*, 356.

156. Personal letter from Johannes Hoifjeld to G. M. Bruce on June 2, 1954, G. M. Bruce File, Luther Seminary Archives, St. Paul, MN.

157. *Lutheran Herald*, 1957, 211.

to cooperation leading to merger. Such openness to merger put him at odds with some members of Hauge's Synod as did his criticism of lack of organizational cohesion within that church body. Yet Bruce, despite his more "churchly" character among the Haugeans, still found himself out of place on the seminary faculty. Nevertheless, Bruce continued his involvement at the seminary and in the broader life of the NLCA, downplaying and discouraging continued factionalism. Even so, Bruce reacted defensively in a confrontation with O. G. Malmin regarding Malmin's misstatement. In a lengthy editorial submitted to Malmin for publication, Bruce expressed his dismay at the ignorance surrounding the history of Hauge's Synod, desiring to set the record straight. Being sarcastic, Bruce told Malmin that the ELC, because the body had changed its name in 1946, only began in that year.[158] His point was to emphasize that Hauge's Synod, though it had changed its name in 1876, was actually the continuation of the church body founded in 1846.

Malmin responded to Bruce's work a few days later, criticizing both the length of the article and its confusing content:

> My first difficulty is its great length. It would be rather hard for me to justify using more than two pages in order to discuss a single historical inaccuracy in an editorial.... My second problem is that I find the first page and three fourths exceedingly confusing. To be quite truthful, it was not until I read that part of your contribution the third time that I was completely sure that you were being facetious. If my reaction was that, I am quite sure that most of our readers would have the same difficulty.[159]

Malmin sought to correct the matter, but his response expressed confusion over Bruce's reaction. He considered his mistake to be a minor oversight blown out of proportion by Bruce:

> I find myself a little puzzled by this whole thing, Dr. Bruce. As a matter of fact, it was from your own book that I concluded that the proper date was 1875.... I drew the conclusion that, since an organization was perpetuated with the same name and the same constitution, that constituted a continuation of the so-called Eielsen Synod. The Hauge's Synod, with a different name and a different constitution, I interpreted to be a new

---

158. Editorial from G. M. Bruce to O. G. Malmin on April 9, 1957, G. M. Bruce File, Luther Seminary Archives, St. Paul, MN.

159. Personal letter from O. G. Malmin to G. M. Bruce on April 11, 1957, G. M. Bruce File, Luther Seminary Archives, St. Paul, MN.

body. However, I certainly see the force of what you say, and I will be happy to publish a correction if you will kindly prepare one which is short enough and simple enough to fit into the available space.[160]

This response from Malmin did not end the matter, however. Bruce responded later that month with a tone that is best described as one of pent-up frustration about the misrepresentation of the history of Hauge's Synod. By this time, Bruce had been retired for a number of years, and possibly for that reason felt free to be more vocal about the heritage of Haugeanism in the ELC. In particular, he criticized the work of O. M. Norlie and Magnus Rohne for failing to represent faithfully the history of Hauge's Synod:

> Thanks for the letter. . . . It was quite interesting and rather amusing. . . . I did not intend to be facetious, as you say, but I did mean to be both satirical and dramatic in the hopes of sounding the death-knell to the Norlian obsession about the time of the organization of Hauge's Synod before we enter into our new and enlarged relationships, so as to have the records clear. This Norlian obsession was adopted by Rohne, who says in so many words that Hauge's Synod was organized in 1875 (see p. 190 of his History of Norw. Am. Lutheranism), and it erupts every now and then, both orally and in print, in persons who are not familiar with the historical backgrounds in the case, and simply jump at conclusions. Mere arguments don't seem to count against such individuals, so I decided to employ the satirical and dramatic technique, to which the history of the ELC lent itself so admirably. I think I did a splendid job on it, and I certainly didn't mean it as a joke.[161]

Bruce also perhaps felt free to be more vocal about his true convictions knowing that the days of the ELC were numbered, a fact to which he refers. Three years later, the ELC would merge with the ALC and the UELC to form TALC. At its heart, Bruce's response reveals a certain sorrow over the lack of understanding and appreciation for the tradition of Hauge's Synod, and his comment concerning "the satirical and dramatic technique, to which the history of the ELC lent itself so admirably" perhaps refers obliquely to a lack of trust among the Haugeans of the NLCA/

---

160. Personal letter from O. G. Malmin to G. M. Bruce, April 11, 1957.

161. Personal letter from G. M. Bruce to O. G. Malmin on April 29, 1957, G. M. Bruce File, Luther Seminary Archives, St. Paul, MN.

ELC regarding the way in which their tradition was treated throughout the years.

In Books

Once again, the year 1932 figures prominently in the story of the Haugean tradition in the NLCA. As already noted, that year witnessed the closing of RWS, and a number of former members of Hauge's Synod went on record as protesting the action. Even prior to this, there was a significant minority within Hauge's Synod that resisted the merger of 1917. One member of this minority committee was the layperson O. H. Oace, whose name reappears in 1932 as the author of a Norwegian language book with the colorful title *Hauges synode (revsede men ikke ihjelslagne)*, translated as *Hauge's Synod: Chastised but not Beaten to Death*.

The Norwegian language of the book as well as the Gothic script of the text has made this book largely inaccessible to modern readers. Yet the title, content, and year of publication make Oace's book important for understanding the legacy of Haugeanism within the NLCA. There can be little doubt that the publication of his book was tied to the concern for the survival of the Haugean tradition in the wake of the closing of RWS. Beginning with a general overview of the history of Hauge's Synod, highlighting the work of Eielsen, the founding of Eielsen's Synod in 1846, the strength of lay activity in the organization, and the work of the China Mission, the book sheds light on some struggles within Hauge's Synod not available from other sources. For example, Oace discusses the conflict between Meland and Bergsland mentioned in the third chapter. He claims that the struggle related to the accusation by Meland that Bergsland was a synergist.[162] Hence, part of the history of Hauge's Synod needs to be understood in light of the thorny issue of the power of the human will.

Yet the tone of Oace's work is not one of objective history. Rather, the tone is combative and accusatory, highlighting how the Haugean element of the NLCA had been mistreated. With the loss of RWS fresh in the memory, his comments regarding the issue are more than pointed. Noting that the union articles established a place for RWS in the NLCA as a pro-seminary, he goes on to say: "But now it must cease to be a school at all.... Broken promises come as a rule from dishonest people.

---

162. Oace, *Hauges synode*, 38. These translations from Oace's book are my own.

Is this to be how faith in love works?"[163] When discussing the fate of JLC, he makes similar comments. He notes that the school was handed over to the NLCA in 1917, "with promises that it be continued in unmodified form." Yet he notes that "it was long ago abandoned."[164] In the following paragraph, he concludes his historical sketch of Hauge's Synod and Haugeanism:

> And so we have quite a number of broken promises. But such is the case when dealing with human beings. God is not so! Never! What he promises is eternally fixed! And he desires that we also resemble him in this and keep what we promise.[165]

In a brief overview of his book toward the back of the volume, Oace seeks to identify the continuing legacy of Haugeanism in North America. Having earlier acknowledged the loss of Hauge's Synod in 1917 and the later loss of its educational institutions within the NLCA, he lifts up the existence of the HLIMF as carrying the banner of Haugeanism: "Hauge's Synod ceased to function as an organization at the meeting on June 8, 1917. But Haugeanism is still in business. Now it takes the appearance of an inner mission society, with most of the societies working under the name of the Hauge Lutheran Inner Mission Federation."[166] He further acknowledges the enduring legacy of Hauge's Synod through the continued mission work in China before concluding with the words of C. J. Eastvold at the concluding convention of Hauge's Synod in 1917. By quoting Eastvold's address, Oace appears to be encouraging the Haugeans in their role of providing continued spiritual leaven within the NLCA:

> Now we as an organization go over into a larger organization, but not on the basis of abandoning what we have built or the principles on which we have stood. We take them with us as our contribution to the large Norwegian Lutheran Church of America that we now shall organize.[167]

Yet the quote from Eastvold was only penultimate. The last quotation in Oace's work was from Hauge himself, in which Hauge reflected on his spiritual life amid persecution in the year 1803. In it, Hauge acknowledged his persecution, yet he joyfully looked toward "the city of eternal

---

163. Oace, *Hauges synode*, 63.
164. Oace, *Hauges synode*, 67–68.
165. Oace, *Hauges synode*, 68.
166. Oace, *Hauges synode*, 95.
167. Oace, *Hauges synode*, 98.

life" where the persecution would end and "enemies" would be no more. That Oace chose to end his book in such a manner is another indicator of the friction that existed between the Haugeans and others in the NLCA as well as the way in which they viewed their role in the organization.

In the following years, there were two other attempts during the era of the NLCA/ELC in the form of books to provide the Haugeans themselves with a sense of identity. As Oace encouraged continued vigilance in serving as leaven in a larger batch of dough through the work of the HLIMF, it is not surprising that the organization produced these books that were obviously intended to help self-identified Haugeans interpret their history. In so doing, they contributed to the edification of readers and communicated that their emphasis on spiritual life was not in vain. In general, these books helped the Haugeans understand themselves not as a defeated tradition, as the situation with RWS might suggest, but rather as a living and active force for good within the church establishment in much the same way that Norwegian Haugeanism functioned within the Church of Norway.

Such is the case with *The Hauge Movement in America*, published by the HLIMF in 1941. In seeking to recount the history of North American Haugeanism, the authors of the book begin by emphasizing the continuity of their tradition with that of the early Christian Church. Lifting up the faith of the early Christians at Pentecost, the authors articulated what they considered a pure form of Christianity, congruent with the concerns of Haugeanism. For example, the authors make the claim that worship in the early church "was done joyfully and in holy simplicity – no special vestments, no chanting, no high church ceremonies. But the Spirit-filled prayers, simple songs of praise, and the testimony of God's people could be heard on every hand."[168] True to the heritage of Haugeanism, the authors from the HLIMF emphasized lay ministry among early Christians, pointing out that the biblical book of Acts describes ordinary believers witnessing to their faith. In what can be described as mild anti-intellectualism and anticlericalism, the authors criticize the academy by claiming that "education and theological learning are worshipped" and that ecclesiastical titles are a hindrance, for "we are all saints in Jesus."[169]

Overall, the book emphasizes that those who stand for historic Haugean principles will face resistance and even outright persecution.

---

168. Hauge Inner Mission Federation, *Hauge Movement*, 11.
169. Hauge Inner Mission Federation, *Hauge Movement*, 13.

Likening the witness of Haugeanism to the witness of Stephen the first martyr, they state that "those who are chosen to live apart from the world will be hated . . . and the pietists and lay-people of all ages certainly have had their share of it." Continuing by criticizing "ritualistic customs," they state that "these customs are the idols of the people. If you try to knock down their idols, they will turn fiercely against you at any time and any age."[170] In the following pages of the book, the authors grudgingly acknowledge that some level of church administration is necessary, but that the purpose of such church offices was "to help along the gifts of grace, not to hinder them" among the "universal priesthood."[171] Accordingly, the HLIMF authors lift up the followers of Peter Waldo from southern France in the Middle Ages as role models for Haugeans of their era. The Waldensians, they claim, were forerunners to Haugeans in that they founded "the First Inner Mission Federation" of true believers devoted to spiritual life within the church establishment. The authors emphasized the loyalty of the Waldensians to the establishment if their freedom to witness was respected.[172] The rest of the book is devoted to recounting the history of American Haugeanism from the year 1825, after the first Norwegian immigrants arrived in North America, and onward. From their place in 1941, their interpretation of events reflects a history of friction with church establishment and a bias against an overemphasis on church order at the expense of spiritual life. In reflecting on the history of Hauge's Synod itself, they interpret the reorganization of 1875 and 1876 as being the result of greater focus on institutional life rather than on the quality of spiritual life. The removal of the second paragraph from the Old Constitution regarding truly converted membership was to blame for this, they claim.[173] Hence, it is not surprising that the authors later emphasize the Haugean movement as a pan-Lutheran phenomenon, refusing to lift up Hauge's Synod in particular as a pristine model of spiritual life. For a group of Haugeans, most of whom were connected to the NLCA, who had experienced some disenfranchisement in the NLCA, their interpretation of their history and present self-understanding makes sense:

---

170. Hauge Inner Mission Federation, *Hauge Movement*, 21.
171. Hauge Inner Mission Federation, *Hauge Movement*, 23.
172. Hauge Inner Mission Federation, *Hauge Movement*, 31.
173. Hauge Inner Mission Federation, *Hauge Movement*, 73.

The history of the Hauge movement after 1864 proves still more emphatically that the Hauge movement cannot be kept within the limits of any one church body. Even within the Hauge Synod itself, which bore the name of our spiritual father, H. N. Hauge, were to be found some of the worst enemies of the revival movement, while some of its best friends were found in other church bodies. So when the Haugeans of the various church bodies began to form Inner Mission Societies in 1884 and the Hauge Federation was launched in 1920, they wisely decided that all members should also, as a rule, be members of some Lutheran church, thereby dismissing all ideas of forming new church bodies or new congregations.[174]

The Hauge Movement in America concludes by acknowledging the presence of true spiritual life outside of the Lutheran fold, a tendency that had been present in Hauge's Synod throughout the years and that was resisted by others in the development of the NLCA, especially regarding the issue of "fellowship" with "Reformed" church bodies. The authors acknowledged the important role non-Lutherans played in stimulating revival among Lutherans at different points, as in the case of Norwegian Methodists.[175] Other groups mentioned are the Norwegian Salvation Army, the Evangelical Free Church, and the Pentecostal movement. Despite differences in doctrine, the HLIMF considered it possible for such non-Lutheran groups to serve as true Christian witnesses and even as role models for Lutherans: "These spiritual movements have carried on in a somewhat more happy and courageous spirit than we low-church Lutherans have often done. They are sinners saved by grace like the rest of us." Quoting an inscription over the grave of a Methodist in London, which speaks of the faith of the deceased as being rooted in his knowledge of himself as sinner and Christ as sufficient for him, the authors simply state, "On this point the best Lutheran and the best Reformed theology agree."[176] This ecumenical focus on "inner mission," true spiritual life existing within church establishments and across confessional and denominational boundaries, is expanded on in the second publication of the HLIMF in 1948 entitled *Innermission Church History* by P. Ljostveit. This work has already been quoted in reference to the life of Hauge's Synod, and so it naturally speaks of the Norwegian-American

---

174. Hauge Inner Mission Federation, *Hauge Movement*, 89.
175. Hauge Inner Mission Federation, *Hauge Movement*, 510.
176. Hauge Inner Mission Federation, *Hauge Movement*, 512.

experience. However, the book recounts the author's view of the history of spiritual life more generally, which includes representatives of many other traditions. Most significantly, however, the publication of this book speaks to the self-identity of the Haugeans in the ELC in the late 1940s. The book begins by arguing that religion can exist without salvation and that most religion in fact is of this type. When Jesus Christ appeared, Ljostveit argues, the world was filled with religion that did not bring true life with God.[177] There are references to this kind of religion throughout the book, in one place called the colorful label of "dead churchianity."[178] That Ljostveit, a former member of Hauge's Synod, had the Lutherans of his time in mind, presumably especially many of those in his own church body of the NLCA, with his denouncements is demonstrated by his interpretation of Lutheran history regarding the authors of the *Formula of Concord*:

> It had been worked out in 1577 at Magdeburg in order to bring peace and harmony in the Lutheran camp and to unify Lutheranism against all dissenting "isms." The Augsburg Confession of 1530 was not enough; they had to get a stronger and stricter confession – condemning the Anabaptists on some 22 points, the Schwenkfeldians on 8 points, the Calvinists and Crypto-Calvinists (in the Supplement) on 22 points. The ultra-Lutheran views were being stressed by an ultra-Lutheran party. The Lutherans, who went more by the Spirit than by the letter and wanted a hand stretched out to Christians of other denominations, were also condemned. They were called Philippists, after Melanchthon's first name. They were branded as Calvinists or Crypto-Calvinists, and were even persecuted. These strict Lutherans, calling themselves genuine Lutherans, are still with us.[179]

CONCLUSION

Thus, late into the life of the NLCA/ELC, one can observe that many Haugeans, having lived through a fair amount of friction within that church body, began to understand their history and continued role as serving as leaven in the larger batch of dough in the NLCA/ELC, though

---

177. Ljostveit, *Innermission Church History*, 3.
178. Ljostveit, *Innermission Church History*, 29.
179. Ljostveit, *Innermission Church History*, 198.

not limited to that particular Lutheran tradition or necessarily Lutheranism at all. This is congruent with the understanding of some Haugeans who desired the merger of 1917, though many of those did not expect the loss of their educational institutions. They therefore, despite lack of trust of the church establishment, continued their focus on spiritual life within, all the while appealing to the persecution experienced by Hauge and other movements throughout history in their own effort at self-understanding.

5

Congregational Life

CHURCH HISTORY ALWAYS RUNS the risk of overemphasizing institutional life and powerful personalities at the expense of examining how historical events impacted laypeople on a congregational level. This tendency, though in some ways unavoidable, is understandable, as historical survey books have precious little space to devote to the supposedly mundane after thoroughly evaluating significant leaders and events, making such histories "about the generals and not about the privates."[1] Yet this tendency, perhaps a by-product of the emphasis placed on merger in American Lutheranism, ignores the very concerns that occupied the Haugeans, which were related to individual and congregational spiritual life. Therefore, to obtain a more complete picture of the enduring legacy of Haugeanism in North American Lutheranism, this chapter addresses the fate of the congregations of Hauge's Synod after the merger. To be sure, much of the information available about congregations, if any historical information can be found at all, has been compiled by amateur historians, and the limitations of such works are often the opposite of those discussed above; the tendency is often to focus overly on local concerns detached from wider synodical developments. Furthermore, one must approach such congregational histories and reminiscences with a critical eye, as the authors of such works frequently lack broad historical knowledge and are therefore prone to making factual errors and unhelpful generalizations. Both the quantity and quality of available congregational information is uneven. At times, there are significant archival records available. At other times, the only information available about the life of a congregation is

1. Harrisville, Interview by Thomas E. Jacobson.

from a congregational website. Nevertheless, to proceed, one must work within such limitations.

Though many of the 342 congregations of Hauge's Synod as of 1916 have closed or merged with other congregations throughout the years, examining the fate of these congregations confirms in part what has already been established; there existed among many parts of the former Hauge's Synod a certain friction with the church establishment that in time led a significant percentage of these congregations outside of the "mainstream"[2] and into alternative Lutheran church bodies perceived as friendlier to their piety. However, such an exodus occurred gradually over the decades rather than as a single group at a particular moment, as was the case with the ELS. This is consistent with the point already established, which is that many Haugeans viewed their role as leaven in a larger batch of dough and continued to carry out their activity within the church establishment despite disagreement with its emphases. At the same time, not all former Hauge's Synod congregations can be fit neatly into a single category, and this chapter will identify different categories into which such congregations can be said to fall. The Haugean heritage of these congregations along with historical circumstances produced a fair amount of diversity of expression among them, which one can observe at present.

THE IMPACT OF THE MERGER ON PARISH LIFE

On a congregational level, the merger of 1917 had an immediate impact. Especially where a number of small congregations existed in a given area, these congregations of the different predecessor bodies often formed parish relationships with one another or merged outright. In 1923, H. G. Stub noted in his annual presidential report to the NLCA that the merger carried out six years prior had the practical benefit of uniting small and struggling congregations in a given area:

> Furthermore: where formerly two or even three congregations by constant struggles and tribulations managed to eke out a

---

2. The term "mainstream" is used in reference to church bodies and their predecessor organizations that were a product of the series of twentieth-century American Lutheran mergers, namely the ELCA and ELCIC. The quotation marks indicate that those congregations that have chosen to belong to alternative church bodies should not necessarily be viewed as sectarian. Rather, they have simply chosen to express their Lutheran identity in organizations viewed as more theologically and socially conservative.

precarious existence, there is now one congregation only, with one minister and one church. The people live together as brethren in Christian unity as if there never had been any divisions among them.³

Numerous examples could be cited, but one in particular illustrates well this common phenomenon. In Clearwater County, Minnesota, located in the northwestern part of the state, the congregations of *Betania norsk evangelisk lutherske menighet* of Hauge's Synod, *Saron skandinavisk lutherske menighet* of the UNLC, *Samhold menighet* of the UNLC, and *Borgund norsk evangelisk lutherske menighet* of the Norwegian Synod all existed in the vicinity of Gonvick, Minnesota. Shortly after the union, *Borgund* and *Samhold* formed a merged congregation called Samhold Lutheran Church, and *Betania* and *Saron* eventually merged to form United Lutheran Church. As a result of the union, Samhold and United soon found themselves in a parish relationship and served by the same pastor. In time, a third congregation evidently established after 1917, Bethlehem Lutheran Church, joined the parish as well. The congregational history of Samhold Lutheran Church states explicitly that the 1917 merger was responsible for creating the new parish configuration.⁴ Therefore, all three of the traditions of the predecessor bodies of the NLCA were present in the Gonvick Lutheran Parish. Stories about the coexistence of these various traditions in congregations and parishes are difficult to find given that congregational record-keeping and chronicling is a haphazard affair most often undertaken by at best amateur historians. One can imagine, however, the difficulty created by some of these congregational mergers and parish relationships, which causes one to question Stub's optimistic appraisal of life within merged congregations. How would a former Hauge's Synod congregation react to being served by a former Norwegian Synod pastor? How would a former Hauge's Synod pastor manage to maintain his own tradition of worship while serving a former UNLC or Norwegian Synod congregation? Especially given the minority status of the former Hauge's Synod in the NLCA, one can assume that the Haugeans would have experienced difficulty maintaining their tradition in many instances.

This is demonstrated by the example of *Markers norsk evangelisk lutherske menighet*. Markers Lutheran Church in Rice County, Minnesota,

---

3. NLCA, "Report of the General President."

4. Congregational history of Samhold Lutheran Church of Gonvick, MN, 1999, T. Jacobson Dissertation Reference, Luther Seminary Archives, St. Paul, MN.

near the towns of Faribault and Cannon City, ended its independent life shortly after the 1917 merger when it merged with two other congregations. Founded in 1869, this small congregation nonetheless boasted many prominent Haugeans as its pastors throughout the years: Ø. Hanson, H. N. Rønning, N. J. Løhre, M. G. Hanson, and G. M. Bruce.[5] In a reflection on the history of the congregation from an unknown date, likely later in the life of the NLCA/ELC, former member Lorraine Brekke Bjorlie expressed her view that the Haugean tradition of Markers Lutheran Church had been lost in the process of congregational merger. With a tenor of sadness, she also expressed consolation at the fact that Haugeanism continued to be influential in the NLCA at large after 1917:

> The Haugean ideas about worship and lay preaching were to fade away in the years to come, but the many people who learned to know their Saviour [sic] through Haugean organizations were to be a constant influence on the Norwegian Lutheran Church in the United States in its task of preaching the "good news". [sic] Markers Lutheran Church is gone, but its message lives on. . . . Those of us who are now members of the North Grove Cemetery Association are proud of this little Church and cemetery, but most of all we are grateful to our ancestors who established this Church and for their deep interest and devotion to God.[6]

In the case of the Gonvick Lutheran Parish mentioned above, which is close to my own experience,[7] there is a noticeable difference between the two congregations in terms of liturgical practice to the present day, with United Lutheran Church, containing the Haugean element, resisting the use of chanted liturgy, insisting on simplicity in worship, and therefore dismissing the suggestion to purchase new hymnals produced by the official church publishing house. Though not prohibiting the use of clerical vestments, members of United Lutheran Church have expressed confusion about their meaning as well as discomfort with them. Samhold Lutheran Church, on the other hand, though not especially "high church" by comparison with some parts of American Lutheranism, has a much greater affinity to structured liturgy and openness to official denominational worship resources. Pastors of the Gonvick Lutheran Parish have tended over the years to favor liturgical formality, and though there are a

---

5. Norlie, *Norsk Lutherske Menigheter i Amerika*, 1:472.

6. Bjorlie, Reflection on the History of Markers Lutheran Church.

7. I served as pastor of Samhold Lutheran Church and United Lutheran Church in and near Gonvick, MN, from 2006 to 2010.

variety of local issues involved, this is likely one factor in the sometimes contentious relationship between the two congregations of the parish. More detailed work on the coexistence of the different Norwegian-American Lutheran traditions in merged congregations and multipoint parishes would likely yield more insight. Stub's 1923 comment, in any case, indicates the pervasiveness of the phenomenon of congregational merger in the early years of the NLCA. The examples of Markers Lutheran Church and the congregations near Gonvick, Minnesota, are a small yet helpful part in the search for the continuation of the Haugean tradition in American Lutheranism.

Another important consideration related to the issue of congregational merger is the size of congregations. It has been observed that prior to the merger, Hauge's Synod consisted of "mostly small" congregations.[8] An evaluation of the most recent membership numbers of each congregation confirms this.[9] These membership numbers were most often reported to O. M. Norlie within the three years prior to the merger, though occasionally only older numbers are available. Additionally, a few congregations reported no membership numbers at all. Even with these limitations, these numbers are telling. Out of 342 congregations, well over half of them reported fewer than one hundred members. A large number of those congregations reported fewer than forty-nine members. Holding the title of the Hauge's Synod congregation with the smallest membership before entering the merger was *Salem norsk evangelisk lutherske menighet* in Kingman, Alberta, apparently a mission congregation founded in 1910, reporting only seven members as of 1914. Well over a hundred congregations could be described as "medium-sized," reporting between 100 and 399 members. Only a handful of congregations, seven in total, boasted more than four hundred members. The largest of these was *Salem evangelisk lutherske menighet* of Roland, Iowa, reporting 767 members in 1914, followed closely by *Singsoos norsk evangelisk lutherske menighet* just outside of Hendricks, Minnesota, though on the South Dakota side of the border, reporting 750 members in the same year. A concentration of larger congregations could also be found in Lac qui Parle County, Minnesota, in and near the towns of Dawson and Madison. Yet another larger congregation was *St. Pauli norsk evangelisk lutherske menighet*, an urban congregation in Minneapolis, Minnesota.

8. Gisselquist, *Called to Preach*, 35.

9. The table in Appendix C lists the congregations that were members of Hauge's Synod as of 1916, including reported membership numbers for each congregation.

Awareness of the generally small size of Hauge's Synod congregations is a significant part of evaluating the legacy of Hauge's Synod and Haugeanism in American Lutheranism. To be sure, the Norwegian Synod and the UNLC had many smaller congregations as well. However, there were many more of them than congregations of Hauge's Synod, and in situations involving congregational merger as with the Gonvick Lutheran Parish mentioned above, the Norwegian Synod and UNLC representation greatly outnumbered the Haugeans, possibly leading to internal friction in the new congregation in addition to the likely loss of Haugean identity.

EVALUATION OF THE FATE OF THE CONGREGATIONS

Determining the fate of individual congregations is challenging. Thanks to the internet, various congregational websites, and miscellaneous archival material, one can uncover at least part of the history of many of the 342 congregations of Hauge's Synod after 1917. At the very least, one can learn in many cases whether and when a particular congregation merged with other congregations or when a congregation dissolved. Even so, information on many of the congregations remains elusive. Indeed, the fate of 197 congregations out of 342 remains undetermined.[10] What is known is that such congregations no longer exist as independent entities, but it is not clear how such congregations ceased to exist. Such congregations obviously merged with others at some point or simply closed. Unfortunately, nothing short of extensive local research in numerous locations beyond the scope of this work can uncover the fate of these 197 congregations. It can be determined that twenty-eight congregations merged with other congregations shortly after 1917 or merged into other congregations at some point after that. Further, it can be determined that fourteen congregations dissolved at some point after 1917, ending their existence as a part of the NLCA/ELC.

Remaining are 103 former Hauge's Synod congregations still in existence that maintained an independent life after the merger of 1917. More than half of these congregations, sixty-three in total, remain a part of the "mainstream" of the Evangelical Lutheran Church in America (ELCA) or the Evangelical Lutheran Church in Canada (ELCIC). The existence of these congregations should not be ignored in any evaluation of the

---

10. See the table in Appendix C of this book.

continuation of the Haugean tradition. However, telling is the fact that 39 percent, a total of forty congregations, of the surviving 103 at present find themselves affiliated with church bodies outside the "mainstream" of the ELCA and ELCIC. The largest collection of these forty congregations, sixteen in total, presently associate with Lutheran Congregations in Mission for Christ (LCMC). Generally understood to be more theologically and socially conservative than the ELCA and the ELCIC, LCMC was founded in 2001 by a small group of congregations that resisted the passage of the 1999 ecumenical agreement between the ELCA and the Episcopal Church USA. In reaction to the requirement that Lutherans conform to the Anglican understanding of a threefold ordained ministry, LCMC organized itself as a decentralized association of congregations rather than as a traditional denomination with a synodical structure. The membership of LCMC grew modestly in the years after its establishment, but it spiked significantly in the years immediately following the 2009 decision of the ELCA to change its standards for ordained ministry by allowing pastors to serve who are in lifelong, monogamous same-sex relationships. LCMC understands itself as an international association of congregations, counting over 900 member congregations around the world. However, most of those, around 750, are in the United States.

The decision of these sixteen former Hauge's Synod congregations to join LCMC reveals two things about the continuation of the Haugean tradition in American Lutheranism. First, one sees in this choice of affiliation an emphasis on congregational autonomy. Of course, Hauge's Synod did possess a synodical structure of its own, which differentiated it from the Lutheran Free Church, but as has been observed, there was within Hauge's Synod a notable sense of disconnect among the congregations and lack of interest in the synod as an institution and in synod-related activities. Even with the synodical structure of Hauge's Synod, there was an emphasis, articulated by M. O. Wee, on congregational autonomy. All this is understandable for a group rooted in the Haugean concern for spiritual life rather than institution building. Additionally, the historic friction experienced by the Haugeans with the leadership of the NLCA/ELC would make LCMC, with its minimal administrative structure, a natural home for these congregations. Second, since LCMC was founded somewhat recently, these former Hauge's Synod congregations obviously remained a part of the "mainstream" for quite some time before making the decision to depart for a church association friendlier to their convictions and piety.

The second largest group of congregations to join an alternative organization elected to join the AFLC, which also understands itself as an association of congregations rather than a traditional denomination. As noted in the introduction, the AFLC, which originally consisted mostly of congregations of the Lutheran Free Church that declined to join TALC in 1962, understands itself to be rooted in the Haugean and other Scandinavian revival traditions. The roots of the AFLC in Scandinavian Pietism make the organization a natural home for many former Hauge's Synod congregations. Also, as in the case of LCMC, the decentralized nature of the AFLC likely appealed to some of them. The roots of the AFLC predate the formation of LCMC by nearly four decades, however. This means that many of the twelve former Hauge's Synod congregations that now count themselves members of the AFLC left the "mainstream" earlier than those that joined LCMC.

Much smaller numbers of the forty former Hauge's Synod congregations joined other church bodies over the course of the decades. Four became members of the CLBA, which was also heavily influenced by the Haugean tradition of Norway from the founding of the group in 1900. Three Canadian congregations of Hauge's Synod are now affiliated with the Canadian Association of Lutheran Congregations (CALC). The CALC is a church body of currently thirty-three congregations that was formed as an alternative to the ELCIC in 1992. Two congregations are now members of the North American Lutheran Church (NALC), which presently consists of over four hundred congregations. The NALC was established in 2010 for congregations in both the United States and Canada desiring an alternative church body from the "mainstream," the immediate, though not exclusive, impetus for its formation being the 2009 decisions of the ELCA regarding human sexuality. The NALC has been caricatured as "high church" both in terms of its organization and the preferred worship style of most of its congregations. Yet like all caricatures, there is some truth contained in this description. The NALC has a synodical structure with clearly organized leadership, and many, though not all, of its congregations and pastors prefer liturgical formality. This explains why many more former Hauge's Synod congregations found a home in LCMC than in the NALC. One congregation joined the American Association of Lutheran Churches (AALC). The AALC was formed in 1987 by a small group of congregations from TALC that refused to join the merger with the LCA and the AELC that produced the ELCA the following year. The AALC considers itself to be a continuation of the conservative confessional tradition of TALC, and of special concern for them was the omission of the word "inerrant" regarding the Scriptures in the proposed constitution of the ELCA. As of 2007, the AALC has been in a relationship of altar and pulpit fellowship with the LCMS. Finally, one former Hauge's Synod congregation is a member of the Alliance of Renewal Churches (ARC). The ARC is a network of Lutheran congregations and pastors who embrace a charismatic emphasis on the presence of the Holy Spirit in worship in addition to a Lutheran sacramental focus.

Categories of Congregations

A thorough evaluation of the life of each former Hauge's Synod congregation currently in existence is not possible both because of space limitations as well as the lack of information and written material available about many of them. In view of these limitations, it is possible however to provide brief information about a sampling of these congregations to observe the various ways they have either maintained their Haugean heritage or how they have been influenced by other movements throughout the years. To accomplish this, such congregations are placed into three broad categories based on the time of their departure from the "mainstream." It has been established that former Hauge's Synod congregations, rather than departing as a group to form a dissenting synod, continued their lives within the NLCA after 1917. Though a large number remained within the "mainstream" for several decades either to continue to remain within it or to depart after the year 1998, it has also been noted that a good number of congregations departed from the "mainstream" in the first few decades after 1917. Therefore, the first category includes congregations that departed from the NLCA/ELC/TALC/ELCA between the years of 1917 and 1998. The second category includes congregations that departed from the ELCA and ELCIC as a result of more recent controversial developments in and after the year 1999. The third category includes congregations that remain a part of the "mainstream" to the present. Far from an exhaustive history of each congregation chosen, what follows are glimpses of the experiences of these congregations. At times, historical information about these congregations is abundant and includes archival material and information provided by the congregation itself. At other times, the only information available is from a congregational website. As much as possible, the featured congregations have been chosen because of an abundance of information about their histories. However, another factor influencing their inclusion in the sampling below is what a particular congregation demonstrates about the continuation of the Haugean tradition in North American Lutheranism.

The First Category

Among those congregations that departed from the "mainstream" between 1917 and 1998, there appears to be no particular event that prompted the exodus, perhaps reflective of an attitude of congregational independence. That no discernable pattern can be detected is perhaps partially due to the limited information available about these congregations. In many cases, exactly when a particular congregation chose an alternative affiliation is unknown. What is known, however, is that such departures occurred on both ends of the chronological spectrum. For example, *Green Lake norsk evangelisk lutherske menighet* of Hauge's Synod near Spicer, Minnesota, elected to remain outside of the NLCA from the beginning, eventually finding its way into the AFLC where it remains today. At least two other examples from much later indicate that the Haugean friction with the official church establishment remained a part of these former Hauge's Synod congregations throughout the decades. What follows is a brief and limited look at the lives of six congregations falling in the first category with reflection on how the Haugean tradition is carried on among them today.

Emmanuel Lutheran Church of Kenyon, Minnesota

Immanuels norsk evangelisk lutherske menighet, known today in English as Emmanuel Lutheran Church, is currently a member of the AFLC and is one of the few congregations falling in the first category with a fair amount of information available about its history. Located in the tiny, unincorporated village of Aspelund, Minnesota, its mailing address is from the neighboring town of Kenyon. It was and remains in a parish relationship with another former Hauge's Synod congregation, also of the Kenyon area, *Hauges norsk evangelisk lutherske menighet*, known today as Hauge Lutheran Church.

Records indicate that a rocky relationship between Emmanuel Lutheran Church and the leadership of TALC began as early as 1966. In that year, Fredrik Schiotz, the last president of the ELC and first president of TALC, gave an address to the Southeastern Minnesota District convention of TALC regarding "the doctrine of the Word," apparently addressing the topic of how to understand the inerrancy of Scripture.[11] The pastor of the congregation, R. L. Larson, then began a discussion with Melford S. Knutson, at the time the president of the Southeastern Minnesota District of TALC. According to Knutson, Larson had previously printed an article in a certain publication in which he accused Schiotz of heresy. The following year, a gathering for preretirement pastors in the district was focused on issues of health in the retirement years. The speaker promoted "alcohol in moderation" as having "a healthful effect," which prompted a woman from Emmanuel Lutheran Church to write a six-page letter to Knutson about the sin of drunkenness. In his report about his interaction with Emmanuel Lutheran Church, Knutson provided a quote from his response letter to the woman: "It so happens that I am a teetotaler. But, the accusations you have made about drunkenness have almost driven me to drink."

In the rest of his report, Knutson recounted the proceedings of a meeting on January 30, 1968, held with members of both Emmanuel and Hauge Lutheran congregations regarding their concerns about the teachings of TALC and trends within the church body. On the whole, the conversation as reported by Knutson centered on the issue of biblical inerrancy and concerns about the "neo-orthodoxy" being taught in seminaries of TALC. From his report of the meeting, it is clear that the members of these congregations had been influenced by the organization called Lutherans Alert, discussed in greater detail in the following chapter. Knutson reported an adversarial and combative tone coming especially from Larson, the pastor. When articulating his view that inerrancy refers to the content of the gospel found in the Scriptures rather than the minutiae of the text itself, Knutson attempted to clarify that this more flexible view of biblical authority predated the rise of neo-orthodoxy and was taught by his own father. In the context of this comment, Knutson interestingly referred to his own Haugean background while arguing with Larson. When Larson suggested that Knutson must feel out of place among a group of Haugeans, Knutson quickly retorted:

---

11. Melford Knutson, Report of Meeting with Hauge and Emmanuel Congregations. The information in this paragraph is derived from this report by Melford Knutson.

And I immediately interrupted him to say, "This is not hard on Dr. Knutson. I understand Hauge people full well. I was raised in a Hauge home. I know their life, I know their habits, their attitudes, and I am perfectly at home with them. I feel very comfortable here. I want you to understand that."[12]

Yet Knutson suggested after the meeting that Larson and his followers actually did not faithfully represent Haugeanism, being critical especially of Larson's judgmental attitude:

> Pastor Larson, as your pastor, I want to tell you that if Hans Nielsen Hauge didn't turn over in his grave tonight, it would be a great surprise to me. As far as I am concerned, there wasn't one single evidence of any spiritual life present here tonight. There was no glory for Jesus Christ. And as your pastor, I want to assure you that I am going to pray that the Holy Spirit will help you to preach a positive Gospel; that He will enable you to glorify Jesus Christ, rather than spend your efforts and time on negatives and criticisms.[13]

Two years later, Emmanuel Lutheran Church severed its ties with TALC and presumably joined the AFLC shortly thereafter. In a sharply worded letter to Knutson, congregational president Arnold Grimsrud stated:

> On Monday evening, Sept. 14th., Emmanuel Lutheran Congregation of Kenyon, Minnesota, by a vote of 72 to 13, voted to sever all relationships with the American Lutheran Church. . . . For two years and more Emmanuel congregation has been in a "state of confessional protest." Within the past two years two letters of protest have been sent to the District President, but those letters have not been acknowledged by him. It is very obvious that the American Lutheran Church is promoting doctrines contrary to the Confession of Faith as set forth in our constitution.[14]

Furthermore, the letter claimed that Emmanuel Lutheran Church was not required to vote twice for disaffiliation from TALC as stipulated in the constitution of the church body both because the Emmanuel Lutheran Church constitution differed from the TALC constitution on that

---

12. Melford Knutson, Report of Meeting with Hauge and Emmanuel Congregations.
13. Melford Knutson, Report of Meeting with Hauge and Emmanuel Congregations.
14. Letter from Emmanuel Lutheran Church to Melford S. Knutson on October 12, 1970, Emmanuel Lutheran Church File, Luther Seminary Archives, St. Paul, MN.

point as well as the fact that Emmanuel Lutheran Church considered that TALC had violated its own constitution because of its teachings. In a response by Knutson, he rebuffed their claim that they were not required to vote twice, noting the necessity of such a vote in order to maintain tax-exempt status for the church.[15]

Obtaining a complete picture of the life of Emmanuel Lutheran Church is unfortunately not possible. As evidenced by the vote to disaffiliate with TALC, there was some diversity of opinion in the congregation that must be borne in mind, at least regarding its relationship with TALC. What the story of Emmanuel Lutheran Church reveals, at least in part, however, is that suspicion of and friction with the church establishment continued strongly in this former Hauge's Synod congregation many decades after the merger of 1917. Curiously, much of the conflict centered on issues of doctrine and concern for biblical inerrancy, as evidenced by the influence of Lutherans Alert. As has been established, such concerns were often foreign to the Haugeans, who placed greater emphasis on the quality of spiritual life than on precise doctrinal formulations. It is understandable, however, given the unfolding history of the Haugean element in the NLCA and the lack of trust among many Haugeans of the church establishment that a former congregation of Hauge's Synod such as Emmanuel Lutheran Church would find an affinity for a protest movement such as Lutherans Alert, even if its expressed concerns were somewhat different than those of historic Haugeanism.

Blom Prairie Lutheran Church of Toronto, South Dakota

Another aspect of the enduring legacy of the Haugean tradition in North American Lutheranism can be observed from the example of *Blom Prairie evangelisk lutherske menighet*. Formerly of Hauge's Synod, Blom Prairie Lutheran Church in the town of Toronto, located in far eastern South Dakota, now counts itself a member of the CLBA. In the case of Blom Prairie Lutheran Brethren Church, the uneven nature of the quantity of available congregational information can be observed; the only available information is from the congregation's website, and even that

---

15. Letter from Melford Knutson to Emmanuel Lutheran Church on November 2, 1970, Emmanuel Lutheran Church File, Luther Seminary Archives, St. Paul, MN.

information is scant.[16] According to a phone conversation with the pastor, the Blom Prairie congregation joined the CLBA in 1962. Therefore, the congregation was a member of the NLCA/ELC throughout its existence, departing from the "mainstream" shortly after the merger that produced TALC. The 1946 NLCA annual report confirms that "Bloom [sic] Prairie" of Toronto, South Dakota, was indeed a member of the NLCA as of that year.[17] Given the timing of the congregation's departure from TALC, it should be considered that the decision was made out of concern that a larger church establishment like TALC would diminish focus on local responsibility and spiritual life.

Though there is not much that one can report about the life of this congregation specifically, its membership in the CLBA is important to note as a part of the enduring legacy of Haugeanism. At present, the only information on its website is its statement of faith, which is taken directly from the CLBA synodical organization itself. Beginning with the CLBA belief in the Bible as the "verbally and plenarily inspired Word of God," being "free from error in the whole and in the part," and therefore "the final authoritative guide for faith and conduct," it then goes on to articulate orthodox Christian doctrines such as the Trinity and the fallen nature of humanity. Reflecting its Lutheran heritage, the statement of faith of this congregation as well as the CLBA as a whole touches on issues of law and gospel, justification, and the sacraments. Specifically reflecting its Norwegian Lutheran background, the website states its official acceptance of only the *Augsburg Confession* and the *Small Catechism*. Reflecting the historic concern of the CLBA for "converted membership" and the broader Haugean concern for "living Christianity," the discussion of baptism affirms the baptism of infants and children yet also carefully articulates the necessity of subjective appropriation of the promises of baptism, stating that those who are baptized must come to demonstrate "a clear conscious personal faith in Christ as their Lord and Savior."

The historic connection between the Haugean focus on subjectivity and the founding of the *Brodersamfund* has already been noted. Hence, it is not surprising that a congregation such as Blom Prairie would come to find a home in the CLBA. Yet perhaps most interestingly, the church polity of the CLBA can be said to bear resemblance to that of the former Hauge's Synod. Though synodical in its structure, there was an emphasis

---

16. Blom Prairie Lutheran Brethren Church, "Statement of Faith."
17. NLCA, *1946 Annual Report*, 776.

in Hauge's Synod, articulated by M. O. Wee, on congregational freedom in governing its own affairs. Even so, Hauge's Synod as an organization had the authority to administer certain cooperative endeavors of the congregations. This is similar to what is stated by the CLBA:

> The Church of the Lutheran Brethren practices the congregational form of church government and the autonomy of the local congregations. The synodical administration has an advisory function as it relates to the congregation, and an administrative function as it relates to the cooperative efforts of the congregations.[18]

Jevnaker Lutheran Church of Borup, Minnesota

Jevnager menighet, now known as Jevnaker Lutheran Church, is located in the northwestern Minnesota town of Borup. Like Blom Prairie Lutheran Brethren Church, it is one of the four former Hauge's Synod congregations now affiliated with the CLBA. Unlike its CLBA counterpart of Blom Prairie, the congregational website of Jevnaker Lutheran Church provides information specific to its congregational life. The congregational website does not make clear what year it departed from the "mainstream" and joined the CLBA. However, it is clear from lists of congregations that have departed from the "mainstream" more recently that Jevnaker Lutheran Church joined the CLBA sometime prior to the more recent controversies in the ELCA. Indeed, the 1946 annual report lists Jevnaker Lutheran Church in Borup among congregations of the NLCA.[19] The brief historical overview provided on its website discusses the founding of the congregation, the construction of the building, and changing pastoral leadership, yet it says nothing of the congregation's relationship to various church bodies over the years.

More significantly, however, the congregation does provide some information about its life and attitude toward the world, and one can detect some congruence between these comments and the historic Haugean tradition. Like Blom Prairie, presumably reflective of the congregation's association with the CLBA, the website points out that "Jevnaker Lutheran Church has continuously upheld the Bible as the verbally inspired, revealed Word of God and the only infallible and authoritative, rule and

---

18. Blom Prairie Lutheran Brethren Church, "Statement of Faith."
19. NLCA, *1946 Annual Report*, 678.

guide for Christian faith, doctrine and conduct."[20] The mission statement of the congregation also emphasizes the empowerment of laity in "exercising the gifts of grace" through "training them to share their faith," and "equipping them to establish others in faith."[21] As much as can be determined from a congregational website, it is clear that this congregation carries forward the historic concern of Hauge's Synod for lay preaching and witnessing.

Finally, the Haugean heritage of this congregation is expressed in its description of its worship life, which emphasizes a "low-church" model similar to the experience of much of the historic Hauge's Synod:

> Our Worship Service provides a traditional, yet non-liturgical, worship experience where the proclamation of God's Word is the central focus of our worship. A blend of traditional hymns, and praise and worship choruses, are incorporated into the worship experience. Our order of worship is structured in such a way that we hear God's Word throughout and respond to that Word through prayer, our gifts and music.[22]

Zion Lutheran Church of Dexter, Minnesota

Zion evangelisk lutherske menighet, formerly of Hauge's Synod, still exists today as Zion Lutheran Church of rural Dexter, Minnesota. This congregation in southeastern Minnesota, unlike the examples of Emmanuel Lutheran Church, Blom Prairie Lutheran Church, and possibly Jevnaker Lutheran Church, departed from the "mainstream" somewhat later, though the exact year is not known. Like Emmanuel Lutheran Church, Zion Lutheran Church is now a member of the AFLC.

Archival records indicate that Zion Lutheran Church experienced friction with the "mainstream" church establishment as early as 1988, though it had roots in earlier experiences. Just a few months after the merger that produced the ELCA in 1988, the pastor of Zion Lutheran Church, Timothy Carlson, sent a handwritten letter to Glenn Nycklemoe, the bishop of the Southeastern Minnesota Synod of the ELCA. According to the tone of the letter, the concerns among the congregation described by Carlson were not shared by him; he wrote only to describe

---

20. Jevnaker Lutheran Church, "About Us," para. 5.
21. Jevnaker Lutheran Church, "About Us," para. 7.
22. Jevnaker Lutheran Church, "About Us," para. 9.

to Nycklemoe the current state of affairs and to invite him to a meeting with the congregation where he could be a "listening ear."[23] In preparation for the upcoming meeting, Carlson's letter described the state of affairs at Zion Lutheran Church, noting that it was a small congregation, averaging between fifteen to twenty people in worship on a given Sunday, and also noting that the small size of the congregation perhaps contributed to the defensive attitude in the congregation at large. Later in the letter, for example, Carlson mentioned a series of issues that might come up in the scheduled meeting, one of which was concern about the attitude of the ELCA toward small congregations and whether they could trust the ELCA in matters of retention of congregational property. Other issues cited by Carlson as areas of concern were the ordination of pastors with a homosexual orientation and "the authority of Scripture," given the omission of the words "inerrant" and "infallible" from the constitution of the ELCA.

Beyond this, Carlson's letter to Nycklemoe sought to inform him of the background of the congregation. Notably, Carlson felt it necessary to point out the Haugean background of Zion Lutheran Church. Apparently, he considered it to be a pertinent detail among other information: "Zion has roots in the Hauge Lutheran Church. It has been very evangelical in a healthy, positive way. It has a low church style of worship with no chanting and little liturgy."[24] After this, Carlson explained that some members of the congregation harbored a deep distrust of the church establishment of TALC and its successor body of the ELCA: "Zion has some members who seem to have been personally offended by contacts with the ALC on the district and national level." He provided a few examples, which included concerns related to Lutheran Social Services showing "sexually explicit films" to adolescents who were in trouble with the law and the rejection that the member received at the convention when raising the concern. Yet another member was upset that his request to view the financial report of the pension fund of TALC was denied, which he interpreted "as an example of the ALC and now the ELCA desire to accumulate wealth secretly, at the expense of congregations such as Zion."

There is no record of Nycklemoe's meeting with Zion Lutheran Church. What is clear is that any attempt to assuage feelings of bitterness and distrust toward the church establishment met with little success, as

---

23. Letter from Timothy Carlson to Glenn Nycklemoe on June 22, 1988, Zion Lutheran Church File, Luther Seminary Archives, St. Paul, MN.

24. Letter from Timothy Carlson to Glenn Nycklemoe on June 22, 1988.

Zion Lutheran Church became a member of the AFLC at some point within the next few years. Today, Zion Lutheran Church apparently remains a small yet vital congregation. Information about the congregation and its worship life on its website is vague, yet one can deduce that the Haugean tradition of simplicity in worship has been retained. Its emphasis on a "relaxed and comfortable" and "family friendly" atmosphere conveys that impression.

East Immanuel Lutheran Church of St. Paul, Minnesota

Østre Immanuels menighet, now known as East Immanuel Lutheran Church, was organized as a congregation of Hauge's Synod in St. Paul, Minnesota, in 1888. The initial pastor was the prominent Haugean M. G. Hanson. Another notable Haugean among its membership was O. H. Oace,[25] who would go on to oppose the merger of 1917 and write his book about Hauge's Synod in 1932. Nevertheless, the congregation's history from its fiftieth anniversary simply states that the congregation became a member of the NLCA at the time of the merger.[26] In 1940, the pastor of East Immanuel Lutheran Church, Clarence M. Hansen, resigned to assume the role of evangelist within the evangelism program of the NLCA.[27] Though this decision is not necessarily reflective of the attitude of the entire congregation, it is an indication that at least some within the congregation, while honoring their Haugean heritage, still took their relationship with the wider NLCA seriously. In that spirit, the same congregational history records that the congregation's purchase of the new *Service Book and Hymnal* in 1958 was a sign that "the members of East Immanuel were anxious to move ahead with the planned merger with the American Lutheran Church and the United Evangelical Luthern [sic] Church in 1960."[28] It is not clear how this hymnal was used, however, and whether it led the congregation to adopt a liturgical style of worship.

A turning point in the life of East Immanuel Lutheran Church came in 1970. Its history reports a two-week "spiritual emphasis time" of prayer

---

25. East Immanuel Lutheran Church, Fiftieth-Anniversary Book.
26. East Immanuel Lutheran Church, Fiftieth-Anniversary Book, 10.
27. East Immanuel Lutheran Church, One-Hundredth-Anniversary Book.
28. East Immanuel Lutheran Church, One-Hundredth-Anniversary Book, 15.

and Bible study that led to a time of renewal among members. Though the description is vague, it is reported that "the Holy Spirit fell as in the book of Acts, chapter two, with signs and wonders accompanying the preaching of the Word." Further, this neo-Pentecostal or charismatic emphasis is described as having contributed to "a significant increase in the lay ministry of East Immanuel members at prisons, retirement homes, homes for the retarded, and private homes."[29] The relationship of the congregation to TALC began to deteriorate in the early 1980s, however, when East Immanuel Lutheran Church voted in 1982 to withhold and redirect benevolence from the Southeastern Minnesota District of TALC because of that district's support of the Minnesota Council of Churches, "which condoned the practice of homosexuality as a valid Christian lifestyle." In 1985, the congregation "voted overwhelmingly to withdraw membership from the American Lutheran Church" after studying the "Narrative Description for a New Lutheran Church," a document that outlined plans for the creation of the ELCA in 1988. The stated concern was that "the proposed Constitution fell short in its statement concerning God's Word" and the "liberalism that had crept into the proposed constitution which is in opposition to clear statements in the Bible." The congregation's history expresses pride that it "took a stand for the infallibility and inerrancy of the Word of God in all matters of faith and life."[30]

For a number of years after its withdrawal from TALC in 1985, East Immanuel Lutheran Church remained an independent congregation. Around the turn of the century, however, the congregation affiliated with the ARC, a clear sign that its charismatic focus remains a part of its identity. It is likely that the Haugean background of simplicity and spontaneity in worship provided an environment where a charismatic emphasis could take root. The focus on lay activity can also be said to reflect a continuation of the Haugean spirit. As with other congregations in this category, one also observes a concern for expressing biblical authority in terms of "inerrancy" and "infallibility," which differentiates it from many congregations in the second category.

---

29. East Immanuel Lutheran Church, One-Hundredth-Anniversary Book, 16.
30. East Immanuel Lutheran Church, One-Hundredth-Anniversary Book, 19.

CONGREGATIONAL LIFE

Kongsvinger Lutheran Church of Oslo, Minnesota

Adding further color to the diverse fate of former Hauge's Synod congregations is the curious example of Kongsvinger Lutheran Church of rural Oslo, Minnesota. *Kongsvinger evangelisk lutherske menighet* was established in 1880 as an independent congregation and joined Hauge's Synod the following year. It also boasted prominent Haugeans such as M. G. Hanson, N. J. Løhre, and G. O. Mona as its pastors throughout the years.[31] Mona, it will be remembered, was one of the leading voices in opposition to the merger of 1917. Nevertheless, the congregation became a member of the NLCA in 1917 as well as TALC in 1960. It also followed TALC into the ELCA in 1988, but it remained associated with the ELCA for only a short time.

According to a brief congregational history by a longtime member of Kongsvinger Lutheran Church, the congregation underwent more than one shift in piety throughout the decades.[32] Mathsen notes that the congregation from early on participated in the revival piety that was typical of the Haugeans, which he claims bore some resemblance to the modern charismatic movement. Also, though ordained pastors were available, he reports that some of these should be more accurately categorized as a "licensed lay ministers" by today's standards, perhaps a reflection of the blurred line between clergy and laity that existed within Hauge's Synod. The Haugean personal piety continued in the congregation well into the twentieth century, with the congregational constitution as late as 1978 enumerating personal lifestyle requirements for members to remain in good standing. This also impacted the practice of the Lord's Supper in the congregation. As Mathsen reports, although the "Exhortation before Communion" in the *Lutheran Hymnary* and the *Concordia Hymnal* did not focus on personal holiness as a prerequisite for reception of the Lord's Supper, there was an emphasis, possibly having its origin in the congregational preaching, on "worthiness" being tied to an individual's morality. Even with the infrequent administration of the Lord's Supper in the congregation, many confirmed members would abstain from the sacrament because of feelings of unworthiness.

With a generational shift in the middle twentieth century, Mathsen reports that Kongsvinger began to adopt, with some resistance from the

---

31. Norlie, *Norsk Lutherske Menigheter i Amerika*, 1:706.

32. Mathsen, "The Haugean Influence." The information about Kongsvinger Lutheran Church is derived from this brief historical reflection.

older members, a stronger liturgical worship life, the impetus of which was the advent of the *Service Book and Hymnal* in 1958. A part of the generational shift was a new generation of pastors who tended to emphasize formality in worship and sacramental life, downplaying the ethical seriousness of previous generations. Mathsen describes the pastoral leadership of the latter part of the twentieth century as minimizing the importance of doctrine and presenting a "comfortable Christianity." Yet members began to question "liberal trends" in the wider TALC and especially the ELCA after 1988. Because of the small size of the congregation, a decision was made to cease operations as a congregation for three months to discern whether there was enough vitality for continued congregational life. The decision was made to remain in existence, but Kongsvinger Lutheran Church began openly to explore alternative affiliations. Mathsen reports that the Northwestern Minnesota Synod of the ELCA informed the congregation at that point that they could not assist them in securing a new pastor due to the fact that several other ELCA congregations existed within a ten-mile radius of Kongsvinger. This seems to imply that they viewed the presence of Kongsvinger as unnecessary in light of the presence of the other nearby congregations, but it should also be considered that the officialdom sensed the inevitability of Kongsvinger's disaffiliation from the ELCA and sought to make the exit as easy as possible.

In the end, the congregation chose to affiliate with the AALC, which was newly formed by a group of diverse congregations from TALC who refused to join the ELCA. These congregations viewed themselves as more conservative than the ELCA, in particular rejecting the ordination of women as pastors. Yet there was considerable diversity in emphasis and piety among these congregations, with some combining social conservativism with a strong Lutheran confessional focus and others with a charismatic emphasis on the "gifts of the Spirit" in worship. From 1988 to 2013, Mathsen reports that Kongsvinger Lutheran Church was served by pastors from the charismatic camp and that this low-church style of worship appealed to some who were influenced by a residual Haugean emphasis. In 2014, however, the new pastor was of a different character and emphasized Lutheran confessional theology. Mathsen reports that the residual Haugeanism in the congregation created some tension, especially regarding the level of authority that the pastor claimed for himself. The new confessional emphasis on the sacraments as means of grace began to replace the Haugean spiritual subjectivism that was present at Kongsvinger from the beginning.

At present, Mathsen reports that Kongsvinger Lutheran Church is recognized as a "confessional Lutheran community" with an emphasis on God's objective Word and little focus on personal spiritual life. Its website reflects and confirms this analysis, with direct statements concerning subscription to creeds and Lutheran confessional documents.[33] The history of Kongsvinger Lutheran Church therefore adds important diversity in the search for the continuation of the Haugean spirit in American Lutheranism.

The Second Category

This second category of former Hauge's Synod congregations consists of those that departed from the "mainstream" after the more recent controversies in the ELCA and ELCIC, from 1999 to the present. As with the previous category, these six congregations have been chosen both because of the amount of available information about them and what these congregations demonstrate about the continuation of the Haugean tradition in North American Lutheranism. These congregations all departed from the "mainstream" after the 2009 decision of the ELCA regarding the issue of human sexuality. For that reason, they embody the Haugean tendency to exist within ecclesiastical organizations as leaven in a larger batch of dough. However, the decision regarding human sexuality appears to have been the "last straw" on top of other issues that have troubled them over the years. Also, at least as far as can be determined from available information, the congregations in this category, although emphasizing a general concern for biblical authority, differentiate themselves from the first category through their lack of emphasis on articulating the exact nature of that authority. In most cases, these congregations do not use the words "inerrant" and "infallible" to describe the Scriptures.

SINGSAAS CHURCH OF HENDRICKS, MINNESOTA

Already mentioned as one of the largest congregations of the former Hauge's Synod prior to the 1917 merger, *Singsoos norsk evangelisk lutherske menighet* was founded in 1874 and joined Hauge's Synod two years

---

33. Kongsvinger Lutheran Church, lines 38–43.

later at the time of the reorganization of the synod. Though technically located on the South Dakota side of the border, the nearest community to Singsaas Church is the Minnesota border town of Hendricks. After its departure from the ELCA in 2009, Singsaas became a member of the AFLC. Today, however, this once prominent congregation of Hauge's Synod has left behind its Lutheran heritage and considers itself a "non-denominational" church.

The prominent place that this congregation occupied within Hauge's Synod was enhanced by the fact that its long-term pastor Jakob Jakobson Eske also served as president of Hauge's Synod from 1915 to 1917 as well as on the union committee the year before the merger. The congregation takes its name from the town of Singsås, Norway, just south of Trondheim. It will be remembered that Hauge himself was imprisoned in Trondheim during Christmas of 1799, and the congregation's written history emphasizes its roots in Hauge's awakening in that region of Norway.[34] It also makes note of the fact that the initial pastor of the congregation, Anfin Olsen Utheim, was ordained for service under Eielsen's leadership.[35] At least for a time, the Haugean heritage lived on strongly in the memory of Singsaas Church.

The informal written history of the congregation interestingly notes the participation of the congregation in an ecumenical worship service with a nearby Methodist congregation on the occasion of the departure of soldiers for World War I, held on June 5, 1917. Of interest is that the Methodist Episcopal minister who led the service was Theodore Sigvaard Mondale, the father of future United States Senator and Vice President Walter Mondale.[36] More significantly, however, this is a reflection of the ecumenical openness of Hauge's Synod. On the same page, the history claims that Singsaas Lutheran Church played a prominent role in the union movement that same year. Though it does not elaborate on the details of the congregation's role in the movement, this is presumably because of the presence and influence of J. J. Eske. Hence, the congregation evidently entered into its life in the NLCA without significant reservations. It continued its affiliation with the "mainstream" throughout the life of the NLCA/ELC, into TALC, and into the ELCA, eventually finding

---

34. Singsaas Lutheran Church, "Congregational History Book." At the time of this writing, this congregational history is incomplete. Nevertheless, it provides important information about the congregation and its self-understanding.

35. Singsaas Lutheran Church, "Congregational History Book," 10.

36. Singsaas Lutheran Church, "Congregational History Book," 24.

itself in a parish relationship with a congregation in the town of Hendricks. Curiously, the history, at least in incomplete form, says nothing of the dissatisfaction that led it to sever ties with the ELCA. However, the congregation moved quickly toward disaffiliation from the ELCA after the sexuality vote in August of 2009. By November of 2010, the congregation decided to affiliate with the AFLC, viewing this organization as a return to its Haugean roots, declaring that the congregation was "Once Again a Free Lutheran Church":

> Two weeks ago the Singsaas Congregation unanimously voted to affiliate with the Association of Free Lutheran Congregations (AFLC or Free Lutheran Church). The next day, the AFLC received Singsaas as a member church. Today's service is our first as a Free Lutheran Church. We celebrate returning to our historic roots and establishing a foundation built firmly on the Word.[37]

After its affiliation with the AFLC, the congregation's worship style closely resembled the typical pattern followed by Hauge's Synod. A bulletin template intended to familiarize guest preachers with the format of Sunday worship indicated that the practice of laity offering public testimony remained a part of congregational life. Furthermore, the format allowed for a certain amount of spontaneity and did not follow a liturgical format from any hymnal. Requests for particular hymns were taken during the worship service, and special music providers were encouraged to offer "comments on why this song inspires them, or similar comments."[38]

First Lutheran Church of Pontiac, Illinois

One of the two congregations served by G. M. Bruce between 1910 and 1911, during which time he began the publication the *Lutheran Intelligencer*, First Lutheran Church of Pontiac, Illinois, is now one of the two former Hauge's Synod congregations that count themselves members of the NALC. First Lutheran Church's affiliation with the more structured NALC along with its history with G. M. Bruce makes it worth mentioning among this sampling of former Hauge's Synod congregations. Unfortunately, available information about First Lutheran Church and its

---

37. Singsaas Lutheran Church, Worship Bulletin.
38. Singsaas Lutheran Church, Worship Bulletin Template.

history is scant. Its website provides some information about congregational activities, but there is no reference to its Haugean past.[39] A congregation of reasonable size, First Lutheran Church holds three worship services each weekend, two of which are labeled "traditional" and one of which is labeled "contemporary." The Lord's Supper is offered weekly at each worship service. From experience in worship at this congregation, it is clear that First Lutheran Church is an example of a former Hauge's Synod congregation that has adopted a number of contemporary ecclesiastical trends somewhat foreign to its heritage. It uses, for example, the liturgy found in the *Lutheran Book of Worship*. However, a social conservativism remains, as the congregation voted nearly unanimously to disaffiliate from the ELCA early in 2011. Indeed, the website displays the Common Confession, adopted in 2005 by the conservative renewal organization within the ELCA called Lutheran CORE. This Common Confession, which addresses a number of theological and social issues that conservatives in the ELCA viewed as necessary to state explicitly, is now enshrined in the constitution of the NALC.

St. Paul's Lutheran Church of Minneapolis, Minnesota

St. Pauli norsk evangelisk lutherske menighet was a prominent urban congregation of Hauge's Synod in Minneapolis, Minnesota. Perusing the list of its pastors throughout the years, one notes two familiar names already mentioned in this book: I. Eisteinsen and N. J. Løhre.[40] Now a member of LCMC, the congregation is currently located in the Phillips Neighborhood at 1901 Portland Avenue, having switched locations to the building of a derelict Presbyterian church after the construction of the interstate highway system displaced the congregation from its initial location. The remodeling of this church building was accomplished in 1964. According to its pastor as of 2017, the congregation elected to remain in the city at that point rather than retreat to the suburbs, sensing a call to minister to the inner city.[41]

The story of St. Paul's Evangelical Lutheran Church occupies an important place in an evaluation of the continuation of the Haugean tradition in American Lutheranism, as the congregation continues to

---

39. First Lutheran Church of Pontiac, lines 13–23.
40. Norlie, *Norsk Lutherske Menigheter i Amerika*, 1:550.
41. Wells, "Pastor Wells' History Articles."

emphasize many historic Haugean principles. According to the pastor, the congregation was instrumental in the development of the LBI. The historical reflection provided by the pastor also notes the involvement of the congregation in many of the independent ministries discussed in the previous chapter: the WMPL and its antecedent the South American Mission Prayer League, the LEM, and the Lutheran Colportage Society.[42] It also intentionally remained within the "mainstream" for the purpose of serving as positive leaven. The pastor made the following observation about the character of St. Paul's Evangelical Lutheran Church, which is congruent with the Haugean emphasis on providing a spiritual witness within larger ecclesiastical organizations:

> We did not stay in the ELCA because of what we were getting out of it.... We stayed in to be a sea anchor for the ELCA in the midst of the storm. We stayed in, very self-consciously, for the sake of the faithful remnant in every ELCA church.... After the Minneapolis vote, we had no choice. We would've lost 80% of the congregation. Our die was cast long before, so we jumped to LCMC with deep regret.[43]

Indeed, the congregation's policy, adopted in October of 1990, stated that should the ELCA adopt changes in its policy regarding the ordination of persons in same-sex unions, the congregation would move immediately toward disaffiliation from the ELCA. With the changes in ordination policy approved in August of 2009, St. Paul's Evangelical Lutheran Church held its first vote to disaffiliate from the ELCA as early as late September of 2009.[44]

It is well-known that St. Paul's Evangelical Lutheran Church clings strongly to its historic Haugean identity and that its constitution prohibits the use of clerical vestments in worship. Firsthand experience with this congregation confirms that the low-church, nonliturgical worship style has been retained over the years. Yet it would be a mistake to characterize the Haugeanism of the congregation solely in terms of resistance to liturgical formality. According to the pastor, the congregation exemplifies the historic Haugean focus on personal faith as well as on local and global outreach. Emphases of the congregation are a "warm Pietistic faith, with

---

42. Wells, "Pastor Wells' History Articles."

43. Email correspondence from Roland Wells Jr. to Thomas E. Jacobson on February 1, 2016.

44. Mayfield and Mador, "Minneapolis Church Votes."

its emphasis on prayer, personal commitment, world missions, caring for human need and small groups."[45] Notably, the pastor also describes a certain charismatic emphasis in worship, with a focus on the gifts of the Holy Spirit. However, the Haugeanism of the congregation is also demonstrated through its ecumenical focus. Though the pastor identifies a "firm foundation in the Lutheran Confessions" as a mark of the congregation, a certain ecumenical openness can be observed, especially in the context of welcoming various ethnic ministries to utilize the church building. An article in the Minneapolis *Star Tribune* from 2015 highlighted the work of the congregation in ministering to a diverse context. In addition to the regular worship of the congregation conducted in English, a Spanish-speaking Baptist congregation also utilizes the facility, as does an Oromo congregation and an Ethiopian congregation that worships in the Amharic language. Quoting the pastor, the article states: "The Bible says that in the end, there will be every tribe and nation worshiping God together. We've got a taste of that here."[46]

One final thing to note about the manner in which Haugeanism is expressed at St. Paul's Evangelical Lutheran Church is its understanding of biblical authority, an issue that sometimes distinguishes Haugean congregations in the first category from those in the second. At least from the pastor's perspective, the issue of how to articulate biblical authority has been a troubling and divisive one in American Lutheranism at large:

> Within the Lutheran church, the central unanswered challenge remains to develop a clear, consistent understanding of the function and authority of Scripture. This, the hermeneutical task of how Scripture functions as Scripture, of how its authority and centrality can best be upheld in the church, remains as central and yet unanswered as it has for the last entire century. Our seminaries, for the most part, ignore the question. No central attempt is made to articulate this in the midst of an America with many competing and contradictory voices. No greater challenge faces the American church. Lutherans are probably best suited to provide some answers, but so far, those voices have not been heard.[47]

---

45. Email correspondence from Roland Wells Jr. to Thomas E. Jacobson, February 1, 2016.

46. Hopfensperger, "Many Faiths Come Together."

47. Wells, "Chapter of Reflection."

The attitude of the whole congregation toward biblical authority cannot be known for certain, but the pastor's reflection indicates his awareness of the different ways that American Haugeanism has approached the issue and its divisive nature.

Bardo Lutheran Church of Tofield, Alberta

Already mentioned in the third chapter is *Bardo menighet*, which was featured in *Budbæreren* on the occasion of the dedication of its first church building in 1908. Originally known as *Norman menighet*, the name was changed at the time of the dedication. Oddly, the congregation experienced the loss of its building on two different occasions as the result of fires from lightning strikes, first in 1921 and then in 1965.[48] One of three former Hauge's Synod congregations now affiliated with the CALC, it is located in the small town of Tofield, Alberta, several miles east of Edmonton.

Like all congregations of Hauge's Synod, Bardo Lutheran Church was required to consider in 1916 whether to join the new NLCA the following year. Its congregational minutes, though lacking in detail, indicate some hesitation on the part of the membership toward the merger:

> The question of Church Union was next. The Church Union articles and Constitution were read and some opinions expressed. Since the feeling was that we were not ready to vote on this it was decided to hold another meeting on Fri. the 11th of March for a decisive vote. Meeting adjourned.[49]

For unknown reasons, the meeting to consider the union articles was not held until March 24. The minutes record that the union articles were read point by point so as to provide opportunity for commentary by members of the congregation. Afterwards, it is stated that the union articles were unanimously approved.[50] Hence, Bardo Lutheran Church entered the "mainstream" in 1917, also becoming a member of TALC in 1960. When the Canadian District of TALC formed the independent Evangelical Lutheran Church of Canada (ELCC) in 1967, it naturally affiliated with that new church body. Similarly, when the ELCC merged with the Canada

---

48. Town of Tofield, Alberta, "Churches," lines 25–26.
49. Bardo Lutheran Church, congregational minutes, February 25, 1916.
50. Bardo Lutheran Church, congregational minutes, March 24, 1916.

Section of the LCA to form the ELCIC in 1986, Bardo Lutheran Church entered the union.

However, the participation of this congregation in the life of the "mainstream" should not be interpreted as support of the emphases and decisions of the church bodies. According to the current pastor, Bardo Lutheran Church has a long history of friction with these church bodies, described as "an 'over-against-the-church' kind of attitude and feeling."[51] Evidence of this attitude, according to the pastor's letter, is found in the resistance of some members to include benevolence to the denomination in the congregational budget, desiring to leave the decision of denominational financial support to individual members. However, the pastor notes that this attitude has changed since the congregation voted to leave the ELCIC in 2012 over general concerns about the authority of Scripture and more specific concerns about the blessing of same-sex unions.

However, the pastor's insights note that the Haugean identity of Bardo Lutheran Church transcends its social conservatism. Consistent with its Haugean heritage, it has resisted the use of clerical vestments and the liturgical order of its hymnal. This preference for a low-church worship style is confirmed by worship bulletins available on the congregation's website, which indicate no chanted liturgy and an order of worship that departs significantly from the typical format of modern hymnals and denominational worship resources.[52] Also significant for this congregation's Haugean identity is its strong support over the years for a variety of the independent ministries already discussed in this book: the HLIMF, the LEM, the LBI, and the WMPL.[53]

Franklin Lutheran Church of Viroqua, Wisconsin

The *Franklin menighet* near the town of Viroqua, Wisconsin is yet another former Hauge's Synod congregation that sought for a number of years to maintain its Haugean identity within the "mainstream" through the series of twentieth-century mergers. Yet the congregation finally departed from the "mainstream" in 2011 when it joined LCMC. After this, Thomas Fortney, a longtime member of the congregation, wrote a brief

---

51. Personal letter from Kevin Langager to Thomas E. Jacobson on November 4, 2015.

52. Bardo Lutheran Church, worship bulletin, October 1, 2017.

53. Personal letter from Kevin Langager to Thomas E. Jacobson on November 4, 2015.

handwritten history of Franklin Lutheran Church in which he emphasized the enduring legacy of Haugeanism in the congregation. Fortney makes a point of noting that the congregation was able to maintain its Haugean identity for decades after 1917 in that it "insisted on Hauge ministers." Hence, the distinction between the Haugean tradition and its other Norwegian-American counterparts is clear in his mind:

> Franklin Church had been a "Hauge" church almost continuous [sic] since it was started in 1870. The Hauge Synod was disbanded in 1917, but Franklin Church insisted on Hauge ministers. D. T. fit right in. After he retired we hired Peder Nordsletten, also a Hauge minister so we had Hauge ministers for 40 years after that synod was discontinued.[54]

Though it cannot be known how widely Fortney's views are held in the congregation, his interpretation of the history of Franklin Lutheran Church sheds important light on the issue of Haugean self-understanding in North American Lutheranism. He highlights the story of Hauge's persecution by the Church of Norway in the context of the decision of Franklin Lutheran Church to disaffiliate from the ELCA. In so doing, he understands the Haugean tradition as something clearly distinct and often at odds with the church establishment. He understands the disaffiliation of the congregation from the ELCA in 2011 to be the culmination of the underlying friction that existed over the years between the Haugeans and the "mainstream" church establishment:

> Hans Nielsen Hauge was an evangelist Christian. He never became an ordained minister. . . . Hardly anyone was going to church any more since no one could see eye-to-eye with the state church which was dictatorial in many ways. . . . You can see now how the "Hauge" theme has stayed rooted in Franklin congregation all these years and how dropping out of the E.L.C.A. and joining L.C.M.C. when the decision was made in the ELCA to hire homosexual ministers was just the thing to do.[55]

South Zumbro Lutheran Church of Kasson, Minnesota

Also choosing to depart from the ELCA and join LCMC in 2011 was *Søndre Zumbro menighet* near Kasson in southeastern Minnesota, now

---

54. Thomas Fortney, Franklin Lutheran Church history.
55. Thomas Fortney, Franklin Lutheran Church history, 14.

known as South Zumbro Lutheran Church. Its congregational website makes note of its history as a member of Hauge's Synod as well as the fact that it was for a time in its history in a parish relationship with Zion Lutheran Church of Dexter, which was mentioned in the first category.[56]

The same brief description of congregational life on its website notes the ways that it understands the Haugean tradition to have been maintained in South Zumbro Lutheran Church over the years. In particular, a nonliturgical worship style with an emphasis on preaching and hymns is emphasized as is strong lay leadership and a focus on support of missionaries. A phone conversation with the long-term former pastor confirmed these insights, and he noted that the congregation maintained its Haugean-style worship life even when other former congregations of Hauge's Synod in the area adopted a liturgical emphasis. In describing the history of South Zumbro Lutheran Church, the pastor recalled an attempt to introduce the *Service Book and Hymnal* of 1958, which was not well received. In place of this official worship resource, the congregation utilizes an independent hymnal called *Great Hymns of the Faith*. The pastor's description of congregational life indicates that the Haugean tradition remains a part of South Zumbro Lutheran Church in other ways, such as the "free flowing" nature of worship evidenced by the eagerness of laity to offer announcements and updates. The practice of laity offering spiritual testimony is also retained at South Zumbro Lutheran Church. According to the testimony of a guest preacher,[57] the congregation maintained a "Hauge Festival" as late as the 1990s, and the guest preacher was encouraged to wear a suit rather than an alb.

The Third Category

Having considered a sampling of former Hauge's Synod congregations that have departed from the ELCA and ELCIC at various points throughout the decades after 1917, it is important to acknowledge the existence of the sixty-three congregations that remain a part of the "mainstream." Doing so provides greater color to an evaluation of the continuation of the Haugean tradition in North American Lutheranism. Even though this group of congregations outnumbers those falling within the first and

---

56. South Zumbro Lutheran Church, "About South Zumbro," para. 1.

57. This anecdote is shared with the permission of the guest preacher, Mark Granquist, Professor of The History of Christianity at Luther Seminary, St. Paul, MN.

second categories combined, there is less available information about those who remained. Many do not have a website, and requests by letter to some of these congregations for access to congregational documents and histories went unanswered. Though information from which to draw is limited, it is curious to observe how certain congregations appear to have embraced a broadly "liberal" approach to theology, accompanied by a strong denominational identity. Three examples of these "mainstream" former Hauge's Synod congregations are provided below.

Emmanuel Lutheran Church of Beresford, South Dakota

The community of Beresford, South Dakota, has already been mentioned as a significant center of activity for Hauge's Synod, being the home of its orphanage and nursing home facility. Naturally, this community was also home to one of the synod's congregations. Emmanuel Lutheran Church of Hauge's Synod was founded in Beresford in 1893.

Unfortunately, a congregational website is the sole source of information available about Emmanuel Lutheran Church today, and a more detailed evaluation of the congregation and its history would reveal more about how its Haugean heritage is lived out among its membership today. However, it is noteworthy that the congregational website makes no reference to Emmanuel's Haugean past. Instead, the website emphasizes the congregation's membership in the ELCA and its South Dakota Synod. Under the title "Who We Are," there is little description of life within the congregation other than its mission statement. In place of that, there is a detailed enumeration of facts about the denomination of the ELCA and the South Dakota Synod in particular. The description simply concludes with a note of welcome: "This is Christ's Church. There is a place for you here."[58] A congregation of reasonable size, evidenced by its two worship services each Sunday, it appears that Emmanuel Lutheran Church understands itself as an expression of the larger "mainstream" of the ELCA, emphasizing "being nurtured in Word and Sacrament," but also social justice themes often associated with "liberal" churches, such as upholding "human dignity," "sharing compassion with all who suffer," and "feeding all whose bodies lack nourishment."[59] Such a social focus

---

58. Emmanuel Lutheran Church, "Emmanuel's Mission Statement," para. 2.
59. Emmanuel Lutheran Church, "Emmanuel's Mission Statement," para. 3.

is not foreign to the historic Haugean tradition, however. With the community of Beresford serving as home to the two signature social outreach ministries of Hauge's Synod, this focus of Emmanuel Lutheran Church is understandable.

Trinity Lutheran Church of Madison, Wisconsin

Even more explicit in its adoption of "liberal" ecclesiastical trends is Trinity Lutheran Church of Madison, Wisconsin. Founded as *Trefoldigheds norsk evangelisk lutherske menighet* of Hauge's Synod in 1906, this urban congregation is located in the historic Haugean stronghold of Dane County, Wisconsin, which also happens to be home to the University of Wisconsin-Madison.

As with Emmanuel Lutheran Church of Beresford, South Dakota, Trinity Lutheran Church of Madison, Wisconsin makes no reference on its website to its roots in Hauge's Synod. Also like Emmanuel, Trinity emphasizes its relationship with the ELCA. The congregation's membership in the Reconciling in Christ organization, which seeks to affirm "people of all ages, ethnic backgrounds, sexual orientations, gender identities, political persuasions, physical and mental abilities, educational backgrounds, marital or partnered status, and economic conditions,"[60] certainly sets it apart as "liberal" in contrast to the more theologically and socially conservative congregations in the first and second categories. Notably absent for a former Hauge's Synod congregation is any emphasis in its mission statement concerning personal faith and morality. Instead, it "lifts up all people as children of God." Concern for morality appears to be expressed through an emphasis on addressing societal ills such as racism. For example, in honor of the five-hundredth anniversary of the Reformation in 2017, the congregation hosted an event sponsored by its ELCA South-Central Synod of Wisconsin entitled "Martin Luther and the Reformation Meets Black Lives Matter and Liberation Theology," encouraging people to "Join us for an informative discussion on a timely topic!"[61]

---

60. Trinity Lutheran Church, "Welcome," para. 1.
61. Trinity Lutheran Church, "Mission," lines 11–12.

Scandia Lutheran Church of Centerville, South Dakota

Scandia evangelisk lutherske menighet of Hauge's Synod was founded in 1908 in the eastern South Dakota town of Centerville, which was for a time the home of the prominent Haugean pastor and evangelist J. O. Gisselquist. Like a number of other former Hauge's Synod congregations, it remains a part of the "mainstream" of the ELCA to the present. Like the previous two congregations, there is no mention of the congregation's roots in Hauge's Synod on its website.

Working within the limitations of its congregational website, however, one notes the existence of some diversity of piety within this third category of congregations. Though its website makes note of its relationship with the ELCA, the pastor's comments indicate a congregational piety that is more "spiritual" rather than "earthly," emphasizing worldly service yet not neglecting a personal piety grounded in the atonement of Christ:

> Gathering in faith is a commitment that is made every day of our lives as we live out our faith and worship our God through our every action and our every word. Gathering in faith means that the one thing we have in common with the entire church around the world is our faith in a God who loves us so much that he was willing to live, suffer, die and be resurrected so that we would not have to die in our sin. As we gather in faith we confess that it is not by our own strength or power that we receive this gift, but only through the blood of Jesus our Lord.[62]

Of course, one obtains an incomplete picture of a congregation from a website, but these remarks demonstrate more congruence with historic Haugeanism than the "liberal" focus of Trinity Lutheran Church of Madison, for example.

CONCLUSION

The merger of 1917 was more than an agreement among ecclesiastical officials. It brought congregations of the three merging traditions into fellowship with one another and thereby facilitated the formation of parishes and merged congregations. In the process, the distinct tradition of

---

62. Scandia Lutheran Church, "From the Pastor," para. 1.

Hauge's Synod was required to coexist with that of the UNLC and the Norwegian Synod and understandably encountered difficulty maintaining its tradition given its minority status and the small size of most of its congregations. Out of the 342 congregations that existed as of 1916, the fate of many of them cannot be precisely determined. It can be determined that some of these congregations dissolved or merged with other congregations at some point after 1917. However, there are 103 former Hauge's Synod congregations that still exist as independent entities. Thirty-nine percent, a total of forty of these congregations, now find themselves outside of the "mainstream" of the ELCA and ELCIC. However, consistent with the Haugean ethos of providing spiritual leaven in a larger batch of dough, these congregations did not depart from the "mainstream" as a single group at a single time. Some departed at different times in the decades following 1917, joining a variety of church bodies such as the AFLC, the CLBA, the AALC, and the ARC. Many, however, departed after the more recent controversies in the ELCA and ELCIC, especially after the 2009 ELCA decision regarding human sexuality, to join primarily the church association of LCMC. An evaluation of some of these congregations in the first and second categories confirms that the friction between the Haugeans and the officialdom of the "mainstream" church bodies existed on a congregational level. However, there is considerable diversity among these congregations, with a variety of influences coloring their piety at present. It must also be remembered that many former Hauge's Synod congregations have remained a part of the "mainstream," with some expressing strong "liberal" tendencies.

6

Haugeanism Today

HISTORIANS ARE RIGHTLY CAUTIOUS when writing about events too close to them in historical distance, but a necessary part of evaluating the continuation of American Haugeanism is discussion of more recent developments in the broader North American Lutheran tradition in which Haugeanism functioned as leaven in a larger batch of dough. Attempting to find an organized Haugeanism today is challenging because Haugeanism, as has been established, was much less concerned with institution building than it was with the quality of spiritual life. Self-identified Haugeans demonstrated as a part of their tradition a strong ecumenical focus, desiring to work with those perceived as kindred spirits in other synodical organizations and in at least some circumstances with those in other Christian traditions. As time went on, this ecumenical commitment expanded beyond the Norwegian-American Lutheran environment, especially after the transition to the English language was realized. For this reason, American Haugeans were often strong contributors to various independent ministries, many of which continue to exist to this day. Identifying organizations at present that can definitively be labeled "Haugean" is difficult both because of this ecumenical focus of Haugeanism as well as the fact that the passage of time tends to erode distinctions in piety. Nevertheless, one can observe at present the continued existence of organizations heavily influenced by the Haugeanism of former times as well as at least one attempt to perpetuate explicitly the name and tradition of Haugeanism. Observing the work of these organizations in more recent decades reveals in many cases that a sense of friction continued to characterize the relationship between such organizations and the "mainstream" church establishment. At the same time, these independent organizations continue to demonstrate willingness to relate to members of the "mainstream." These organizations also came to and continue to exert a great deal of influence on Lutheran organizations outside of the "mainstream." Their independence gives them freedom to relate to various church bodies as leaven in a larger batch of dough.

OVERVIEW OF AMERICAN LUTHERANISM AFTER 1960

The fourth chapter provided a brief overview of the broader American Lutheran environment in which the Haugean tradition would function, highlighting significant developments after the merger of 1917. Discussion in the fourth chapter dealt largely with events within the NLCA/ELC, which ceased to exist with the merger of 1960 that produced TALC. It is now necessary to consider developments after this time, up to the present. Though a number of these developments after 1960 have been referred to already in the fifth chapter concerning congregational life, a basic overview of key events in this period provides the narrative backdrop of the story of the continuation of the Haugean spirit.

Related to the transition to the English language discussed earlier, Lutherans in North America began in the early twentieth century to move gradually out of various ethnic enclaves and into a unified American identity. This was true especially in the post– World War II era.[1] This was a time of tremendous numerical growth for the United States in particular, and Lutheran growth, stemming in part from a strong focus on home mission, mirrored or exceeded that of the country as a whole. It can be argued that the Haugean tradition was no small contributor to this focus on home mission and therefore of Lutheran growth, at least among the ELC. In 1952, the Commission on Evangelism of the ELC led by George Aus established a program of parish evangelism that was nicknamed "the P-T-R," standing for "Preaching-Teaching-Reaching."[2] This program was carried out as an evangelistic strategy involving multiple congregations in a given area and made use of laypeople who were trained to visit the unchurched. A "religious canvass" of a community was used to identify those who would be reached by this program. The

---

1. Granquist, *Lutherans in America*, 263. Discussion in this section is based on pages 261 to 290 in this volume.
2. Nelson, *Lutheran Church*, 2:266–67.

shape of this "P-T-R" program had its roots in the ministry of J. O. Gisselquist in Centerville, South Dakota. It then became a part of the LEM, at which point it was adopted by the ELC.[3]

In addition to the various intra-Lutheran cooperative ventures that had been established after World War I, such as the NLC and the American Lutheran Conference, many Lutheran synods began to associate with broader Lutheran and ecumenical federations established after World War II, such as the Lutheran World Federation, the National Council of Churches, and the World Council of Churches. The transition to the English language being largely complete, coupled with participation in these ecumenical ventures, meant that the move toward American Lutheran merger was all but inevitable. As the old ethnic lines began to blur, the reasons to perpetuate the ethnically based denominations seemed fewer. Fearing "unionism," however, the Lutheran synods affiliated with the Synodical Conference remained aloof from these cooperative ventures.

Yet it was not exactly clear what form the merger process would take. It was not only the Synodical Conference that expressed concerns about theological integrity in the merger process; a group of "middle synods," including the NLCA/ELC, had formed the American Lutheran Conference in 1930. Though these synods participated in the broader NLC along with the large ULCA, which was considered more liberal, the American Lutheran Conference excluded the ULCA from its membership. For this reason, some consider the American Lutheran Conference to have been a defensive alliance against the larger and more liberal ULCA, a means of distinguishing themselves theologically. Two issues in particular were sources of contention. The first had to do with the language of "inerrancy" regarding the Scriptures, which the American Lutheran Conference synods held in common with the Synodical Conference but which the ULCA lacked. The second had to do with the degree of agreement required for church fellowship. The ULCA, influenced by Erlangen confessional theology, was open to merger negotiations on the basis of a shared commitment to the Lutheran confessional documents, whereas the American Lutheran Conference synods and the Synodical Conference required subscription to extraconfessional theses that further articulated theological positions. Most synods of the American Lutheran Conference were open to a merger process involving the fellow members of that cooperative federation but that excluded the ULCA.

---

3. Gisselquist, *Called to Preach*, 81.

The Augustana Evangelical Lutheran Church, of Swedish origin, though a member of the American Lutheran Conference, desired that merger negotiations be open to all interested parties, including the ULCA. Historically, the Swedish Augustana Synod, which was renamed in 1948, was a member of the General Council, though it chose to pursue an independent course in 1918 rather than enter the merger that produced the ULCA.

For this reason, there emerged two different merger processes leading up to 1960. In the end, the Augustana Evangelical Lutheran Church chose to honor its heritage in the General Council by entering the merger process with the ULCA. Those two church bodies were joined by the much smaller Finnish Suomi Synod and the even smaller American Evangelical Lutheran Church, the smaller of the two Danish Lutheran synods. The four bodies merged in 1962 to form the LCA. In the meantime, the synods of the American Lutheran Conference pursued their own merger process. The largest of these bodies was the Norwegian ELC, which was joined by the slightly smaller German ALC and the much smaller Danish UELC. These three merged in 1960 to form TALC. The Lutheran Free Church lacked the votes internally to join TALC that year. They mustered enough support in 1962, however, and that body joined TALC in 1963. A significant percentage of its congregations, however, resisted the movement toward merger and met in 1963 to form their own organization known as the AFLC.

Hence, though there remained a number of small Lutheran synods, there were as of the early 1960s three major-sized Lutheran denominations in North America of similar size, all of which had membership numbers rising above two million: the LCA, the LCMS, and TALC. Though the merger process of this era resulted in two separate groups rather than a larger merged body, the hope of many was that there would eventually be another merger that would unite all three larger church bodies. An encouraging sign was that the *Service Book and Hymnal* of 1958 was in widespread use throughout both TALC and the LCA, providing some unity of worship practice. Also, with the mergers complete, maintaining the NLC was no longer practical, as the number of church bodies connected to it was now reduced to two.[4] In its place, there formed a new organization that came to include the participation of the LCMS as well: the Lutheran Council in the USA (LCUSA). The LCUSA,

---

4. Granquist, *Lutherans in America*, 296. Discussion in this section is derived from pages 291 to 318.

like the NLC, sought to coordinate various "external" activities of the three church bodies, thereby allowing for the participation of the LCMS. Another significant move toward unity in this era was the establishment of altar and pulpit fellowship between the LCMS and TALC in 1969.

Perhaps in reaction to this greater ecumenical openness in the LCMS, there emerged within that church body a struggle between conservatives and moderates. These moderates cannot be described as liberal but were simply more open to cautious cooperation with other Lutherans and engagement with modern intellectual trends, including more recent developments in biblical scholarship. In 1974, the conflict resulted in division. After most students and faculty walked out of Concordia Seminary in St. Louis on February 19 of that year, an alternative church body was formed in 1976 called the Association of Evangelical Lutheran Churches (AELC). Though hopes were high among some that a sizeable number of LCMS congregations would join the AELC, only around 250 did so. Those "exiled" from the LCMS came to form relationships with members of TALC and the LCA, especially on the level of seminary education. With the conservatives in control of the LCMS, the relationship between the LCMS and TALC and the LCA began to deteriorate, a situation exacerbated by the fact that both TALC and the LCA had begun in 1970 the practice of ordaining women to the office of pastor. The relationship of altar and pulpit fellowship between the LCMS and TALC ended in 1981 when the LCMS voted to discontinue it. It became increasingly clear that the LCMS would not pursue a merger process with the other larger bodies, and the AELC moved toward closer fellowship with TALC and the LCA. In the early 1980s, plans were underway for a merger of the small AELC with TALC and the LCA, which was realized in 1988 with the formation of the ELCA. The ELCA began with well over five million members and brought for the first time a majority of Lutherans in the United States into a single church body. A small number of congregations, mostly from TALC, elected not to join the new ELCA and formed the alternative AALC. Despite that, the formation of the ELCA was heralded as a significant accomplishment and was accompanied by excitement on the part of many. However, the ELCA experienced a number of conflicts of its own in the first twenty-five years of its existence, especially over the doctrine of the ministry and the issue of human sexuality. Congregations and individuals began leaving the ELCA in large numbers beginning in the year 2000, and LCMC was established that year as an alternative church association for pastors and congregations unwilling to accept the requirement of episcopal ordination in accordance with the 1999 ecumenical agreement with the Episcopal Church USA. The 2009 decisions related to human sexuality increased the exodus from the ELCA, and the NALC was formed in 2010 as yet another alternative church body for dissenters.

HAUGEANISM IN THE AMERICAN LUTHERAN CHURCH

Understanding the basic story of American Lutheran merger and other significant developments in the period in question is important for establishing the context in which Haugeanism functioned. Yet overly focusing on external developments such as merger is contrary to the spirit of Haugeanism, which tended to express indifference toward such developments, demonstrating greater concern for spiritual life within larger organizations. For that reason, it is important to consider the continuation of the Haugean tradition after 1960, at which point the ELC became a part of the larger TALC.

The Ministry of Seth Eastvold

Seth Clarence Eastvold figures prominently in the memories of those active in the ELC and TALC in the late 1950s and early 1960s. When David Preus, former president of TALC, was asked what individuals from the former Hauge's Synod played a prominent role in the life of the ELC, he understandably mentioned G. M. Bruce, but the first and only other name he mentioned was that of Seth Eastvold, the son of prominent Haugean C. J. Eastvold.[5] Seth Eastvold has already been mentioned in chapter four in the context of the presidential election in the ELC to succeed J. A. Aasgaard. Harrisville claims that Seth Eastvold was a "big shot" who "ran" against Fredrik Schiotz, who was ultimately elected.[6] Retired pastor and missionary James Knutson remembers Seth Eastvold during a trip that Eastvold and his wife took around the world. In particular, he recalls that Seth Eastvold was an outspoken critic of the World Council of Churches and that "you could write an interesting book about Seth

---

5. David Preus, Interview by Thomas E. Jacobson.
6. Harrisville, Interview by Thomas E. Jacobson.

Eastvold. Maybe somebody will."⁷ Preus mentions that Seth Eastvold "was indistinguishable as particularly Haugean," but an examination of some of his writings indicates that Haugean piety continued to play a role in his work in the later years of the ELC and into TALC and that he experienced some friction with the perspectives of others, possibly because of his Haugean background. Serving for a time as a pastor in Eau Claire, Wisconsin, he went on to become the president of Pacific Lutheran College (PLC) in Tacoma, Washington. This position of prominence helps explain his candidacy for the presidency of the ELC.

Former students of PLC remember Seth Eastvold as a strong administrator and fundraiser for the college who cared about the students. But they also remember him for his attention to morality among students and his "pietist form of religion."⁸ He reportedly sought to provide alternative activities for students, such as parlor games, in lieu of dances, and he considered jazz music an "abomination." Where Seth Eastvold apparently ran into some difficulty, however, was in the issue of required chapel attendance for students at PLC. In a 1952 address that was published by the ELC the same year, Seth Eastvold argued for the position of mandatory chapel attendance at church-related colleges such as PLC, arguing that such a requirement was a major part of what distinguishes a Christian school from a secular one. Living in what he described as "a lawless age," Seth Eastvold articulated his understanding of Christian freedom; while many viewed freedom as the ability to choose to attend chapel at church-related colleges, he argued that allowing worship on college campuses to be neglected led to a loss of freedom in the most important definition of the word:

> Our freedom has been founded upon law and order. The value of the individual and the dignity of man can only be understood in the light of the Gospel of Jesus Christ. It is our business to get this truth across to our entire College family. If this is to be done, we must gather to hear and learn. Little by little America is losing that point of view. Many Christian colleges have made full surrender of the principles of their founders. Instead of finding freedom, they are enslaved by the gods of this world. Time is running out. A critical decision faces us in the few remaining really Christian colleges in America.⁹

---

7. Knutson, Interview by Thomas E. Jacobson.
8. Schaffner, Interview with Dave and Marilyn Knudson.
9. Eastvold, *Let Us Go to Chapel*, 4.

Seth Eastvold never mentioned specifically any particular colleges that had embraced the practice of voluntary chapel attendance, but it is reasonable to assume that other colleges of the ELC were in his mind. Differences between the Haugeans and others in the vision of what a Christian college should be were not new, as has been observed in the case of JLC shortly before it closed in 1924.

Seth Eastvold's comments on this issue were pointed and passionate, indicating the seriousness of debate. He lamented that the German model of education, which in his view divorced spirituality from learning, had begun to replace the British and American model, which placed college chapels in the center of campuses.[10] He further argued that it was just as appropriate for a Christian college to require chapel attendance as it was for them to require the study of particular subjects. His vision for worship services in the college chapel was that they would provide proper spiritual focus to learning that would impact daily living. To that end, he desired that "chapel services should always consist of song, prayer, scripture, and a brief address setting forth the ideas of the Christian life."[11] His Haugean background shines through in this focus on Christian life and morals, but it also finds expression in his ecumenical vision of "a Christ centered program" where "every true evangelical Christian will feel at home."[12] For Seth Eastvold, the existence of church-related colleges was only justified if the education there encouraged an active Christian faith that would impact the world:

> There is too much lethargy and shoddiness on the average Christian campus. There is too much difference between our theory and our practice. Christian education sounds wonderful in the catalog. The test comes as we see our product emerge from college into the university of hard knocks. We must acquaint our students with an experienced Christian life wherein are the roots of democracy. Sir Richard Livingstone has said, "The influence of the universities on the world is disappointingly limited."[13]

In reflecting on his life and ministry from an unknown date, likely toward the end of his presidency of PLC in the late 1950s or early 1960s, Seth Eastvold revealed his Haugean background by expressing his ecumenical

10. Eastvold, *Let Us Go to Chapel*, 8.
11. Eastvold, *Let Us Go to Chapel*, 20.
12. Eastvold, *Let Us Go to Chapel*, 21.
13. Eastvold, *Let Us Go to Chapel*, 21.

Lutheran focus as well as his focus on the importance of conversion in Christian life. Pointing out that he was a committed Lutheran and no friend of "unionism," his reflection nonetheless argues that "there is a lot of lattitude [sic] in approach" in how Lutheranism is expressed. This perhaps reflects the spirit of the "Interpretation" of the union articles of 1917. He appears to refer to his Haugean background as something unfamiliar to many Lutherans of his time as he provided an apology for his emphasis on conversion in Christian life:

> We have many backgrounds. It is easy to sense that some of my Lutheran brethren are strangers to some of the things that I know—with fifty years in my background, the kind of pastors I had, the kind of schools I attended, the kind of churches I served as pastor, the kind of people I lived with. But we meet at the altar of God—we are different in some respects, but there is room for practical differences.[14]

In that spirit, Seth Eastvold did not expect that everyone would experience conversion in the same way. He acknowledged that while some experience a dramatic and conscious conversion, others exhibit a relationship with God from childhood. At the same time, he admonished the Lutherans of his era not to despise the principle of conversion properly understood in a Lutheran theological framework, and he warned of espousing a comfortable Christianity. He clearly sensed that large parts of American Lutheranism were downplaying the reality of personal spiritual struggle, and he emphasized the traditional Haugean theme of the importance of living faith:

> In the second place, the baptized do fall away—not all. I think I've been a Christian always, and yet I am converted daily. ... But I do know some people who have fallen from grace to become the children of the devil, and they do need conversion—a coming back to God. . . . Conversion is necessary, and the Lutheran Church has whole pages in its dogmatics dealing with the doctrine of conversion. Let's never surrender that doctrine to the Reformed sects, or to those who are of a radical type. That's apostolic Christianity and belongs to us as Lutherans.[15]

---

14. S. C. Eastvold, Personal reflection.
15. S. C. Eastvold, Personal reflection.

He went on to criticize the practice of giving false assurance of salvation to people who are struggling, granting absolution without reckoning with sin, which was a historic concern of the Haugeans:

> There is a pastor here in the west who told me that while he was at a Lutheran Seminary he did not have peace with God. He went to one of his theological professors, and the professor didn't know what he was talking about. Now that can happen in a Lutheran Seminary, and it has happened. It was disturbing to his faith, but that professor shouldn't have told him, "There's nothing the matter with you. You're all right, you're a Christian." The student knew he didn't have peace with God. . . . <u>We do not easily fool the guilty sinner with absolution!</u>[16]

Despite Preus's assertion that Seth Eastvold was not distinguishable as a Haugean, his emphases show an affinity for that tradition all the while demonstrating the continuing friction between that tradition and other parts of American Lutheranism. The opposition to his candidacy for president of the ELC discussed in the fourth chapter can be understood in light of the Haugeanism he expressed and the negative reaction to it.

Lutherans Alert

Though the merger process of the late 1950s and early 1960s was taken by many as an encouraging sign of Lutheran unity in North America with hopes for an even larger merger at some point in the future, there were signs of internal disunity in the early years of TALC. The conflict centered on the teaching of biblical "inerrancy." As a part of the heritage of TALC in the American Lutheran Conference, the word "inerrant" in reference to the Bible was included in the constitution of TALC. Yet revealing the limited value of the word "inerrant" for upholding the authority of the Scriptures in the denomination, there emerged a conflict concerning the meaning of the term.

In 1966, an organization called Lutherans Alert was formed to combat the perceived liberal trends that they saw as gaining ascendancy in TALC. The organization's president, R. H. Redal, stated the purpose of Lutherans Alert in the first issue of its magazine:

---

16. S. C. Eastvold, Personal reflection.

> With this first issue of LUTHERANS ALERT the invitation goes out to men and women everywhere to participate in the promulgation of truth. We invite a sleeping Church to awaken from its apathy and indifference. The teaching that the Bible is the Word of God is slowly being taken away from us today. We invite you to BE ALERT to this trend.[17]

Redal went on to elaborate on the situation and the perspective of Lutherans Alert:

> It is not the will of this magazine to be schismatic or negative. Our aim is simply to remind all of us to BE ALERT to the presence of false doctrine and questionable teachings that can so easily and so subtly gain entrance into the Churches of our land. We feel that the lay people of our congregations (and even some of the pastors) are not well enough informed concerning the inroads that neo-orthodoxy, liberalism and Rationalism are making within our Church body. We intend to inform them. If you are concerned for The American Lutheran Church, if you are concerned that the Bible continue to be proclaimed as the written Word of God from cover to cover, and if you realize that there are always possibilities of error creeping into any Church body, then we invite you read this magazine and to subscribe to it![18]

In general, the perspective of Lutherans Alert was that the Bible should be considered "inerrant" as a whole. They were critical of attempts to nuance the meaning of "inerrancy" by limiting such inerrant authority to matters of "faith and life." They argued that the wording of the constitution of TALC should be understood in light of the Minneapolis Theses of 1925 rather than the later United Testimony on Faith and Life of 1952.[19] They were further critical of Frederik Schiotz, president of TALC, for claiming that "inerrancy" should refer to the overall message of the Bible and not to the text itself.

> To be more specific, in the first place Dr. Schiotz attempts to divide the text and the truth of the Bible into two alternatives. Inerrancy refers to one but not the other. This cannot be done! If the text is faulty, the truth is faulty. We communicate by means of words! If the words are wrong the message is garbled. Either

---

17. Redal, "You Are Invited," 1.
18. Redal, "You Are Invited," 1.
19. Redal, "You Are Invited," 5.

the text *and* the truth are inerrant or the text and the truth are errant—false—wrong. You cannot divide the two for the text is the message. Logically, the position Dr. Schiotz has taken is indefensible.[20]

Again, they appealed to the perspectives and confessions of the predecessor bodies such as the ALC and the ELC, claiming that the understanding that these church bodies held of "inerrancy" was different from that articulated by Schiotz.

As can be seen, the concerns of Lutherans Alert were doctrinal in nature, and those concerns led them to establish an alternative theological seminary in Tacoma, Washington, in 1969. Faith Evangelical Lutheran Seminary eventually became a nondenominational institution, but it began among Lutherans in TALC concerned about the issue of biblical "inerrancy." Though the concerns of Lutherans Alert had to do with doctrine, it has already been seen, in the case of Emmanuel Lutheran Church of Kenyon, Minnesota, that Lutherans Alert was influential in at least some former Hauge's Synod congregations. The generally combative tone of the magazine might well have found a willing readership among many Haugeans who felt disenfranchised by the "mainstream," even if the stated concerns of the organization were of a somewhat different nature than the emphasis of historic Haugeanism. Yet it is clear that Lutherans Alert appealed to a broader constituency, which included some who were influenced by the Haugean concerns of former times. Leonard Conrad Masted, a pastor, evangelist, and missionary who was ordained in the NLCA in 1927, offered critical comments about the state of affairs in TALC that same year, which reflect the influence of Haugeanism. L. C. Masted's father, Ludvig Larson Masted, was ordained in 1900 as a part of the UNLC, yet he was educated at RWS. This was evidently the source of the Haugean influence on L. C. Masted.

L. C. Masted began by criticizing the doctrinal confusion that he saw within TALC, noting the presence of "neo-orthodoxy," which he equated with liberal theology, and he sarcastically suggested that TALC should seek reunion with the Roman Catholic Church if doctrine is a matter of such indifference. Yet his remaining comments deviated from a focus on doctrine. He touched on issues of worship, morality, and repentance that troubled him:

---

20. "Editorial," 5. Italics in the text are in the original.

> Is the High-Churchly, liturgical movement going to make an impassable gulf between Clergy and Laity? Must every morning service be exactly the same? Is it always the sermon that must be cut in case there is lack of time? Will empty people, of whom the Church is full, tire of dead forms and leave the Church, as they have in Europe? How soon will Communism, which stands for something, push over a people who will stand for nothing? We had better stop "playing Church."[21]

One senses in the above quote a longing for simpler and more spontaneous worship life of the Haugean tradition, which he viewed as more authentic. He was also critical of the lack of focus on personal morality in TALC:

> Is dancing now to be accepted, since even some of our Church Colleges are sanctioning it? When Israel forsook the Lord, she danced around a calf of gold. What's wrong with the Church when conditions prevail like that reported by one pastor to the effect that about 25 out of 30 members of his Youth Society admitted they had been having illicit sex relationships?[22]

Finally, L. C. Masted lamented the lack of focus on repentance and conversion in the preaching prevalent in TALC: "And what about secularism? Have 90% of our people ever met the Lord in true godly sorrow for sin, repentance and faith? Do our sermons reach the conscience?"[23]

L. C. Masted's comments, although brief, indicate that the tradition of Haugeanism continued to play a role in the broader TALC, though its connection with Lutherans Alert indicates as well that Haugeanism of this era experienced a sense of homelessness within the "mainstream" as it sensed its emphases had no voice among the officialdom. That these concerns were more than the isolated fears of one individual is indicated by the opening comment of L. C. Masted, where he presumes to speak on behalf of "many sincere pastors, missionaries and laymen who are asking these same questions."[24]

---

21. Masted, "Earnest Plea to Our Pastors," 10.
22. Masted, "Earnest Plea to Our Pastors," 10.
23. Masted, "Earnest Plea to Our Pastors," 10.
24. Masted, "Earnest Plea to Our Pastors," 10.

Affiliation of Lutheran Movements

When considering the Haugean presence and influence in the era of TALC and the LCA, brief note must be made of a cooperative organization known as the Affiliation of Lutheran Movements (ALMS). Formed in 1974, the ALMS originally consisted of three schools in the LBI movement, namely LBI of Canada, LBI of Seattle, and the Lutheran Bible School of California, as well as the LEM, Lutheran Youth Alive, Lutheran Youth Encounter, and the WMPL. Later, after the Zion Society for Israel was renamed Good News for Israel in 1975, that organization became a part of the ALMS in 1978. The Latin American Lutheran Mission joined the ALMS that same year, followed by Lutheran Lay Renewal of America in 1981.[25]

References to the presence of the ALMS organization appear sporadically in reports of the LEM in the 1970s and 1980s, but reports about the actual work of the ALMS cannot be found. Nevertheless, the existence of this organization as a cooperative fellowship of like-minded independent ministries connected to the Lutheran denominations of North America is an important part of evaluating Haugean self-understanding and the continuation of that tradition. Though the origin of a few of these organizations connected with the ALMS cannot be precisely determined, many of these ministries have been shown to have strong Haugean roots. In the constituting document of the ALMS, the organization was envisioned as one that would connect various renewal, discipleship, and mission movements within the broader Lutheran family of North America and provide a place where such movements could be mutually supportive in the task of providing an important witness within the established church bodies. The preamble of the constituting document emphasizes this focus on renewal within the established denominations:

> Whereas God in His sovereign grace has brought about within our Lutheran family movements of Bible study, evangelism, mission, and youth ministry: . . . Whereas God has laid on our hearts a burning concern for renewal and discipleship within this body: . . . Whereas God has laid on us a common concern for the strengthening of each other's ministries as well as sharing together in our togetherness: we hereby agree to share with each other in the following manner.[26]

---

25. "Affiliation of Lutheran Movements."
26. Affiliation of Lutheran Movements, "Terms of Reference."

The founders of the ALMS organization were careful to emphasize in the constituting document that the purpose of this fellowship of renewal movements was to support and enhance the work of the denominations rather than compete with them. They viewed their organizations as being of service primarily to congregations, with:

> An overarching and undergirding call to spiritual renewal. We find our deepest well of togetherness in our commitment to a constant revival within our Lutheran Church. This we give ourselves to as expendable agents.[27]

At the same time, two things indicate the existence of friction between the ALMS organizations and the church establishment. First, the stated need for "spiritual renewal" and "repentance and faith" among members of congregations indicates the belief that the spiritual life within congregations of the "mainstream" was deficient and in need of renewal. Second, the fact that the ALMS felt the need to emphasize its Lutheran confessional focus indicates that the constituent movements were not viewed as authentically Lutheran by at least some:

> Our stance is complementary and non-competitive to official Lutheran structures and confessional. We are not a power structure but service oriented and within our Lutheran confessions are committed to a radical and total discipleship to the Person of Jesus Christ as Lord and Savior.[28]

More work on the ALMS organization itself can and should be done. It is simply noteworthy for present purposes that many of these organizations heavily influenced by historic Haugeanism found themselves working together in a type of independent spiritual alliance as they sought to carry forward their emphases within the "mainstream."

The Lutheran Evangelistic Movement

One of the constituent members of the ALMS was the LEM, which continued its work into the era of TALC and the LCA. Its stated purpose in this period reflected the Haugean concern for ministering both to those within and outside of the established church bodies:

27. Affiliation of Lutheran Movements, "Terms of Reference." Underlined text is in the original.

28. Affiliation of Lutheran Movements, "Terms of Reference." Underlined text is in the original.

> The Lutheran Evangelistic Movement is a free, spontaneous movement within Lutheranism which has as its purpose, by God's grace, to revive and deepen the spiritual life and fellowship of believers, to reach and win the lost for Christ, and to encourage the use of spiritual gifts for the extension of Christ's kingdom.[29]

Its records from this time provide an important glimpse of the activity of this historic Haugean organization. Notably, official reports of the LEM from the 1970s and 1980s often mention former Hauge's Synod congregations or historic strongholds of Haugeanism as locations of the organization's activity. For example, the executive committee of the LEM met in April of 1975 at St. Paul's Lutheran Church of Minneapolis, Minnesota. The names of Eagle Grove, Iowa and Viroqua, Wisconsin also make appearances in official reports as locations of gatherings as do the Haugean strongholds of northwestern Minnesota and north central Iowa, indicating that the LEM continued to speak to the concerns of those shaped by the Haugean tradition. That the LEM maintained its connection with Haugeanism is also demonstrated by its connection with the activities of the HLIMF and its "tent meetings" in Kasson, Minnesota.[30]

The LEM continued its activity in the decades of the 1970s and 1980s, holding its summer Deeper Life camps, its Midwinter Conferences, and evangelistic meetings in various congregations. Though LEM evangelists were often active in rural areas, including Haugean strongholds, the LEM also began a program in 1975 focused on urban evangelism. This "Skyways Chaplaincy" initiative was focused on reaching out to people in downtown Minneapolis, Minnesota, in particular those involved with businesses in the IDS building and others connected to it via the network of skyway pedestrian bridges. The annual report of the LEM that year spoke of its Skyways ministry in the following way: "There is a great need to help people in the downtown area in their times of crisis and need by counsel, and seeking to lead them to Jesus Christ."[31] According to Kenneth Ellingson, who served as the initial Skyways chaplain, the evangelism carried out by the program was focused both on witnessing to unbelievers and on encouraging revival among Christians themselves, a focus congruent with historic Haugeanism. Ellingson commented in his report concerning the Skyways ministry: "The measure of its worth is

---

29. Lutheran Evangelistic Movement, "The Ministry of Area Conferences."
30. Lutheran Evangelistic Movement, "Annual Report."
31. Lutheran Evangelistic Movement, "Annual Report."

found primarily in lives dramatically changed and the sensing of a spirit of revival surfacing among downtown believers."[32] This dual focus found expression in the three-pronged strategy of the evangelistic program, which was first devoted to sharing testimony "with whoever will listen." It then focused on providing "warning" by calling the spiritually indifferent to repentance and faith. Finally, the Skyways ministry provided education in the form of Bible studies both in the ministry office itself and in various workplaces, all of which presumably were intended to minister to both seekers and existing Christians.

Records of the LEM from this period also reveal significant friction between its emphases and those of the established Lutheran denominations. This friction centered on the perceived misunderstanding of the role of baptism in Christian life. While affirming the importance of baptism, the LEM sought to communicate the necessity of faith for baptism to be effective. This is consistent with the historic Haugean focus on subjectivism in faith. In a form letter from 1979 intended to articulate the philosophy of LEM to potential evangelists, the topic of baptism is addressed among other issues:

> We also believe that "he who believes and is baptized shall be saved, but he that believes not shall be damned" (even though he is baptized) March [sic] 16:16. We believe that Christ saves through baptism – 1 Peter 3:21 – but we also believe that one can fall away from baptismal grace and become lost. We do not trust in our baptism but in the Christ we receive as Savior, who gives grace to believe in Christ (Eph. 2:8–9) for salvation. These are some of the basic beliefs the Lutheran Evangelistic Movement stands for.[33]

As will be seen, this concern for articulating the proper relationship between baptism and faith continued to present itself in the following years, and friction with representatives of the established "mainstream" continued to play a role in the work of the LEM. At the same time, the LEM leadership sought despite the friction to make clear their commitment to Lutheran identity as they understood it. In 1982, associate director Dick Erickson commented about his planning for the Midwinter conference,

---

32. Lutheran Evangelistic Movement, "Annual Report."

33. Lutheran Evangelistic Movement, "The Distinctives of an LEM Evangelist-Teacher."

"It is not easy to find speakers who are Lutheran and maintain the truly evangelical distinctive."[34]

Reports of the LEM evangelists of this era also reveal friction between their emphases and those of "mainstream" pastors as they sought to serve as positive spiritual leaven in various congregations. In October of 1982, evangelist Nels Pedersen commented on his visit to one of his own former congregations, which he lifted up as an example of the challenge of spiritual stagnation within the "mainstream." He articulated the historic Haugean concern for converted membership within established congregations:

> I had the privilege of sharing the morning message at one of the churches I served over 30 years ago. This was another chapter of what is taking place in the Lutheran church today. There were only a few people left of the professing Christians. They had several pastors over the years who were liberals, who didn't believe in personal experience of salvation. The conflict got to the point that the Christians were asked to leave, so the Covenant church in the area received another group of Lutheran members. The present pastor questioned me on the whole idea of personal commitment, and personal salvation. He, too, was of the opinion we received it all in Baptism.[35]

Yet the relationship between the LEM and the "mainstream" church establishment was not always contentious in this era and was at times complementary to the work of the church establishment. In 1985, LEM evangelist Paul Gunderson conducted a church growth seminar at a congregation in Rockford, Iowa. This was reportedly a troubled congregation, where some members had asked the pastor to leave. Gunderson reported that he had communicated with the bishop of the Iowa District of TALC about his coming visit: "The Iowa Bishop, David Brown, called me one day and wished me well because his own staff had been fruitless in their endeavors at reconciliation."[36] Gunderson further commented on his visit:

> Every afternoon we went out calling on [the pastor's] members and I led three of them to personal assurance of salvation. Three others received inner healing in counseling sessions. Pastor Sevig was very appreciative of the week, his church's response, and

34. Erickson, "Associate Director's Report to the Executive Committee."
35. Pedersen, "Report to the Executive Committee."
36. Gunderson, "Report to Executive Committee."

what he, himself, was able to learn. He wrote a glowing evaluation to the office, and I have since sent a summary letter to Dr. Brown.[37]

The response of the bishop indicated his appreciation for the work of the LEM in facilitating healing in that congregation:

> Dear Pastor Gunderson: I thank you for your very insightful letter. I want to thank you for what you were able to accomplish at Rockford, evidently with both the people and the pastor. I think you put your finger on several things that need examining. I like the way you go about to help them in the study of who they are and what they might become. Thank you for sharing the correspondence. It helps us understand better where the pastor is coming from. I wish we had more opportunities to match pastor and people.[38]

Despite examples of positive cooperation with representatives of the "mainstream," the LEM continued to combat what it saw as a pervasive cultural Christianity in the established Lutheran church bodies. This friction took place mostly within the context of discussions regarding the efficacy of baptism for salvation. In March of 1984, handwritten notes on the agenda of the LEM executive committee meeting make the following comments: "If not born of God you are a child of the Devil. Until born of God, you are a creature of God, <u>not</u> a child of God. Baptism <u>must</u> be coupled w/ faith to be effective."[39] The following year, the LEM addressed this issue directly in its official organ *Evangelize*. The editor Jim Boline reported to the LEM executive committee, informing them of an upcoming article focused on the importance of emphasizing revival and living faith within established churches, even among those who have already been baptized:

> The September/October issue will be centered on the theme, "Baptism, Decisions and Lutherans." I will be reprinting portions from some articles printed in the ALMS booklets from 1982 and 1983 on "The Evangelization of the Baptized," and "Preaching Evangelism."[40]

37. Gunderson, "Report to Executive Committee."

38. Personal letter from David Brown to Paul Gunderson on May 6, 1985, Lutheran Evangelistic Movement Papers, Luther Seminary Archives, St. Paul, MN.

39. Lutheran Evangelistic Movement, "Executive Committee Meeting Agenda." Underlined text is in the original.

40. Boline, "Editor's Report to the Executive Committee of LEM."

Evidence indicates, however, that the LEM continued to encounter difficulty in its work of articulating a proper understanding of baptism, including open resistance from some pastors. In August of 1985, Paul Gunderson reported on his summer experience at Canadian Bible camps.

> The week of June 17–20 I participated with the training camp of the summer camp team. On Saturday, June 29, my family I [sic] left for two weeks of Bible camps in Canada. The first one was in Midale. The pastors in this area have a very heavy emphasis on baptism. I had received a letter stating that I was not to give an 'altar call.' I did, however, announce my availability for counseling and several people took advantage of the opportunity.[41]

RECENT DEVELOPMENTS

As a conclusion to this chapter, it is important briefly to note the present existence of the various independent ministries related to historic Haugeanism. In some cases, these organizations note explicitly their connection with the Haugean tradition as they seek to relate to established church bodies. The existence of these organizations stands as a testimony to the continuation of the Haugean spirit in North American Lutheranism. At the same time, the distinction between the darker and more legalistic form of Haugeanism and the more evangelical Haugean emphasis colored by the Rosenian tradition can be observed especially when comparing one of these organizations with the others. As is the case with many modern organizations, much of what can be learned about them is available only electronically on websites.

The Hauge Lutheran Inner Mission Federation

When considering the various organizations that seek to perpetuate the Haugean spirit among Lutherans of North America, one is naturally drawn to the HLIMF, as their use of the name "Hauge" makes their identification with the Haugean tradition unmistakable. Founded originally in 1920 to preserve the Haugean witness after the merger that produced the NLCA in 1917, the HLIMF continued throughout the years to exist as a network of various Haugean "inner mission" societies. The organization continues its existence today, and though more work on the history

---

41. Gunderson, "Report to the Executive Committee."

of the HLIMF can and should be done, what can be learned about it from its website reveals much about how this organization understands itself in relation to the established church bodies. Unfortunately, requests to view historical records of the HLIMF have gone unanswered. It seems clear, however, that the HLIMF remains especially active in communities with historic ties to Haugeanism. The website lists Kasson, Minnesota as a location of one of its recent Bible conferences. As of November of 2017, two of the officers of the organization were from the southeastern Minnesota communities of Kenyon and Dexter, respectively.[42]

The HLIMF continues its monthly publication of *Morning Glory*, with the historic emphases of the organization still emblazoned on its front page: "Experienced Salvation, Christian Fellowship, Simplicity in Worship." The HLIMF also continues to promote its historic books *The Hauge Movement in America* and *Innermission Church History*, published in 1941 and 1948, respectively. Other devotional articles and pamphlets are available on its website as well. Consistent with the ecumenical focus of historic Haugeanism, recognizing the presence of true spiritual life in other parts of the Christian world, the HLIMF promotes Calvinist theologian Jonathan Edwards's sermon "Sinners in the Hands of an Angry God" among its various tracts and publications. The organization's website acknowledges that its work is unfamiliar to many people today and seeks to clarify its roots and purpose. The roots of the HLIMF in the Haugean awakening of Norway are noted in its vision to serve the Lutheran community in North America in a way similar to the work of the Norwegian Haugeans. The HLIMF clarifies that it is not in itself an established church body, but rather an independent movement for the promotion of spiritual life among existing church bodies:

> The Hauge Lutheran Innermission Federation is: A FREE MOVEMENT AMONG LUTHERANS FOR SPIRITUAL LIFE. It is not to be confused with any church body or synod. Rather, it is a fellowship of Lutheran Christians working for revival and spiritual life within the existing church and throughout the Christian community.
>
> The "Hauge connection" identifies the movement historically with the Haugean revivals in Norway which had such a powerful impact upon that nation in the early nineteenth century. The Hauge Federation today exists as a REVIVAL

---

42. *Morning Glory*, November 2017, 2.

MOVEMENT, stressing the desperate need of spiritual awakening and new life in Christ.[43]

The independence of the HLIMF, through which the organization seeks to serve as positive spiritual leaven within established church bodies, is evidently cherished by the organization. It emphasizes again its status in relation to the broader Lutheran community:

> The Hauge Federation desires to be a spiritual resource providing assistance to pastors and churches in their evangelistic efforts. As an inter-Lutheran fellowship, the Federation is not bound by synodical affiliations, but is supportive of all Lutheran church bodies that are faithful to the Word of God.[44]

Working toward the end of enriching spiritual life and calling for revival within the church establishment, the HLIMF naturally emphasizes its publications such as *Morning Glory*. Yet it also lists its various current ministries: "Spiritual Life Rallies in various areas, Evangelistic meetings, Bible conferences and an annual Weekend Retreat. Smaller fellowship/testimony meetings are encouraged."[45] It is also noteworthy that the HLIMF today understands itself to be driven by lay leadership and oriented toward encouraging spiritual life among the laity. It lifts up the example of Hauge himself and emphasizes his role as a lay leader:

> A LAY-WITNESS MINISTRY IN THE HAUGEAN TRADITION. Following his conversion to Christ as a young farm boy, Hans Nielsen Hauge promptly felt the call to be a witness for Christ. He began at once sharing the Gospel with his neighbors and friends, and ultimately throughout the length and breadth of Norway.
>
> The Hauge Federation today is essentially a lay-movement encouraging spiritual life and leadership among the laypeople. While the involvement of pastors and of church leaders is always welcome, the work is directed largely by laymen.[46]

Theologically, though the HLIMF understands itself as a Lutheran organization, it continues to emphasize the Haugean theme of experienced salvation through personal conversion. Not surprisingly, the organization takes a position on the role of baptism in Christian life similar

---

43. Hauge Lutheran Inner Mission Federation, "For Your Information," paras. 3–4.
44. Hauge Lutheran Inner Mission Federation, "For Your Information," para. 7.
45. Hauge Lutheran Inner Mission Federation, "For Your Information."
46. Hauge Lutheran Inner Mission Federation, "For Your Information," paras. 5–6.

to that of the LEM described above. In the May 2008 issue of *Morning Glory*, Jim Haga wrote a brief article in which he criticized the baptismal focus of many Lutheran congregations. Not denying baptism as a means of grace, he nonetheless emphasized subjective appropriation of baptismal grace through faith:

> Many Lutheran pastors and church leaders are telling their people, "Remember your baptism," or "Look to your baptism.". . . It can even carry to the point where pastors will put the baptismal fount in front of the casket at a funeral. . . . We in the Lutheran Church believe that the Scriptures teach that baptism is a means of Grace. . . . Yet, there still must be a personal conversion in the life of the baptized, or there will be no spiritual life. It is the same as the Word of God. . . . The grace of God is present through the Word (as in baptism), but are we going to say then that every one [*sic*] who has heard the Word of God is saved? No, it is only those who personally respond to the offered grace who come alive spiritually. So is the case with baptism.[47]

The HLIMF also maintains a presence on the social media website Facebook, and the content shared on that page reveals much about the theological focus of the organization. Aside from posting the monthly publication of *Morning Glory*, the Facebook page consists entirely of shared articles and blogs from both Lutheran and non-Lutheran sources. The content emphasizes the countercultural nature of the Christian faith while at the same time criticizing modernistic, liberal trends in contemporary Christianity that minimize or negate entirely the tension between a converted life and the surrounding culture. For example, on July 9, 2017, an article by conservative commentator Matt Walsh was shared on the page entitled "God's Word hasn't become less true just because it has become less popular."[48] Another theological issue emphasized as important is that of the substitutionary atonement of Christ. Attempting to walk the fine line between valuing its Lutheran heritage and acknowledging the existence of true spiritual life in other places, especially contemporary "evangelical" churches, the HLIMF shared an article on June 1, 2017, entitled "There is already a church that is both evangelical and sacramental."[49]

---

47. Haga, "Where Are You Looking?"
48. Walsh, "God's Word."
49. Veith, "There is already a church."

Yet despite its concern for doctrine, the Facebook page of the organization betrays its historic Haugean concern for morality among Christians, emphasizing the salutary function of the law in Christian life. A comic book–style cartoon shared on May 25, 2017 lifts up God's commands as a "guardrail" in front of a cliff that many mistake for a fence that unnecessarily restricts their activity. Specific issues addressed are those related to sexual morality, abortion, and even gluttony. Surprisingly, criticism of the practice of dancing among Christians still finds a place in the HLIMF at present.[50] It can be argued that this emphasis on law by the HLIMF demonstrates an affinity for the darker and more legalistic form of Haugeanism discussed earlier. Two other issues that distinguish the HLIMF from other contemporary movements influenced by historic Haugeanism are its insistence on a literal historical reading of the creation accounts in the biblical book of Genesis[51] and its clear stance against the ordination of women:

> The United Church of Christ is very likely the most liberal of liberal denominations in America. Furthermore, the Bible is quite clear that a pastor is to be "the husband of one wife," not the wife of one husband (1 Tim. 3), which makes the pastoral office a distinctly male role.[52]

Perhaps for these reasons, the work of the HLIMF appears to find a greater audience among Lutherans in the AFLC and is somewhat detached from the work of more centrist Lutheran organizations such as LCMC and the NALC. Criticism of the ELCA is common in the pages of *Morning Glory* and on the organization's Facebook page, and though the HLIMF would tend to agree with many of the emphases of these newer centrist Lutheran organizations, their perspectives on the two issues mentioned above generally differ from the convictions of the HLIMF. The strong connection between the HLIMF and the AFLC is demonstrated by the fact that its most recent annual conference was held in June 2017 at Grace Free Lutheran Church of the AFLC in Bagley, Minnesota.[53]

---

50. Aahus, "An Awakening," 1.
51. Morris, "Creation with the Appearance of Age," 11.
52. "Despite Criticism," 8.
53. *Morning Glory*, May 2017, 16.

The Lutheran Evangelistic Movement

The LEM, referred to earlier in this chapter as well as in the fourth chapter, continues its existence at present under the name "LEM Deeper Life," with the accompanying slogan of "Making Disciples. Being Disciples." Unfortunately, information about its current activity is limited. It seems clear that the LEM continues to understand itself as an independent Lutheran ministry that seeks to enrich the spiritual life of existing Lutheran church bodies. At present, however, four of the seven listed leaders of the LEM are pastors associated with LCMC. Nevertheless, the LEM does not view itself as only serving the association of LCMC. There are apparent connections to the AFLC as well. According to the website, a presentation on the recent written history of the LEM, *Our Fathers Saw His Mighty Works*, was given in 2014 for the AFLC pastor's conference. The pan-Lutheran nature of the work of the LEM can be seen in the organization's vision statement, which includes no reference to particular church bodies: "The Lutheran Evangelistic Movement has as its purpose by God's grace to revive and deepen the spiritual life and fellowship of believers, to save the lost, and to encourage the use of spiritual gifts for the extension of Christ's kingdom."[54]

The current activity of the LEM apparently differs somewhat from its historic focus on evangelistic meetings and offering Deeper Life and Midwinter Conferences, however. To be sure, the current LEM website seeks to preserve the history of the organization by offering the texts and occasionally audio recordings of sermons and lectures by former LEM evangelists such as J. O. Gisselquist and Evald Conrad. Yet the LEM today embraces a four-tiered approach to its ministry, described by board member Tom Hilpert as consisting of preaching, offering pastoral retreats for renewal, church planting, and communicating the Christian message through creative media.[55] According to Hilpert, the creative media produced by him and other members of the leadership seek to present the Christian faith in ways that are culturally relevant. Modeling their work after Jesus's practice of storytelling, the LEM seeks to convey spiritual truths through the writing of short stories and novels as well as creating computer games based on those stories, among other initiatives. It can be argued that just as many historic Haugeans sought to adapt

---

54. Lutheran Evangelistic Movement Deeper Life, "Mission and Vision."

55. Lutheran Evangelistic Movement Deeper Life, "Making Disciples Through Media," para. 1.

to their surroundings through the use of English for the sake of more effectively spreading the faith, the LEM carries on that tradition through their desire to present the faith in a culturally relevant manner.

Perhaps the most visible way in which the LEM carries out it work, however, is through their ministry known as Life Together Churches (LTC). The work of LTC is focused on assisting Lutherans in the creation of small group worshipping communities, often known as "house churches." According to its website, the LCT network "provides everything needed to enable a local group to quickly and effectively start a small group worshiping community and sustain its life and growth."[56] It can be argued that this focus on small group gatherings has, in light of the Haugean roots of the LEM, a connection with the historic Haugean focus on conventicles and edifying gatherings. More significant for the continuation of the Haugean tradition, however, is the stated purpose of creating these "house churches." The goal is not the creation of large congregations and elaborate buildings. Rather, the goal is to encourage spiritual life and commitment among participants through "authentic relationships." The LTC network does not operate according to a Christendom model and instead views itself as a means to foster individual and communal discipleship:

> Life Together Churches are like rescue boats launched for the purpose of saving people on the open sea and bringing them safely into the Kingdom. We are quick to plant new churches, even knowing that we cannot assure their long-term survival. Our aim is not to plant churches that stand the test of time, but to make disciples who stand the test of time.[57]

In addition to having an informal connection with LCMC and the AFLC, the work of the LEM through its LTC network is recognized as an official "ministry partner" of the NALC, assisting that church body in the creation of "house churches." There is a certain irony in the fact that the NALC, which has been caricatured as "high church," utilizes the LTC network as an important part of its life, a testimony to the wide influence of Haugeanism on American Lutheranism more generally. The connection between the LEM and the more centrist Lutheran bodies of LCMC and the NALC also demonstrates the diversity of Haugean expression at present. In contrast to the HLIMF, which as evidenced by its

---

56. Life Together Churches, "Mission and Vision," para. 1.
57. Life Together Churches, "Mission and Vision," para. 4.

stance on the ordination of women and its focus on morality and prohibited amusements, exhibits a darker and more legalistic piety, the LEM focuses more on positive evangelism, perhaps reminiscent of the Rosenian influence on the Haugeanism of former times. The LEM certainly does embrace a high view of the authority of Scripture, using the word "inerrant" in the statement of faith of the LTC network. Nevertheless, they appear to understand biblical authority somewhat differently than their counterparts in the HLIMF, evidenced in part by their apparent acceptance of the ordination of women to the office of pastor. To be sure, different groups of Christians come to a variety of different conclusions on a number of issues, even when claiming adherence to biblical inerrancy. Nevertheless, the LEM expresses its view of biblical authority in ways that reflect a greater focus on positive evangelism, as seen in their emphasis on the message derived from the text rather than on the text itself, as in the following quote:

> LEM has always been about the work of trying to communicate the gospel in effective, culturally relevant ways. We believe in the objective truth of the Bible. We strive to be relentlessly consistent in our Christian orthodoxy. But as we seek to reach new generations for Jesus, there is nothing as timelessly relevant as a story. ... Jesus himself used storytelling extensively. His stories were often not true in the sense of being factual. Have you ever stopped to realize that there was no actual Good Samaritan? The Good Samaritan is a fictional character, made up by Jesus. ... Even so, we remember the Good Samaritan, and more importantly, we remember the truth that this make-believe story teaches us. The story of the Good Samaritan itself isn't true, and yet is a powerful tool to communicate eternal truth.[58]

The World Mission Prayer League

The WMPL continues its existence to the present as well, and like the LTC network of the LEM, this historic Haugean mission organization is included among the official ministry partners of the NALC. The WMPL maintains its independence, however, noting its Lutheran identity in its handbook, yet emphasizing the pan-Lutheran nature of its constituency: "We are a Lutheran community in mission. . . . We undertake our

---

58. Lutheran Evangelistic Movement Deeper Life, "Making Disciples Through Media," para. 17. Bold text is in the original.

mission as Lutherans. We proceed from a variety of Lutheran synodical backgrounds, in which we participate gladly."[59] Nevertheless, the work of the WMPL appears to be connected more strongly to the centrist conservative Lutheran community. Its statement of faith articulates a high view of biblical authority, yet it does so in such a way that allows for more flexibility in biblical interpretation than one would find in the HLIMF, for example. The words "inerrant" and "infallible" are used as descriptors of the Bible, but specifically only as the "norm for doctrine and living."[60]

The brief written history of the WMPL in its handbook makes no specific reference to the organization's Haugean roots, instead briefly summarizing what has been stated in the fourth chapter. However, the WMPL carries forward some important historic emphases of Haugeanism. The statement of faith of the WMPL affirms both the historic creeds of the Christian church as well as the normative nature of the Lutheran confessional documents, with primacy given to the *Small Catechism* and the *Augsburg Confession*, perhaps a vestige of its background in Norwegian Lutheranism. It also strongly affirms traditional Lutheran themes of substitutionary atonement, the sacraments as means of grace, and justification by grace through faith. Yet the WMPL emphasizes the subjective appropriation of grace, noting that such grace gives "complete access to God's every gift and benefit – for all who repent and put their faith in Jesus Christ alone for salvation."[61] Furthermore, the WMPL emphasizes the Haugean concern for "living faith," expressed in the following words: "We believe in . . . the indwelling presence and transforming power of the Holy Spirit, who gives to all believers a new life and the spiritual gifts necessary for a calling to obedient service."[62]

In its independent Lutheran mission work that today encompasses twenty different countries, the WMPL continues to emphasize its historic desire to maintain a lean organization as well as its commitment to carry out its work "along the frontiers." It will be remembered that the WMPL was often critical of the mission work of the established Lutheran synods for overly focusing on the comfort of the missionaries and lack of focus on indigenization. Accordingly, the WMPL describes its work in the following way:

---

59. World Mission Prayer League, *Handbook*, 2.
60. World Mission Prayer League, *Handbook*, 5.
61. World Mission Prayer League, *Handbook*, 5.
62. World Mission Prayer League, *Handbook*, 5.

> We understand that this commitment exacts a cost – and we purpose to bear it, by the grace of God. We will ready ourselves for suffering. We will turn away from costly comforts, a larger income, material possessions, and places of personal privilege or honor. We will choose instead to embrace the way of poverty, loss, suffering, and humiliation – whatever it takes to bring the Gospel of Jesus to as many people as possible.[63]

In this spirit, the WMPL published in 2015 a collection of stories from its missionary personnel throughout the years, which recount both the joys and the hardships of the missionaries a well as God's provision in their work. Inspired by the story of the prophet Elijah from the biblical book of 1 Kings, the book is entitled *Food from Ravens*, and the following story can be regarded as typical. Noteworthy is that stories such as this emphasize both courageous evangelism and a rejection of cultural, nominal Christianity:

> My desire and dream to be a missionary in Pakistan brought great trouble and distress to my family – especially my parents. My mom and dad were not Christians and, understandably, could not comprehend my sense of call. There was much sorrow, crying and prayer before God. One day during lunch my dad told me, "Gaby, the place that you have chosen to go is certainly dangerous and the countries around it are dangerous, too. But, I read a verse in the Bible last night that mentions that even when thousands surround us, the Lord protects us. . . . I was astonished! You see, my father had become a Christian and was now beginning to understand. . . . How good is our God![64]

Consistent further with the historic Haugean focus on emphasizing spiritual life rather than institution building, the WMPL pledges to work with existing church bodies for the deeper purpose of spreading the faith, but it emphasizes that its goal is not one of long-term institution building. Rather, it focuses on the work of planting the faith:

> As for ourselves and our work, we intend to be mobile. We pledge ourselves to expendability. We will not ensconce our persons or our organization permanently in any of our areas of work. We understand ourselves as scaffolding; but when a building is completed, the scaffolding must be removed. In all

---

63. World Mission Prayer League, *Handbook*, 3.
64. Tollefson and Manson, *Food from Ravens*, 21.

of our work, we will plan for our own dismantling, in order to help build up the church in another area.⁶⁵

China Service Ventures

Another independent Lutheran ministry with roots in historic Haugeanism is China Service Ventures (CSV), and like the previous two organizations, CSV is recognized by the NALC as an official "ministry partner." Presumably because of the policy of the Chinese government toward Christian mission organizations, CSV does not specifically reference its Lutheran identity on its website, nor does its website articulate evangelism as the purpose of the organization. Rather, its stated purpose is to express the Christian faith through service to the poor in the Henan province of China: "The mission of China Service Ventures is to improve the quality of life for the rural poor in Henan, China. We give witness to the Gospel through Jesus' words: 'Not to be served, but to serve.'"⁶⁶ Direct evangelism is prohibited by the Chinese government. For this reason, CSV administers a number of service programs to the population of Henan. If asked questions about the motivation of the organization in providing such services, the workers are then permitted to speak about their faith. The services provided by CSV fall under four foci: providing educational scholarships for poor children, operating summer camps, providing English-as-a-second-language teachers, and operating a service for Chinese children whose parents are absent for work. Though the website of CSV is vague on many details about its history, again presumably because of Chinese government regulations, it is clear that CSV, officially incorporated in the year 2000, understands itself to be a continuation of the various Haugean China mission endeavors begun in the late nineteenth and early twentieth centuries:

> The roots of China Service Ventures run deep in the center of China. In 1890, a farmer from Iowa with a clear call to missionary service in China, sold his farm and all his possessions and left for China with $500 in his pocket.... By the time the Bamboo Curtain of communism closed China to the work of foreign missionaries in the early 1950's, 25 missionaries had served in this part of China, and built churches, schools, and

---

65. World Mission Prayer League, *Handbook*, 4.
66. China Service Ventures, "Our Mission."

hospitals. . . . CSV continues God's work in the same place where it began in 1901.⁶⁷

Chosen People Ministries

As previously noted, the Zion Society for Israel, which was founded in 1878, changed its name to Good News for Israel in 1975. Continuing its mission of Christian outreach to Jews at home and abroad, the organization recently merged with another Christian outreach ministry to Jewish people known as Chosen People Ministries. As Good News for Israel was headquartered in the Twin Cities suburb of St. Louis Park, the merger, which was effected on July 1, 2016, meant that Good News for Israel became "the Minnesota branch of Chosen People Ministries" as of that date.⁶⁸

In promotion of the merger of these ministries, the website of Chosen People Ministries notably makes reference to the Haugean roots of Good News for Israel:

> Good News for Israel was founded by the disciples of Hans Nielsen Hauge (1771–1824); a carpenter, lay clergy, and founder of the great Norwegian "Hauge Revival," which eventually led to the founding of The Zion Society for Israel in 1878 and later renamed Good News for Israel in 1975.⁶⁹

Their description of the history of Good News for Israel, through its reference to Martin Luther, hints at the Lutheran background of the organization, but it also does not emphasize it. It emphasizes instead the importance of being rooted in the message of the Scriptures, spiritual revival, and evangelism.

> Hans has been called the Martin Luther of Norway. God used him to dramatically transform the spiritual landscape of Scandinavian Europe and America. He emphasized the importance of people reading the scriptures for themselves. During a prayer revival, the followers felt inspired to start an evangelical

---

67. China Service Ventures, "Our History." Bold text is in the original.

68. Chosen People Ministries, "Chosen People Ministries + Good News for Israel," para. 4.

69. Chosen People Ministries, "History of Good News for Israel," para. 1.

outreach to the Jewish community called The Zion Society for Israel.[70]

The connection between Good News for Israel and Chosen People Ministries can be understood as a contemporary example of the ecumenical focus of historic Haugeanism. To be sure, the doctrinal statement of Chosen People Ministries articulates an orthodox Christian understanding of God as Trinity, as well as general Protestant convictions such the Bible as the foundation of Christian teaching and salvation by grace through faith. However, though the organization appears to be pandenominational, it is clear that its roots are not Lutheran, even though the doctrinal statement is sufficiently ambiguous as to allow for participation from a variety of Christian backgrounds. Endorsements of the organization come primarily from representatives of Baptist and evangelical institutions, such as Gordon-Conwell Theological Seminary and Dallas Theological Seminary.[71]

Lutheran Lay Renewal of America

One final organization to note when considering the contemporary presence of Haugeanism in American Lutheranism is Lutheran Lay Renewal of America (LLRA). Like some of the aforementioned organizations, LLRA, though an independent ministry, is classified as an official "ministry partner" of the NALC. LLRA was not founded until 1971, so its roots are obviously not found directly in historic Haugeanism. However, LLRA bears mentioning here, as it became one of the constituent members of the ALMS organization mentioned earlier. One assumes that it therefore demonstrated some affinity with the piety of the other member organizations.

Indeed, even though LLRA does not specifically mention Haugeanism as an influence in its ministry, its work is congruent with important aspects of the Haugean movement in both Norway and North America. First, like the other ministries already mentioned, LLRA operates independently of, yet in service to, established Lutheran church bodies: "It has always been our policy to serve all Lutheran congregations, regardless of denominational affiliation, and we also are willing to serve any

---

70. Chosen People Ministries, "History of Good News for Israel," para. 2.
71. Chosen People Ministries, "Endorsements."

Christian congregation that would like to utilize our ministry."[72] Second, the movement is focused on the development of spiritual life among the laity within established congregations. The assumption of the organization is that mere outward membership in a Christian congregation is inadequate; church members need added depth to their spiritual lives. Such a supplementary renewal ministry to congregations is reminiscent of the practice of Haugean conventicles:

> The renewal weekend has been our main ministry since 1971. We offer the pastor and church leadership the opportunity to strengthen and renew their people for greater involvement in ministry. . . . Everything we do on a weekend falls into five categories: worship, prayer, sharing our faith stories, small group discussions, and fellowship . . . What can a church expect to happen as a result of a renewal weekend? 1. Deeper commitments to Jesus as Lord and Savior 2. Building Christian community on a deeper, more spiritual level 3. Greater commitment to being involved in lay ministry 4. People being empowered for ministry and emboldened to share their faith with others 5. The launching of new ministries.[73]

Third, LLRA, though desiring to work with established church bodies, is critical of the phenomenon of spiritual stagnation and nominal membership in such Lutheran church bodies in ways similar to the critique of historic Haugeanism. One of its recent newsletters provides a lengthy defense of historical Pietism, especially as expressed in the German awakening movement of the eighteenth century. Conceding that Pietism has at times fallen into an excessive legalism, Dave Luecke nonetheless argues that Lutherans of the present day are in need of evangelical renewal and that such congregations tend to overemphasize justification at the expense of the necessary accompanying spiritual renewal:

> I propose it is time for a 21st century re-renewal of emphasis on the Good News not only of justification by grace through faith but also on God's action in sending the Spirit to renew hearts and produce his special fruit. . . . Christian theology is recognized as the art of keeping a balance among different biblical emphases. Lutherans are rightfully known for our stress on Paul's teaching that we are saved by grace through faith, not by works. We are, I believe, out of balance with our insufficient

---

72. Lutheran Lay Renewal of America, "Who We Are and What We Do," para. 2.
73. Lutheran Lay Renewal of America, "Renewal Weekend."

emphasis on the Holy Spirit's work of awakening and motivating new life in Christ.[74]

CONCLUSION

Even through the merger movements of the latter part of the twentieth century, which produced first TALC and then the ELCA, Haugean influence, though not always directly identified as such, continued to exert itself in various ways, sometimes exhibiting a darker and more legalistic piety and other times exhibiting a more positive evangelical focus. Through it all, the sense of friction that characterized the relationship between the Haugeans and the broader church establishment continued, with suspicion on both sides. At the same time, the affinity of Haugeans for establishing movements for mission and service independent of the established church bodies came to play an important role in the church life of the "mainstream" and especially the lives of the more centrist conservative Lutheran bodies of LCMC and the NALC. Lacking the resources for creating their own separate departments for mission work and not desiring to "reinvent the wheel," congregations of LCMC and the organization of the NALC have partnered with such organizations in carrying out home and foreign missions. The admittedly brief overview of the variety of mission organizations with roots in historic Haugeanism stands as testimony to the enduring legacy of Haugeanism, serving as leaven in a larger batch of dough.

---

74. Luecke, "The Weak Link in Our Gospel Presentation."

7

Conclusion

WHAT CAN BE SAID about the heritage of Haugeanism and the continuation of the Haugean spirit in North American Lutheranism? This concluding chapter will provide a summary of the content of this work, which has sought to answer this question. Beyond the task of shedding further light on the tradition of Haugeanism and the small organization of Hauge's Synod, several summary conclusions can be drawn from the preceding chapters. First, it is clear that a renewed and more extensive analysis of the American Haugean tradition was needed in light of the paucity of material about the topic as well as in response to Nelson and Meuser's optimistic assessment of the coexistence of the different traditions that fed into what became the NLCA. Nelson's 1952 comment commended to future historians the task of evaluating the "working out" of the arrangement of the 1917 merger, an arrangement that he lauded as a remarkable accomplishment. Meuser claimed in his 1975 comment that the situation produced by the merger was harmonious and devoid of difficulty. As the preceding chapters demonstrate, this assessment was incorrect. Many representatives of the minority Haugean element entered the merger with reservations about the survival of their tradition, and the subsequent years revealed significant friction between them and their more formal, churchly counterparts. Whether this oversight on Meuser's part was the product of the historiographical bias of his era or simply the result of an unintentional oversight of a small minority tradition is unclear. Nevertheless, concern for historical honesty demands recognition of this friction.

Second, as the discussion of Hauge's activity in Norway demonstrates, Haugeanism functioned in that country as a nonseparatist spiritual movement devoted to the promotion of "experienced Christianity" within the Church of Norway, which would impact the way that Haugeanism expressed itself on American soil. The Haugean revival of Norway served, through its emphasis on conscious faith and lay preaching, to empower the working class to exercise authority in both spiritual and civil matters. Yet the spiritual authority they exercised took place initially outside the official auspices of the Church of Norway. Despite the commitment of Hauge and his followers to function within the established church, providing a supplementary spiritual witness, friction at times characterized the relationship between the Haugeans and the church establishment, especially in the early years after Hauge's death. When Haugeanism was transplanted in North America by Norwegian immigrants, the absence of the state church in the new land necessitated an adjustment on the part of the Haugeans; without a structured church organization in which they could function as spiritual leaven, supplementing the ritual life of the Church of Norway, they were required to combine their tradition of edifying gatherings with sacramental worship and accompanying church order. This resulted in an attempt at providing at least some ecclesiastical order among the American Haugeans in the form of Eielsen's loosely organized "Evangelical Lutheran Church in America." Yet the primary concern of the Haugeans was on spiritual life rather than the building of church organizations and institutions. The "Old Constitution" of Eielsen's Synod was inadequate in providing ecclesiastical order, which was one factor that led to the reorganization of that group as Hauge's Synod in 1876. Even with this reorganization and slightly greater focus on institutional life, however, evidence indicates that Hauge's Synod struggled to balance its focus on spiritual life with a healthy sense of organizational life, as many within it expressed indifference to the work of the synod. Their roots as leaven within the larger batch of dough of the Church of Norway meant that the American Haugeans were at a disadvantage in their attempt to found and maintain church institutions in the new land.

Third, important for understanding the enduring legacy of Haugeanism in North America is the established point that what is described as Haugeanism was not a monolithic movement. Perhaps partially a result of the lack of institutional focus described in the second point, there existed no centralized authority to define its boundaries. Hence,

CONCLUSION

one observes throughout the years a fair amount of diversity among the American Haugeans. The movement of the New Tendency against the Old Tendency in Eielsen's Synod was an expression of this diversity. Likely the result of the influence of Johnsonian and Rosenian emphases on Norwegian Haugeanism, some American Haugeans expressed concern for greater church order, focus on Lutheran theology, and positive evangelism. Some, however, exhibited a darker and more legalistic focus, showing greater aversion to cooperation and merger with other church bodies, especially suspicious of their "high-church" counterparts. At the same time, the lack of centralized organization among the Haugeans at times makes the sorting out of the different emphases among them challenging.

Fourth, returning to the point concerning friction between the Haugeans and others in Norwegian-American Lutheranism, it has been seen in the preceding chapters that suspicion and at times an even adversarial relationship emanating from both sides existed between the Haugeans and other Norwegian-American Lutherans, especially members of the Norwegian Synod. This suspicion was enough to keep Hauge's Synod from participating in the merger of 1890, and though there were voices among the Haugeans in opposition to or at least expressing reservations about the merger of 1917, Hauge's Synod elected to end its independent existence to join with the UNLC and the Norwegian Synod in forming the NLCA. Evidence shows, however, that this move among some of the Haugeans was taken with the understanding that their perspectives would be taken seriously and influence the spiritual life of wider organization of the NLCA, perhaps in a way similar to the influence of Norwegian Haugeanism on the Church of Norway. Further, it has been shown that friction between the Haugeans and others continued after the consummation of the 1917 merger, with many Haugeans feeling especially disenfranchised at the loss of their educational institutions. Though it certainly is possible that the leadership of the NLCA intentionally neglected these educational institutions, there is evidence to suggest that the lack of administrative talent among the Haugeans was at least partially responsible for the demise of their schools. Amid this, one also observes strong Haugean involvement in a variety of ministries for mission and evangelism, some of which predated the formation of the NLCA. Though the Haugeans were not entirely opposed to participation in denominationally supported ministries, a number of these ministries were independent of official control of the NLCA and were in fact pan-denominational in their membership. It has been observed that one possible reason for this was the desire for freedom among the Haugeans to carry out their spiritual life unhindered by the perspectives and regulations of the officialdom of the NLCA. At the same time, many of these Haugeans remained a part of the NLCA even despite their sense of disenfranchisement. By providing opportunities for service outside of official control of the denomination, however, they sought to serve as a witness within the larger church body, similar to the witness of the Norwegian Haugeans on the Church of Norway.

Fifth, an evaluation of the fate of former Hauge's Synod congregations after 1916 reveals that a large percentage of these congregations departed from the "mainstream" to join other church bodies friendlier to their piety, which is yet another indicator of the existence of friction between the Haugeans and other members of the NLCA. Yet in keeping with the lack of institutional focus as well as the desire to serve as positive spiritual leaven within the NLCA, these congregations departed at different times and joined different organizations over the years rather than forming a single dissenting organization. Furthermore, this analysis reveals the diversity within the Haugean tradition discussed earlier, with different congregations exhibiting different emphases, comparable to the division between the "sweeter" and more positive Rosenian focus and the darker and more legalistic Haugeanism.

Finally, how can Haugeanism be said to exist today? The process of twentieth-century merger among Lutherans in North America naturally tends to overlook a small minority tradition, especially one that has tended to express indifference to the emphasis on merger that has preoccupied their more formal, churchly counterparts. Answering this question in terms of an enduring institutional presence leads one to conclude that Haugeanism was indeed a defeated tradition in American Lutheranism, to which the derelict JLC and RWS stand as witness. Yet the loss of these institutions did not have the effect of eradicating the influence of Haugeanism, and its presence as a spiritual movement within larger institutions continues to serve as positive leaven for some and pain in the belly for others. Indeed, one observes that the Haugean tradition continues to be influential in North American Lutheranism in a deeper way more congruent with its roots. A number of organizations for mission and evangelism founded or influenced by the Haugeans continue to exist today, some of which note explicitly their roots in that tradition. From the history recounted in this study, one can assert that

CONCLUSION

the Haugeans were in many ways ill-suited for the task of institution building. At the same time, true to its origins in Norway, the Haugean emphasis on the importance of experienced and personal faith, integrity, mission, and evangelism continues to exert influence on yet independent of the various Lutheran church establishments. The continuation of the Haugean tradition in North American Lutheranism is best understood as a spiritual movement rather than an institution, one which continually provides an important witness to the institutional church, calling it back to the central concerns of the faith, serving, like the Norwegian Haugeans, as leaven in a larger batch of dough.

Appendix A

The "Old Constitution." Church Constitution for the Evangelical Lutheran Church at Jefferson Prairie, etc., in North America

THE TRANSLATION OF THE "OLD CONSTITUTION"

Notes on the Translation

As DISCUSSED IN THE second chapter of this book, Elling Eielsen's church body that was originally founded in 1846 was governed by a document commonly known as the "Old Constitution." According to J. Magnus Rohne, the original document underwent revisions between 1846 and 1850. The text of Rohne's translation of the 1850 version, found on pages 107 to 110 of his volume *Norwegian American Lutheranism up to 1872*, is provided here for reference, especially for comparison with the revised constitution that became the governing document of Hauge's Synod in 1876, which is provided in Appendix B. Rohne notes that the original document was written in less than eloquent Norwegian, and he sought to replicate this poor linguistic style in his English translation. His translation is reproduced here as printed, except for slight adjustments of spelling, italicizing, and capitalization, which bring the text in line with modern English. These adjustments do not change the wording or meaning of the original. Also, the article numbers are listed here as Roman numerals for consistency with Appendix B. Finally, the manner of biblical citation in the translation has been changed to the method used elsewhere in this book.

The Text of the Constitution

Article I

Whereas we, the united ones, have by the grace of our Lord Jesus Christ united and joined ourselves together into an official church body in the Lutheran Church, be it hereby firmly resolved and decided, that this our church body shall forever continue to be, just as it now is, in conformity to the genuine Lutheran faith and doctrine, and built on God's Word in the Holy Scriptures in conjunction with the Apostolic and Augsburg Articles of Faith, which together with the Word are the rule for our church order, and for our faith and confession, as living members under our Savior Jesus Christ, who is the Head of our Church.

Article II

In accordance with the order and method which the Holy Scriptures teach and convince, that nothing common or unclean can enter the New Jerusalem (Rev 21:27, etc.), no one ought to be accepted as a member of our body, except he has passed through a genuine conversion or is on the way to conversion, so he has a noticeable sorrow for his sins, and hunger and thirst after righteousness, from which must follow an improvement in his conduct as a testimony of the living faith's activity in soul and heart, about which the Scriptures witness so expressly that they are the inescapable necessity for every true member of the true church body.

Article III

Every member in the church must consequently strive, in virtue of the power of faith, to walk piously and blamelessly, and have constantly a wakeful eye upon himself, because he in love must remind others, who walk faultily (Gal 6:1). Not to pass harsh and merciless judgments on his failing brother, as one who sees the mote in his brother's eye but is unaware of the beam in his own; but as a Christian, to whom it is becoming to seek the pure truth; and then one cannot possibly say good about the evil.

Article IV

One should according to Jesus's Word in Mt 18:15-17, remind and punish the failing between himself and him alone, and not trumpet forth his hidden faults to his harm and to the offense of others; if he hear you, you have won your brother. But if he does not hear, then take one or two others with you, that the whole matter may be established at the mouth of two or three witnesses. But if he does not hear them, then tell it to the congregation; but if he does not hear the congregation, then he shall be for you as a heathen.

Article V

He who, with the prodigal son, repents of his trespass before God and man, he should be taken in again in the church body, and the church must not refuse that also that one is given absolution, that is, assurance of God's grace in Christ.

Article VI

With popish authority and also the common ministerial garb we henceforth have absolutely nothing to do, since there is no proof in the New Testament that Jesus or his disciples have used or enjoined it. On the contrary, we can read in Mt 23:5, Mk 12:38, and Lk 20:46 that Jesus chastised those who went about in long clothes and performed [acts of] piety to be well thought of by men. Experience also teaches, that both minister and hearer [worshiper] often place a blind confidence in the dead church ceremonies and clerical garb, and through this do away with God's command because of their custom (Mt 15:6).

Article VII

We believe that there is only one Master, who has left us an example to follow in doctrine, life and relations, namely, Jesus Christ, the Righteous One, who entered into the Holy [Place], and found an eternal propitiation.

Article VIII

We also believe that the teaching estate is a holy estate, and instituted by God; as Paul says: "We are ambassadors in Christ's stead, as though God did beseech you by us; we pray you in Christ's stead, be ye reconciled to God" (2 Cor 5:20). But this estate is abused by many as a deadly poison, so that they cheat both themselves and also others of the hope of salvation, until they awake in hell (Isa 3:12; Mt 7:15).

Article IX

Teachers or preachers ought to be elected by the congregation in such a way that they at least are taken on trial one year before they are permanently and rightly elected. Those who are talented for aptitude for teaching must procure the necessary knowledge, as far as the circumstances permit; but this, as everything else, must be subject to the Lord in faith and obedience, that not ours but His will is done. Paul says: "Jesus Christ is the same yesterday and today yea and forever" (Heb 13:8). He himself chose lay and unlearned men to proclaim his Gospel, which also was done with such power and wisdom, that the worldly wise in surprise had to ask: Are not all these which speak Galileans? And how hear we, every man in our own tongue, wherein we were born? (Acts 2:7-11, 4:13). Jesus likewise says, that He not only will be with His apostles to the end of the world, but also with all those who, on account of their words, believe on Him; and that He will give all those the Holy Ghost who humbly ask Him for it.

Article X

The young should be instructed in God's Word from their early youth. The A B C Book, Luther's Small Catechism of the older unadulterated editions, and E. Pontoppidan's *Sanhed til Gudfrygtighed* should be learned and be explained for the young, so they can be enlightened concerning all of God's plan of salvation. Each master and mistress should diligently instruct their children and members of their household, and by prayer and the meditation on God's Word help along as much as they by God's grace are able, that they, as living branches, can grow into the true vine, into which they are grafted; and likewise become accustomed to prayer and to call upon the Lord, since the children especially are more easily induced to pray than grown-ups. The grown-ups should pray with a reverent mien; because also this will have influence on the hearts of the young and attune their minds to more sobriety; especially ought to be held forth the sweet love of Jesus toward those who call on him.

Article XI

We should make it a point to further schools and instruction, and, as Christ's true followers, let God's Word dwell richly among ourselves, and, besides, do good to all, but most to those of the household of faith, who are united to help the needy as well in their physical as their spiritual need.

Article XII

It shall also be the minister's duty, with the help of the congregation, to procure the necessary books, the wealthy paying the bill, since the needy must have them free of charge, who have not the means to pay.

Article XIII

The children must be educated in both languages, but in the mother tongue first, though in such a way that the district school is not neglected.

Article XIV

We united ones repudiate altogether the fearful sin of giving our consent to the slave traffic; but rather use all possible diligence in bringing about, and supporting, opposition to it, to the freeing of the negroes, since Jesus has said, "All things therefore whatsoever ye would that men should do unto you, even so do ye also unto them; for this is the law and the prophets" (Mt 7:12). They are also redeemed with the same blood and intended to inherit the same bliss, as other races. We advise that each one give this matter close consideration.

Article XV

Likewise each one is reminded, who brings on dissension in the congregation and seeks to organize his own party, that those who are confirmed in the Lord and are what the Scriptures call "elders," ought then convene together, and use all possible diligence in bringing about unity in faith, doctrine, and relations. If this bears no fruit on the contentious, then do as Paul says: "A man that is an heretic after the first and second admonition reject; knowing that he that is such is perverted, and sinneth, being condemned of himself" (Titus 3:10-11). About such it is that John says: "They went out from us, but they were not of us; for if they had been of us, they would no doubt have continued with us; but they went out, that they might be made manifest how that they were not all of us (1 Jn 2:19).

Article XVI

Each congregation shall elect "elders," who shall supervise all things in the church, such as the members' daily relations and circumstances, whether the school is rightly conducted, and, besides, see to it that those who speak for edification do not go their own ways, and that they hold fast to the wholesome teaching and such other things as necessity requires; and, finally, that they are subject to one another in godliness.

Article XVII

Likewise ought the congregation to combine to support by freewill gifts those persons who are elected by the congregation to travel about and proclaim God's Word.

Article XVIII

The congregation ought to use all diligence in getting "awakened" and Christian-minded school teachers, who stand with the believers in the unity of faith, to the end that the young might be taught and rightly catechized and be given a true enlightenment in their Christianity, so that they can comprehend and understand it rightly to the renewal of their baptismal covenant, and thereby be renewed and grow in faith and in love to God and their neighbor.

Article XIX

A pastor should, according to Paul's admonition in 1 Tim 3:2, be blameless. If he, accordingly, after his election fall into perverse doctrine or anything worthy of censure, then the same means be used here, as are described in paragraph four above. If the milder ones do not bear fruit, so that one must perforce use the stricter, namely, expulsion from the congregation, then his errors should be publicly proclaimed in accordance with 1 Tim 5:20; 2 Tim 3:7-9, etc., and thus in the name of our Lord Jesus Christ, in the unity of faith, and with the power of our Lord Jesus Christ surrender such an one to Satan, for the destruction of his flesh, that his spirit might be saved on the day of our Lord Jesus Christ (1 Cor 5:4-5). In this, as in all things else, the Holy Scriptures are the only source from which the wholesome teaching flows out, especially when the Holy Spirit can get room to work in the hearts both of the teacher and the hearer, so they become subject to God and each other in the fear of God, and disposed to love each other mutually of a pure heart.

Article XX

The Sacraments of Baptism and the Altar are administered according to the Ritual and Altar Book of the Church of Norway, which we in all parts follow as far as the blessed doctrine is concerned. Nevertheless, the laying on of hands at absolution is not used, since it cannot be seen from Holy Scriptures that Jesus and his apostles have used this at the Lord's Supper; but as Paul reminds each to try himself, and so eat of the bread and drink of the cup. But when the pastor in his preparatory address has made plain the way of life and the way of death, as a true shepherd of souls, he concludes his preparatory address in this wise: "Accordingly, then, from God's Word is declared to all penitent, repentant, and believing souls the forgiveness of sins in the name of the Father, of the Son, and of the Holy Ghost. Amen."

God give us all His grace to unite in Jesus's name and in Jesus's mind, that the power of his suffering and death might show itself in all our ways. Amen.

Appendix B

The Constitution of Hauge's Norwegian Evangelical Lutheran Synod in America

THE TRANSLATION OF THE CONSTITUTION OF HAUGE'S SYNOD

Notes on the Translation

WHAT FOLLOWS IS AN English translation of the constitution of Hauge's Norwegian Evangelical Lutheran Synod in America, provided here for reference. As mentioned in the second chapter of this book, the "Old Constitution" of Elling Eielsen's "Evangelical Lutheran Church in America" was revised in 1876 when the synod reorganized and renamed itself. This translation of the revised constitution was prepared by Gustav Marius Bruce for the June 1913 issue of the *Lutheran Intelligencer*, a short-lived English language periodical of which Bruce served as editor. The version of the constitution provided here is a revision of the original constitution of 1876, adopted between 1909 and 1910. For example, the original constitution declared that the sacraments of baptism and the Lord's Supper were to be administered according to the Norwegian Church Ritual of 1685. This updated version of the constitution stated that the sacraments were to be administered according to the Ritual of 1889. However, this is the only existing English translation of the constitution of Hauge's Synod and, mindful of revisions made from the original text, is still useful for comparison with the "Old Constitution." The text of the constitution is reproduced in almost the same form as printed in the June issue of *The Lutheran Intelligencer*. Exceptions are that the words "article" and "section" are abbreviated in the original and are here written as complete words. There are also occasional instances of capitalization and punctuation errors and archaic spellings of words that have been corrected for modern readers, which do not change the meaning of the original. Names of documents have been italicized. The manner of biblical citation has been changed to that used elsewhere in this book.

The Text of the Constitution

Article I – Name

The Church Society which was organized by Hauge's friends, April 13-14, 1846, at Jefferson Prairie, Rock County, Wisconsin, and which has hitherto been known as "The Evangelical Lutheran Church in America," hereby adopts the name: Hauge's Norwegian Evangelical Lutheran Synod in America.

Article II – Of Confession

As we united have by the grace of our Lord Jesus Christ united and joined ourselves together into an organized Church Society of the Lutheran Church in America, so be it hereby firmly resolved and declared that this our Church Society shall ever remain as it now is in accordance with the true Lutheran faith and doctrine, built upon the Word of God, the Holy Scriptures, the canonical books of the Old and New Testament, as the only source and rule for faith, doctrine, and life. We accept as a true exhibition of the principal doctrines of the Word of God the three oldest symbols, the Apostolic, Nicene, and Athanasian, the Unaltered Augsburg Confession, and Luther's Small Catechism.

Article III – Of Object

The Society's object is the extension and establishment of the Kingdom of God by: a) the preaching of the Word of God and the administration of the sacraments for the awakening of spiritual life, regeneration, and sanctification among our people, the gathering and organization of Lutheran congregations, assisting these to obtain pastors and teachers, and encouraging the Christian laymen's activity; b) the training of future pastors and teachers of religion for the ministry in the congregations and the instruction of the young; c) promoting the dissemination and perusal of the Holy Scriptures, Lutheran devotional literature, textbooks, and hymnals; d) adjusting ecclesiastical differences and giving advice and decisions in ecclesiastical questions when the congregations request the Synod's assistance; e) encouraging and directing one another mutually in brotherly love in accordance with the Word of God, and f) providing for the abundant spreading of the Word of God among the heathen and the Jews by a vigorous missionary activity.

Article IV – Of Admission

For admission to the Synod is required that the congregation unreservedly believes and confesses the canonical books of the Old and New Testaments to be the Holy Word of God, accepts those in Article II mentioned confessions, and subscribes to this constitution in its entirety. The same requirements shall apply to individuals, and, in addition, that they live Christian lives. Furthermore, we believe that he alone is a true member of the Church who is converted and regenerated, remains in the state of grace, and bears the fruits of faith.

Article V – Of Discipline

Every member must in the strength of faith strive to live a holy and blameless life, constantly have a watchful eye directed upon himself, not mercilessly judge a failing brother, but as befits a Christian determine what is truth, and in love admonish the one who has trespassed (Gal 6:1). The rule to be followed in such cases is given in the words of Jesus, Mt 18:15-17. Church discipline proper belongs to the local congregation. A breach of the Constitution and the decisions of the Synod is a transgression against the Synod, which it may chastise. If such chastisement does not avail, the offending party, whether a congregation or an individual, may be excluded from the Synod. If the offending party repents, forgiveness shall be granted according to the Word of God.

Article VI – Of the Ministry

The Ministry is a holy office, instituted by God, as Paul says: "We are ambassadors therefore on behalf of Christ, as though God were entreating by us: we beseech you on behalf of Christ, be ye reconciled to God (2 Cor 5:20).

Article VII – Of the Pastor

Pastors are chosen by the congregation. The one who is called, must before his appointment be found to be a truly believing Christian, as far as man is able to judge, have a clear insight into the saving doctrine of the Word of God and ability to present it to others, possess the necessary educational attainments, and be rightly ordained.

Article VIII – Of the Instruction of the Young

It devolves upon every congregation with care to provide for the instruction of the young in the Word of God, Vogt's Bible History, Luther's Small Catechism, and Pontoppidan's Explanation of the same, or a good epitome of it, should be taught the young, that they may be enlightened in all God's counsel unto salvation.

Article IX – Of Controversy

Should controversy arise in regard to the accepted faith, doctrine, and ritual, the Synod shall earnestly seek to adjust it in accordance with the Word of God, and admonish the erring ones. If admonishment proves futile, the Synod shall sever its connection with such parties.

Article X – Of Church Government

The Synod charges every congregation to elect elders, who shall have supervision over all things in the congregation, as the daily walk and life of the members, the right management of the school, see to it that those who preach unto edification do not walk according to their own way, but cleave to sound doctrine, are subject to one another in the fear of God, and such other matters as may be necessary.

Article XI – Of the Support of Evangelists

The congregation shall also support by voluntary gifts those persons who by the Synod are chosen to travel about and preach the Word of God.

Article XII – Of School Teachers

Every congregation in the Synod shall in the choice of teachers exercise care as far as possible so as to secure such as have trustworthy testimonials of true Christianity and that they yield full submission to the faith and doctrine of the Synod.

Article XIII – Of the Disciplining of Pastors

A pastor shall according to the admonition of Paul in 1 Tim 3:2, be without reproach. If he, following his election as pastor, should fall into false doctrine or anything else that is blameable, then the congregation shall employ the same means as mentioned in Article V. If the milder procedure mentioned in this Article proves futile, then the more severe shall be employed, and the case presented to the Synod for final adjudication.

Article XIV – Of Ceremonies

Section 1

Our Synod does not employ all the ceremonies of the public worship of the State Church of Norway, as the clerical vestments, the intonation, and the laying on of hands in the public absolution.

Section 2

The Sacraments of Baptism and the Altar, confirmation, the solemnization of marriages, and funeral services shall be performed according to the Norwegian Altar Book of 1889.

Section 3

Confession and absolution shall be diligently employed, but shall not be placed as requirements for participation in the Lord's Supper.

Section 4

Congregations that desire to retain the connection between absolution and the Lord's Supper will follow the practice hitherto in vogue.

Article XV – Of What the Synod Consists

The Synod consists of Congregations and individuals who have been admitted into the Synod and have subscribed to this constitution.

Article XVI – Of Voting

The following have the right to vote at the annual meetings of the Synod: Delegates chosen by the congregations; pastors belonging to the Synod, who are actively engaged in the ministry, serve the Synod in some capacity, or have retired from the ministry on account of sickness or age; the theological professors at Red Wing Seminary, and members of the board of trustees.

Article XVII – Of the Annual Meeting

The Synod shall hold its annual meeting at such place as the previous meeting may determine, and shall begin on the first Wednesday after the first Tuesday in June, provided that the time for the opening of the meeting shall not be earlier than June 4.

Article XVIII – Of Representation

The congregations of the Synod shall be represented (at the annual meeting) by one or two representatives. If the congregation is too small or too poor to send a representative, it may send one jointly with one or more sister congregations, where circumstances will allow it. Every representative must present credentials to the meeting.

Article XIX – Of Officers

Section 1

The officers of the Synod are the following: A president, a vice-president, a secretary, a treasurer, and a board of trustees, consisting of nine members.

Section 2

To attend to the Synod's various activities, the following boards shall be elected: A board of school directors, composed of seven members; a church council, composed of nine members, consisting of the president of the Synod, three pastors, and five laymen; a home mission board, composed of seven members; a China Mission board, composed of seven members; an orphan's home board, composed of seven members; a board of publication, composed of seven members; an English board, composed of five members; an auditing committee, composed of three members, together with district presidents.

Section 3

These officers, boards, district presidents, and auditing committee shall perform their work in accordance with the Synod's regulations and the acts passed at the Synod's annual meetings.

Section 4

All officers, boards, and district presidents shall be elected by ballot. Their term of office shall be three years.

Article XX – Of Vote Required

The amendment of the Synod's constitution, the election of permanent theological professors, and the discharge of officers and professors require a two-thirds vote. All other elections and resolutions shall require only a majority vote. In the case of a tie, the president's vote shall decide the issue.

Article XXI – Of Schism

Should, which God in mercy prevent, a schism take place in the Synod, then the united congregations which abide by the constitution shall constitute the Synod and retain all its real and personal property.

Article XXII – Of the Settlement of Doctrinal Questions

Questions of doctrine and conscience shall not be decided by vote, but only in accordance with the Word of God and the symbolical books.

Article XXIII – Of Amendments

This constitution may be amended by a two-thirds vote, provided the proposed amendment has been publicly considered at a previous meeting and is not contrary to the provisions of the unalterable articles I, II, XX, and XXI, as well as the present article.

  The Lord grant us grace and peace, that we may be united unto one mind and heart in Christ Jesus, our Savior, that the power of His life and death may manifest itself in all our conversation. Amen.

By-Laws

Article I – Duties of the President

The president shall issue the call for the annual meeting and preside over it, examine candidates for the ministry in conjunction with the church council, and provide for their ordination, preserve peace and order in the Synod, visit the district presidents, and report to the annual meeting in regard to his activities and the status of the Synod.

Article II – Duties of the Vice-President

The vice-president shall perform the functions of the president when he cannot because of sickness or other cause perform his duties.

Article III – Duties of the Secretary

The secretary shall keep proper record of the proceedings of the Synod and publish them when the Synod so decides, execute all documents for the Synod upon its order or that of its president, publish the time and place of the annual meeting together with the matters for consideration, and be the custodian of the Synod's seal and documents.

Article IV – Duties of the Treasurer

The treasurer shall collect all moneys for the funds entrusted to him in accordance with the Synod's resolutions, pay out money upon vouchers signed by the president and secretary of the board of trustees, and present to the annual meeting an audited statement of his accounts. He shall give bonds in the sum fixed by the board of trustees.

Article V – Duties of the Church Council

The church council shall adjust all controversies within the congregations, when so requested. If brotherly admonition proves futile, the case shall be presented to the Synod for settlement. If shall also issue the call for extraordinary synod meetings, when necessary.

Article VI – Adjudication of Controversies

The Synod shall settle all such matters for the church council as mentioned in Article V, and shall summon the accused before the public synod meeting. If all admonitions are without avail, the accused parties shall be excluded from the Synod, whether it be individuals or congregations. All members and congregations thus excluded forfeit all their right to the real and personal property of the Synod.

Article VII – Duties of the Trustees

The board of trustees shall have charge of the Synod's (financial) affairs in accordance with the resolutions passed by the annual meetings. It shall organize as soon as the annual meeting has elected the new members by choosing from among its own number a president, vice-president, and secretary. The president shall call as many special meetings as he shall find necessary. Five members of the board shall constitute a quorum.

Appendix C

Congregations of Hauge's Norwegian Evangelical Lutheran Synod in America

THREE TABLES OF CONGREGATIONAL INFORMATION

Explanation of Tables

THE FIRST TABLE CONTAINS information about the congregations of Hauge's Norwegian Evangelical Lutheran Synod in America as of 1916, just prior to the merger of 1917 that produced the NLCA. This information is derived from the two volumes of Olaf Morgan Norlie's *Norsk Lutherske Menigheter i Amerika, 1843 – 1916*. These volumes contain statistical information in varying detail on every Norwegian-American Lutheran congregation in the United States and Canada that existed between 1843 and 1916. Norlie's volumes are written entirely in Norwegian. Though this does not create a significant barrier in understanding the table below, for clarification, the Norwegian word *menighet* is translated as "congregation." The word *prækeplads* is translated as "preaching point."

Additionally, the names of the various church bodies listed in the "membership number" section require some translation. The word *Forenede* means "united" and refers to the United Norwegian Lutheran Church (UNLC) that was formed in 1890. This was one of the church bodies with which Hauge's Synod merged in 1917. *Norske synode* refers to the Norwegian Synod, the other body with which Hauge's Synod merged in 1917. *Frikirken* refers to the Lutheran Free Church, the association of congregations that was formed in 1897 after departing from the UNLC largely over a dispute about the status of Augsburg College and its relationship to Augsburg Seminary in that church body. The Lutheran Free Church, also known for its roots in the Haugean tradition, did not merge with other Norwegian-American Lutheran synods in 1917, but continued an independent existence until it voted to join the American Lutheran Church (TALC) in 1962. Congregations desiring to continue an independent existence at that point formed a group known as the Association of Free Lutheran Congregations (AFLC) in 1963. The word *Konferensten* refers to "The Conference," the largest of the church bodies that merged to form the UNLC in 1890. *Dansk forenede* refers to the United Danish Evangelical Lutheran Church (UDELC), which took complete form with a merger of two groups of "sad Danes" in 1896. As Danish immigration to the United States was considerably smaller than Norwegian immigration, many Danes found a home in Norwegian-American Lutheran congregations because of their shared Scandinavian heritage. In time, however, many of these Danes departed to join the distinctly Danish UDELC. Finally, the word *utenom* means "independent," indicating that a congregation belonged to no particular church body. At times, however, these independent congregations were loosely associated with one or more church bodies, as the pastors who served these congregations were members of a particular synod.

In the first table, those congregations listed in regular type were members of Hauge's Synod as of 1916. Those listed in italics were members of Hauge's Synod at some point in history before joining a different Norwegian-American Lutheran denomination prior to 1916. Those listed in bold type are "preaching points," meaning that they were considered by Hauge's Synod to be less formal worshipping communities rather than fully-fledged congregations. Often, though not always, these "preaching points" among Norwegian-American Lutherans were worshipping communities connected to various institutions, such as colleges, seminaries, hospitals, or other care facilities.

In addition to the name of the congregation, the first table lists the county, city, and state or province of its location. For those interested in further information about a particular congregation, the volume in which a congregation is listed in Norlie's work is also provided as well as the specific page number in that volume. To provide the reader with a sense of the size of these congregations as of 1916, the most recent membership figure for the congregation that Norlie provides is listed under "membership number." The first number listed is the number of *sjaele*, translated as "souls," who were members of the congregation. The second number listed is the year in which the membership number was reported. Finally, where such information could be obtained, the table lists the current status and denominational affiliation of the congregation. Some of these congregations are now defunct, and this status is noted where it could be determined with reasonable certainty. In a number of cases, the exact fate of a congregation could not be determined without extensive local research that is beyond the scope of this work. In all likelihood, these congregations labeled as "undetermined" ceased to exist at some point or merged with neighboring congregations at some point after 1917. Otherwise, the table provides as much information as available about the current status of a congregation, noting, for example, when a congregation left a denomination and joined a different one. The meaning of acronyms can be found in the "abbreviations" section in the front matter of the book.

The second table provides numerical information derived from the first table, listing information such as how many congregations were members of Hauge's Synod as of 1916, how many of those congregations are now members of the ELCA, and how many of those congregations now belong to various other Lutheran organizations.

The third table, also derived from the first, lists the number of congregations of Hauge's Synod as of 1916 by US state and Canadian province.

Table 1: Hauge's Synod Congregations as of 1916

Congregation Name	County	City	State/Province	Norlie Volume	Norlie Page	Membership Number	Current Status
Hauges norsk evangelisk lutherske menighet	La Salle Co.	Norway	Illinois	1	44	115; 1914	AFLC; Merged into Fox River Lutheran in 1917
Trinity Lutheran Church (Trefoldighed)	Cook Co.	Chicago	Illinois	1	51	253; 1915	Undetermined
Immanuels norsk lutherske menighet	Cook Co.	Chicago	Illinois	1	51	200; 1915	Undetermined

APPENDIX C

St. Paul English Evangelical Lutheran Congregation	Cook Co.	Chicago	Illinois	1	51	487; 1915	Undetermined
Hauges norsk evangelisk lutherske menighet	Cook Co.	Chicago	Illinois	1	52	254; 1914	Undetermined
Ebenezer norsk lutherske menighet	Cook Co.	Chicago	Illinois	1	52	175; 1915	Undetermined
Elim norsk evangelisk lutherske menighet	Cook Co.	Chicago	Illinois	1	52	64; 1915	Undetermined
Irving Park lutherske mission	Cook Co.	Chicago	Illinois	1	52	Unknown	ELCA
The Lutheran Church of the Redeemer	Cook Co.	Chicago	Illinois	1	53	Unknown	Undetermined
Norsk evangelisk lutherske menighet av den uforandrede Augsburgske Konfession	Kendall Co.	Plattville	Illinois	1	70	200; 1914	ELCA
Newark evangelisk lutherske menighet	Kendall Co.	Newark	Illinois	1	71	295; 1914	AFLC; Left ALC before ELCA merger
Rook's Creek Lutheran Church (The Rook Creek Evangelical Lutheran)	Livingston Co.	Pontiac	Illinois	1	75	100; 1914	ELCA; Merged into St. Paul Lutheran
First Lutheran Church	Livingston Co.	Pontiac	Illinois	1	75	200; 1914	NALC; Left ELCA in 2011
Den norsk evangelisk lutherske menighet ved Creston, Ill.	DeKalb Co.	Creston	Illinois	1	79	300; 1914	LCMC; Renamed Calvary Lutheran
Vor Frelsers evangelisk lutherske menighet	DeKalb Co.	Sandwich	Illinois	1	80	35; 1914	ELCA

St. Johns norsk evangelisk lutherske menighet	Ogle Co.	Creston	Illinois	1	83	100; 1914	ELCA
Norsk evangelisk lutherske menighet	Will Co.	Joliet	Illinois	1	83	102; 1905	LCMC; Renamed Messiah Lutheran in 1961
Hauge norsk evangelisk lutherske menighet	Dane Co.	New Glarus	Wisconsin	1	102	145; 1914	ELCA; Merged with Primrose Lutheran
Hauges norsk evangelisk lutherske menighet i Perry	Dane Co.	Daleyville	Wisconsin	1	107	125; 1914	ELCA
Trefoldigheds norsk evangelisk lutherske menighet	Dane Co.	Madison	Wisconsin	1	110	100; 1914	ELCA
Hauges norsk evangelisk lutherske menighet i Deerfield	Dane Co.	Deerfield	Wisconsin	1	112	95; 1914	Undetermined
Hauges norsk evangelisk lutherske menighet i Cambridge	Dane Co.	Cambridge	Wisconsin	1	112	45; 1914	Undetermined
Bethel norsk evangelisk lutherske menighet	Dane Co.	Mt. Horeb	Wisconsin	1	113	44; 1914	Undetermined
Morrisonville Lutheran Congregation	Dane Co.	Morrisonville	Wisconsin	1	113	114; 1914	Undetermined
Den 1ste Hauges evangelisk lutherske menighet	Milwaukee Co.	Milwaukee	Wisconsin	1	120	130; 1914	Undetermined
Hauges evangelisk lutherske menighet	Columbia Co.	Lodi	Wisconsin	1	130	180; 1914	Undetermined

APPENDIX C

Den evangelisk lutherske menighet paa Bonnett Prairie i Hauges synode	Columbia Co.	Rio	Wisconsin	1	133	126; 1914	Dissolved in 1947
Spring Prairie evangelisk lutherske menighet	Columbia Co.	Keyeser	Wisconsin	1	134	119;1915	Undetermined
Den evangelisk lutherske Roche a Cree menighet	Adams Co.	Arkdale	Wisconsin	1	151	50; 1914	ELCA; Merged into Trinity Lutheran in 1919
West Prairie menighet	Vernon Co.	West Prairie	Wisconsin	1	153	112; 1915	LCMC
Franklin menighet	Vernon Co.	Viroqua	Wisconsin	1	158	225; 1915	LCMC
Immanuels menighet	Vernon Co.	Viroqua	Wisconsin	1	158	45; 1915	ELCA
Zion menighet	Vernon Co.	Genoa	Wisconsin	1	160	135; 1915	Undetermined
Eidsvold menighet	Pierce Co.	Esdaile	Wisconsin	1	179	229; 1915	ELCA
Bethlehem menighet	Pierce Co.	Bay City	Wisconsin	1	181	165; 1915	ELCA
Elk Creek Valley norsk evangelisk lutherske menighet	Trempealeau Co.	Osseo	Wisconsin	1	228	140; 1914	ELCA
Osseo evang. Lutherske menighet	Trempealeau Co.	Osseo	Wisconsin	1	229	142; 1914	ELCA
Tabitha norsk evangelisk lutherske menighet	Burnett Co.	Grantsburg	Wisconsin	1	244	75; 1915	Undetermined
Norsk evangelisk lutherske menighet	Kenosha Co.	Kenosha	Wisconsin	1	319	15; 1911	Undetermined
Den evangelisk lutherske menighet (McGregor)	Clayton Co.	McGregor	Iowa	1	337	43; 1915	Undetermined
Stavanger norsk lutherske menighet	Fayette Co.	Ossian	Iowa	1	340	371; 1914	ELCA

West Union norsk lutherske menighet	Fayette Co.	West Union	Iowa	1	341	65; 1914	Undetermined
Lincoln norsk evangelisk lutherske menighet i Slater og Huxley, Iowa	Story Co.	Huxley og Slater	Iowa	1	345	382; 1914	Undetermined
Bethel menighet	Story Co.	Story City	Iowa	1	348	175; 1915	LCMC
Salem evangelisk lutherske menighet	Story Co.	Roland	Iowa	1	349	767; 1914	LCMC
Bethania evangelisk lutherske menighet	Story Co.	McCallsburg	Iowa	1	349	135; 1915	LCMC
Nathanaels evangelisk lutherske menighet	Emmet Co.	Wallingford	Iowa	1	364	125; 1914	Undetermined
Nazareth norsk evangelisk lutherske menighet	Emmet Co.	Armstrong	Iowa	1	364	108; 1914	ELCA
Josvas evangelisk lutherske menighet	Emmet Co.	Forsyth	Iowa	1	364	40; 1904	Undetermined
Norway evangelisk lutherske menighet	Humboldt Co.	Eagle Grove	Iowa	1	379	117; 1914	Undetermined
Clear Lake og Ellsworth norsk evangelisk lutherske menighet	Hamilton Co.	Jewell	Iowa	1	390	125; 1914	Undetermined
Nazaret norsk lutherske menighet	Hamilton Co.	Radcliffe	Iowa	1	390	125; 1914	Undetermined
Bethesda evangelisk lutherske menighet	Hamilton Co.	Jewell	Iowa	1	391	354; 1913	ELCA
Elim menighet	Hamilton Co.	Randall	Iowa	1	391	350; 1914	LCMC

APPENDIX C

Tabitha norsk evangelisk lutherske menighet	Hamilton Co.	Williams	Iowa	1	391	300; 1914	LCMC; Merged into St. Paul Lutheran
Betania evangelisk lutherske menighet	Hamilton Co.	Radcliffe	Iowa	1	391	180; 1914	Undetermined
Immanuels norsk lutherske menighet	Hamilton Co.	Ellsworth	Iowa	1	392	40; 1914	Undetermined
Zion evangelisk lutherske menighet	Hamilton Co.	Jewell	Iowa	1	392	101; 1914	Undetermined
St. Johannes evangelisk lutherske menighet	Woodbury Co.	Sioux City	Iowa	1	402	350; 1914	ELCA
Zion norsk evangelisk lutherske menighet (Sion)	Hardin Co.	Garden City	Iowa	1	404	310; 1914	ELCA
Stavanger norsk lutherske menighet	Hardin Co.	Garden City	Iowa	1	405	225; 1914	AFLC
Petri norsk lutherske menighet (St. Petri)	Hardin Co.	Radcliffe	Iowa	1	405	130; 1914	Undetermined
Bethlehem menighet	Wright Co.	Holmes	Iowa	1	419	160; 1915	Undetermined
Samuel menighet (Salem?)	Wright Co.	Eagle Grove	Iowa	1	420	140; 1915	NALC
Jewell College prækeplads	**Hamilton Co.**	Jewell	Iowa	1	435	N/A	N/A
St. John's Hospital og Deaconess Home prækeplads	**Woodbury Co.**	Sioux City	Iowa	1	435	N/A	N/A
Arendahl evangelisk lutherske menighet (Arendal)	Fillmore Co.	Peterson	Minnesota	1	441	325; 1915	ELCA

351

Peterson norsk evangelisk lutherske menighet	Fillmore Co.	Peterson	Minnesota	1	445	136; 1915	ELCA; Merged with Our Savior's in 1951 to form Grace
Bethelehem norsk evangelisk lutherske menighet	Fillmore Co.	Le Roy	Minnesota	1	448	107; 1914	Undetermined
Bethania norsk evangelisk lutherske menighet	Mower Co.	Le Roy	Minnesota	1	452	140; 1914	Undetermined
Zion evangelisk lutherske menighet (Sions)	Mower Co.	Dexter	Minnesota	1	453	55; 1913	AFLC
Immanuels norsk evangelisk lutherske menighet	Goodhue Co.	Kenyon	Minnesota	1	465	250; 1914	AFLC; Left ALC in 1971
Hauges norsk evangelisk lutherske menighet	Goodhue Co.	Kenyon	Minnesota	1	465	200; 1914	AFLC
St. Peters norsk lutherske menighet (St. Petri)	Goodhue Co.	Red Wing	Minnesota	1	466	392; 1915	ELCA; Merged into United Lutheran in 1931
Størdahl norsk evangelisk lutherske menighet	Goodhue Co.	Zumbrota	Minnesota	1	467	260; 1914	ELCA
Søndre Zumbro menighet i Olmsted og Dodge Cos.	Olmsted Co.	Kasson	Minnesota	1	470	233; 1914	LCMC; Left ELCA in 2011
Markers norsk evangelisk lutherske menighet av Faribault og Cannon City	Rice Co.	Faribault	Minnesota	1	472	83; 1914	Merged with two other congregations near Fairbault after the 1917 merger
Salør menighet (Solør)	Rice Co.	Webster	Minnesota	1	474	170; 1915	ELCA

APPENDIX C

Immanuels norsk evangelisk lutherske menighet (Etter)	Dakota Co.	Etter	Minnesota	1	478	44; 1915	Dissolved
Zion menighet	Dakota Co.	South St. Paul	Minnesota	1	478	65; 1915	ELCA
Nannestad Hauges norsk evangelisk lutherske menighet	Kandiyohi Co.	New London	Minnesota	1	501	36; 1914	ELCA; Merged with East Norway Lake
Betania norsk lutherske menighet	Kandiyohi Co.	Spicer	Minnesota	1	502	78; 1914	Dissolved
Green Lake norsk evangelisk lutherske menighet	Kandiyohi Co.	Spicer	Minnesota	1	505	170; 1914	AFLC; Did not enter 1917 merger
Bethania menighet (Frost, Bethany)	Faribault Co.	Frost	Minnesota	1	517	275; 1915	ELCA
Emerald norsk evangelisk lutherske menighet (Emmveld)	Faribault Co.	Frost	Minnesota	1	517	65; 1915	Undetermined
Silo norsk evangelisk lutherske menighet	Faribault Co.	Elmgrove	Minnesota	1	518	30; 1891	ELCA
Salem engelsk-norsk lutherske menighet	Faribault Co.	Elmore	Minnesota	1	518	53; 1914	Undetermined
Skandinavisk evangelisk lutherske menighet	Faribault Co.	Kiester	Minnesota	1	518	75; 1915	Undetermined
Bethlehem menighet	Faribault Co.	Bricelyn	Minnesota	1	518	65; 1915	Undetermined
Hauges menighet	Jackson Co.	Jackson	Minnesota	1	529	237; 1913	ELCA; Apparently merged with Belmont
Salem norsk evangelisk lutherske menighet	Jackson Co.	Heron Lake	Minnesota	1	530	80; 1914	Undetermined

St. Pauli norsk evangelisk lutherske menighet	Jackson Co.	Lakefield	Minnesota	1	531	150; 1914	Undetermined
Belmont norsk evangelisk lutherske menighet	Jackson Co.	Lakefield	Minnesota	1	532	120; 1914	ELCA
Des Moines Valley menighet	Jackson Co.	Jackson	Minnesota	1	533	229; 1914	Undetermined
Our Redeemer's Lutheran Church	Hennepin Co.	Minneapolis	Minnesota	1	549	35; 1915	ELCA
St. Pauli norsk evangelisk lutherske menighet (St. Pauls)	Hennepin Co.	Minneapolis	Minnesota	1	550	400; 1915	LCMC
First Lutheran Church (St. Louis Park)	Hennepin Co.	St. Louis Park	Minnesota	1	550	Unknown	Undetermined
Immanuels norsk evangelisk lutherske menighet	Ramsey Co.	St. Paul	Minnesota	1	563	150; 1914	ELCA
Østre Immanuels menighet	Ramsey Co.	St. Paul	Minnesota	1	564	225; 1915	ARC
Hauges menighet	Renville Co.	Franklin	Minnesota	1	575	295; 1913	Undetermined
Franklin menighet	Renville Co.	Franklin	Minnesota	1	576	139; 1915	Undetermined
Hof evangelisk lutherske menighet	Renville Co.	Sacred Heart	Minnesota	1	576	140; 1915	Undetermined
Zion menighet	Renville Co.	Fairfax	Minnesota	1	578	112; 1915	Undetermined
Opdahl norsk evangelisk lutherske menighet	Renville Co.	Sacred Heart	*Minnesota*	1	578	70; 1914 *Independent as of 1912*	ELCA
Riverside evangelisk lutherske menighet	Lac qui Parle Co.	Dawson	Minnesota	1	589	400; 1914	ELCA; Merged with Trinity in 1961

APPENDIX C

Lac qui Parle evangelisk lutherske menighet	Lac qui Parle Co.	Dawson	Minnesota	1	590	651; 1914	ELCA; Significant split to form LCMC congregation
Ness evangelisk lutherske menighet	Lac qui Parle Co.	Madison	Minnesota	1	593	500; 1914	Undetermined
Solør menighet	Lac qui Parle Co.	Madison	Minnesota	1	595	76; 1915	Undetermined
St. Johannes norsk evangelisk lutherske menighet	Lac qui Parle Co.	Boyd	Minnesota	1	595	60; 1915	Undetermined
Trefoldigheds menighet av Boyd, Minn.	Lac qui Parle Co.	Boyd	*Minnesota*	*1*	596	490; 1914 Forenede as of 1897	ELCA
Løken lutherske menighet (Løken)	Lac qui Parle Co.	Hadenville	Minnesota	1	597	48; 1915	Dissolved
Ten Mile Lake evangelisk lutherske kirke	Ottertail Co.	Dalton	Minnesota	1	598	136; 1914	ELCA; Merged with Our Savior Lutheran
Bethel evangelisk lutherske menighet	Ottertail Co.	Ashby	Minnesota	1	598	95; 1914	Undetermined
Swan Lake norsk lutherske menighet	Ottertail Co.	Fergus Falls	Minnesota	1	598	101; 1914	CLBA
Norwegian Grove menighet (Norway Grove)	Ottertail Co.	Norwegian Grove	Minnesota	1	599	38; 1915	Undetermined
Zion evangelisk lutherske menighet	Ottertail Co.	Fergus Falls	Minnesota	1	607	100; 1914	ELCA
Vang evangelisk lutherske menighet	Ottertail Co.	Fergus Falls	Minnesota	1	612	80; 1914	Undetermined
Friborg menighet (Friberg)	Ottertail Co.	Rothsay	Minnesota	1	613	36; 1915	Undetermined
Søndre Friborg menighet	Ottertail Co.	Fergus Falls	Minnesota	1	613	36; 1915	Undetermined
Lille Bethania menighet	Ottertail Co.	Rothsay	Minnesota	1	613	124; 1915	Undetermined
Ny Trefoldigheds lutherske menighet	Yellow Medicine Co.	Canby	Minnesota	1	624	20; 1911	Undetermined

Bethlehem menighet	Yellow Medicine Co.	Hazel Run	Minnesota	1	624	50; 1915	Undetermined
Israels menighet (Israels evangeliske fremenighet)	Yellow Medicine Co.	Clarkfield	Minnesota	1	625	108; 1915	Dissolved
Hauglum norsk evangelisk lutherske menighet	*Becker Co.*	*Lake Park*	*Minnesota*	*1*	630	90; 1914 Forenede as of 1890	ELCA; But dissolved in 2013
Saron menighet	Becker Co.	Audubon	Minnesota	1	630	215; 1911	Undetermined
Detroit menighet (St. Petri?)	Becker Co.	Detroit	Minnesota	1	631	198; 1915	Undetermined
Callaway menighet	Becker Co.	Callaway	Minnesota	1	633	110; 1911	Undetermined
Zion menighet	Clay Co.	Barnesville	Minnesota	1	637	24; 1915	Undetermined
Bethesda evangelisk lutherske menighet (Hauges)	St. Louis Co.	Duluth	Minnesota	1	666	200; 1914	ELCA; Merged into First Lutheran in 1941
Floodwood skandinavisk evangelisk lutherske menighet	St. Louis Co.	Floodwood	Minnesota	1	672	25; 1914	LCMC; Merged with Finns in 1965, and now Hope Lutheran
Elsborough norsk evangeliske menighet	Murray Co.	Lake Wilson	Minnesota	1	686	175; 1914	Undetermined
Bethania menighet	Norman Co.	Twin Valley	Minnesota	1	690	80; 1914	Undetermined
St. Pauli menighet	*Norman Co.*	Hendrum	*Minnesota*	*1*	693	90; 1915 Forenede as of 1903	*Undetermined*
Trefoldigheds menighet (Trinity)	Norman Co.	Ada	Minnesota	1	693	160; 1913	Undetermined
Landstads menighet (Landsted, Lansted)	Norman Co.	Perley	Minnesota	1	697	112; 1913	Undetermined
Jevnager menighet	Norman Co.	Borup	Minnesota	1	698	84; 1913	CLBA

APPENDIX C

Norman menighet	Norman Co.	Flaming	Minnesota	1	700	80; 1913 Switched between Forenede and Hauge's	Undetermined
Hauges Minde evangelisk lutherske menighet	Polk Co.	Crookston	Minnesota	1	703	68; 1915	ELCA; Merged into Trinity Lutheran in 1938
Kongsvinger evangelisk lutherske menighet	Polk Co.	Birkholz	Minnesota	1	706	236; 1914	AALC
Broderheim menighet	Polk Co.	Erskine	Minnesota	1	717	100; 1915	Undetermined
Bethel evangelisk lutherske menighet (Betel)	Polk Co.	Beltrami	Minnesota	1	717	45; 1910	Undetermined
Hill River Lake evangelisk lutherske menighet	Polk Co.	McIntosh	Minnesota	1	720	32; 1915	Undetermined
Kandata norsk evangelisk lutherske menighet	Todd Co.	Sauk Center	Minnesota	1	736	33; 1915 Formerly Forenede and Frikirken	Undetermined
Eagle Valley norsk evangelisk lutherske menighet	Todd Co.	Eagle Bend	Minnesota	1	738	75; 1915	Undetermined
Freeman Creek norsk evangelisk lutherske menighet	Todd Co.	Clarissa	Minnesota	1	738	61; 1909 Formerly Forenede	Undetermined
Bethel norsk evangelisk lutherske menighet	Todd Co.	Clarissa	Minnesota	1	739	70; 1915	Undetermined
Bethlehem evangelisk lutherske menighet	Marshall Co.	Newfolden	Minnesota	1	772	63; 1914	ELCA
Zion norsk evangelisk lutherske menighet (Viking)	Marshall Co.	Viking	Minnesota	1	773	55; 1914	ELCA

Bethlehem norsk lutherske menighet	Crow Wing Co.	Brainerd	Minnesota	1	774	119; 1905 Frikirken as of 1906	ELCA
Egelund evangelisk lutherske menighet	Crow Wing Co.	Brainerd	Minnesota	1	774	32; 1882 Frikirken as of 1906	Undetermined
Deer Wood skandinavisk evangelisk lutherske menighet	Crow Wing Co.	Brainerd	Minnesota	1	774	51; 1914 Frikirken as of 1896	Undetermined
Trefoldigheds norsk evangelisk lutherske menighet	Pennington Co.	Thief River Falls	Minnesota	1	778	57; 1914	Undetermined
Immanuels evangelisk lutherske menighet	Pennington Co.	Thief River Falls	Minnesota	1	778	53; 1915	Undetermined
Zoar norsk evangelisk lutherske menighet	Pennington Co.	Brunkeberg	Minnesota	1	781	52; 1914	Undetermined
Ekelund evangelisk lutherske menighet	Pennington Co.	Erie	Minnesota	1	781	85; 1914 Norske synode as of 1910	ELCA
Little Oak norsk lutherske menighet (Lille Oak)	Pennington Co.	Neptune	Minnesota	1	782	35; 1915	Undetermined
Mykland norsk lutherske menighet	Pennington Co.	Goodridge	Minnesota	1	782	35; 1915	Undetermined
Zion menighet (Ihlen, Zion frimenighet)	Pipestone Co.	Ihlen	Minnesota	1	792	67; 1914	Undetermined
Opdal norsk evangelisk lutherske menighet	Roseau Co.	Badger	Minnesota	1	798	59; 1914	Undetermined
Moland norsk evangelisk lutherske menighet	Roseau Co.	Greenbush	Minnesota	1	798	98; 1914	ELCA; Merged to form Bethel Lutheran

APPENDIX C

Bethlehem norsk evangelisk lutherske menighet (Bethlehem)	Roseau Co.	Greenbush	Minnesota	1	799	147; 1914	Undetermined
Midland norsk evangelisk lutherske menighet	Roseau Co.	Haug	Minnesota	1	800	39; 1915	Dissolved
Gustav Adolf menighet (Gustav Adolf frimenighet)	Roseau Co.	Strathcona	Minnesota	1	802	80; 1914	ELCA
Nannestad norsk evangelisk lutherske menighet	Roseau Co.	Badger	Minnesota	1	803	66; 1915	Undetermined
Emanuels evangelisk lutherske menighet	Clearwater Co.	Queen	Minnesota	1	806	70; 1915	Dissolved; Merged with Bang to form Bethlehem in 1921
Sion menighet	Clearwater Co.	Leonard	Minnesota	1	808	50; 1913	Undetermined
Betania norsk evangelisk lutherske menighet	Clearwater Co.	Berner	Minnesota	1	810	83; 1915	NALC; Merged with Saron to form United
Immanuels menighet	Kanabec Co.	Ogilvie	Minnesota	1	827	55; 1913	ELCA
Comfort Norwegian Lutheran Free Church of Kanabec Co.	Kanabec Co.	Mora	Minnesota	1	827	44; 1914	Undetermined
Bethlehem menighet	Cook Co.	Grand Marais	Minnesota	1	829	80; 1915	ELCA
Trefoldigheds evangelisk norsk lutherske menighet	Cook Co.	Hovland	Minnesota	1	830	60; 1915	ELCA
Zoar evangelisk norsk lutherske menighet (Tofte)	Cook Co.	Tofte	Minnesota	1	830	56; 1915	LCMC
Red Wing Seminary prækeplads	**Goodhue Co.**	**Red Wing**	**Minnesota**	**1**	**835**	**N/A**	**N/A**
Vor Frelsers norsk evangelisk lutherske menighet	Muskegon Co.	Muskegon	Michigan	1	864	205; 1914	ELCA

Bethania skandinavisk evangelisk lutherske menighet	Montcalm Co.	Amble	Michigan	1	869	37; 1914	Undetermined
Bethesda menighet	Kent Co.	Grand Rapids	Michigan	1	883	40; 1913	Undetermined
Wyoming Park lutherske mission	Kent Co.	Grand Rapids	Michigan	1	883	50; 1913	Undetermined
Roseni menighet	Union Co.	Beresford	South Dakota	1	899	338; 1915	ELCA
Emmanuel's Lutheran Church	Union Co.	Beresford	South Dakota	1	900	113; 1914	ELCA
St. Peters menighet	Clay Co.	Vermillion	South Dakota	1	902	97; 1914	Undetermined
Trondhjem evangelisk lutherske menighet	Yankton Co.	Volin	South Dakota	1	906	208; 1915	AFLC
Meldahl evangelisk lutherske menighet (Meldal)	Yankton Co.	Mayfield	South Dakota	1	908	152; 1915	Independent; Merged into Calvary Lutheran
Salem kristelig lutherske menighet	Yankton Co.	Irene	South Dakota	1	908	103; 1914	Independent; Merged into Calvary Lutheran
Irene skandinavisk lutherske menighet	Yankton Co.	Irene	South Dakota	1	908	80; 1914	Independent; Merged into Calvary Lutheran
Elim norsk lutherske menighet	Yankton Co.	Irene	South Dakota	1	909	75; 1914	Undetermined
Romsdal norsk evangelisk lutherske menighet	Lincoln Co.	Beresford	South Dakota	1	912	249; 1915	LCMC
Skrefsrud norsk lutherske menighet	Lincoln Co.	Beresford	South Dakota	1	914	57; 1914	AFLC
Stordahls norsk evangelisk lutherske menighet	Minnehaha Co.	Dell Rapids	South Dakota	1	920	106; 1914	Undetermined
Highland norsk evangelisk lutherske menighet	Minnehaha Co.	Sherman	South Dakota	1	921	37; 1914	ELCA

APPENDIX C

Salem norsk evangelisk lutherske menighet	Minnehaha Co.	Sherman	South Dakota	1	923	21; 1914	Undetermined
Singsoos norsk evangelisk lutherske menighet	Brookings Co.	Lake Hendricks	South Dakota	1	929	750; 1914	Left ELCA to join AFLC in 2011; now "nondenominational"
Bethania menighet (Volga)	Brookings Co.	Volga	South Dakota	1	931	70; 1914	Dissolved
Imanuels norsk evangelisk lutherske menighet	Turner Co.	Centerville	South Dakota	1	933	68; 1914	AFLC
Melhus menighet	Turner Co.	Centerville	South Dakota	1	933	55; 1914	ELCA; Merged with Scandia in 1944
Bethlehem menighet	Turner Co.	Hooker	South Dakota	1	936	55; 1912	Dissolved
Scandia evangelisk lutherske menighet	Turner Co.	Centerville	South Dakota	1	936	85; 1914	ELCA
Astoria prækeplads	**Deuel Co.**	**Astoria**	**South Dakota**	**1**	**938**	**N/A**	**Undetermined**
Blom Prairie evangelisk lutherske menighet	Deuel Co.	Toronto	South Dakota	1	938	173; 1914	CLBA
Rome evangelisk lutherske menighet	Deuel Co.	Goodwin	South Dakota	1	940	34; 1914	Undetermined
Estelline lutherske menighet	Hamlin Co.	Estelline	South Dakota	1	950	125; 1915 Forenede until 1903	Undetermined
Recaboth lutherske menighet	Grant Co.	Albee	South Dakota	1	951	75; 1916	Undetermined
Wilson evangelisk lutherske menighet	Grant Co.	Revillo	South Dakota	1	952	46; 1899	Undetermined
Zoar evangelisk lutherske menighet	Grant Co.	Marietta/ Revillo	South Dakota	1	952	89; 1916	ELCA

Lake Preston menighet (Lake Preston)	Kingsbury Co.	Lake Preston	South Dakota	1	954	30; 1914	ELCA
Trefoldigheds menighet (Trinity)	Kingsbury Co.	Oldham	South Dakota	1	954	145; 1915	Undetermined
James norsk lutherske menighet	Brown Co.	James	South Dakota	1	976	35; 1914	Undetermined
Victor norsk evangelisk lutherske menighet	Davison Co.	Mt. Vernon	South Dakota	1	978	136; 1914	Dissolved
Vor Frelsers evangelisk lutherske menighet	Spink Co.	Redfield	South Dakota	1	983	77; 1915	ELCA
Stavanger evangelisk lutherske menighet	Brule Co.	Dunlap	South Dakota	1	985	10; 1914	Undetermined
Clark Center norsk evangelisk lutherske menighet	Clark Co.	Clark	South Dakota	1	987	132; 1915	Undetermined
Good Hope norsk lutherske menighet	Clark Co.	Naples	South Dakota	1	988	90; 1914	Undetermined
St. Pauli norsk evangelisk lutherske menighet	Clark Co.	Clark	South Dakota	1	989	35; 1915	ELCA
Carpenter norsk evangelisk lutherske menighet	Clark Co.	Carpenter	South Dakota	1	989	Unknown	Undetermined
Bailey norsk lutherske menighet	Hand Co.	Bailey	South Dakota	*1*	989	48; 1884 Frikirken as of 1904	*Undetermined*
Franke menighet (Francke)	Charles Mix Co.	Bloomington	South Dakota	1	991	26; 1915	Undetermined
Morningside menighet	Charles Mix Co.	Geddes	South Dakota	1	993	54; 1914	Undetermined
Tabor evangelisk lutherske menighet	Charles Mix Co.	Platte	South Dakota	1	993	62; 1914	Undetermined

APPENDIX C

Salem norsk lutherske menighet	Day Co.	Pierpont	South Dakota	1	994	58; 1914	Undetermined
Bethlehem norsk evangelisk lutherske menighet (Bethlehem)	Day Co.	Pierpont	South Dakota	1	997	92; 1914	LCMC
St. Ansgari evangelisk lutherske menighet (St. Ansgar)	Day Co.	Lily	South Dakota	1	998	35; 1915 Forenede as of 1915	Dissolved
Langford norsk lutherske menighet	Marshall Co.	Langford	South Dakota	1	1000	273; 108	Undetermined
Elm Creek menighet	Walworth Co.	Glenham	South Dakota	1	1004	62; 1914 Frikirken as of 1904	Undetermined
Ebenezer evangelisk lutherske menighet (Ebenezer)	Douglas Co.	Corsica	South Dakota	1	1009	68; 1914	Undetermined
Trefoldigheds menighet	Pennington Co.	Quinn	South Dakota	1	1012	26; 1915	Undetermined
Israels norsk evangelisk lutherske menighet	Sanborn Co.	Artesian	South Dakota	1	1016	70; 1914	Undetermined
Trefoldigheds norsk evangelisk lutherske menighet	Haakon Co.	Nowlin	South Dakota	1	1017	26; 1915	Undetermined
Bonesteel norsk evangelisk lutherske menighet	Gregory Co.	Bonesteel	South Dakota	1	1018	32; 1914	Undetermined
Rosebud skandinavisk evangelisk lutherske menighet	Gregory Co.	Herrick	South Dakota	1	1019	20; 1914	Undetermined

Nathanael lutherske menighet	Harding Co.	Cox	South Dakota	1	1020	55; 1916	Undetermined
Lodgepole lutherske menighet (Lodgepoli)	Harding Co.	Ludlow	South Dakota	1	1020	30; 1916	Undetermined
Bethel skandinavisk lutherske menighet	Harding Co.	Buffalo	South Dakota	1	1022	18; 1916	Undetermined
Høiland evangelisk lutherske menighet	Harding Co.	Ladner	South Dakota	1	1022	125; 1916	Undetermined
Bethlehem lutherske menighet	Harding Co.	Bullock	South Dakota	1	1022	30; 1916	LCMC
South Creek menighet (South Chrich)	Jackson Co.	Kadoka	South Dakota	1	1027	32; 1915	ELCA; Became Concordia Lutheran
Bethesda børnehjem prækeplads (Bethesda barnehjem)	Lincoln Co.	**Beresford**	South Dakota	1	1029	N/A	N/A
Bethesda alderdomshjem prækeplads	Lincoln Co.	**Beresford**	South Dakota	1	1029	N/A	N/A
St. Paul evangelisk lutherske menighet	Greenwood Co.	Eureka	Kansas	1	1034	28; 1907	Undetermined
Fall River norsk lutherske menighet	Greenwood Co.	Eureka	Kansas	1	1034	84; 1907	ELCA; Merged and now part of Christ Lutheran
Otter Creek evangelisk lutherske menighet	Greenwood Co.	Climax	Kansas	1	1034	39; 1907	Undetermined
Bethlehem skandinavisk evangelisk lutherske menighet	Sonoma Co.	Santa Rosa	California	1	1054	87; 1914	ELCA

APPENDIX C

Shell Creek evangelisk lutherske menighet	Madison Co.	Newman Grove	Nebraska	1	1067	279; 1915	ELCA
Zion evangelisk lutherske menighet (Sion)	Custer Co.	Mason City	Nebraska	1	1071	50; 1889 Danske forenede kirke as of 1891	Undetermined
Niobrara norsk evangelisk lutherske menighet	Knox Co.	Niobrara	Nebraska	1	1073	69; 1914	ELCA; Merged to form Niobrara Evangelical Lutheran Church
North Branch menighet	Boone Co.	Petersburg	Nebraska	1	1076	105; 1915	Undetermined
Fron evangelisk lutherske menighet	Cass Co.	Horace	North Dakota	2	14	217; 1914	ELCA; Now Horace Lutheran Church
Hemnes evangelisk lutherske menighet (Hemnæs)	Richland Co.	Christine	North Dakota	2	19	27; 1915	Undetermined
Mayville evangelisk lutherske menighet	Traill Co.	Mayville	North Dakota	2	31	82; 1914	ELCA; Merged to form Mayville Lutheran Church
Trefoldigheds norsk evangelisk lutherske menighet	Traill Co.	Portland	North Dakota	2	36	94; 1914	Undetermined
Ny Stavanger menighet (My Stavenger)	Traill Co.	Buxton	North Dakota	2	39	224; 1914	AFLC
Valdheim evangelisk lutherske menighet (Kathryn, Waldheim)	Barnes Co.	Kathryn	North Dakota	2	43	100; 1914 Previously Forenede	ELCA
Kathryn norsk evangelisk lutherske menighet	Barnes Co.	Kathryn	North Dakota	2	46	30; 1914	Undetermined

Nordre Trefoldigheds norsk evangelisk lutherske menighet	Walsh Co.	Grafton	North Dakota	2	47	81; 1914 Previously Konferensten and Utenom	Undetermined
Vor Frelsers evangelisk lutherske menighet	Walsh Co.	Grafton	North Dakota	2	48	120; 1914	ELCA
St. Pauli menighet (St. Pauls)	Walsh Co.	Edinburg	North Dakota	2	52	60; 1914	Undetermined
Hvidesø menighet (Hvidsø)	Walsh Co.	Edinburg	North Dakota	2	52	161; 1915	Undetermined
Silvesta menighet (Selvesto, Silvista)	Walsh Co.	Fairdale	North Dakota	2	56	98; 1914	Undetermined
St. Peters menighet (St. Petri)	Walsh Co.	Edinburg	North Dakota	2	56	70; 1914	Undetermined
Vang menighet	Walsh Co.	Adams	North Dakota	2	57	73; 1915	Undetermined
Trefoldigheds evangelisk lutherske menighet	Grand Forks Co.	Grand Forks	North Dakota	2	61	123; 1915	Undetermined
Logan menighet	Grand Forks Co.	Fergus	North Dakota	2	69	40; 1913 Forenede as of 1904	*Undetermined*
Betania norsk evangelisk lutherske menighet (Bethania)	Steele Co.	Finley	North Dakota	2	73	70; 1914	Undetermined
St. Petri norsk evangelisk lutherske menighet (St. Peters)	Steele Co.	Pickert	North Dakota	2	73	49; 1914	Undetermined
Nordland menighet (Rutland)	Sargent Co.	Rutland	North Dakota	2	75	65; 1914	Undetermined
Trefoldigheds menighet	Sargent Co.	Forman	North Dakota	2	77	178; 1914 Forenede as of 1890	*ELCA*

APPENDIX C

Stiklestad	Ransom Co.	Fort Ransom	North Dakota	2	84	85; 1914	Undetermined
Lisbon evangelisk skandinavisk lutherske menighet	Ransom Co.	Lisbon	North Dakota	2	85	150; 1914	Undetermined
Nidaros menighet	Ransom Co.	Englevale	North Dakota	2	87	60; 1914	Undetermined
Lyster norsk evangelisk lutherske menighet (Hannaford)	Griggs Co.	Hannaford	North Dakota	2	93	29; 1912	Undetermined
Norway norsk evangelisk lutherske menighet	Nelson Co.	Aneta	North Dakota	2	100	85; 1914	Undetermined
Stefanus menighet (Stefani)	Cavalier Co.	Milton	North Dakota	2	102	75; 1915	Undetermined
Pomona Valley evangelisk lutherske menighet (Pomona)	Lamoure Co.	Kulm	North Dakota	2	111	29; 1914	Undetermined
Zoar menighet	Lamoure Co.	La Moure	North Dakota	2	111	30; 1914	ELCA
Ruso evangelisk lutherske menighet	McLean Co.	Ruso	North Dakota	2	116	59; 1914	Undetermined
St. Hans menighet	Ramsey Co.	Edmore	North Dakota	2	123	133; 1915	ELCA; Building destroyed by fire in 1986 and joined Concordia
Norway evangelisk lutherske menighet	Dickey Co.	Oakes	North Dakota	2	126	40; 1914	Undetermined
St. Ansgars norsk evangelisk lutherske menighet	Dickey Co.	Fullerton	North Dakota	2	127	80; 1914	Undetermined
Norwich norsk lutherske menighet	McHenry Co.	Norwich	North Dakota	2	135	40; 1901	ELCA
North Prairie evangelisk lutherske menighet (Nord Prærie)	McHenry Co.	Velva	North Dakota	2	135	74; 1914	Dissolved

Name	County	Town	State				Status
South Prairie evangelisk lutherske menighet (Syd Prairie)	McHenry Co.	Velva	North Dakota	2	136	29; 1913	Undetermined
Velva norsk evangelisk lutherske menighet	McHenry Co.	Velva	North Dakota	2	136	35; 1913	Undetermined
Ebenezer norsk evangelisk lutherske menighet	McHenry Co.	Norwich	North Dakota	2	139	64; 1916	Undetermined
Emmanuels norsk evangelisk lutherske menighet	Morton Co.	Fleak	North Dakota	2	142	23; 1914	Undetermined
Ox Creek norsk evangelisk lutherske menighet	Rolette Co.	Rolette	North Dakota	2	143	161; 1914	Undetermined
Vestland menighet	Rolette Co.	Rolette	North Dakota	2	144	83; 1914	Undetermined
Immanuels norsk lutherske menighet	Ward Co.	Minot	North Dakota	2	148	50; 1914	Undetermined
Zion menighet (Sion)	Ward Co.	Berthold	North Dakota	2	151	115; 1914	ELCA
Rose Valley menighet	Ward Co.	Grelland	North Dakota	2	153	81; 1914	ELCA
Lake View menighet	Towner Co.	Egeland	North Dakota	2	160	62; 1914	AFLC
Manger norsk evangelisk lutherske menighet	Bottineau Co.	Bottineau	North Dakota	2	164	61; 1914	Undetermined
St. Peters menighet	Benson Co.	Minnewaukan	North Dakota	2	177	80; 1914	ELCA
Emanuels menighet	Benson Co.	Maddock	North Dakota	2	180	290; 1914	ELCA
Zion norsk lutherske menighet	Benson Co.	Maddock	North Dakota	2	181	66; 1914	CLBA
Bethania norsk lutherske menighet	Benson Co.	Esmond	North Dakota	2	182	70; 1914	Undetermined

APPENDIX C

Bethel norsk lutherske menighet	Wells Co.	Heimdal	North Dakota	2	189	173; 1914	Undetermined
Ray norsk evangelisk lutherske menighet	Williams Co.	Ray	North Dakota	2	191	80; 1911	ELCA
Wheelock norsk evangelisk lutherske menighet	Williams Co.	Wheelock	North Dakota	2	192	75; 1914	Undetermined
Epping norsk evangelisk lutherske menighet	Williams Co.	Epping	North Dakota	2	192	125; 1915	ELCA
Hauges menighet	Williams Co.	Williston	North Dakota	2	194	30; 1913	Dissolved
Sandy Creek menighet	Williams Co.	Marmon	North Dakota	2	195	95; 1914	Undetermined
Rainbow Valley norsk evangelisk lutherske menighet (Rambon)	Williams Co.	Ray	North Dakota	2	195	85; 1914	ELCA
Temple norsk evangelisk lutherske menighet (Temple)	Williams Co.	Temple	North Dakota	2	195	68; 1914	Dissolved
River View menighet	Williams Co.	Wheelock	North Dakota	2	196	30; 1914	Undetermined
Lindahl menighet	Williams Co.	McGregor	North Dakota	2	199	90; 1915	Undetermined
Ploom Creek (Ploone Creek)	Williams Co.	Williston	North Dakota	2	199	91; 1915	Dissolved
Zion evangelisk lutherske menighet	Mountrail Co.	Lundsvalley	North Dakota	2	211	190; 1914	Undetermined
Threfoldigheds menighet (Trefoldigheds norsk evangelisk lutherske)	Mountrail Co.	Manitou	North Dakota	2	211	65; 1914	Undetermined
Beauty Valley menighet	Mountrail Co.	Purdon	North Dakota	2	212	90; 1914	Undetermined
Kristiansand menighet	Mountrail Co.	White Earth	North Dakota	2	214	60; 1914	Undetermined
Saron menighet	Mountrail Co.	White Earth	North Dakota	2	216	40; 1914	Undetermined

Bethel skandinavisk evangelisk lutherske menighet	Mountrail Co.	Lunds Valley	North Dakota	2	216	80; 1914	Undetermined
Skandia evangelisk lutherske menighet	Mountrail Co.	Lostwood	North Dakota	2	217	61; 1915	AFLC; Now First English Lutheran
Brush Hill norsk evangelisk lutherske menighet	Divide Co.	Colgan	North Dakota	2	227	50; 1915	Undetermined
Farland norsk lutherske menighet	McKenzie Co.	Arnegard	North Dakota	2	231	45; 1914	ELCA; Merged into Banks Lutheran
Zoar norsk lutherske menighet	McKenzie Co.	Arnegard	North Dakota	2	231	73; 1914	Undetermined
Garden norsk lutherske menighet	McKenzie Co.	Watford	North Dakota	2	231	106; 1914	ELCA
Timber Creek norsk lutherske menighet	McKenzie Co.	Rawson	North Dakota	2	232	54; 1914	Undetermined
Cherry norsk lutherske menighet	McKenzie Co.	Watford	North Dakota	2	232	48; 1914	Undetermined
Mamre skandinavisk luthersk menighet	Bowman Co.	Reeder	North Dakota	2	237	95; 1914	Dissolved
Little Missouri menighet	Bowman Co.	Marmarth	North Dakota	2	237	9; 1913	Undetermined
Bethania menighet	Bowman Co.	Rhame	North Dakota	2	238	80; 1914	Undetermined
Our Savior's English Lutheran (Bowman?)	Bowman Co.	Bowman	North Dakota	2	239	50; 1915	Undetermined
St. Paul skandinavisk evangelisk lutherske menighet	Adams Co.	Bucyrus	North Dakota	2	241	25; 1915	Undetermined
Zion norsk evangelisk lutherske menighet	Adams Co.	Leigh	North Dakota	2	242	53; 1915	Undetermined

APPENDIX C

Whetstone Butte norsk lutherske menighet (Whitstone)	Adams Co.	Reeder	North Dakota	2	242	36; 1915	Undetermined
Zion English Evangelical Lutheran Congregation	Adams Co.	Spring Butte	North Dakota	2	243	35; 1909	Undetermined
Bethel norsk evangelisk lutherske menighet	Adams Co.	Chandler	North Dakota	2	245	36; 1914	Undetermined
Bethania menighet	Hettinger Co.	Watrous	North Dakota	2	248	33; 1914	Undetermined
Regent norsk evangelisk lutherske menighet	Hettinger Co.	Regent	North Dakota	2	248	24; 1913	Undetermined
Selbu menighet	Whitman Co.	La Crosse	Washington	2	311	100; 1914	ELCA
St. Petri menighet	Latah Co.	Moscow	Idaho	2	322	55; 1914	Undetermined
Golden West norsk evangelisk lutherske menighet	Chouteau Co.	Sollid	Montana	2	349	31; 1914	LCMC
Farmington norsk evangelisk lutherske menighet	Teton Co.	Choteau	Montana	2	352	25; 1914	ELCA; Merged with Trinity Lutheran
Valier norsk lutherske menighet	Teton Co.	Valier	Montana	2	354	Unknown	LCMC
Pondera norsk evangelisk lutherske menighet	Toole Co.	Galata	Montana	2	359	30; 1915	Undetermined
Immanuels norsk evangelisk lutherske menighet	Sheridan Co.	Westby	Montana	2	364	50; 1915	Undetermined
Pauce Coupe menighet	Yale-Cariboo P. D.	Hudson Hope	British Columbia	2	410	Unknown	Undetermined
Bardo menighet (Norden menighet)	Vegreville P. D.	Bardo	Alberta	2	412	62; 1897	CALC

Bethel menighet (Iquity)	Vegreville P. D.	Ryley	Alberta	2	413	75; 1915	ELCIC
Amisk Creek menighet (Amosk Creek)	Vegreville P. D.	Ryley	Alberta	2	413	Unknown	Undetermined
Skandia norsk evangelisk lutherske menighet (Scandia)	Camrose P. D.	Armena	Alberta	2	415	105; 1914	ELCIC
Immanuels norsk evangelisk lutherske menighet	Camrose P. D.	Camrose	Alberta	2	415	78; 1914	Undetermined
St. Josephs norsk evangelisk lutherske menighet	Camrose P. D.	Hay Lake	Alberta	2	418	53; 1914	ELCIC
Bethesda norsk evangelisk lutherske menighet	Camrose P. D.	New Norway	Alberta	2	418	53; 1914	ELCIC
Bethlehem norsk evangelisk lutherske menighet (Pretty Hill)	Camrose P. D.	Dinant	Alberta	2	418	65; 1914	Undetermined
Nazareth menighet	Camrose P. D.	Bawlf	Alberta	2	418	19; 1915	Undetermined
Throndhjem (Trondhjem)	Camrose P. D.	Round Hill	Alberta	2	419	210; 1913	CALC
Salem norsk evangelisk lutherske menighet (Kingman)	Camrose P. D.	Kingman	Alberta	2	419	7; 1914	CALC
Vigs menighet	Lacombe P. D.	Bentley	Alberta	2	421	96; 1914	Undetermined
Scanavia menighet (Aspelund, Scandia)	Lacombe P. D.	Blackfalds	Alberta	2	421	56; 1914	Undetermined
Vor Frelsers norsk lutherske menighet (Sylvan Lake)	Lacombe P. D.	Eckville	Alberta	2	421	60; 1914	Undetermined

APPENDIX C

Zion menighet	Wainwright P. D.	Irma	Alberta	2	429	50; 1915	Undetermined
Den 1ste skandinavisk lutherske menighet	Edmonton P. D.	Edmonton	Alberta	2	432	98; 1913	Undetermined
Zion norsk lutherske menighet	Medicine Hat P. D.	Pakowski	Alberta	2	433	39; 1915	Undetermined
Bethania norsk lutherske menighet	Medicine Hat P. D.	Pakowski	Alberta	2	434	47; 1915	Undetermined
Nazareth English Congregation	Medicine Hat P. D.	Pakowski	Alberta	2	434	21; 1915	Undetermined
Solør norsk evangelisk lutherske menighet	Acadia P. D.	Cereal	Alberta	2	438	75; 1915	ELCIC
Excel norsk evangelisk lutherske menighet	Acadia P. D.	Excel	Alberta	2	438	Unknown	Undetermined
Vor Frelsers norsk evangelisk lutherske menighet	Acadia P. D.	Cereal	Alberta	2	438	Unknown	Undetermined
Benville skandinavisk lutherske menighet	Peace River P. D.	Benville	Alberta	2	439	Unknown	Undetermined
Northfield norsk lutherske menighet	Peace River P. D.	Benville	Alberta	2	439	Unknown	Undetermined
Valhalla norsk lutherske menighet (Walhalla)	Peace River P. D.	Grand Prairie	Alberta	2	439	Unknown	Undetermined
Camrose College prækeplads	Camrose P. D.	Camrose	Alberta	2	439	N/A **Dual affiliation with Forenede**	N/A
Rose Valley evangelisk lutherske menighet	Tramping Lake P. D.	Denzil	Saskatchewan	2	488	35; 1911	Undetermined

373

Table 2: Fate of Hauge's Synod Congregations

Overview	
Active congregations as of 1916 that were members of Hauge's Synod	342
Congregations that switched from Hauge's Synod to other synods before 1916 (noted in italics)	14
Preaching points as of 1916	7
Total	***363***
Fate of the 342 congregations	
Undetermined	197
Merged into or with other congregations	28
Dissolved	14
Total undetermined, merged, and dissolved	***239***
Total determined and active today (not including congregations that have merged)	**103**
ELCA	58
ELCIC	5
Total ELCA and ELCIC	***63***
LCMC	16
AFLC	12
CLBA	4
CALC	3
NALC	2
AALC	1
ARC	1
"Nondenominational"	1
Total non ELCA and ELCIC	***40***

APPENDIX C

Table 3: Number of Hauge's Synod Congregations by State/Province as of 1916

State/Province	Number of Congregations
Minnesota	98
North Dakota	82
South Dakota	53
Alberta	25
Iowa	25
Wisconsin	22
Illinois	17
Montana	5
Michigan	4
Kansas	3
Nebraska	3
British Columbia	1
California	1
Idaho	1
Saskatchewan	1
Washington	1

Bibliography

Aahus, Alice. "An Awakening that Stopped the Dancers." *Morning Glory*, May 2017.
Aarflot, Andreas. *Hans Nielsen Hauge: His Life and Message.* Translated by Joseph M. Shaw. Minneapolis: Augsburg, 1979.
Aasgaard, J. A. "Hans Nielsen Hauge." *Lutheran Herald*, 1932.
"Affiliation of Lutheran Movements." In *Christian Cyclopedia*.
Affiliation of Lutheran Movements. "Terms of Reference." 1974: Lutheran Evangelistic Movement Papers, Luther Seminary Archives, St. Paul, MN.
Anderson, Jonathan D. *Our Fathers Saw His Mighty Works: The Lutheran Evangelistic Movement and a Forgotten Mid-20th Century Revival.* Newfolden, MN: Mercy and Truth, 2013.
Arden, G. Everett. *Four Northern Lights: Men Who Shaped Scandinavian Churches.* Minneapolis: Augsburg, 1964.
Arntzen, Arnliot M. *The Apostle of Norway: Hans Nielsen Hauge.* Minneapolis: The Lutheran Free Church, 1933.
"Baptism Is Necessary." *Lutheran Intelligencer*, August 16, 1911.
Bardo Lutheran Church. Congregational minutes, February 25, 1916. T. Jacobson Dissertation Reference, Luther Seminary Archives, St. Paul, MN.
———. Congregational minutes, March 24, 1916. T. Jacobson Dissertation Reference, Luther Seminary Archives, St. Paul, MN.
———. Worship bulletin, October 1, 2017. http://bardolutheranchurch.weebly.com/uploads/2/3/7/0/23706690/bulletin_-__pentecost_17_-_october_1_2017.pdf.
Barstad, B. K. "What the Inner Mission People Have Meant to Me." *Morning Glory*, June 1934.
Berge, Selmer A. *Evangelism in the Congregation.* Minneapolis: Faith in Action Movement, 1944.
Bergendoff, Conrad. *The Church of the Lutheran Reformation: A Historical Survey of Lutheranism.* Saint Louis: Concordia, 1967.
Bjorlie, Lorraine Brekke. Reflection on the History of Markers Lutheran Church. [unknown date], Markers Lutheran Church File, Luther Seminary Archives, St. Paul, MN.
Blom Prairie Lutheran Brethren Church. "Statement of Faith." http://blomprairie.org/about/what-we-believe.
Boline, Jim. "Editor's Report to the Executive Committee of LEM." Minneapolis, June 21, 1985. Lutheran Evangelistic Movement Papers, Luther Seminary Archives, St. Paul, MN.

BIBLIOGRAPHY

Boraas, Julius. "Red Wing Seminary: As Julius Boraas Knew It in 1886-90, 1895-9." [ca. early twentieth century]. RWS File, St. Olaf College Archives, Northfield, MN.

Brorson, Hans Adolf. "My Heart Is Filled with Wonder." In *ReClaim: Lutheran Hymnal for Church and Home*. St. Paul, MN: ReClaim Resources, 2013.

Bruce, Gustav Marius. *Lutheran Intelligencer*, May 3, 1911.

———. "Editorial." *Lutheran Intelligencer*, September 11, 1911.

———. "Editorial." *Lutheran Intelligencer*, August 16, 1911.

———. "Editorial." *Lutheran Intelligencer*, January 1912.

———. "Editorial." *Lutheran Intelligencer*, February 1912.

———. "Editorial." *Lutheran Intelligencer*, April 1912.

———. "Editorial." *Lutheran Intelligencer*, July 1912.

———. "Editorial." *Lutheran Intelligencer*, October 1912.

———. "Editorial." *Lutheran Intelligencer*, April 1913.

———. "Editorial." *Lutheran Intelligencer*, June 1913.

———. "The Influence of Hauge on Norwegian Lutheran Christianity and Church Life in America." In *Hans Nielsen Hauge in Retrospect*, translated by Lars Walker, 89-98. Minneapolis: Augsburg, 1926.

Burton, Louise. "The Lutheran Evangelistic Movement: The Reappearance of Pietism and Its Subsequent Contribution to American Lutheranism." MA thesis, Wheaton College Graduate School, 1999.

Carlsen, Clarence J. "Elling Eielsen, Pioneer Lay Preacher and First Norwegian Lutheran Pastor in America." MA thesis, University of Minnesota, 1932.

China Service Ventures. "Our History." https://www.chinaserviceventures.org/history/.

———. "Our Mission." https://www.chinaserviceventures.org/our-mission/.

Chosen People Ministries. "Chosen People Ministries + Good News for Israel." https://chosenpeople.com/site/good-news-for-israel/.

———. "History of Good News for Israel." https://chosenpeople.com/site/history-of-good-news-for-israel/.

———. "Endorsements." https://chosenpeople.com/site/our-mission-statement/endorsements/.

Christofferson, Karen. "History of Immanuel Lutheran Church: Presentation to the Annandale History Club." http://www.annandaleonline.com/History/HistoryClub/Programs/KChristofferson-ImmanuelChurch-2001.htm.

"Church News." *Lutheran Intelligencer*, August 1913.

"Church Union." *Lutheran Herald*, 1915.

"Church Union and the Synod." *Lutheran Herald*, 1914.

Clark, G. G. "An Interesting Statement." *Lutheran Intelligencer*, April 1913.

Curtiss-Wedge, Franklyn. "Reverend Thomas Hanson." In *The History of Renville County Minnesota*, 2:1258-59. 2 vols. Chicago: H. C. Cooper Jr., 1916.

"Den Retfærdiggjores salige Tilstand." *Budbæreren*, 1910.

"Despite Criticism, Faith Leaders Embrace New Planned Parenthood Facility." *Morning Glory*, April 2017.

Dunkley, E. H. *The Reformation in Denmark*. London: SPCK, 1948.

East Immanuel Lutheran Church. Fiftieth-Anniversary Book. 1938. T. Jacobson Dissertation Reference, Luther Seminary Archives, St. Paul, MN.

East Immanuel Lutheran Church. One-Hundredth-Anniversary Book. 1988. T. Jacobson Dissertation Reference, Luther Seminary Archives, St. Paul, MN.

BIBLIOGRAPHY

Eastvold, Carl Johann. *A Sermon on Baptism.* Red Wing, MN: Hauge's Synod Printing Office, 1909.

Eastvold, Carl Johann et al. "*En Henvendelse til Prester og Menigheder.*" [An appeal letter to pastors and congregations] [ca. November 1919]. M. O. Wee File, St. Olaf College Archives, Northfield, MN.

Eastvold, Seth Clarence. *Let Us Go to Chapel.* Minneapolis: Board of Christian Education, Evangelical Lutheran Church, 1952.

———. Personal reflection. [unknown date]. Seth Clarence Eastvold File, Luther Seminary Archives, St. Paul, MN.

"Editorial." *Lutherans Alert*, August-September 1966.

Emmanuel Lutheran Church. "Emmanuel's Mission Statement." https://web.archive.org/web/20161014075921/http://beresfordemmanuel.org/about/4588317700.

Engelbrecht, Edward A., ed. *The Church from Age to Age: A History from Galilee to Global Christianity.* St. Louis: Concordia, 2011.

Erb, Peter C., ed. *Pietists: Selected Writings.* New York: Paulist, 1983.

Erickson, Dirk. "Associate Director's Report to the Executive Committee." November 19, 1982. Lutheran Evangelistic Movement Papers, Luther Seminary Archives, St. Paul, MN.

"Facts about Hauge's Synod." *Lutheran Intelligencer*, June 1913.

"Farewell, Red Wing Seminary." *Morning Glory*, June 15, 1938.

Fevold, Eugene L. *The History of Evangelism in the Evangelical Lutheran Church: 1917-1960.* Published by the author, 1963.

———. *The Lutheran Free Church: A Fellowship of American Lutheran Congregations, 1897-1963.* Minneapolis: Augsburg, 1969.

First Lutheran Church of Pontiac. http://firstlutheranpontiac.org/.

"Forening og lägmandsvirksomhed." *Budbæreren*, 1913.

"Foreningssagen." *Budbæreren*, 1888.

———. *Budbæreren*, 1912.

———. *Budbæreren*, 1916.

Fortney, Thomas. Franklin Lutheran Church personal congregational history. 2017. T. Jacobson Dissertation Reference, Luther Seminary Archives, St. Paul, MN.

"General Notes." *Lutheran Intelligencer*, May 1913.

Gisselquist, Orloue. *Called to Preach: The Life and Ministry of Rev. J. O. Gisselquist, 1888-1968.* Published by the author, 1999.

Graebner, Theodore. "The Ghost of Pietism." *Concordia Theological Monthly*, April 1932.

Granquist, Mark A. *Lutherans in America: A New History.* Minneapolis: Fortress, 2013.

———, ed. *Scandinavian Pietists: Spiritual Writings from 19th-Century Norway, Denmark, Sweden, and Finland.* New York: Paulist, 2015.

———. "The Sociological Factor Is Not to Be Underestimated: Swedes, Norwegians, and American Lutheran Merger Negotiations, 1920-60." In *Norwegians and Swedes in the United States: Friends and Neighbors*, edited by Philip J. Anderson and Dag Blanck, 160. St. Paul: Minnesota Historical Society, 2012.

Gray, Dennis, ed. *Rise Up and Build.* Newfolden, MN: Mercy and Truth, 2014.

Grell, Ole Peter, ed. *The Scandinavian Reformation: From Evangelical Movement to Institutionalisation of Reform.* Cambridge: Cambridge University Press, 1995.

Grindal, Gracia. *Thea Rønning: Young Woman on a Mission.* Minneapolis: Lutheran University Press, 2012.

BIBLIOGRAPHY

Gunderson, Paul. "Report to Executive Committee." May 1985. Lutheran Evangelistic Movement Papers, Luther Seminary Archives, St. Paul, MN.

———. "Report to the Executive Committee." August 1985. Lutheran Evangelistic Movement Papers, Luther Seminary Archives, St. Paul, MN.

Haga, Jim. "Where Are You Looking?" *Morning Glory*, May 2008.

Harrisville, Roy Jr. Interview by Thomas E. Jacobson. Falcon Heights, MN, September 3, 2014. Transcript, Luther Seminary Archives, St. Paul, MN.

———. "Luther Theological Seminary, 1876-1976." In *Thanksgiving and Hope: A Collection of Essays Chronicling 125 Years of the People, Events, and Movements in the Antecedent Schools That Have Formed Luther Seminary*, edited by Frederick H. Gonnerman, 35-57. St. Paul, MN: Luther Seminary, 1998.

Hauge, Hans Nielsen. *Autobiographical Writings of Hans Nielsen Hauge*. Translated by Joel M. Njus. Minneapolis: Augsburg, 1954.

Hauge Inner Mission Federation. *The Hauge Movement in America*. Minneapolis: The Lutheran Free Church, 1941.

Hauge Institute. *The Hauge Institute: Imperative Principles*. Oslo: Hauge Institute, 2016.

Hauge Lutheran Inner Mission Federation. "For Your Information." http://www.haugeinnermission.com/site/default.asp?sec_id=180000037.

Hauge's Norwegian Evangelical Lutheran Synod in America. *Reports to the 55th Annual Convention*. Red Wing, MN.

———. *Reports to the 56th Annual Convention*, Red Wing, MN.

———. *Reports to and Minutes of the 58th Annual Meeting*, Red Wing, MN.

———. *Reports and Proceedings of the 60th Annual Convention*, Red Wing, MN.

Helland, Andreas. *The American Santal Mission: Notes on Its History*. Minneapolis: The American Santal Mission, 1948.

———. *Georg Sverdrup: The Man and His Message*. Minneapolis: The Messenger, 1947.

"History of Kindred Lutheran Church, Kindred, ND." [ca. 1960]. Kindred Lutheran Church File, Luther Seminary Archives, St. Paul, MN.

"Historical Survey." *United Lutheran*, July 2, 1915.

Hopfensperger, Jean. "Many Faiths Come Together in Minneapolis Church." *Star Tribune*, April 5, 2015.

"An Introduction...with Remarks." *Morning Glory*, February 16, 1939.

Irvin, Dale T., and Scott W. Sunquist. *History of the World Christian Movement. Vol. 1, Earliest Christianity to 1453*. Maryknoll, NY: Orbis, 2001.

Jacobson, Thomas. "Hauge's Norwegian Evangelical Lutheran Synod in America and the Continuation of the Haugean Spirit in Twentieth Century American Lutheranism." PhD diss., Luther Seminary, 2018.

Jevnaker Lutheran Church. "About Us." https://jevnakerlc.weebly.com/about-us.html.

Johnson, Elmer. "The School on the Hill That Was Closed." *Morning Glory*, March 1936.

Keyser, L. S. "Objections to the Licensed Saloon." *Lutheran Intelligencer*, May 1912.

Kibler, Ray F., III. "The Lutheran Bible Institute and the Augustana Synod, 1918-1932." PhD diss., Fuller Theological Seminary, 2008.

Klungtvedt, Nils. "Red Wing Seminary." *Morning Glory*, February 1937.

Knutson, James. Interview by Thomas E. Jacobson. St. Paul, MN, September 5, 2014. Transcript, Luther Seminary Archives, St. Paul, MN.

Knutson, Melford S. Report of Meeting with Hauge and Emmanuel Congregations at Kenyon, MN. January 30, 1968. Emmanuel Lutheran Church File, Luther Seminary Archives, St. Paul, MN.

BIBLIOGRAPHY

Kolb, Robert, and Timothy Wengert, eds. *The Book of Concord: The Confessions of the Evangelical Lutheran Church*. Minneapolis: Fortress, 2000.

Kongsvinger Lutheran Church. http://www.kongsvingerchurch.org/.

"*Kredsmöde, foreningssagen.*" *Budbæreren*, 1916.

"The Language Situation in the United Church." *United Lutheran*, 1914.

Lee, Robert Lloyd. *A New Springtime: Centennial Reflections on the Revival in the Nineties among Norwegian-Americans*. Minneapolis: Heirloom, 1997.

Life Together Churches. "Mission and Vision." http://www.lifetogetherchurches.com/purpose/196.

Ljostveit, Peder. *Innermission Church History*. Hauge Lutheran Inner Mission Federation, 1948.

Luecke, Dave. "The Weak Link in Our Gospel Presentation: An Interpretation of Heinrich Schwan's 'Propositions on Unevangelical Practice.'" http://lutheranrenewal.com/files/125083895.pdf.

Lundeberg, K. O. "Haugeanism in Norway." *Lutheran Herald*, 1942.

Luther Theological Seminary Catalog:1919-1920. St. Paul, MN: Luther Theological Seminary, 1919.

Luther Theological Seminary Catalog: 1922-1923. St. Paul, MN: Luther Theological Seminary, 1922.

Luther Theological Seminary Catalog: 1930-1931. St. Paul, MN: Luther Theological Seminary, 1930.

Luther Theological Seminary Catalog: 1936-1937. St. Paul, MN: Luther Theological Seminary, 1936.

Lutheran Bible Institute. *L. B. I. Memoirs: 1919-1934*. Minneapolis: Lutheran Bible Institute, 1934.

Lutheran Evangelistic Movement. "Annual Report." 1975. Lutheran Evangelistic Movement Papers, Luther Seminary Archives, St. Paul.

———. "The Distinctives of an LEM Evangelist-Teacher." 1979. Lutheran Evangelistic Movement Papers, Luther Seminary Archives, St. Paul, MN.

———. "The Ministry of Area Conferences." [ca. 1975]. Lutheran Evangelistic Movement Papers, Luther Seminary Archives, St. Paul, MN.

———. "Executive Committee Meeting Agenda." March 16, 1984. Lutheran Evangelistic Movement Papers, Luther Seminary Archives, St. Paul, MN.

Lutheran Evangelistic Movement Deeper Life. "Making Disciples Through Media." http://lemdeeperlife.org/deeper-life-resources/making-disciples-through-media/a60.html.

———. "Mission and Vision." http://www.lemdeeperlife.org/.

The Lutheran Hymnary. Minneapolis: Augsburg, 1913.

Lutheran Lay Renewal of America. "Renewal Weekend." http://lutheranrenewal.com/files/124391065.pdf.

———. "Who We Are and What We Do." http://www.lutheranrenewal.com/.

Malmin, Rasmus, et al., trans. and rev. *Who's Who among Pastors in All the Norwegian Lutheran Synods of America: 1843-1927*. Minneapolis: Augsburg, 1928.

Masted, L. C. "An Earnest Plea to Our Pastors." *Lutherans Alert*, August-September 1966.

Mathsen, Don. "The Haugean Influence in the Past and Recent History of Kongsvinger Lutheran Church." 2016. T. Jacobson Dissertation Reference, Luther Seminary Archives, St. Paul, MN.

Mayfield, Cathy, and Jessica Mador. "Minneapolis Church Votes to Leave ELCA over Gay Clergy." *Minnesota Public Radio News*, September 30, https://www.mprnews.org/story/2009/09/30/church-leaves-elca.

"*Mit syn paa Foreningssagen.*" *Budbæreren*, 1889.

Molland, Einar. *Fra Hans Nielsen Hauge til Eivind Berggrav: Hovedlinjer i Norges kirkehistorie i det 19. og 20. århundre* [From Hans Nielsen Hauge to Eivind Berggrav: Principal Themes in Norway's Ecclesiastical History in the Nineteenth and Twentieth Centuries]. Oslo: Yldendal, 1968.

Mona, G. O. "Open Letter." 1916. G. M. Bruce File, Luther Seminary Archives, St. Paul, MN.

Montgomery, Ingun. "Norway." In *Oxford Encyclopedia of the Reformation* 3:155–158.

Morris, John D. "Creation with the Appearance of Age." *Morning Glory*, December 2016.

Mulder, William. *Homeward to Zion: The Mormon Migration from Scandinavia*. Minneapolis: University of Minnesota Press, 1985.

Nass, Martin E. "Jewell Lutheran College." October 27, 2002. JLC File, St. Olaf College Archives, Northfield, MN.

Nelson, E. Clifford. *The Lutheran Church among Norwegian Americans: A History of the Evangelical Lutheran Church. Vol. 2, 1890-1959*. Minneapolis: Augsburg, 1960.

———, ed. *The Lutherans in North America*. Philadelphia: Fortress, 1975.

———. "The Union Movement among Norwegian-American Lutherans from 1880 to 1917." PhD diss., Yale University, 1952.

Nelson, E. Clifford, and Eugene L. Fevold. *The Lutheran Church among Norwegian Americans: A History of the Evangelical Lutheran Church. Vol. 1, 1825-1890*. Minneapolis: Augsburg, 1960.

Nichol, Todd W. "The American Lutheran Church: An Historical Study of its Confession of Faith According to its Constituting Documents." ThD diss., Graduate Theological Union, 1988.

———, ed. *Crossings: Norwegian-American Lutheranism as a Transatlantic Tradition*. Northfield, MN: Norwegian-American Historical Association, 2003.

Norlie, Olaf Morgan. *Elling Eielsen: A Brief History*. Norway, IL: The Elling Eielsen Centennial, 1940.

———, ed. *Norsk Lutherske Menigheter I Amerika: 1843-1916* [Norwegian Lutheran Congregations in America: 1843-1916]. *Vol. 1*. Minneapolis: Augsburg, 1918.

———, ed. *Norsk Lutherske Menigheter i Amerika: 1843-1916* [Norwegian Lutheran Congregations in America: 1843-1916]. *Vol. 2*. Minneapolis: Augsburg, 1918.

Norwegian Lutheran Church of America (NLCA). *1923 Annual Report*. Minneapolis: Augsburg, 1923.

———. *1923 Annual Report: District Conventions*. Minneapolis: Augsburg, 1923.

———. *1924 Annual Report*. Minneapolis: Augsburg, 1924.

———. *1924 Annual Report: District Conventions*. Minneapolis: Augsburg, 1924.

———. *1926 Annual Report*. Minneapolis: Augsburg, 1926.

———. *1932 Annual Report*. Minneapolis: Augsburg, 1932.

———. *1936 Annual Report*. Minneapolis: Augsburg, 1936.

———. *1946 Annual Report*. Minneapolis: Augsburg, 1946.

———. "Report of the General President and the Church Council." *1923 Annual Report*. Minneapolis: Augsburg, 1923.

Oace, Ole H. *Hauges synode (revsede men ikke ihjelslagne) samt et foredrag af H. H. Bergsland om forsoningen* [Hauge's Synod: Chastised but not Beaten to Death, with a Lecture from H .H. Bergsland Concerning the Atonement]. St. Paul: 1932.
"Other Lutheran Synods." *United Lutheran*, 1914.
"Our Amusements." *Lutheran Intelligencer*, June 1912.
"Our Debt to Interdenominational Movements." *Lutheran Intelligencer*, February 1913.
Pedersen, Nels. "Report to the Executive Committee." October 15, 1982. Lutheran Evangelistic Movement Papers, Luther Seminary Archives, St. Paul, MN.
Pettersen, Wilhelm. *The Light in the Prison Window: The Life Story of Hans Nielsen Hauge*. Minneapolis: The Christian Literature Company, 1926.
Preus, David. Interview by Thomas E. Jacobson. St. Paul, MN, September 5, 2014. Transcript, Luther Seminary Archives, St. Paul, MN.
Preus, Herman Amberg. *Vivacious Daughter: Seven Lectures on the Religious Situation among Norwegians in America*. Translated by Todd W. Nichol. Northfield, MN: The Norwegian-American Historical Association, 1990.
Preus, J. C. K., et al., eds. *Norsemen Found a Church: An Old Heritage in a New Land*. Minneapolis: Augsburg, 1953.
Preus, Linka. *Linka's Diary: A Norwegian Immigrant Story in Words and Sketches*. Translated by Marvin G. Slind. Minneapolis: Lutheran University Press, 2008.
"Proceedings of the Sixty-eighth Annual Conference of Hauge's Synod, June 4-11, 1913." *Lutheran Intelligencer*, June 1913.
"Proposal for Merger of the Santal Mission with the American Lutheran Church." January 10, 1971. Santal Mission File, WMPL Archives, Minneapolis, MN.
"Proposed Conditions from Santal Side." October 16, 1970. Santal Mission File, WMPL Archives, Minneapolis, MN.
Quam, John Elliott. "Jørgen Erickssøn: A Study in the Norwegian Reformation, 1571-1604." PhD diss., Yale University, 1968.
Red Wing Seminary Alumni Association. "Seminary Newsletter." June 1939. RWS File, St. Olaf College Archives, Northfield, MN.
Redal, R. H. "You Are Invited." *Lutherans Alert*, January 1966.
Reitan, J. O. "A Pietistic Lutheran Institution." *Morning Glory*, July 1934.
Rholl, Arthur, ed. *Red Wing Seminary: Fifty Years of Service*. Red Wing, MN: Red Wing Seminary, 1930.
Rohne, J. Magnus. *Norwegian American Lutheranism up to 1872*. New York: Macmillan, 1926.
Rønning, N. N. "An Abiding Spiritual Influence: The Memory of Red Wing Seminary. Address at the Sixtieth Anniversary of St. Olaf College." June 4, 1934. RWS File, St. Olaf College Archives, Northfield, MN.
———. *Lars O. Skrefsrud: An Apostle to the Santals*. Minneapolis: The Santal Mission in America, 1940.
———. "Our First Church Body." *Lutheran Herald*, 1946.
Satre, Lowell J. "The Hauge's Synod: Education for Awakening." In *Striving for Ministry: Centennial Essays Interpreting the Heritage of Luther Theological Seminary*, edited by Warren A. Quanbeck et al., 81-96. Minneapolis: Augsburg, 1977.
Scandia Lutheran Church. "From the Pastor." http://scandialutheran.com/From_the_Pastor/#sthash.uBbv1rVo.dpbs.

BIBLIOGRAPHY

Schaffner, Sarah. Interview with Dave and Marilyn Knudson. October 13, 1997. Seth Clarence Eastvold Papers, Pacific Lutheran University Archives, Tacoma, WA.

Schiotz, Fredrik A. *One Man's Story*. Minneapolis: Augsburg, 1980.

Semmingsen, Ingrid. *Norway to America: A History of the Migration*. Translated by Einar Haugen. Minneapolis: University of Minnesota Press, 1978.

Shall Red Wing Seminary Be Closed? Why? Red Wing, MN: Red Wing Printing Company, 1932.

Shaw, Joseph M. *Bernt Julius Muus: Founder of St. Olaf College*. Northfield, MN: The Norwegian-American Historical Association, 1999.

———. *John Nathan Kildahl*. Northfield, MN: Highland, 2014.

———. *Pulpit under the Sky: A Life of Hans Nielsen Hauge*. Minneapolis: Augsburg, 1955.

Singsaas Lutheran Church. "Congregational History Book." 2017. T. Jacobson Dissertation Reference, Luther Seminary Archives, St. Paul, MN.

———. Worship Bulletin, November 28, 2010. T. Jacobson Dissertation Reference, Luther Seminary Archives, St. Paul, MN.

———. Worship Bulletin Template. 2010. T. Jacobson Dissertation Reference, Luther Seminary Archives, St. Paul, MN.

"*Smuler fra Bardo i Alberta*." *Budbæreren*, 1908.

Solberg, Carl Knutson. *A Brief History of the Zion Society for Israel*. Minneapolis: The Zion Society for Israel, 1928.

Solberg, Richard W. *Lutheran Higher Education in North America*. Minneapolis: Augsburg, 1985.

South Zumbro Lutheran Church. "About South Zumbro Lutheran Church." http://szlc.org/About.aspx.

Sovik, Ansgar E. "Elling Eielsen and Some Elements of the Church Strife among Norwegian-American Lutherans in the 1840's and 1850's." MTh thesis, Princeton Theological Seminary, 1946.

Stageberg, Susie W. "Red Wing Seminary: Pioneer Institution of Learning among Lutherans in America," [unknown date]. RWS File, St. Olaf College Archives, Northfield, MN.

Svanoe, Atle. *The Work of Laypersons in Lutheran Perspective*. Translated by Gordon Gunderson. Madison, WI: Omnipress, 1989.

Svendsbye, Lloyd A. *I Paid All My Debts: A Norwegian-American Immigrant Saga of Life on the Prairie of North Dakota*. Minneapolis: Lutheran University Press, 2009.

Syrdal, Rolf. "American Lutheran Mission Work in China." PhD diss., Drew University, 1942.

Tengbom, Mildred. *The Spirit of God Was Moving: The World Mission Prayer League: Its Beginnings*. Minneapolis: World Mission Prayer League, 1985.

Thompson, Jesse. "A Cursory History of Jewell Lutheran College" [ca. 1950s]. JLC File, St. Olaf College Archives, Northfield, MN.

Tollefson, Jan, and Wanda Manson, eds. *Food from Ravens: Stories of God's Power and Provision Through Prayer*. Minneapolis: World Mission Prayer League, 2015.

Town of Tofield, Alberta. "Churches." http://tofieldalberta.ca/services/churches/#blc.

Trinity Lutheran Church. "Mission." https://web.archive.org/web/20160130103444/https://tlcmsn.org/about/.

"The Union and the Synod." *Lutheran Herald*, 1914.

"Union of Norwegian Lutherans." *Lutheran Intelligencer*, February 1914.

BIBLIOGRAPHY

"The Union of Norwegian Lutherans." *Lutheran Intelligencer*, April 1914.

"The Union Question." *Lutheran Intelligencer*, June 1913.

Van Lieburg, Fred, and Daniel Lindmark, eds. *Pietism, Revivalism and Modernity, 1650-1850*. Newcastle, England: Cambridge Scholars, 2008.

Veith, Gene Edward. "There is already a church that is both evangelical and sacramental." Facebook, June 1, 2017, http://www.patheos.com/blogs/geneveith/2017/06/there-already-is-a-church-that-is-both-evangelical-and-sacramental-draft/.

Walker, Larry J., ed. *Standing Fast in Freedom*. Minneapolis: The Association of Free Lutheran Congregations, 2000.

Walsh, Matt. "God's Word hasn't become less true just because it has become less popular." Facebook, July 9, 2017. https://www.theblaze.com/contributions/matt-walsh-gods-word-hasnt-become-less-true-just-because-it-has-become-less-popular.

Wee, David. Interview by Thomas E. Jacobson. Northfield, MN, November 28, 2016. Transcript, Luther Seminary Archives, St. Paul, MN.

Wee, Mons Olson. *Haugeanism: A Brief Sketch of the Movement and Some of Its Chief Exponents*. St. Paul: Published by the author, 1919.

———, ed. *Inter-Synodical Evangelical Lutheran Orient Mission Society: Addresses Delivered at the Mission Conference*. St. Paul: Lutheran Orient Mission Society, 1921.

———. *Urgent Needs of Our Times*. St. Paul: Published by the author, 1923.

Wee, Morris Sr. Interview by Morris Wee Jr. Northfield, MN. 1991. Transcript, T. Jacobson Dissertation Reference, Luther Seminary Archives, St. Paul, MN.

Wells, Roland Jr. "Chapter of Reflection and the Beginning of the 21st Century." 2014. T. Jacobson Dissertation Reference, Luther Seminary Archives, St. Paul, MN.

———. "Pastor Wells' History Articles – A Collection: Published for the Fiftieth Anniversary at 1901 Portland." April 13, 2014. T. Jacobson Dissertation Reference, Luther Seminary Archives, St. Paul, MN.

Wentz, Abdel Ross. *A Basic History of Lutheranism in America*. Rev. ed. Philadelphia: Fortress, 1964.

"What Others Say." *Lutheran Intelligencer*, April 19, 1911.

World Mission Prayer League. *Handbook*. Minneapolis: World Mission Prayer League, 2015.

www.ingramcontent.com/pod-product-compliance
Lightning Source LLC
Chambersburg PA
CBHW071141300426
44113CB00009B/1048